THE PORTERS
OF LONDON

THE PORTERS
OF LONDON

WALTER M. STERN

LONGMANS

LONGMANS, GREEN AND CO LTD
6 & 7 CLIFFORD STREET, LONDON W1
THIBAULT HOUSE, THIBAULT SQUARE, CAPE TOWN
605–611 LONSDALE STREET, MELBOURNE C1
443 LOCKHART ROAD, HONG KONG
ACCRA, AUCKLAND, IBADAN
KINGSTON (JAMAICA), KUALA LUMPUR
LAHORE, NAIROBI, SALISBURY (RHODESIA)
LONGMANS, GREEN AND CO INC
119 WEST 40TH STREET, NEW YORK 18
LONGMANS, GREEN AND CO
20 CRANFIELD ROAD, TORONTO 16
ORIENT LONGMANS PRIVATE LTD
CALCUTTA, BOMBAY, MADRAS
DELHI, HYDERABAD, DACCA

© WALTER M. STERN 1960
First Published 1960

Printed in Great Britain by
Spottiswoode Ballantyne & Co. Ltd.
London & Colchester

To My Parents

PREFACE

THIS account traces the history of the Porters who performed transport services in the port and City of London. Theirs was an essential occupation at all times; their origins reach back to the Middle Ages, and faint traces of them survive to this day. Substantially the story covers the period of their corporate existence, which begins in the later sixteenth century and draws to a close at the end of the nineteenth.

Though individually members of City Companies, Porters ranked low on the social scale and belonged to the yeomanry, never to the livery of their guilds. As Porters they were organized in fellowships; the status of a fellowship *vis-à-vis* a guild can be likened in present-day terms to that of a trade union *vis-à-vis* a professional organization. However, while trade unions owe their origin to a spontaneous movement towards self-help among their members, fellowships were established by the City Corporation as a means of limiting and disciplining a difficult and fluctuating labour force. The attempts to combine an adequate labour supply and a controlled level of charges for essential work with a reasonable amount of social provision for the men engaged in it provide one of the story's chief interests.

It would be an error to assume that everybody described as a Porter carried burdens. This may have been the beginning, but by the sixteenth century, if not earlier, two types of Porters existed: the burden carriers and those who arranged for burdens to be carried, that is to say the transport contractors. That the same description should serve for employers and employees does not help to make the story easier to understand. There were four main groups: Tacklehouse Porters, the chief representatives of the employer type of Porters; Street Porters, who confuse the picture further by changing their name to Ticket Porters in the middle seventeenth century; Fellowship or Billingsgate Porters; and Aliens' Porters, a group of men working for and under a City officer known as the Packer and Porter of Aliens' Goods. Porters who do not come within one of these categories concern the present story only in passing; the development of the four main groups forms the subject of this study.

vii

Writing a book within the framework of a large university department, I was privileged to have at my disposal so much help that I cannot be sure whether I deserve any credit the outcome may merit. My gratitude goes out to Professor T. S. Ashton and Mr. H. L. Beales, to whom among others I owe my introduction to economic history; to Professors F. J. Fisher and W. Ashworth who, first as teachers then as colleagues, awakened and deepened my understanding, and who have read this book in typescript and suggested improvements; similarly to my colleague Dr. T. C. Barker who twice put me in his debt for similar help. Another colleague, Dr. A. R. Bridbury, kindly gave advice on the medieval part of my story in which I felt least at home, and Miss Olive P. Coleman deciphered for me the medieval manuscripts.

But my obligation extends beyond university walls. I welcome the opportunity of expressing my gratitude for the generosity of the Marc Fitch Fund which assisted the publication of this book by a grant. I have had much encouragement and assistance from the staff of the City of London Guildhall Library Records Office and Muniment Room, among whom I owe particular thanks to Messrs. P. E. Jones, M. F. Chandler and Dr. A. E. J. Hollaender, not only for the patience with which they made their records available to me, but also for suggestions of further sources. The excellence of the City of London Corporation Records and the generosity and willingness with which they are put at the disposal of research workers inspired a special footnote of praise in a book written half a century ago; the acknowledgement is as well-deserved now as it was then. Mr. B. Stewart, Librarian of the Port of London Authority, kindly made his help available to me in this, as he had done in a previous piece of work. Where my indebtedness relates to particular aspects of research, I have tried to acknowledge it in the appropriate notes. There is, however, one general debt which can find no proper expression here, that to my wife. While not directly associated with this work, she had to bear with the black moods and depression incidental to a first book. Without her support, it would never have been finished, and in that sense her share in it is the largest of all.

The London School of Economics and Political Science
September 1958.

CONTENTS

MAP
between pages 120 and 121
Area of London Porters' Principal Activities

GLOSSARY OF TERMS

ALIENS' PORTERS: Porters employed by the Packer and Porter of Aliens' Goods (*q.v.*) to carry the goods of alien merchants.

ASSISTANT: officer of a Fellowship (*q.v.*) endowed with a limited degree of authority for purposes of management and discipline.

BALLIAGE (or BAILLAGE): toll paid for the delivery of merchant strangers' goods, including porterage, landing and shipping.

BEADLE: subordinate officer of City Companies and Fellowships (*q.v.*) who acts as messenger, hall-keeper and general factotum.

BERTH, TO GO ON: to register at the proper office for work in order of arrival and seniority.

BILLINGSGATE PORTERS: *see* Fellowship Porters.

BLACKWELL PORTERS: Porters employed to carry woollen cloth at Blackwell Hall.

BOUNDS: territorial limits within which precedence of seniority operates in staffing teams for work.

BROTHERHOOD: *see* Fellowship.

CANTING: overboard work from barge to barge.

CATCHING A FOX: going on a job and finding that it has been cancelled and will not be paid for.

CITY GAUGER: City official whose function it was to measure the quantities of liquor and other gaugeable liquids changing hands.

CITY PACKER: *see* Packer and Porter of Aliens' Goods.

CITY PORTERS: Porters free of, and licensed by, the City of London who work within the area of the City and the Port of London.

COAL UNDERTAKER: middleman between collier, bringing coal to London by sea, and coal retailer.

COCQUET: Lord Mayor's permit authorizing against payment of a fee the entry of waterborne goods into the Port of London.

COMMON PACKER: *see* Packer and Porter of Aliens' Goods.

COMPANY OF WOODMONGERS: City Company of fuel merchants.

COMPENSATION COMMISSIONERS: commissioners set up under the West India Docks Act, 1799 (39 Geo. III, cap. LXIX), to compensate interests adversely affected by the establishment of wet docks in the Port of London.

CONSIGNED WORK: goods unloaded on behalf of the purchaser.

CORN METERS IN TRUST, BOARD OF: a Board of ten Common Councilmen of London, elected by their fellow members, charged with supervision of corn measuring in the Port of London.

COTCHEL: a small consignment of corn, amounting to 20 quarters or less.

COURT OF REGISTERS AND RULERS: body responsible for management and discipline within the Society of Tacklehouse and Ticket Porters.

COURT OF RULERS AND ASSISTANTS: body responsible for management and discipline within the Fellowship of Billingsgate Porters.

CUT INTO A JOB: join a working team, thereby displacing a junior Porter.

DEPUTY METER: actual measurer of commodities in the Port of London on behalf of the Meter (*q.v.*).

DRAFT: amount of merchandise which a crane can lift in one operation.

FELLOWSHIP: an organization established by Act of Common Council for workers in an occupation.

FELLOWSHIP PORTERS: members of the Fellowship of Billingsgate Porters, also known as the Fellowship of Corn, Salt and Coal Porters.

FILLAGE: charge levied by a Deputy Meter (*q.v.*) for his labour in filling the bushel.

FOREIGN PORTERS: men working as porters in London, though not possessing the freedom of the City.

FREE PORTERS: men working as Porters in London who possess the freedom of the City.

GANGS: permanent combinations of Porters working on particular commodities or in a particular locality.

HEAVER AND GOER: a Porter joining a working team which was already complete.

HOLDSMAN: man measuring, or working on, cargo in ship's hold.

INN PORTERS: men employed by innkeepers to perform porterage services on their behalf.

KEYMEN: the six senior Rulers of the Fellowship of Billingsgate Porters.

LASTAGE: charge payable for the benefit of the Meters' Pension and Sickness Fund, levied on all corn unless coming from Essex, Kent, the river Ware or out of granary.

MASTER TACKLE PORTER: the highest rank of Wine Tackle Porter (*q.v.*)

METAGE: charge payable to the City Corporation for metering.

METAGE ON GRAIN COMMITTEE: committee set up to supervise voluntary measuring of grain in the Port of London by virtue of the Metage on Grain (Port of London) Act, 1872 (35 & 36 Vict., cap. c).

METER: man appointed by the City Corporation to exercise on its behalf functions of measuring commodities within the Port of London.

ONION BILL: group of Fellowship Porters (*q.v.*) of medium seniority reached after approximately 25 years' membership of the Fellowship.

OPEN WORK: porterage work not organized according to seniority.

OUTLIER: member of the Fellowship of Billingsgate Porters not working regularly at porterage labour.

PACKAGE (or PACCAGE): toll paid for the oversight or survey of merchant strangers' goods imported or exported.

PACKER AND PORTER OF ALIENS' GOODS: City Officer exercizing the power of supervising and portering all goods belonging to alien merchants.

PACKER'S PORTERS: *see* Aliens' Porters.

PENNYMAN: full-time executive officer of the Fellowship of Billingsgate Porters.

PITCHING: unloading or putting down of goods.

PLACED MEN: the 18 senior Deputy Corn Meters.

PORTERS OF LEADENHALL: Porters employed in the Leadenhall area of the City who were free of the City, but not incorporated in a Fellowship.

PUT BY: indict a Porter before his Court of Rulers.

PUT INTO: join a job of work.

QUARTERMAN: the most junior grade of Fellowship Porter (*q.v.*)

QUEEN'S PORTERS: a group of unfree and unlicensed porters working in London in the sixteenth century.

REGISTER: finance officer of the Society of Tacklehouse and Ticket Porters.

RULER: elected member of the body responsible for management and discipline of a Fellowship (*q.v.*).

RUN ON THE JOB: join work irregularly out of turn, without prior notification of the proper Porters' Office.

SCAVAGE: toll paid to towns or ports in respect of merchant strangers' goods displayed and exposed for sale.

SERVANT PORTER: the lowest rank of Wine Tackle Porter (*q.v.*).

SHIFTER: paymaster of the Fellowship of Billingsgate Porters.

SHOOTING UP: storing corn in a granary for future sale.

SKINS AND ALL: grain delivery in the sacks in which it was transported.

SOCIETY, THE: *see* Fellowship.

STREET PORTERS: name of Ticket Porters (*q.v.*) during the early stage of their existence.

STRIKE: instrument for levelling corn in the bushel during metering.

SUFFERANCE WHARF: a wharf licensed by the Customs authorities on a temporary basis for the discharge of dutiable commodities.

TACKLEHOUSE PORTER: porterage contractor on behalf of a major City Company.

TICKET PORTER: Porter working at certain stations either at the waterside or at a stand in the City, carrying goods not allotted to other groups of Porters; at the early stage a member of the Society of Street Porters, subsequently organized in a joint Society with Tacklehouse Porters (*q.v.*).

TURN IN, HAVING HIS: taking an authorized place in a working team.

TURN LABOUR: porterage work organized according to seniority.

UPPER RULER: chairman of the Court of Rulers and Assistants (*q.v.*).

UPTOWN PORTER: Ticket Porter (*q.v.*) whose work is away from the waterside.

VESSEL, TAKING UP A: collecting the fees for all porterage work done on a ship.

VINTNERS' PORTERS: *see* Wine Tackle Porters.

WATERSIDE PORTER: Ticket Porter (*q.v.*) who works at the wharves and quays.

WAY, BREAKING THE: taking up the gang planks.

WAY, MAKING THE: putting down the gang planks.

WEIGHERS' PORTERS: Porters employed by the various Customs Weighers, who were free of the City, but not incorporated in Fellowships.

WINE TACKLE PORTERS: Porters employed by the Vintners' Company for the carrying of wines.

WOOL PORTERS: *see* Blackwell Porters.

I

THE HEYDAY

1

GENERAL

(a) Scope of Porterage in London

To any port or market, the transport of merchandise is an important concern. On its availability and cost depends the decision of traders to use one centre rather than another; as part of the selling price of commodities, freight and handling charges affect the general price level of the locality. In a gradually expanding town the demand for transport services increases, while the task of moving goods grows more complicated as longer distances have to be covered. Before competitive enterprise could be relied upon to provide transport services at the lowest possible price, their availability and cost would fall to the responsibility of municipal and port authorities. On the success with which this duty was discharged depended the competitive importance of business centres in a period of expanding trade.

A city like London realized this duty at an early date. It required transport services of two kinds, by water and by land. Water transport in due course was subdivided, lightermen undertaking the moving of goods, watermen the carriage of persons. Land transport involving long distances became the duty of carmen—drivers of carts in the City and beyond. These methods of moving goods implied simple mechanical aids: watermen and lightermen had to handle boats, a task requiring some skill where the river was crowded; carmen had to steer their carts along equally congested, narrow and badly-surfaced streets. There remained the most primitive form of land transport, the carrying of goods by human agency without the aid of any mechanical device. This was the task of the City's Porters.*

* In order to distinguish authorized and licensed porters from men merely undertaking porterage services, the former have been spelt with a capital P throughout.

Goods were carried by the Porters either on their backs or on their heads, by means of slings or suspended from bars resting on the shoulders of two Porters. These modes of carriage resisted mechanization for many centuries, particularly as they had arisen in connection with such intricate operations as the loading and unloading of vessels. Goods arrived in ships' bottoms, whence they had to be hauled on deck, handled into lighters or carried on shore over planks thrown from ship to land, sometimes over a number of other ships. It was in their capacity as stevedores and dockworkers, to give them their modern names, that Porters made their earliest appearance in City records. But though Porters loaded and unloaded vessels, this never constituted more than part of their activities. Once landed, goods had to be carried to granaries or other stores and suitably stacked. Commodities for dispatch had to be similarly moved in the opposite direction before being stowed in ships' holds. Such merchandise was not brought to, nor collected from, the waterside in carts, which would have left Porters to concentrate merely on ship-to-shore activities.

The original reason for the absence of such a division of labour is undoubtedly chronological: Porters plied their trade long before wheeled vehicles were brought into use; hence Porters grew accustomed to carrying goods not only on to and from ships, but also between the waterside and their destinations before ever carmen existed. But even when carts and carmen made their appearance, they did not for a long time contest the Porters' privilege of carrying cargoes unloaded from or loaded on to ships. Wharf space was very limited; even a single horse and cart, if brought close to the vessel, would have considerably obstructed the working of the wharf, whereas no arrangement contributed less to congestion than a Porter carrying each load from the vessel not only to the wharf, but across it townwards to its destination. Newer quays and wharves were constructed, some wide enough to accommodate carts, especially coal wharves used by woodmongers, but not until the eighteenth century did direct discharge of goods from vessels into carts call in question the Porters' privileges. The scope of carts within the City was equally restricted by the width of the carriage-way. They could move along the broader streets, but narrow alleys, passages and courtyards precluded their use. Here

Porters enjoyed a natural monopoly in the transport of loads. They became carriers of goods within the City as well as in the waterside-to-warehouse traffic; a special branch of the trade, the Uptown Porters, engaged in carriage of commodities at a distance from the waterside. At a period when absence of good postal facilities often called for special delivery services, they became predecessors of latter-day special messengers.

Like other centres, London from early times constituted a market for a wider area. To London came from the surrounding country-side goods, above all foodstuffs, for display and sale in the town's various specialized markets. Such markets were situated in the City centre; to have the merchandise available there in time for market opening and to remove it after sale, without in the process paralysing all other traffic, proved no easy task. Where country carts and wagons drove straight to the market, they had to be unloaded quickly and withdrawn as soon as possible. Far more difficult though more common was the discharge when country carts carried goods for various con-signees, sometimes even for different markets. They required a distributing agent in London to take delivery of mixed loads, sort them and direct the various consignments to their destinations. This function was assumed by the innholders who, in addition to accom-modating travellers, developed a considerable trade in accommodating, directing and supervising merchandise on its way to markets. Inn-yards formed islands of refuge where goods, without obstructing the high-ways, could be unloaded, sorted and made ready for onward dispatch. Either the innholder's own cart or a Porter would assume responsibility for the last lap of the commodities' journey to market; even if con-veyed in the cart, such goods upon arrival at the market were unloaded by Porters who soon came to know the various salesmen's stalls as well as where and when goods would be wanted in any particular section of the market. Market portering developed into an important branch of the porterage business, even though the City Porters never had the whole field to themselves; in some market branches, guilds employed men of their own to carry their goods. Nor do Porters ever appear to have enjoyed much of the business of removing goods from markets after sale; though they were available to do the work, the majority of buyers preferred to carry their purchases away themselves or through their own servants, as they were entitled to do.

Porters were more than mere human beasts of burden, at least in theory: they occupied a position of trust and responsibility. Wherever bulky goods changed hands, their quantities had to be authoritatively ascertained; this might happen on board ship or in a granary or store. In an age of unreliable weights and measures the duty had to be discharged by an impartial body. The authority administering a port or market was the obvious choice. To be measured, bulky goods had to be carried to and poured into official containers, nor could the measurer be certain that containers had been fairly and truly filled unless impartial porters, owing allegiance and showing favour to neither buyer nor seller, were employed in the work. Hence City Porters throughout their history are found by the side of City Meters—men who at the working level had usually been elevated to their office from the Porters' ranks and were expected to employ licensed Porters only. By thus guaranteeing fair measure, the market authority fulfilled another of its duties.

(b) Nature and Strength of the Labour Force

The carrying of heavy loads is an unpleasant, depressing, and largely unskilled occupation. Men engage in it because they have been unable to acquire any skill valued more highly by society, or because the exercise of such skill has not afforded them and their families a livelihood. So much is the porter identified with unskilled labour that in primitive societies the word 'porter' is often used to designate every type of unskilled labourer,[1] on the assumption that he will mostly be employed in the carriage of burdens. In any economy offering alternatives, recruits to this trade are therefore drawn from two groups: the bulk consists of physically strong representatives of the lowest stratum who, lacking ability or social opportunity of acquiring any skill, are therefore driven to employing themselves in an occupation which makes use of their brawn; a minority are skilled craftsmen fallen on bad times and resorting to porterage as a measure of despair because all else has failed. A labour force thus composed raises a number of problems. It suffers from chronic instability. Craftsmen gladly and eagerly return to their crafts at the slightest indication that circumstances have changed in favour of earning their living as well, or better, by plying their crafts than by portering; Porters work at their jobs, not because their occupation inspires them with pride, but because they know of no other way of earning their living. However essential a link in the chain along which goods pass from the producer to the customer, the Porter does not occupy an honoured place in society and is only too ready to vacate it if he sees a chance. Moreover, many members of the labour force have to drop out of portering prematurely because the strain overtaxes their strength. Accidents take a considerable toll, but in any case porterage is a young man's work; constant carrying of heavy loads ages men prematurely, and a Porter cannot look forward to a long working life without loss of vigour and capacity. This is true of those taking up porterage in their youth; it bears far more heavily on men whom necessity drives to this occupation later in life. None of the organizations set up to deal with porterage succeeded in solving satisfactorily the problem of ageing Porters.

If an authority responsible for satisfactory goods transport may at times have to contend with an outflow of labour assuming proportions which jeopardize the maintenance of adequate standards of service, the dangers of an unstable labour force will far more often manifest themselves in the opposite direction. As the last resort of the unsuccessful seeker after employment, porterage tends to attract a shifting and shiftless population washed up by the tides of political and social change. By rendering employment scarcer and more precarious, each trade depression sweeps additional elements of this uprooted population into portering. London suffered from an increase in the number of poor who settled in various parishes or remained just outside the City boundaries in an attempt to avoid supervision by the City authorities. Sturdy beggars troubled the capital even more than the rest of the country, and in the late 1570s London parish constables received orders to administer whippings to vagrants and newcomers who could not support themselves, before sending them away. Such orders were issued shortly after a committee of Aldermen had investigated complaints of disorders daily instigated by the Porters of the City. Migrants from a distance, unfamiliar with employment prospects, not sure as yet whether to attempt settlement or to pass on to other areas, saw an easy way of making a little money by porterage which required neither training nor tackle nor much local knowledge. Whether adequate or not, a porterage labour force is exposed to a periodical inflow of such human flotsam and jetsam, unsettling and often underbidding those who have made a living as Porters for some time. Neither is such inflow regulated to any significant extent by the rewards offered, nor the demand exercised, for porterage services; hunger and absence of alternative methods of earning a living, not employment opportunities in porterage, determine the number of men offering themselves as porters. This threat found clear expression in a mayoral proclamation of 1617 which explained that lenience and toleration towards a few unauthorized porters by the City authorities

hath beene an occasion of late to invite and draw many other slight and vagrant People from all Parts of the Kingdome unto this Citty, who here (presuming of the like Favovour) become Lodgers and Inmates; and wthout any Order, Admittance, or Allowance, daily intrude themselves into the Labour of Porters in Blackwell Hall, Leadenhall, and all other Market Places, Streetes, Lanes, Corners, Wharfes, Keyes, and Innes, in and about this Citty; many of them being also Hucksters, Forestallers, and Regraters; and others of them being Brokers for Regraters and Forestallers of all sorts and kinds of Victualls and other Merchandizes comming to this Citty by Land or by Water to be solde, whereby many Inconveniences dayly grow and increase to this Citty and Cittizens thereof, and others resorting to the same, by the inhancing of the Prizes of Victualls, Rents of Houses, and otherwise, by reason of the Multitude of this sorte of People.[2]

Indigence and low social esteem are poor incentives to law-abiding behaviour, nor does a shifting population pay excessive respect to laws in a locality where they feel themselves to be but birds of passage. Porterage attracts the physically strongest specimens of a class most likely to take the law—or at least what they regard as the law—into their own hands. The existence of a labour force engaged in portering, however necessary to keep trade moving, constituted a constant threat to public order and a permanent irritant to authorities charged with police duties. Until the nineteenth century the position of these authorities remained very weak; they commanded no regular forces of any strength whose unremitting supervision could divine a potential danger to public safety and nip it in the bud. Yeomen of the Waterside, ward constables or bailiffs were no match for crowds of unruly Porters on mischief bent, especially if gang warfare broke out among themselves or between them and groups of men who had been forced into similar employment by equally unpropitious circumstances, such as the watermen. Unable to summon outside forces of sufficient strength to intimidate and discipline Porters, the City fell back on the only feasible method of enforcing order upon the Porters—by enrolling them in an organization controlled by men of their own trade under City supervision. The means by which the City imposed this discipline was privilege. The Crown having granted the City Corporation exclusive jurisdiction in the Port of London, a jurisdiction which included sole rights of porterage,[3] no Porter could exercise his trade in the Port of London (an area far wider than the City of London) unless licensed by the City Corporation. Provided the number of Porters so licensed remained larger than that of intruders, the City in any test of strength could rely on commanding the bigger battalions.

(c) The Fellowship Form of Organization

Guilds are a familiar feature of craft organization. By forming a guild, craftsmen protected their skill against outsiders; they also regulated conditions of work and employment within the craft and disciplined members. Theirs was a self-governing organization; more than that, as nominees of their guilds, craftsmen participated in municipal administration. It was from the liverymen of the guilds that cities recruited their governments. Porters were the least skilled of labourers, occupying too lowly a position in City society to aspire to similar functions. Guilds grew into City Companies, many with royal charters. Porters were organized into mere fellowships, owing their existence to nothing more impressive than Acts of Common Council; the life which the Common Council had given, it could take away again at pleasure if the child revolted against its progenitor. Fellowships had their own governing bodies, composed of Porters, but always at their head stood one or several City Aldermen, chosen not by the Porters themselves, but superimposed by Common Council legislation or by election in the Court of Aldermen.

By using the weapon of privilege for the purpose of organizing Porters, City authorities were able to pursue other desirable ends, besides introducing an element of much-needed discipline. Demand for porterage labour fluctuated in ways which, apart from seasonal variations, remained unpredictable: hazards reflected in the volume of goods changing hands could be meteorological, such as the influence of wind and weather on the arrival and departure of ships; political, such as the effect of naval warfare, especially privateering, on sea-borne trade; or purely economic, as in trade fluctuations. Employment in porterage was therefore casual in more senses than one. On demand conditions for porterage services the City could exercise no influence, but by limiting the total number of Porters licensed it curtailed the supply and thus contributed to the decasualization of employment. To keep the system reasonably flexible, Common Council Acts fixed maximum membership figures for each fellowship, but these could be increased by amending Acts to correspond with permanent expansion of trade; if labour was required at short notice, unlicensed men could be admitted on a temporary basis.

To become a member of a City guild, a man had to take up the freedom of the City of London. To any craftsman this represented an indispensable condition for exercizing his craft in London which he would not seek to call in question. Not so an unskilled labourer who had no prospect of participating in the exercise of City government; he could see little advantage in becoming a freeman of the City, and the expenditure necessary entailed for him a far more real sacrifice. With numbers of unskilled increasing faster than those of skilled, London ran the risk of degenerating into a City in which only a small upper layer of skilled craftsmen and large traders had taken up their freedom and conducted the government, whereas the majority of the governed remained permanently excluded from both. To attach privileges to the freedom of the City enhanced its value; by making freedom a condition of entry into a fellowship of Porters, the City found a means of compelling certain groups of unskilled labourers to acquire a freedom with which they would otherwise have willingly dispensed.

Although the Port of London, as defined from the early charters onwards, covered a very wide area, the trade employing Porters in the Middle Ages was concentrated in a small sector, the neighbourhoods of Queenhithe and Billingsgate. Porters were stationed at these centres to deal with the work. As trade spread, the Port as a whole became busier, though the area west of London Bridge roughly up to Blackfriars continued to be the point of maximum concentration. Porters tended to collect there rather than at the periphery of business activities where jobs occurred less frequently and at irregular intervals. Had this situation been left to the free interplay of supply and demand, either no Porters at all would have been available at the periphery or those stationed far from the centre would have had to charge proportionately higher fees for their services to compensate themselves for the diminished volume of employment falling to their lot. It is at least arguable that this would have done harm to the development of the Port by strengthening the propensity towards concentrating activities in a small part and making insufficient use of the remainder. The City authorities did not permit this to happen. Through the fellowships they guaranteed the availability of Porters in whatever part of the Port their services were needed; though Porters did not take up permanent stations in outlying areas, they could be compelled to journey there and perform porterage labour whenever a job required it. Moreover, however distant the locality and however small the quantity of work to be done, porterage had to be performed at the standard rates fixed for the Port (with very slight locational variations). In enforcing this rule, the City authorities did their best to spread utilization of Port facilities over the widest possible area.

Poor men themselves, Porters often carried valuable loads. This raised the question of liability if through the Porter's fault employers suffered damage or loss. The Porter was a common carrier, liable as a bailee, but the Porter's liability proved of little interest to merchants painfully aware of the fact that, even if apprehended, he could not pay.[4] Just as Porters had a duty to perform services, merchants were under an obligation to use licensed Porters—an obligation which could hardly be enforced upon merchants unless they were provided with a more substantial prospect of compensation than that derived from the

liability of individual Porters. Here again the fellowships proved use-
ful: as a condition of membership, Porters could be made to find
securities for good behaviour and to enter into bonds. From such
bonds, funds were formed to accept collective liability for any damage
caused by a member to a customer.

The City's claim to make porterage in London a prerogative of its
freemen did not pass unchallenged. Of Porters plying their trade in
London, not all were prepared or able to acquire the City's freedom.
The transition from free to licensed porterage had of necessity to be
gradual. Unlicensed porters, however, divined danger and, knowing
the City Corporation to be bent on their gradual elimination, in 1579
petitioned the Privy Council for protection; not being admitted in
London, petitioners adopted the general title of Queen's Porters. The
Privy Council referred the complaint to the Lord Mayor, and the
Court of Aldermen buried it in a committee; not even an angry
reminder from the Privy Council could resurrect it. Having decided
on its solution to the porterage problem, the City was not to be shaken
in its determination to reserve the employment to its freemen.

That considerations of public order predominated in the decision of
the City Corporation to regulate Porters, becomes apparent from the
period at which it was put into operation. The year 1579, outstanding
in City annals on account of the increase of the poor and the consequent
difficulty of keeping the peace, saw the organization of two of the
principal groups of Porters. Previous measures had amounted to no
more than spasmodic regulation of limited aspects of porterage activity,
principally charges and geographic scope. In terms of commodities,
these early rules applied to imports of corn and salt, necessities of life
the price of which must always have been a matter of concern to
the City Corporation, which hence, in the late thirteenth century, led
to some supervision of their Porters which fell into disuse in the course
of the following centuries and was resumed only in the 1540s, at the
request of the Porters themselves, who at that period felt in need of
City protection from the influx of paupers into London setting up in
competition. Porters concerned with overseas trade were organized in
1579. Many of them under the terms of their privileges dealt also with
coastwise goods; Porters discharged corn arriving in the Port of

London, whether from the Baltic or from Essex and Kent, and the same group of Porters was also entitled to unload coal vessels from the Tyne. This makes it impossible to fix an exact date when porterage in the coastwise trade became fully organized. The last—because the least important—type of porterage to attract close supervision by the Court of Aldermen was that which took place in the streets at a distance from the waterside, but even here a first attempt at organization had been made by 1584. Thus during the six years between 1579 and 1584 every type of City Porter was brought within disciplinary reach of the City authorities. Nor were Porters the only unskilled labourers to whom the City applied this treatment; in 1580 similar regulations by the Court of Aldermen, no doubt for similar reasons, dealt with the City's carmen.[5]

(d) The Four Classes of London Porters

There emerged in the course of this regulation the four classes of Porters which will provide the main headings of the present study: Aliens' Porters, Tacklehouse Porters, Street (later known as Ticket) Porters, and Billingsgate Porters. Of these groups no two were organized in identical manner. The form of organization most familiar to the City, the guild, had evolved in response to the needs of skilled occupations, and was appropriate neither to the requirements nor to the social status of unskilled labourers. The City took advantage of existing guilds so far as it could use them as instruments of supervision: wherever Porters performed work on behalf of a particular City Company, that Company could be charged with responsibility for the men and their equipment. Tacklehouse Porters thus grew up within the framework of the major City Companies which maintained waterside tacklehouses as bases from which these Porters operated. As members of major City Companies, Tacklehouse Porters quickly achieved an economic and social status superior to all other types of Porters. The laborious and irksome character of the work ensures that no Porter will continue to port, once he has gone up in the world; a well-to-do Porter is a man who sets others to work carrying loads on his behalf and for his account, in fact a porterage contractor. This development transformed Tacklehouse Porters from a group of specialists within the porterage trade into an important section of Porters' employers.

The City's Packer and Porter of Aliens' Goods, to give him his full title, was not in the same category; though he partook of the description of Porter, at no time did he personally carry goods, but was always the lessee of one of the functions granted to the City by the early charters, employing Porters to work under his orders. These Aliens' Porters were not organized, merely licensed, and thus experienced City supervision in its loosest and least burdensome manner. As in the instance of the guilds, the City had in the person of the Packer and Porter a responsible authority to whom to delegate such supervision.

The remaining two groups of Porters, not working under known and trusted management, required more rigid and elaborate organization. For the Corn, Coal and Salt (also known as Billingsgate) Porters, this took the form of constituting them into a fellowship under aldermanic control. If not conspicuously successful, this organization proved at least enduring: it served the Billingsgate Porters through three centuries of corporate existence. When the City repeated the experiment by establishing a similar fellowship of Street Porters—the type of Porters originally confined to uptown work and later on usurping additional business not specifically assigned to other groups of Porters— the weakness of the device became clear: like the guild of which it represented an inferior copy, a fellowship relied largely on self-government and depended for discipline on the responsibility of its leading members. This amount of self-discipline was not attained in an organization recruited from the lowest stratum of unskilled and unsettled labourers, nor were spasmodic attentions given by two Aldermen to grievances and abuses sufficient to impart the amount of supervision needed. In its search for a more appropriate solution the City retraced its steps. In their early stages, it had supervised the Tacklehouse Porters through their guilds. Now that Tacklehouse Porters had become respected guild members and in their capacity as porterage contractors large employers of the Street Porters, why not impose upon them responsibility for supervision and discipline of the latter? A precedent for such a solution existed: in 1580, when the City had felt compelled to strengthen control of the carmen, their rule and guidance had been entrusted to the Fellowship of Woodmongers who as fuel suppliers provided them with their principal loads. Similarly the City in 1609 formed the Society of Tacklehouse and Ticket Porters. While it would be going too far to suggest that it thereby harnessed Pegasus to the same yoke as the ox, the combination of porterage employers and labourers in a single society—a novelty in the organization of Porters—can be explained only as an attempt to fix responsibility for discipline and government of the Ticket Porters on Tacklehouse Porters. This device, however irksome to both parties, met with more success than independent incorporation of the labouring element.

The beginning of the seventeenth century thus saw in existence four separate bodies of Porters: the Aliens' Porters, licensed men working under the City Packer; the Tacklehouse and the Ticket Porters, men with different functions and privileges, but forcibly united in a single society; and the Billingsgate or Fellowship Porters, a fellowship of Porters concerned with the carriage of measurable commodities. All of them had been in existence before 1600, but owed definite organizational form to the pressure of social change in the later sixteenth century.

(e) The Rights of Different Classes of Porters

The seventeenth and eighteenth centuries represented the heyday of London Porters, during which their prerogative, derived from the City of London's monopoly of the provision of services throughout the Port of London, never suffered serious challenge. On the contrary, the City Corporation's rights found more complete and detailed expression than ever before in its charter granted in 1605 by James I, the text of which was repeated in the *Inspeximus* charter of Charles I in 1638. When Charles II in 1681 confiscated the City charters by virtue of a King's Bench judgment that all City liberties were forfeited to the king, a few merchants quickly saw an opportunity of breaking the Porters' monopoly by refusing to pay established rates or even by introducing unlicensed porters. The Billingsgate Porters promptly petitioned the Privy Council, which took the view that London metage and porterage rights now vested in the king. By confirming

the appropriate Common Council legislation, James II in 1686 restored
the Fellowship Porters' privileges until City rights in their entirety
were re-established by an Act of Parliament in 1690. A court of law
may be thought to have called them in question in deciding (upon a
suit brought by the City Chamberlain in 1704) that, while municipal
by-laws might compel all porters within the City to be freemen, they
could not compel strangers coming to the City to employ City
Porters only. It gave as its reasons that strangers could neither recognize
authorized Porters as such nor force such City Porters to work for
them, nor would strangers have any remedy against a city which failed
to appoint an adequate porterage force. Though the judgment was not
reversed, it had no effect on the employment of City Porters, particularly as a suit by a subsequent City Chamberlain twenty-four years
later elicited a verdict that the City's privileges relating to free Porters
remained valid.

While Porters did not suffer from diminution of their overall
privileges, demarcation disputes between different groups of Porters
interrupted trade throughout the period. Allocation of work among
different Porters' organizations could be effected according to one of
four criteria: type of merchant requiring services; type of goods
handled; locality where services were required; places of origin or
destination of goods involved. Singly, any of these might have served,
though the second and third were far more satisfactory than the first
and fourth. The City of London however used all four: Aliens' and
Tacklehouse Porters served specified groups of merchants, while
Fellowship Porters concerned themselves with measurable goods only;
certain Ticket Porters were entitled to all work done at a distance from
the waterside, while the prerogative of both Tacklehouse and waterside Ticket Porters depended on the origin or destination of merchandise. Criteria in such profusion could not avoid overlapping; nothing
contributed more to endless conflicts, physical and legal, between
different groups of City Porters than the confusion caused by mutually
non-exclusive definitions of Porters' rights. Time and again complaints
reached the Court of Aldermen, which decided particular issues
arbitrarily, without establishing as a general principle that a single
criterion ought to rule the allocation of work to all Porters.

Not that even a more judicious division of available labour among the claimants could have completely avoided demarcation disputes. Two centuries constitute too long a period of validity for any ruling based on trade; in these particular two centuries England developed from being a growing but peripheral commercial country in Europe to becoming its foremost trading nation, with the changes in the volume and structure of trade which this implied. Certain types of goods, once of great importance, faded out of international trade; others, unknown when regulations had first been formulated, came to occupy a prominent place. As the commodity structure and direction of trade changed, so, simultaneously, the fortunes of different groups of Porters waxed and waned.

In these circumstances it was fortunate for the City Porters that, whatever modifications commerce in particular goods or with particular countries underwent, the overall volume of employment increased. At all times the Port of London accommodated a substantial proportion of the country's total sea-borne trade. No single measure of the increase in commerce passing through London Porters' hands is available, especially in a century as exposed to trade fluctuations and wars as the eighteenth. In 1796 the Inspector General of Customs furnished to the Select Committee on Accommodation for Trade and Shipping in the Port of London a table showing the expansion of imports and exports for that port:

	Imports*	Exports*
1700	4,875,539	5,387,787
1710	2,894,737	4,622,371
1720	4,958,102	5,008,246
1730	6,224,882	6,344,766
1740	4,904,249	5,593,734
1750	5,540,564	8,415,218
1760	7,063,396	10,726,709
1770	8,889,868	9,267,709
1780	6,794,021	6,837,960
1790	12,275,547	10,716,549
1794	14,863,238	16,578,803

* Expressed in sterling to the nearest complete pound.

C

Compilers of commercial statistics in the eighteenth century based values of goods on a rate-book established in 1696 and infrequently adjusted for subsequent price changes. This renders their figures useless for purposes of estimating values. But even as an indication of volume, aggregate amounts collected on this basis are imperfect, owing to changes in the type of goods carried in commerce. In addition to overseas trade, Porters were, moreover, concerned with coastwise trade, which remains unrepresented in this table.

The background of fluctuations against which expansion took place is better delineated by a table drawn from a modern source. Throughout the eighteenth century seamen suffered deductions of 6d. a month from their wages to support the Greenwich Hospital for disabled seamen. Mr. Ralph Davis has pointed out that the receipts of the Receivers of Sixpences in different ports constitute an indication of the numbers of merchant sailors employed and, implicitly, of the number and size of merchant ships plying there. In order to avoid the impact of short-term fluctuations, Mr. Davis's calculations of receipts by the Receiver of Sixpences in London have been turned into ten-year annual averages. The usefulness of these figures is reduced because only mariners serving on ships of British ownership were liable to these deductions, whereas Porters concerned themselves equally with alien-owned ships. As Britain in the eighteenth century gained on Holland as a maritime carrier and the tonnage of British shipping in the Port of London increased relative to that of Dutch, this table overstates the expansion in Porters' employment, the error becoming larger in later decades.

Annual Average Receipts by the Receiver of Six-pences in London (£)

1707–1709	3,449	1750–1759	3,310
1710–1719*	3,948	1760–1769	4,318
1720–1729	4,018	1770–1779	3,896
1730–1739	3,651	1780–1789	5,123
1740–1749	3,009	1790–1799	5,119

* 1714–1716 missing.

The great majority of Porters engaged in waterside work during part or the whole of their working time. The above figures furnish evidence for the increase in their employment; at no time of their existence were City Porters more prosperous than in the eighteenth century. This may well excuse the error of the anonymous author of *A General Description of all Trades digested in Alphabetical Order* in describing Porters as a City Company, the ninetieth in precedence; there never was a City Company of Porters. Setting out what he knew about the trade in 1747, he continued:

> The Use of these every Gentleman, Merchant, and Trader knows; but they differ greatly, according to the Nature of the Business they follow; some being for downright Labour and heavy Work in various Shapes, others middling, and some very little or none, as those belonging to the Inns of Court, Companies and Noblemen; but most of them get good livelihoods, and some live very handsomely.

However unassailable the legal position of freemen Porters in the City, attempts occurred now and then on the part of unauthorized porters working in the London area to encroach upon their work. In 1613–14 such unlicensed porters enjoyed the protection of justices of the peace of Middlesex and Surrey, much to the disgust of the City authorities. Sir John Swinnerton, Lord Mayor in 1613, called a meeting of Aldermen and of London, Middlesex and Surrey magistrates in order to hammer out an agreement. When country justices subsequently attempted to depart from its terms, the City Remembrancer was promptly instructed to remind them of these proceedings. Nor did non-free porters working in the suburbs succeed in enlisting the City Corporation's sympathy against those only recently admitted Porters.

On another plane, authorized Porters vindicated their legal position when learned counsel in the eighteenth century made it clear that they had the right, while in the employment of merchants, to enter any wharves, even if it were only for the purpose of carrying merchandise across the wharf. No wharfinger was entitled to deny them access while they acted in the exercise of their employment.

(f) A Corporation of London Porters?

There existed in London other Porters free of the City who did not
form part of the Porters' bodies mentioned above. Such were the
Porters of Leadenhall. Theirs must have been considered offices of
profit. On one occasion a servant of the Lord Mayor was appointed to
their number, on another a Merchant Taylor surrendered a place
which was given to a Haberdasher without prejudice to a reversion
previously granted. Porters also served the Master Weighers of the
King's Beam at the waterside and of the Iron Beam in Thames Street.
Yet another category worked at Blackwell Hall under a Clerk and
Master Porter against whom the 'poor Porters that carry forth Essex
Bays out of Blackwell Hall' would occasionally lodge complaints with
the City Corporation. These Porters had their remuneration fixed on a
time, instead of an output, basis. Porters organized by the City received
payment in proportion to work done, while Leadenhall, Blackwell and
Weighers' Porters served for fixed hours at a pre-arranged wage.
With these special groups of Porters our story will not be concerned.

Observers of City Porters in their different groupings could not fail
to weigh the advantages of incorporating them in a single organization.
Indeed, the patent of such a Corporation for Porters was transmitted to
the City Chamberlain in 1614, its validity lacking only a seal which the
Lord Mayor had refrained from affixing. Did he realize that his hesita-
tion doomed the scheme to permanent failure? A petition addressed to
the king in 1633 for the incorporation of all Porters in London caused a
committee of Aldermen to consider the proposal afresh. The text of
the 1633 petition is not extant, but a long address to the king five years
later treated as abuses committed by existing Porters' societies the
suspension from porterage employment of members who failed to pay
quarterage, as well as the barring of men who had not been admitted or
had not paid their admission fees, besides accusing the societies of
collecting excessive funds. The remedy suggested—outside control
through the agency of a controller appointed under royal letters patent
—ignored the fact that such outside control was already vested in the
City Corporation. The king was sufficiently impressed to appoint a
royal commission of enquiry, describing unincorporated societies of

Porters as an intrusion upon the royal power and prerogative—an utterance symptomatic of the king's general feeling towards the City of London rather than of his considered judgment. Not surprisingly, nothing resulted from the commission. When the idea was mooted once again in 1691, the interested party wishing to become Controller of a Corporation of Porters by royal appointment, it was referred to the law officers of the Crown. Presumably they disillusioned him.[6]

2

PORTERS OF ALIENS' GOODS

(a) Rights and Duties of Alien Merchants

ALIEN* merchants' activities in medieval England present a difficult problem. National legislation fosters the illusion that statutes and regulations applied to all merchant strangers. Nothing could be further from the truth. Well might laws subject aliens trading in England to certain restrictions or burdens: those merchants from overseas who belonged to powerful organizations or made themselves indispensable to the sovereign soon obtained exemption—exemption embodied in charters if designed to be permanent, or in Privy Council ordinances if of a more temporary character. Accordingly the scope of statutes legislating for aliens is impossible to define; they applied to whoever had failed to contract out.

Treatment of aliens depended on the shifting balance of power between contestants in two political conflicts. Internally king and nobility struggled with municipal authorities, the former cultivating what might without too much exaggeration be called a cosmopolitan outlook: they desired to attract alien merchants to the country and to engage in direct transactions with them. To extend the boundaries of commerce to men with immediate access to foreign merchandise allowed English consumers to benefit from the widening of the market. This was clearly illustrated in 1377 when a curtailment of alien traders' activities resulted in a general rise of merchandise prices in England which caused popular dissatisfaction. These restrictions imposed on merchant strangers had to be rescinded in the following year. But the motives of sovereign and aristocracy were not wholly unselfish. Of potential customers for imported consumption goods they themselves

---

* Throughout this book *alien* denotes a person not of English nationality, whereas *foreigner* means a person not free of the City of London.

formed the largest group; to purchase at the lowest prices accorded with their own immediate interests. The king had a second and even more direct concern: royal revenues depended chiefly on duties imposed on international commerce. That such trade should flourish and increase was a matter of palpable advantage to him.

City and port authorities on the other hand put municipal privileges first. Though far from wishing to ban alien merchants, they relegated them to second place, where they ranked below enfranchised native traders in privileges and opportunities. For this reason municipalities wanted alien merchants to confine themselves to wholesale transactions with traders free of the city. In London, for instance, alien merchants—always excepting those who had succeeded in striking special bargains with the City Corporation—could not until the late thirteenth century own premises or keep servants; their merchandise had to be sold on board their ships, the City providing Porters for their requirements. The aliens themselves had to occupy lodgings where the landlords acted as brokers. Higher fees were often charged for identical services to alien merchants than to enfranchised traders; when national customs duties levied on merchant strangers fell into disuse, municipalities frequently adapted and adopted them as local taxes. If in need of justification for this policy, towns and ports had recourse to the argument of reciprocity, claiming that alien merchants received no worse treatment at their hands than did English traders in the strangers' home countries. Reciprocity proved a potent argument because its exact meaning eluded definition. Not only could alien merchants claim—as did the Hanse traders in England in 1380—that they had no power to guarantee reciprocal treatment, not being the rulers of their home towns; precisely what reciprocity involved could hardly be deduced from their contention that English traders already enjoyed more freedom in Hanse towns than they themselves did in England.

Parliament at first represented the aristocratic point of view favouring freedom for alien merchants. The law of 1225 (9 Henry III, cap. 30) provided clear evidence in this respect. But in proportion as the king was driven by the needs of his war chest to seek financial aid from the municipalities, in particular from the largest of all, the City of London, and as the House of Commons gained in power and importance,

Parliament gradually veered to a more parochial attitude. To trace in detail the fluctuations of this battle would be tedious: during the period when all London's liberties were suspended by the king (1285–1298), aliens enjoyed a large measure of freedom which became more strictly circumscribed as soon as the monarchy was put in commission (1311–1323). The *nova custuma*, embodying aliens' rights, were revived repeatedly in the fourteenth century, alternating with charters granting London and other towns extensive privileges of controlling their trade. London skilfully argued, not that it stood above the royal writ, but merely that royal charters granted to the City Corporation—as London Sheriffs submitted to the Privy Council in 1420—overrode any privileges alien merchants might have obtained. Whether at any one time this interpretation secured acceptance depended on the degree of the sovereign's need to rely on London for finance.

Alien merchants' rights were fashioned not only by the conflict for power within England but also by the contest for domination in the European trading area. Wars and alliances did not affect alien traders in general, but only particular groups of merchants suffering or benefiting from their relationship to powers who at one time acted as allies, at another as enemies of England. Purveyors of essential imports for which substitutes could not be obtained, found it easier than others to strike special bargains. Picardy merchants from Amiens, Corbie, and Nesle who brought to England woad, one of the most important textile dyestuffs, agreed in 1237 to pay the London Corporation a fine of £100 and an annual sum of 50 marks for the right to land and house their woad; Amiens merchants alone enjoyed the further privilege of choosing, jointly with their London counterparts, Meters and brokers of woad, who subsequently took the oath before the Lord Mayor. The porterage arrangements are not known, but may well have been similar to those in Bristol half a century later, when four woad Porters were sworn to the thorough and impartial discharge of their duties. Imported woad had to be lodged in designated warehouses where Porters before sale broke it into little pieces and mixed it four times, stacking it after the fourth mixing in preparation for inspection and grading which determined the price. Porters were selected by agreement between the Bristol municipal authorities and the woad merchants; at least two of them had to be engaged for each sale. They were entitled to fixed fees, higher if employed in the breaking, lower if only in the mixing, receiving twice as much for Toulouse as for Picardy woad. Bristol burgesses had a choice between breaking their own woad or having the work performed by the Porters whom in any case they had to employ for the mixing; all other merchants were compelled to use the Porters' services for both processes at fees higher than those exacted from burgesses. No evidence exists of London Porters being specially assigned to woad, although in two instances of that period Meters of woad were appointed and sworn upon nomination by the woad merchants on the one hand and the dyers of the City on the other.[7]

The strongest organized group of alien merchants with whom English municipalities had to contend in the fourteenth and fifteenth centuries was the Hanse. Not only did its members belong to powerful countries; their own organization represented an important force, at least at times when they were united, and by denying to England and her merchants trading routes and outlets on the Continent could exercise strong pressure. The picture was a complex one, influenced by events in the Hundred Years' War, Hanseatic attempts to obtain the favour of various English sovereigns and the London mobs' resentment of privileges enjoyed by residents in the Steelyard; but in spite of shifting fortunes the balance tipped ever more decisively in the Hanse's favour. At Utrecht in 1474, Edward IV had to concede to the Hanse all their old privileges and liberties as defined by the Hanse's own interpretation of revived agreements. Nor was there any question of London in future overriding Hanse rights by virtue of its own charters: *'non obstantibus aliquibus privilegiis ipsis Londoniensibus concessis, quibus nec contra prefatos mercatores gaudere debebunt'* made it clear that in a clash the privileges granted to Hanse merchants would prevail.

How much bearing has the question of Hanseatic rights on porterage services in London? No direct evidence exists; the use of Porters is never mentioned. Indirectly, porterage was concerned in one of the specific complaints raised by the Hanse envoys at Utrecht which led to the insertion of a paragraph in the final peace treaty. A grant first made to alien merchants by Edward I in 1303 regarding weighing and measuring of commodities had stipulated that only official weights and measures were to be used, sealed with the royal seal and deposited at designated places in all English trading towns and fairs. Before weighing, the scale should be seen to be empty and its pointers set level in the presence of buyer and seller. Having achieved this, the weigher should immediately remove his hands. Two years after this grant London had protested to the sovereign, claiming the right to its own methods of weighing and refusing to treat aliens more favourably than free London merchants (which casts a curious light on London's own opinion of its weighing procedure). Porters loaded goods on and off the scales; their services formed part of the weighing process. Although the grant had originally applied to all alien merchants, only the Hanse traders retained it into the fifteenth century. In the preliminaries to the Utrecht peace treaty they had complained bitterly of London's unfair weighing and measuring procedures at variance with the grant. The king did not want to coerce London more than necessary. In his reply he assured Hanseatic merchants that, since their last departure from England, more satisfactory weighing and measuring methods had been introduced in and by the City of London with which he had no desire to interfere, but he undertook to remedy any specific grievance which might subsequently be brought to his notice. The Hanseatic envoys accepted the king's assurance that weighers and Meters (of the latter only those of cloth received specific mention) would henceforth exercise their functions impartially, justly and faithfully and that, if they offended, the king would provide Hanse merchants with a specially appointed single weigher and a single Meter; in order to remedy imperfections in the scale used, its tongue would be extended beyond the length of one foot.[8]

Certainly Hanseatic merchants, possibly also other alien traders, could once again own houses in London in 1478. Edward IV in that year granted the City Corporation a charter conferring the right of scrutinizing and supervising the handling of all aliens' and denizens'* goods imported into or exported from the Port of London, mentioning specifically carriage and porterage of such goods, to which later enactments added scavage and balliage. All merchants, whether free and native or alien, were obliged to use authorized Porters; that they

* Naturalized aliens or sons of alien-born fathers.

had to employ different groups of Porters could have represented a grievance only to the extent to which substantial differences existed in either the efficiency displayed or the fees charged by various categories of Porters. Of this there is no evidence; charges levied by the Packer's Porters (as the group of Porters employed in the exercise of City rights over aliens' goods came to be called) for some services exceeded and for others merely equalled those made by Porters dealing with English merchants. That naturalization did not affect the status of aliens in this respect was twice confirmed by national legislation.

French merchants made a strong complaint to the king in 1535 about the charges to which the City of London subjected them. The peace treaty of 1514 had not permitted either country to discriminate against the other's merchants, yet the City of London had raised £4,000 to £5,000 a year from complainants by way of scavage duty, and compelled them at a fee of 18d. for every ton to use carts and Porters licensed by the City. Moreover, goods had been ruined while lying in the rain to await the arrival of Porters. Merchants were permitted neither to weigh their goods themselves nor to sell them without weighing; London hostmen gave them false weight to the extent of eight or ten per cent or even more, charging 3d. instead of the former 1½d. for the service of weighing. From every salt ship arriving in London the City levied an unaccustomed tribute of one bushel in every twenty, and the sale of wine was hedged around with restrictions unlike any suffered by English subjects in France. Protesting merchants and their goods were seized by the Lord Mayor even if they offered sureties. To all these charges the City opposed the plea of justification: scavage duty had been fixed by the Privy Council and applied to all merchant strangers; the use of licensed carts and Porters formed part of the public order maintained by the City Corporation, these carmen and Porters undertaking liability for any accident or damage to the goods handled; merchant strangers neither paid fees higher than they had always paid nor than those levied from English merchants, and were treated like the latter in the weighing procedure. The French merchants do not appear to have obtained any satisfaction.[9]

(b) City Packers and Porters of Aliens' Goods and their Men

The City's Packer and Porter of Aliens' Goods, also described as the Common Packer, held his post on a lease from the City Corporation. Yet in one sense he was a royal official in that he played a part in the collection of the royal customs. He received twice a year from the Exchequer Court parchment books containing numbered pages for the entry of all consignments exported on behalf of merchant strangers; these books, with all entries completed, had to be returned to the Exchequer at Easter and Michaelmas. In spite of his importance to customs collection, the king only rarely tried to influence the appointment: in 1524 Henry VIII wrote to the Court of Aldermen to request the reversion of the City Packer's situation for Thomas Sackville, groom porter. Whether the City authorities complied or not, a whole century passed before the Crown concerned itself again with this post. In the sixteenth and seventeenth centuries, competition for the lease and the right to grant it suggests that the office was a profitable one. Starting from Richard Wright, who held the place in the very early seventeenth century and underwent 'much cost and trouble in settling the office for the country's good and performed many good services for the City at his own great charge', most Packers are recorded by name. The reversion passed to Robert, Richard Wright's son who, however, predeceased his father, whereupon James I intervened with the City to transfer the reversion to another son, Lionel. The Corporation complied; Lionel became the next Packer. In 1630, probably at Lionel's demise, Francis Massingbird paid £600 for the office to the City chamber and gave gratuities to the Lord Mayor and the Sheriff. A young man of thirty-six years of age, looking forward to a long tenure, he was annoyed to find Francis Wallworth, scholar of Trinity College, Cambridge, and a clerk in the City Sheriffs' Court, seeking the king's support six years later to obtain a reversion of the office. The king complied, but a secret Court of Aldermen after hearing Massingbird refused to grant the reversion, and in the following year the king agreed to interfere no further with the appointment.

Up to the end of Charles I's reign, the authority within the City responsible for leasing the City Packer's office was the Court of Alder-

men, but the Common Council claimed this right among others during
the Interregnum, when it also halved the Lord Mayor's profits from the
office. Accordingly the Common Council in 1657 appointed Joseph
Dawson as City Packer in succession to John Adams, fixing his payment at £400 p.a., of which £173 6s. 8d. went to the Lord Mayor,
£150 to the Sheriffs, £66 13s. 4d. to the City chamber and £10 to the
Hospital of St. Bartholomew. The right of disposal reverted to the
Court of Aldermen after the Restoration. The value of the office
greatly appreciated; Richard Peirce in 1683 paid a yearly rent of £1,200
for a seven years' lease. Peirce was particularly well placed to execute
the office, being one of the Custom House Searchers; from records
referring to him as Colonel Peirce and from the king's declaring himself 'being well satisfyed with the Loyalty and good Seruices of the
Petr', he appears to have been a regular soldier. His lease was renewed;
he obtained a twenty-one years' grant of office in 1705 at a fine of
£1,000 and an annual rent of £950. Twelve years later he sub-let the
unexpired part of this lease to Daniel Blackwell, John Hall, Griffith
Lloyd and William Bigg. Perhaps he had grown too old to cope with
the work, but this represented the beginning of a century of financial
straits for Packers. He charged the sub-lessees an annual rent of only
£60; the office had suffered considerable loss of income through large-
scale naturalization of aliens who thereupon ceased to require the Packer's
services. By the time Peirce died insolvent, intestate, and in very mean
circumstances in 1722, he owed to the City rent exceeding £2,200. The
City chamber did not suffer a total loss, however, for a Customs officer
who had collected package and scavage duties on Peirce's behalf held a
considerable amount of money to be set against the indebtedness.

The City then cancelled the unexpired portion of Peirce's lease, but
being unaware of the existence of a sub-lease, it appointed a temporary
collector. Thereupon John Hall and William Bigg, the two surviving
sub-lessees, made themselves known and explained that they had paid
no rent since Peirce's death, but were anxious to make good the
arrears, continue the lease and obtain a renewal when it expired in
1726. It is likely that their wish was granted and that they held office
till 1739 when John Standish was appointed for twenty-one years at
the modest annual rental of £105—the amount which Aliens' Porters

paid for the remainder of the eighteenth century. Standish held office for less than eighteen months before assigning half the profits to Nathaniel Major; soon afterwards Standish died insolvent, Major alone continuing as Aliens' Porter. The emoluments of the office had become very exiguous; Major found himself in financial straits in 1746, owing arrears to the City and proving by the submission of accounts that his earnings did not suffice to pay them; nevertheless he was anxious to continue the lease, provided Standish's widow could be prevailed upon to relinquish her interest. After protracted formalities the City granted Major's wish; in 1752 he obtained a new twenty-one years' lease which could be terminated at six months' notice by either party.

Major died, leaving his widow to carry on the office; she appointed one of the Goldsmiths' Tacklehouse Porters, George Reynolds, to act as her deputy. On his death, twelve months before the expiry of the lease, the two other Goldsmiths' Tacklehouse Porters, William Arnold and Fuller White, became deputies and then lessees in their own names for three years. The brevity of the period of lease was due to the validity and value of the Aliens' Porter's office having been called in question in 1772; the three years were to serve as a trial period in which to determine by action at law in the Aliens' Porters' names, but at the City's expense, whether the courts would vindicate the Aliens' Porters' rights. The question had not yet been answered at the end of the period; hence another three years' lease was granted, this time to William Arnold alone. His successor for a seventeen years' term, William Johnson, allowed another goldsmith, Thomas Payne, to exercise the office on his behalf for some time before assigning it to Payne in 1792. Actions to test the validity of the privileges were still pending; in order to pursue them, Payne had to exercise office in his own name, not as assignee. For the remainder of the seventeen years, therefore, Payne became the sole Aliens' Porter. In 1796 the office passed to William Stennett whose successors of the same name were to be the last holders of it.[10]

Information about the Aliens' Porter is easier to obtain than about the men who performed the actual porterage. As for other groups of Porters, City Acts of 1597 and 1608 stipulated that freemen only should be employed. This did not remain a mere paper rule: when William Bancks purchased a place as one of the Packer's Porters for £16 in 1619, he was unable to occupy it because he had not acquired the City's freedom. He presumably had paid the money to his predecessor; for the City Packer to have taken reward or consideration for the admission of a Porter under him would have constituted an offence. In 1694 Peirce was accused of employing under him several non-freemen, one of them being the Daniel Blackwell who became one of his assignees.* Such foreigners, according to allegations made by Tacklehouse and Ticket Porters, were employed at the cut-price rate of 3s. 6d. per week, less than half the wage paid to men engaged by Tacklehouse Porters. Complainants contended that such non-freemen were not originally Packer's Porters, but merely their servants who took their places when the principals died, purchasing the City's freedom only when complaint was made to the Court of Aldermen. It is clear from the sub-lease that by 1717 Blackwell as a member of the Grocers' Company, and Hall and Lloyd as members of the Goldsmiths', had become free of the City; Bigg was described merely as of the parish of St. Mary, Whitechapel, Porter. It appears therefore that the City Packer engaged only free Porters, but that these Porters themselves employed unfree servants. While free Porters were under instructions not to take servants of this description, the servants themselves could not be ordered to desist from such work nor penalized for engaging in it. Only in 1798 did a Common Council Act clearly state that all men employed under the Packer's Porters should be duly admitted Ticket Porters.

(c) Rates and Charges

Only in one instance before 1600 did the City Corporation determine a rate for the work of Aliens' Porters: in 1543 the Court of Aldermen fixed the fee for carrying sugar to the weigh-house at 6d. a chest, whether big or small. Aliens' Porters' rates and charges, unless specifically laid down and published by the City authorities, remained those traditionally levied. A table of rates for Aliens' Porters attached to the charter of 16 Charles I shows them to have been identical with those charged by Tacklehouse and Ticket Porters, a note being appended to

* See p. 29 above.

the effect that these rates had been paid by strangers within these last ten years. This table of charges appeared unacceptable when submitted to royal scrutiny: in 1626 Lord Treasurer Marlborough wrote to the Lord Mayor, annexing a schedule of fees and demanding to know whether they did not exceed those authorized for the City Packer. Indeed, a Crown lawyer suggested that the City had between 1619 and 1636 collected under the headings of package, balliage, and scavage—it is not clear whether he meant to include porterage—£1,000 a year to which it was not entitled. The accusation was designed to pave the way for a grant by the king of package, balliage, and scavage rights in 1633 to a man called Kirke. As the grant conflicted with City privileges, the parties litigated until 1635, when they came to an arrangement. However, the City repudiated this agreement and itself in 1636 submitted its table of rates for package, balliage, scavage and porterage to the Privy Council for confirmation or modification. Many new types of merchandise had been introduced since the table had first been compiled; hence, after an alphabetical list of commodities and rates charged for them, an omnibus clause fixed a fee of 1d. per £1 sterling for any commodities not enumerated; strangers also paid for the making of bales as well as 6d. for every pack-book entry. Proceedings were delayed by an oversight: the Privy Council committee entrusted with the scrutiny had had package, balliage, and scavage, but not porterage fees included in its terms of reference—an error rectified in 1639. It is unlikely that at that date Privy Councillors had much leisure to consider such details. Not until 1650 did the Council of Trade once again press for an up-to-date table of rates. The Court of Aldermen asked for more time, 'as the many and great affairs of this City do not admit so deliberate an examination of this business at the present as the case requires', but a committee within three months began compiling a new table of rates which by the middle of 1651 was ready for submission to the Council of Trade, and eventually formed part of the book of rates given legal force by Act of Parliament in 1660.[11]

(d) Demarcation Disputes

Wool Porters of Leadenhall complained in 1561 of Packer's Porters usurping the work of carrying goods from Leadenhall and other City places to the waterside. Packer's Porters had been restricted to the goods of alien merchants; in no circumstances did they possess the right of interfering with English merchants' goods. No other group of Porters was limited to goods belonging to a particular type of owners only and this criterion confused the Common Council; on the plea that all men should be allowed to choose what workmen they wished to employ, it permitted Packer's Porters in 1579 to be engaged for goods of either alien or English traders. Not until 1597 did the Common Council pass a general Act demarcating the prerogatives of the various groups of Porters. Here again it failed in its task of clarification: while explicitly barring Packer's Porters from handling freemen's goods and defining their duties as concerned with merchant strangers, it left out of account English traders not free of the City. In any case, the Act of 1597 remained valid for one year only; no sooner had it lapsed than the Packer's Porters resumed the carriage of English merchants' goods. The Aldermen expressed the hope that the Act would be re-introduced, confining Packer's Porters to the goods of merchant strangers and such members of the Mercers' Company as would employ them; at this time the Mercers had no tacklehouse of their own. But the Act was not revived until 1606; in its final form in 1608 it at least removed ambiguity by restraining Aliens' Porters from handling the goods of any English merchant, whether or not free of the City.

This was clear as far as it went. It was not made equally plain that, in return for Packer's Porters' keeping their hands off the goods of English merchants, other Porters should leave alien and denizen merchants to the Packer's Porters; by taking advantage of the obscurity of the Act, competitors compelled an amendment in 1619 declaring the goods of such merchants the exclusive prerogative of Aliens' Porters on pain of £5 for each unauthorized interference. Not until 1646 was the Court of Aldermen challenged to define a 'denizen'; in that year Jacob Fortell, English-born son of an alien father, refused the ministrations of the Aliens' Porters on the plea that he was not an alien. In assigning him to the prerogative of the City Packer, the Court of Aldermen was out of step with Parliament, or else it would have been unnecessary to legislate in 1661 against children of aliens under the age of twenty-one being traders or having goods entered in their names.

The question assumed importance because Cromwell's Parliaments had been generous in their grants of naturalization to aliens, who thereupon claimed the right to pay fees only on a par with English-born merchants; the City feared this would lead to the seeking of the same privilege by further alien merchants. Such naturalization made inroads on the earnings of the City Packer and his Porters, driving them to trench on other Porters' prerogatives in the 1690s. The City Packer treated it as an absurdity if his men were suddenly barred from handling the goods of a merchant who had always employed them, merely because he had in the interval obtained naturalization.[12]

It proved no easier to determine alien merchants' goods than alien merchants. The possibility of goods being 'coloured', passed off as somebody else's property, had repeatedly preoccupied Parliament. Customs authorities could not legally clear goods, whether imported or exported on alien or English (in the eighteenth century British) account, until their owner had signed a bill of entry. Apart from pre-vention of fraud, the legislature concerned itself with the protection of British shipping embodied in the Navigation Act of 1660, which defined as aliens' goods a wide range of overseas produce unless im-ported in British ships, thus treating English traders whose merchandise arrived in non-British vessels as aliens for the purpose of customs and scavage duties. Ought they also to employ Aliens' Porters? The City Packer naturally asserted that they should, and claimed such work as his prerogative; the Tacklehouse Porters disputed the claim and arrogated the work to themselves. Counsel's opinion was sought, but Mr. Pengelly would commit himself to nothing more positive than that, if the City Packer sued for such work, he would find the action very difficult to maintain. The City Lands Committee, on the other hand, sided with the Packer and looked upon importation in alien vessels as conclusive evidence that merchandise ought to be treated as aliens' goods. After a five years' delay imposed by Common Council resistance, the Committee carried its point. During the wars which filled much of the eighteenth century, British merchants considered it prudent to import goods in neutral bottoms—one of the changes in commercial practice undermining the Tacklehouse Porters' economic importance by depriving them of merchandise which would otherwise have fallen to their prerogative.

Demarcation disputes between Tacklehouse and Ticket Porters on the one hand and Aliens' Porters on the other flared up every now and again in the seventeenth and eighteenth centuries. They did not crystallize into a serious threat to Tacklehouse and Ticket Porters until in the 1740s Nathaniel Major, first on John Standish's behalf and later in his own name, held the Aliens' Porter's lease*. The master mind behind the scheme may have been Major or John Stansbury, a Goldsmiths' Tacklehouse Porter who joined Major. Whereas each group of Porters was limited to its prerogative, a combination of Porters ranging over all the groups could handle almost any consignment reaching the Port. Some aliens' goods were liable to much higher porterage rates than British goods. By promising to handle their aliens' goods at less than authorized rates, provided they entrusted them with all their merchandise, whether aliens' or otherwise, a partnership of the Aliens' Porter, two Tacklehouse Porters and a Ticket Porter drew merchants importing mixed consignments away from rival Porters who had hitherto dealt with their British goods. The new combine also took advantage of the ambiguous situation of those British-born merchants who prudently used neutral ships for the import of merchandise which in wartime might otherwise have been seized at sea by enemy forces. Against importers who continued to employ other Tacklehouse Porters to unload such commodities, the Aliens' Porter took legal action to recover fees for work which he had not done. As a result of having indemnified merchants against damage, Tacklehouse Porters had to defend such suits at their own expense.

Except to those of the Goldsmiths' Company who formed part of it, the combine's activities constituted a threat to all Tacklehouse Porters. When Major in spite of his ingenuity suffered financial embarrassment in 1746, they tried to restrain the City from assisting him, above all from granting him a new lease unless he undertook to abstain from all association with Tacklehouse or Ticket Porters. The City Lands Committee saw no reason to penalize Major for showing enterprise: the City Packer's lease had been publicly advertised; other Tacklehouse

* See pp. 29–30 above.

Porters had had equal chances of acquiring it. This spelt cold comfort to the Tacklehouse Porters; in 1758 they made another attempt to convince the City authorities that this represented unfair competition, but were merely advised to obtain Counsel's, later the Common Serjeant's, opinion. Worse was to come. Upon Major's death, his lease was assigned to the Goldsmiths' Tacklehouse Porters; instead of merely acting in partnership, Aliens' and Goldsmiths' Tacklehouse Porters had now become the same persons, pursuing ever more energetically the advantages attendant upon the combination of offices. Against this the other Tacklehouse Porters brought forward a scheme which would assign the Aliens' Porter's lease to all of them collectively on condition that they granted a share to the present lessees. The City authorities remained obdurate. No evidence had been adduced that the handling of aliens' goods had in the past been done more cheaply than regulations prescribed, nor that it would in future be better performed, or as satisfactorily accounted for, were it shared out among all Tacklehouse Porters; no grounds existed to penalize Goldsmiths' Tacklehouse Porters for having been more quickwitted than their colleagues. In the later eighteenth century the value of the Aliens' Porters' rights declined so severely that the grievance lost most of its substance.

Like other City Porters, Aliens' Porters found merchants trying to evade their ministrations by discharging or loading goods outside City limits. This arose from misinterpretation of the law. Although the Porters' authority derived from the City Corporation, the latter's jurisdiction in this respect extended far beyond City boundaries. The Lord Mayor of London was Conservator of the River Thames from Teddington in the west to Yantlet Creek in the east; Charles I's charter had explicitly stipulated that goods handled at St. Katherine's, Tower Wharf, Southwark, Dick Shore, Wapping, Rotherhithe, Deptford, Greenwich, Blackwall and other places on either side of the River situated between Blackwall and London Bridge should pay City dues on a par with merchandise handled within the Port of London itself. Merchants could not therefore secure immunity from regulations by avoiding City territory; nevertheless they tried this device again and again under the impression that the City's writ did not run there.

Indeed, merchants were not the only people to harbour this misapprehension. Tacklehouse Porters believed that Aliens' Porters could not, or at least would not, follow their goods beyond the City limits. When the two groups of Porters quarrelled over the combination of the Aliens' with the Goldsmiths' Porters in the later eighteenth century, Tacklehouse Porters, in co-operation with sufferance wharfingers, persuaded alien merchants to land their goods at sufferance wharves on the south shore, assuming that this transferred the merchandise from the Aliens' Porters' prerogative to that of the Tacklehouse Porters. However mistaken this reading of the law, only by prosecution of offending merchants could the Packer enforce his right. The number of expensive lawsuits that this entailed did much to account for the unprofitability of the City Packer's office, particularly as Tacklehouse Porters indemnified an alien merchant against loss from landing his goods on the Surrey side in order to bring a test case. Counsel for the Packer was himself a Customs officer, able to detect evasion with comparative ease; whenever the Packer brought an action, he won it. Yet he almost ruined himself by legal costs, especially as a suit lay only against merchants, not against wharfingers or yard owners who instigated evasion. Geographical avoidance similarly endangered other City rights; hence the City authorities eventually let themselves be persuaded into briefing the City Solicitor to take over prosecutions.[13]

3

TACKLEHOUSE PORTERS AND STREET OR TICKET PORTERS

(a) Growth of Tacklehouses and Tacklehouse Porters

Of the twelve primary Companies of the City of London, some employed Porters of their own before the beginning of historical records. Companies maintained establishments near the waterside known as tacklehouses where tackle and probably also goods were stored on behalf of Company members; Tacklehouse Porters, besides being Porters, acted as warehousemen. First mention of such Company Porters often refers to privileges already enjoyed, as in the case of the Vintners' Company whose Tacklehouse Porters in 1508 possessed sole rights of lowering and setting up all wines imported into the City. There is no evidence of the earliest Companies having sought or received authority to employ such Porters, nor is there any reason why they should have done so. The institution of Tacklehouse Porters was purely traditional and came gradually to be recognized by City Corporation Acts and ordinances. This led the Royal Commission on Municipal Corporations in England and Wales in the nineteenth century to the conclusion that the monopoly of these Porters had no legal basis—a doubtful finding in view of the wide freedom conferred upon the City Corporation to exercise privileges within its area.

Company Porters first received official attention through an application to the Court of Aldermen from the Haberdashers' Company for a tacklehouse and Tacklehouse Porters in 1576—at a time when haberdashers imported large quantities of Spanish wool. The only Companies then legitimately possessing tacklehouses and Tacklehouse Porters were the Grocers, Salters, Vintners and Fishmongers. Members of other Companies requiring waterside porterage services had them

38

performed by these Tacklehouse Porters; this explains their opposition to the appointment of further Tacklehouse Porters, opposition which led to the Haberdashers' application being refused. They nevertheless appointed two Porters and were brought before the Court of Aldermen in the following year for disobeying its order. They had sinned in company with others: the Skinners, too, had very recently appointed Tacklehouse Porters without authority, a state of affairs which had prevailed in the Drapers' Company for five or six years. The older primary Companies charged the newer ones with taking in foreigners and non-members for whom they did not have to find places in their Companies, thus overstocking the trade and disturbing the order hitherto prevalent among Tacklehouse Porters. Though the verdict went against the newer Companies in 1577, it was set aside two years later by the Common Council when Drapers, Skinners, Haberdashers and Clothworkers were authorized to employ Porters and erect tacklehouses. Nor could the Common Council see any reason in principle to deny this privilege to any of the City Companies; but, in order to settle current controversies and prevent overcrowding in the trade, it restrained the remaining four primary companies as well as all lesser ones from appointing Tacklehouse Porters without its own licence. Companies authorized were strictly enjoined to confine appointments to freemen, an injunction not always observed, and repeated in the Common Council Act of 1597.

In objecting to the appointment of new Tacklehouse Porters, older Companies had claimed that old-established Porters kept good order and were promoted by seniority. The Common Council attempted to enforce a similar régime on the new Tacklehouse Porters who were admonished to 'demean themselves towards the merchants, as that they be not thought obstinate in refusing their work', a request which had to be addressed afresh to all members of the Society of Tacklehouse and Ticket Porters in the middle of the seventeenth century; specific fines were subsequently awarded for incivility to employers. Tacklehouse Porters obtained protection against interference with their work; the Water Bailiff's officer was instructed to apprehend any offenders and bring them before the Lord Mayor. Such offenders were foreigners, not freemen; in fact this was the beginning of the Street

Porters, originally foreigners and unadmitted Porters, whose recognition marks the completion of porterage regulation by the City
Corporation.[14]

The first City Company seeking Common Council permission in
the seventeenth century to appoint Tacklehouse Porters was the
Mercers', which had needed porterage services urgently enough to
employ the Aliens' Porters until in 1609 it applied for, and obtained, a
tacklehouse and Porters of its own. The Company of Ironmongers
experienced such need for porters to carry iron and cutlery goods at
Leadenhall that it appointed four porters in 1640. These men were not
Tacklehouse Porters but employees, like the cloth porters of Blackwell
Hall; however, they resembled Porters organized in societies in not
receiving time wages but a piece rate amounting to 6d. per load of a
ton or less and 1d. per pack. Not until 1688 did the Ironmongers apply
to the Court of Aldermen for a tacklehouse. That it was granted, must
be concluded from the report of a committee twenty years later which
mentioned that the Ironmongers had long since disposed of their right
to such a tacklehouse to the Fishmongers' Company. The committee
must have been mistaken: the Fishmongers had been among the
earliest of the Companies to enjoy a tacklehouse in their own right, and
during a period running from 1738 to 1831 both Ironmongers and
Fishmongers regularly appointed Tacklehouse Porters. Following the
Ironmongers' precedent, the Goldsmiths obtained a tacklehouse in
1706. Records do not show when the Merchant Taylors first appointed
Tacklehouse Porters, but they, also, had them throughout the period
1738–1831. Indeed, the only Company which, having once been
granted Tacklehouse Porters, failed during this period to make use of
the privilege was the Vintners'. Tacklehouse Porters did not suit this
Company's purpose and they were therefore replaced at an early date
by Vintners' Porters, also sometimes called Wine Tackle Porters, a
group of labouring men not free of their Company, whose history is
discussed more conveniently in the context of the nineteenth century.*

Tacklehouse Porters gave security to their Companies for goods
handled by them and their servants. Full value had to be paid in respect
of any merchandise lost or damaged; in the early eighteenth century

* See pp. 196–200 below.

the Mercers' Tacklehouse Porters had to defray £60 in respect of a small packet of silk stockings lost, the property of a Hamburg merchant. Should Tacklehouse Porters be unable to pay, as happened to the Goldsmiths' Porters after the loss of a box of jewels worth £1,021 10s. on Custom House Quay in 1769, the owners could sue the Company instead. The sums involved corroborate that Tacklehouse Porters were not porters at all, but porterage and warehousing entrepreneurs; they could be called porters only in the sense of contracting to provide porterage services. 'Persons conversant in matters of trade and whose characters and situations in life have been truly respectable', runs the description given by the Haberdashers' Company in 1794; they had to be men of experience, substance and responsibility, indeed a superior class of tradesmen. Emphasis on their status usually served to distinguish them from the lowlier members of their Society, the Ticket Porters, though this did not prevent the exceptionally successful Ticket Porter from being appointed a Tacklehouse Porter. Even Tacklehouse Porters sometimes came down in the world; several of them after a career as considerable merchants and liverymen of their Companies had by 1745 been compelled by great losses personally to attend to business at the waterside, though this need not be read to mean that they carried loads on their own backs.

The value of a Tacklehouse Porter's place varied greatly according to the Company concerned and the number of Porters it maintained (most Companies appointed two). Compensation proceedings arising out of the establishment of various docks around 1800 caused Tacklehouse Porters to disclose the value placed on their appointments; one of the Goldsmiths' Porters sold his office in 1800 for £80 p.a., and compensation ranged from £600 paid to a Fishmongers' Tacklehouse Porter and £1,600 paid to his colleague from the Grocers to £2,170 received by the Merchant Taylors' holder of the office. Subject to good behaviour, Tacklehouse Porters were appointed for life; compensation to them was assessed on that basis.[15]

(b) A Separate Society of Street Porters

The Court of Aldermen in 1584 constituted five freemen and seven foreigners into a Society—they called it a company, but this description did not imply corporate status—of Street Porters for the purpose of carrying certain imported goods for merchants. Vacancies were not to be filled until the number of members had dropped from twelve to eight; at that figure it was to remain, the servants employed by Tacklehouse Porters being appointed to vacancies. The Common Council Act of 1597, re-enacted in 1608, stipulated for Street as for Aliens' Porters that freemen only should join, excepting foreigners already employed in this capacity; candidates qualified for admission by securing the approval of four Tacklehouse Porters, the Alderman and at least four Common Councilmen of the ward where they resided, or if not domiciled in the City, wherever most of their work was done. Even after admission they had to furnish to the selection committee periodical certificates giving evidence both of good behaviour, to be obtained by testimony from their neighbours, and of their places of abode; the latter to be registered by a senior Tacklehouse Porter at a charge not exceeding 3d.* per entry, any change of address to be notified to this registrar within seven days. This constituted the first step towards the supervision exercised by Tacklehouse over Street Porters which was to lead to a joint Society of Tacklehouse and Ticket Porters.

Beyond such regular admission, the Court of Aldermen reserved the right to grant direct admission as Street Porters to worthy or well-sponsored applicants: as in 1616 to a resident of twelve years' standing in St. Martin's-in-the-Fields who had worked as a porter for seven years and brought a recommendation from the Duke of York; in 1634 to a candidate recommended by the Archbishop of York; to a 'poor labouring man in commiseration of his wants and for other especial reasons' in the following year; and to four men on similar grounds during the years 1645 to 1648. Poverty constituted the chief qualification for admission of Street or Ticket Porters not only on extraordinary occasions. Sir Hubert Llewellyn Smith quotes a printed admission form of 1729 to the Society of Tacklehouse and Ticket Porters which states 'that the bearer hereof . . . being of late fallen to Decay, he is unable at his Trade to maintain himself and his family'. At least as a matter of form this assertion was made on behalf of all

* 1d. in 1597.

candidates for Ticket Porter membership. Many Ticket Porters were to claim in 1786 that they had acquired the City's freedom at great expense, 'but through the decay of trade or other misfortunes in their respective occupations have been reduced to the necessity of becoming Ticket Porters as their last resort to get their Livelihoods', though they had been liverymen and respectable tradesmen in their day. Colquhoun in 1800 described 'scuffle-hunters' in terms which make it probable that he intended to include this category of Porters when he spoke of them as 'men ever ready to offer their assistance to work as porters by the day or the hour, when goods are shipping or landing upon the quays; they come dressed in long aprons which enable them to conceal what they pilfer'.

However humble a trade, there are always some men able to turn it into a stepping-stone to improved conditions. At least one Ticket Porter was known in 1700 to occupy a warehouse where he provided weighing and loading services for merchants and employed a number of men by the week. When the Port of London Compensation Commissioners invited evidence from parties damaged by the construction of the docks a century later, Thomas Green Weed, a Ticket Porter, submitted a memorial showing that he had worked with a contractor transacting the waterside transport business of a firm until he, the Ticket Porter himself, took over the business. Another claimant, Richard Cookes, had been in business as a Master Shipping Landing and Ticket Porter at Water Lane and Porters' Quay for upward of ten years, whereas Stephen Christopher and James Smith had for a number of years by themselves and by their servants worked on the legal quays, wharves and other places for several merchants in the liquor line. Half a dozen Ticket Porters had their claims disallowed by the Commissioners on the ground that none of their income or profit derived from their personal labour—clear evidence that substantial Ticket Porters working as contractors were by no means unknown.

Street Porters were an unruly body of men. Discipline by outside authority was indispensable. The Water Bailiff, entrusted with the task of enforcing it, proved inadequate, and in 1605 the Aldermen deputed to two of their own number the duty of keeping order and deciding disputes among Street Porters. Under the supervision of these two

Governors, twelve Rulers were appointed from among the Street Porters themselves, of whom six were to retire annually. The Rulers exercised discipline with the aid of thirty Assistants, chosen by themselves from among the members and confirmed by the two Governors; Assistants attended meetings convened by the Rulers and had disciplinary powers akin to those of the Rulers. The mere fact that regulating functions devolved upon forty-two individuals proves how large the Brotherhood had grown by 1605.

There was no question of the Society being reduced to, and remaining at, a membership of eight; in view of its expansion it was considered best to grant admission to all whom the selection committee had approved without fixing limits. The only formal disqualification which barred freemen from becoming Ticket Porters was membership of the Fellowship of Billingsgate Porters. Members on admission now paid 6s. 8d., plus 4d. to the Brotherhood's clerk, a fee varied by the Court of Registers and Rulers in 1616 to 2s. 6d. for freemen and 5s. 8d. for foreigners. Sixty years later, complaints about foreigners daily acquiring the City's freedom and being admitted as Porters immediately afterwards prompted a rule which subjected persons acquiring their freedom by means other than apprenticeship to double admission fees. The subscription amounted to 4d. a quarter, half in respect of general funds, the other half for the rent of the meeting place. An adequate fee in the early seventeenth century, it became patently insufficient by the late eighteenth and had to be trebled in 1798.

New members had to furnish sureties to the Governors for their good behaviour in the sum of £100. Friends, relatives or neighbours guaranteeing the sum served as sureties. The great fire of 1666 destroyed all these bonds; merchants defrauded by Porters in subsequent years could obtain no redress and agitated for the provision of new bonds, which was undertaken between 1674 and 1677. Registration of sureties was attended by the payment of fees, the Court receiving £1 1s. and the Clerk 7s., of which 2s. remunerated him for filling up the bond, 5s. for entering the certificate in the records. Bonds could be used for legal action, not only by merchants suffering damage through Porters' misdemeanours, but also by the Society against members defaulting on quarterage. If guarantors died, Porters could be compelled to furnish new securities within six months; if they merely became insolvent, nothing could be done to enforce substitution of a more effective surety. Sometimes guarantors grew nervous and asked to be released from their pledges, but Counsel advised that such requests were invalid unless the Porter concerned acquiesced in them. If a member gave up portering, the security did not protect persons to whom he rendered services in another capacity. Guarantors had to be freemen and house-keepers; in accordance with the Act of 1798 they were neither to be Ticket Porters themselves nor to serve as security for more than two Ticket Porters.

On acquiring membership a Street Porter had to purchase by the next Court Day for 6d. from Charles Anthony, goldsmith, a tin badge which bore the wearer's name and proved his admission to the Brother-hood; when he died, the badge had to be returned to the Society. This was the 'ticket' which led to members being called Ticket Porters. The *General Description of all Trades digested in Alphabetical Order* of 1747 referred to this badge as a pewter ticket hung on the wearer's apron string; its price, subsequently paid to the Beadle, in the eighteenth century amounted to 1s. Ticket Porters' privileges could be asserted only if the badge was worn openly and conspicuously or at the least produced on request, thus identifying the wearer as a public transport employee. The Brotherhood received frequent complaints that Ticket Porters not only did not display their tickets, but had even lost them without taking steps to replace them. A Porter had to testify before the Governor on oath to the genuine nature of his loss in order to obtain a new ticket. More serious than failure to wear the ticket was the lending of tickets to enable unauthorized men to pose as Ticket Porters.

Discipline within the Brotherhood required a range of penalties running from fines in the first place to suspension or even dismissal from the Society. For persistently disobeying the Society's ordinances a member could be committed to prison—which was also the ultimate punishment for refractory behaviour and the use of bad language to Rulers, though legal opinion doubted whether the penalty applied effectively to this offence. Exceptionally, a Ticket Porter was expelled in 1657 for unruliness and misbehaviour to the Court of Aldermen.

To settle conflicts between members within the framework of the organization, elaborate machinery had been designed. They had to resort to the Court of Rulers. If this proved unable to determine the dispute, the Governor had to be consulted. No member of the Society could go to law against another without the Governor's permission. This did not prevent Tacklehouse and Ticket Porters from offering physical violence to each other if one group performed work claimed by another, and a £5 penalty had to be imposed in 1798 on any member usurping work to which he was not entitled.[16]

4

SOCIETY OF TACKLEHOUSE AND TICKET PORTERS

(a) Joint Organization

THE elaborate organizational structure of the Street and Corner Porters which was developed by 1605 could look forward to an independent existence. But that existence lasted for only one year. Early in 1606, 'on account of diverse misdemeanours and disorders committed and daily practised by the late brotherhood of Street Porters', a wrathful Court of Aldermen dissolved the Brotherhood completely, voided all its orders and ordinances, took away its warrants under the Lord Mayor's seal and appointed a committee to keep an eye on the Street Porters until something more permanent be decided about them. Far from proving that these necessary and troublesome individuals could be left to their own devices, the breakdown of the organization showed the desirability of stricter discipline. This led to the Court of Aldermen in 1609 combining the Street and Corner with the Tacklehouse Porters in a joint body and re-enacting the structure of supervision which had existed for Street Porters alone. The two Aldermen Governors were retained until a century later, when disagreement between them led to so much inconvenience that the number was reduced to one. In consultation with the Court of Rulers, the Governor made rules and regulations for the membership at large, attaching penalties of up to 20s. for their breach, but such rules and regulations required endorsement by the Court of Aldermen. Of the twelve Rulers appointed in 1609, half were drawn from the Tacklehouse, the other half from the Street Porters, three of the latter serving as representatives of the Uptown Porters. That the new Fraternity comprised a far larger number of Street than of Tacklehouse Porters found recognition in the Court of Assistants, of whom only six were

47

Tacklehouse and twenty-four Street Porters. At the first appointment of the latter, only eight were free, sixteen being foreigners. The membership register continued to be kept by a Tacklehouse Porter, and within four years this Register (as the registrar was called) engaged in acrimonious disputes with the Street Porters and some of their Assistants. As the office of Register gained importance, it became a growing grievance of the Street Porters that a Tacklehouse Porter occupied it, until in 1645 a constitutional change divided the office between a Tacklehouse and a Ticket Register, both of equal authority, who jointly controlled the Society's financial transactions and submitted to the Governors annual statements of accounts audited by the Rulers. Although responsibility for electing a Register now rested on each group of Porters, the Tacklehouse Porters in 1675 took it upon themselves to ask the Court of Aldermen to disallow the Register elected by the Ticket Porters, on the ground that he was a person unfit to hold that office.

Elaboration of the governing structure had gone too far; the Assistants, whose functions were nearly indistinguishable from those of Rulers, faded out almost as soon as they had been constituted. From being a Court of Rulers and Assistants, the Society's chief disciplinary organ became the Court of Registers and Rulers, the Registers as executive financial officers occupying a position distinct from other Rulers. Before the constitution had been in operation for a year the Rulers were already asking the Court of Aldermen to intervene because of offences and variances in the Brotherhood, but for some time after 1609 they ruled effectively, if not always peaceably. One of the Governors in 1666 or 1667 marked his dissatisfaction with the Registers' and Rulers' conduct of business by prohibiting the holding of further courts without direction from him. He withheld permission for so long that the Registers petitioned the Aldermen, pointing to the damage arising to the Society's affairs from such lengthy suspension of effective government, and the Aldermen accordingly lifted the interdiction. The Ticket Porters in 1681–82 complained that Registers and Rulers were co-opted by the existing office-holders, instead of being elected by the whole body of Porters as the 1609 constitution prescribed. They renewed their attack on the Court's composition in 1793, this time by asking for a larger number of Rulers to be appointed by the general membership, which in effect meant curtailing the Tacklehouse Porters' representation in the government. The demand provoked prompt protests from the Companies of Grocers, Haberdashers, Salters, Clothworkers, Drapers, Goldsmiths and Fishmongers. That the Vintners should have treated the dispute with indifference is not surprising, as they had long ceased to appoint Tacklehouse Porters, but the absence of objections on the part of the Mercers, Skinners and Merchant Taylors is less easy to explain.

There is no mention in the records of the Tacklehouse and Ticket Porters' possessing a hall of their own; yet the Court assembled in Porters' Hall at the beginning of the 1680s. In 1683 the *Unicorn* in King Street formed the meeting place, which within the next fifteen years was transferred to the Embroiderers' Hall in Gutter Lane. The anonymous author of the *General Description* of 1747 knew them to assemble at the Turners' Hall, College Hill, from which they moved to the Founders' Hall in 1759. There they remained for thirty years. In 1790 the Court moved twice: in March from the Founders' to the Plasterers' Hall; in June from there to Guildhall, where it enjoyed the City Corporation's hospitality in the Irish Chamber for the rest of its existence.[17]

Early in 1667 Registers and Rulers held a meeting at the *White Horse* inn, Cripplegate Without, to elect a Clerk to the Society. Four candidates presented themselves and were informed that the electors would make their choice by simple majority. By six votes to five, Thomas Hill was chosen. One Register and two Rulers, outvoted on this occasion, resented their defeat and did their best to prevent Hill's confirmation in office by the Governors. Hill and some aggrieved members of the Society took the matter to the Lord Mayor who confirmed Hill's election, but it prompted the question of how and by whom the Clerk of the Society of Tacklehouse and Ticket Porters should be appointed. A committee of Aldermen which was asked to elucidate the procedure never reported; the minutes of the Court of Registers and Rulers show that this body originally nominated several candidates from whom the Governors made their choice, but by the later seventeenth century merely presented its own selection for

E

approval. In 1737 the Court made a rule that the Clerk be elected annually. If this was ever done, it proved an empty formality; no new Clerk was ever chosen unless the previous holder of the office had died, though the rule was subsequently re-affirmed. The Society also had an Upper and an Under Beadle, both elected by the Court, the former displaying on public occasions the Society's silver badge and chain weighing about twenty-three ounces and engraved with the City arms.

(b) Membership and Funds

To the Society of Tacklehouse and Ticket Porters the two constituent groups contributed very unequal numbers. From the nature of their employment there could not be many Tacklehouse Porters. In two documents addressed to City authorities around 1682 the Ticket Porters gave the number of Tacklehouse Porters variously as thirty and fifty; the former figure is by far the more credible. The same source gave the number as seventy-two in 1707, apparently counting not merely Tacklehouse Porters but also their servants; this explanation is all the more probable since in yet another petition only five years later the Ticket Porters referred to twenty-eight Tacklehouse Porters. By 1793 only twenty-two were left; this remained their number up to 1800.

As against this small group, Ticket Porters in 1645 were estimated to number over 3,000. In an attempt to weed out unadmitted Porters, the Common Council in the following year made a final offer of admission to all foreigners who had for twelve months effectively, though without authority, worked in this capacity and who otherwise fulfilled admission conditions. This led to a considerable influx: in the early 1680s the Ticket Porters estimated their own numbers at 5,000, an estimate which rose to 6,000 in 1707. The Tacklehouse Porters in 1711 supplied detailed figures according to which there might be 9,000 to 10,000 Ticket Porters—an estimate corroborated by the Ticket Porters themselves—but only 2,000 worked actively in that capacity, many others being too old for work, retired or dead, and only a hundred of them did waterside work singly, in addition to another eighty working in quayside gangs. In the next thirty years the unrealistic membership figures were reduced; the whole Society claimed a membership of only just over 2,000 in 1747, a claim repeated in 1786, 1793 and 1794, though the Society had purported to consist of more than 3,000 members in 1791. When Colquhoun in 1800 listed the various workers employed in the Port of London, he mentioned 290 gangsmen and 500 individual Porters classed as Ticket Porters. Titular members accounted for a small proportion of these discrepancies. In the main, however, differences were due to Ticket Porters changing their occupations, retiring, being injured, or dying without the register being amended; hence at any one time Ticket Porters on the books greatly exceeded the number of men who sought to make a livelihood out of the trade.[18]

All the Society's members were obliged to attend what was described as a hall meeting whenever the Rulers chose to call one. Probably such hall meetings were held quarterly for the purpose of collecting quarterage from all members. However adequate while the Society was small, this arrangement was bound to become unsatisfactory once membership ran into four figures. Rulers were exempt from paying quarterage during their period of office—a measure of compensation for the working time lost while attending to the Brotherhood's business; though far less unpleasant, it was also less profitable to exercise rulership functions than to carry heavy loads. Before 1640, Tacklehouse Porters also paid no quarterage, partly in recognition of the fact that they belonged to the Society not for their own benefit, but in order to constitute a disciplinary and restraining counterweight to the Ticket Porters and partly because as members of their Companies they bore all the financial burdens attendant upon such membership. The exemption was revoked in 1640, but Ticket Porters in 1681–82 still accused them of not paying quarterage. The Society had great difficulties in collecting quarterage, particularly as no alternative replaced attendance at general meetings where members had handed over the dues in person. In 1726 the Court of Rulers complained of considerable arrears and threatened to suspend from labour and sue on his bond any member whose quarterage had remained unpaid for nine quarters. But nine quarters imposed a very long waiting period. By 1799 Ticket Porters were barred from beginning ship's work or plying at any uptown stand or corner if their quarterage arrears exceeded one year.

Ticket Porters in 1681–82 estimated the income derived from quarterage at £533, a figure based on the utterly fallacious assumption that 8,000 members had paid their quarterage in full. The real revenue can be ascertained from the Registers' account books which are extant for the whole period from 1673 to 1851 and show the income to have been £66 5s. 1d. in the very year in which the Ticket Porters had stipulated for a gross revenue of £533 6s. 8d. The main impression derived from the accounts painstakingly kept by the Registers over so long a span is the smallness of the amounts involved. The highest gross revenue collected in any one year came to £190 0s. 4d. in 1738–39. If made up entirely of quarterage, this would have represented 2,850 members paying full dues. In fact a certain amount derived not from quarterage but from fines. At a moment when the Brotherhood felt very rich, in July 1715, it used £6 5s. 6d. of money received by way of fines to buy a staff with a silver head. A regrettable incident occurred in 1751: the Ticket Porters' Register of that year, Thomas Ruth, removed from the Brotherhood's cash box £9 11s. 11½d. which he never brought to account; it had to be written off in the following year.

Except where required to defray administrative expenses, funds were devoted to the relief of aged or incapacitated members or of the dependants of deceased Ticket Porters. According to the Registers' accounts, an average of £15 p.a. was dispensed for these purposes during the period 1673 to 1800, annual totals being higher before 1752 and lower thereafter: £27 in 1697–98 and £27 4s. in 1749–50 were the largest annual sums applied to relief. Expenditure on this purpose during several years in the 1790s barely exceeded £6. Among the disbursements for April 1693, an entry reading 'To ye Widd Todde nothing she being a very abusive woman' shows that relief payments were not automatic, but depended on the Court's discretion. Extreme cases like the widow Todd's apart, the Brotherhood admitted a duty to support widows of members as well as blind and aged Ticket Porters. A short-lived Protection Society of Ticket Porters, starting in April 1759 and lasting not quite a month, seemed from its title to imply that Ticket Porters felt the need to provide greater financial assistance than the Brotherhood's relief funds could afford. Although it described itself as a Friendly Society, the Protection Society's rules made no provision for mutual insurance, only for regular meetings, conviviality and contributions; members were to treat each other like blood brothers, settle differences among themselves and take joint action to exclude interlopers from the trade. The largest number of members the Protection Society ever mustered was thirty-two, and when it came to subscribing for the prosecution of an unauthorized porter, only twenty-two members made contributions.

Nothing grieved Ticket Porters more than the unequal partnership with the Tacklehouse Porters forced upon them by the City authorities. Tacklehouse and Ticket Porters were constant rivals for work on merchandise which both claimed as their prerogative; very rarely did the two groups join forces to fight some outside interference. While Tacklehouse Porters did not actively object to an organization which embraced both themselves and the Ticket Porters, the latter in 1621 addressed the first of many petitions for separation from the Tacklehouse Porters to the Court of Aldermen. Twenty years later political conditions appeared to favour the lower orders, and it would have been surprising had the Street Porters failed to take advantage of their opportunity; they weighed in with a strongly-worded petition which went so far as to say that they would consent to nothing short of separation, language to which the Court of Aldermen was not accustomed and to which it replied that 'the Street Porters shall submit themselves to the orders and ordinances of the Tackle House Porters and in all things perform the order of this Court . . . or stand suspended from the execution of their places'.

Even after this sharp rebuke, the Ticket Porters—this is the first occasion on which the more modern name replaces in the records the older one of Street Porters— complained again in 1641, 1642 and 1644, and finding the Aldermen obdurate, in the latter year addressed the Common Council instead. Certain constitutional alterations in the Society in 1645 improved their position, but on their main request, separation from the Tacklehouse Porters, the Common Council was no more amenable than the Aldermen. The Porters may have hoped that the Commonwealth period would be marked by more sympathy with the underdog than could be expected at other times. A renewed petition in 1651 was addressed 'to the right Honble the Lord Maior

with the honble representatives of this Citty of London in Common
Councell assembled'—a deliberate omission of the Aldermen which
offended the Lord Mayor and Aldermen to the point of walking out
and thus putting an end to proceedings when the petition came to be
read.

After this ill-judged attempt to take advantage of the political
situation, Ticket Porters lay low for sixty years before returning to the
attack in 1712 by arguing that in the Brotherhood's government
twenty-eight Tacklehouse Porters were represented as strongly as
10,000 Ticket Porters, enabling Tacklehouse Porters to hold and
misapply quarterage funds contributed by Ticket Porters. Another
reform Act was passed by the Common Council re-defining the working prerogatives of Tacklehouse and Ticket Porters respectively, but as
loth as ever to split them organizationally, and the same failure attended
the last effort on the Ticket Porters' part in 1794 when they enlarged on
the same complaints under four headings and obtained merely another
Act concerned with rights of work. By that time the Ticket Porters
must have realized that their relationship to the Tacklehouse Porters
resembled marriage in a country that knows no divorce.[19]

(c) Working Methods and Conditions

To regulate working methods and conditions was one of the principal
functions for which the Society of Tacklehouse and Ticket Porters
had been established. No Porters were to work on Sundays, except in
Lent when there was fresh fish at the gate. As Tacklehouse Porters did
not themselves work at the trade, but set others to work, they were
mainly concerned with regulations laying down whom they could
employ and on what terms. In principle they were to employ Ticket
Porters only, with one exception: at the outset, they could keep one
servant each, the expression 'servant' here denoting a man employed
on a long-term contract. Not only need such servants not be Ticket
Porters, they could even be foreigners, provided they were City
residents of long standing. It was clearly understood that every place
vacated by such a foreigner had to be filled by a freeman or an admitted
Ticket Porter—the two were not yet quite synonymous by 1646.
Tacklehouse Porters were accused in the 1680s of preventing their

single authorized servants from becoming Ticket Porters—a strange allegation at a period when all such servants ought long ago to have been pensioned off.

It was not always easy to engage Ticket Porters. If able to secure more lucrative work on their own account, Ticket Porters willing to accept employment at prescribed rates might not be found when wanted. Hence the rule prohibiting Tacklehouse Porters from employing outsiders on pain of 12d. for each contravention had to be read with a pinch of salt. Ticket Porters were under an obligation to accept such employment, unless engaged on other work, on pain of dismissal, moderated in 1645–46 to 5s. for each refusal. The City looked upon porterage as a public service which it owed to merchants; in order to enable Tacklehouse Porters at all times to perform it, Ticket Porters had to be coerced to accept engagement. Primarily the Registers and Rulers were in duty bound to furnish labour and to judge of the validity of the reasons a Porter might put forward for not responding to the call. Yet it still remained for Tacklehouse Porters to find Ticket Porters wherever they could; when the latter suggested in 1712 that two stations be appointed between London Bridge and Custom House where Ticket Porters would always be available and willing to work from 6 a.m. to 6 p.m., the proposal was not taken up.

Tacklehouse Porters in any case received higher fees than they paid their workers, but the difference between revenue and expenditure was greater if employees were foreigners not entitled to Ticket Porters' rates; hence the fine for employing such unauthorized men had to be increased from 1s. to 5s. in 1645. Thirteen years later Ticket Porters still complained of employment going not to them but to foreigners, while Tacklehouse Porters countercharged that Ticket Porters could not be procured to work at authorized rates. Tacklehouse Porters in the 1680s were accused of giving employment to 300–400 unlicensed porters a day during 'vintage time', the three or four months of the year when work was most pressing. If Tacklehouse Porters engaged whoever would work at cut prices, whether foreigners, soldiers or anybody else, they could point to the need for moving goods promptly to avoid spoilage and deterioration and the impossibility of waiting until Ticket Porters could be prevailed upon to attend. Justice was done by making Tacklehouse Porters pay 1s. an hour to every Ticket Porter who offered his services while foreigners were actually employed.[20]

Ticket Porters could work only at the place for which they had taken up their tickets, nor could a Ticket Porter change his station without the consent of the Society's Registers and Rulers. Location of work divided Ticket Porters into two branches: Uptown Porters, who occupied stands in various parts of the City waiting to be hired, and waterside Porters working at quays and wharves. At each standing-place Porters came under the supervision of a Ruler or Assistant; it was largely to provide sufficient supervisors that Assistants had first been appointed. The location of Porters' stands changed over the centuries; the list below is compiled from those found to exist at the dates given.

1605	1773-74	1841
	Abchurch Lane	
	Aldermanbury	
	Aldersgate Street	Aldersgate Street
Aldgate	Aldgate	Aldgate
	Bartholomew Lane	
Billingsgate	Billingsgate	
	Birchin Lane	
	Bishopsgate Street	
Bishopsgate	Bishopsgate Within	
	Bishopsgate Without	
	Blackfriars	
	Blackwell Hall	
	Botolph Lane	
	Botolph's Wharf	
	Bow Lane	
	Bread Street	
	Brewers' Quay	
	Broad Street	
	Brooke's Wharf	
	Bucklersbury	
	Bush Lane	
	Cannon Street	

1605	1773–74	1841
	Castle Alley	
	Change Alley	Change Alley
Cheapside	Cheapside	
	Clements Lane	
	Cox's Quay	
	Cornhill	
	Crutched Friars	
Custom House	Custom House	Custom House
	Dice Quay	
	Doctors' Commons	Doctors' Commons
	Dowgate	Dowgate
	Dyers' Hall	
Eastcheap	Eastcheap	
	Exchange Alley	
	Exchange (Royal)	
		Farringdon Market
	Fenchurch Street	
	Fetter Lane	
	Finch Lane	
	Fleet Bridge	Fleet Street
	Fleet Market	
	Fresh Wharf	
	Friday Street	
Gracechurch	Gracechurch Street	Gracechurch Street
	Grocers' Alley	
	Harp Alley	
Holborn Bridge	Holborn Bridge	
	Holborn Hill	
	King Street	
		Lad Lane
Leadenhall	Leadenhall Market	Leadenhall
	Leadenhall Street	
	Ludgate Hill	
	Mansion House	
Mark Lane		

1605	1773–74	1841
	Milk Street	
	Mincing Lane	
		Minories
	Moorfields	
	Moorgate	
Newgate Market	Newgate Market	Newgate Market
	Newgate Street	
		+ North
	Old Change	
Old Fish Street	Old Fish Street	
	Old Jewry	
	Paul's Wharf	
	Porters' Quay	
Queenhithe	Queenhithe	
	Queen Street	
	Ralph's Quay	
	St. Dunstan's Hill	
	St. Helens	
St. Laurence Seat	St. Lawrence Bench	
St. Magnus Corner	St. Magnus	
	St. Mary Axe	
	St. Mary Hill	
	St. Michael's Alley	St. Michael's Alley
St. Paul's Churchyard	St. Paul's	
	St. Swithin's Alley	
	St. Swithin's Lane	
	Shoreditch	
	Smart's Quay	
Smithfield	Smithfield	
	Snow Hill	
	Somers Quay	
Southwark		
	Staple Inn	
Stocks	Stocks Market	
	Temple	

1605	1773–74	1841
Temple Bar	Temple Bar	
	Throgmorton Street	
	Tower Street	Great Tower Street
	Three Cranes	
	Warwick Lane	
	Wood Street	

The number of stands at the three dates illustrates the expansion of the Uptown Porters' business in the seventeenth and eighteenth centuries and its subsequent contraction. In a report made by a committee of the Port of London Compensation Commissioners, the employment of Uptown Ticket Porters was defined as the carriage of packages from the different warehouses in the City to the legal quays, to be shipped. Work of this type formed an important section of the Uptown Porters' activities and may have been the only part to concern the Commissioners, but as a definition of Uptown Porters' employment it was far from exhaustive. Uptown Porters carried, loaded, and unloaded miscellaneous burdens, above all in the City markets, and acted as express letter carriers and messengers.

In the course of their work, Uptown Porters often had to carry loads weighing from one half to three hundredweights for distances of up to three miles. This could not be done without resting at intervals. If they dropped their burdens wherever they happened to be, traffic would be considerably impeded. For this reason pitching-places were distributed at intervals, specially designed for the purpose of allowing Porters of all kinds, particularly Ticket Porters, to take a rest. Each pitching-place was provided with a wooden pitching-block on to which loads could be lowered; to keep these blocks in good repair formed part of the duties of the Brotherhood of Tacklehouse and Ticket Porters. In 1693 the Society obtained permission to erect two, one adjoining the conduit in Cheapside, the other at the Rood Lane corner, but in 1761 it complained of the absence of proper pitching-places in the City and asked for permission to erect five new ones: by the pump in Bishopsgate Without, on the west side of the Mansion House facing Bucklersbury, between the posts on the west side of Bow Church, on the north-west side of St. Paul's Churchyard, and near the pump at the end of Leadenhall Street.[21]

Uptown work, however varied the jobs to be done, followed a simple pattern. A waterside Ticket Porter on the other hand might work as an employee or on his own account; in the latter capacity he might form part temporarily of a team or permanently of a gang. A Tacklehouse Porter employing him could engage him by the hour, the half-day, or the day. The earnings of waterside Ticket Porters working on their own account towards the end of the eighteenth century can be measured roughly by the claims they made for compensation when displaced by the coming of docks. Individuals estimated their loss of annual income at from £5 to £40; by far the largest number accepted lump sums of £100 in satisfaction of their demands. A Ticket Porter working on his own account could become a contractor and employ others to work for him. If he did this, he was under as strict an obligation as any Tacklehouse Porter to engage Ticket Porters only, and forfeited 1s. an hour to any other Ticket Porter waiting and offering his services while an unauthorized person was employed. Foreigners could be taken on only when no Ticket Porter was available, but had to be turned off as soon as any Ticket Porter appeared and demanded the labour, although in that case they had to be paid for whatever work they had done in the meantime.

The discharge of ordinary cargoes was entitled 'ship's work', that of coastwise goods 'jobs'; different rules applied to the two. In 'ship's work' the cargo owner at his choice could either employ a single Ticket Porter as contractor who would hire other Ticket Porters as journeymen, or several Ticket Porters could form a team. Team formation occurred during the 'beginning', the period during which the team remained open to further comers; if the cargo consisted of upwards of eighteen drafts, the 'beginning' extended over the time required to discharge the first six drafts. Of a smaller cargo one third or sixty parcels represented the 'beginning'. A Ticket Porter standing by during the 'beginning' instead of joining in the work was excluded from the team. Nor could a Porter steal a march on his team mates, for instance by surreptitiously sending a lighterman or waterman to fetch part of a cargo on his own behalf; such a subterfuge rendered the whole 'beginning' void. No Porter could validly join in the work once six drafts had been cleared. For entering a lighter or craft discharging goods which did not concern him or for attaching them to a sling or hook, a Porter could be fined 5s.

As soon as the team was complete, one member would be appointed bookkeeper, undertaking to inspect all members' tickets, ascertain their names and count their turns of work. In due course he became paymaster by collecting the team's remuneration from the merchant and dividing it in accordance with the amount of work done by each individual. If a single contractor acted as employer of the remainder, he naturally undertook to be bookkeeper. Whatever agreement he had with the cargo owner, he was not entitled to any share of the rates paid on account of labour unless he actually began working the ship with the other Porters and was not holding any other ship at the same time.

Ticket Porters working in such conditions were tempted to run from ship to ship, joining several teams simultaneously and staying to work wherever conditions looked most rewarding. In 1670 the Court of Rulers ordered any Ticket Porter starting the unloading of an American or West Indian ship and transferring to another vessel before the first ship had been completely discharged, to forfeit his share of remuneration in respect of the first ship. At the end of the eighteenth century this simple rule was greatly elaborated. No Ticket Porter engaged on ship's work could leave the vessel without a written order from the Society's Governor, until less than six drafts of cargo remained to be cleared. The offender forfeited not only his remuneration, but also a 10s. fine; in addition he was disqualified from starting work on any other vessel until the ship deserted by him had been cleared. Once the cargo to be unloaded had been reduced to less than six drafts Ticket Porters were at liberty to start work on another vessel. Where labour consisted not of 'ship's work' but of a 'job', no Ticket Porter was permitted to act as employer, but all Porters arriving in time for the 'beginning' worked as a team on an equal footing. This implied that all of them not only took regular turns, but also carried equivalent loads—a matter difficult to determine unless they used standardized containers. No Porter could carry stone and earthenware unless equipped with a basket 29 inches in depth and having a diameter of

27½ inches at the top and 23 inches at the bottom. Though burdens of this commodity required regulation most urgently, owing to its exceptional weight, standard loads existed for many others also.

(d) Gangs of Ticket Porters

Teams of Ticket Porters formed wherever the handling of cargo required several workers. Gangs on the other hand were permanent partnerships of Ticket Porters working on joint account. Apart from the exceptionally prosperous individual, gangsmen constituted the undoubted aristocracy of Ticket Porters, enjoying earnings and opportunities far in excess of those available to ordinary waterside Porters. No ganging up of Ticket Porters had originally been contemplated. Permanent groupings on their own initiative among men licensed to perform essential duties offended the concept of public service as much as would a present-day association of a number of policemen claiming an exclusive right to patrol certain beats. Not only did the Society's early regulations make no mention of gangs, but when gangs first formed in the middle of the seventeenth century, the Aldermen at large remained unaware of them, although the Society's two Governors approved a minute of the Court of Rulers in 1664 permitting a member of the East Country Gang to draw his share of the gang's earnings even in respect of days when his duties as a Ruler required attendance at the Court and precluded him from working with his gang. This is the first mention of a gang among Ticket Porters; it did not penetrate beyond the Court of Rulers' minute-book.

At the London Sessions of 1675 a Ticket Porter sued three members of a gang to whom he had paid £20 for admission to a share in its work and profits; they had neither admitted him nor refunded the money. The court did not decide on this action, but referred it to the arbitration of two Aldermen. Thus gang formation must have come to the attention of individual Aldermen before it occupied their Court officially in the following year. Twelve Porters, members of a gang of long standing, had admitted four newcomers, demanding £30 from each for such admission. When one of the recruits withheld his entrance fee, they petitioned the Court of Aldermen against him—clearly with no thought that they had anything to hide. The Court of Aldermen, horrified at the discovery that the gang had been in existence for many years, considered the combination unlawful and the admission fees illegally exacted. Gang members were made to repay the entrance money and the gang itself was dissolved. Into a similar category of behaviour fell the practice of old-established Ticket Porters demanding money for drink or other entertainment from members newly admitted to the Society as a condition of permitting them to ply for work. The Court of Aldermen sharply repressed such habits in 1695 when the exactions were described as high. The trouble recurred in 1723 when a recruit to the Society had to pay an unspecified sum in addition to giving a promissory note for 50s. The money seems to have been irrecoverable, but the recipients suffered suspension from employment until they had returned the promissory note.

The tendency to gang formation must have been strong; by 1700 gangs again threatened the interests of Ticket Porters working on their own account, and caused the Aldermen to consider the advisability of a City by-law against gangs. Ten years later, vacancies in Ticket Porters' gangs were worth £50-£60, such gangs existing at every quay from Tower Dock to London Bridge, there being

> 20 men in the gang at Botolph's Wharf
> 5 or 6 ,, ,, ,, ,, ,, Dice Quay
> 4 ,, ,, ,, ,, ,, Smart's Quay
> 14 ,, ,, ,, ,, ,, Wiggins' Quay
> 12 ,, ,, ,, ,, ,, Bear Quay
> 4 ,, ,, ,, ,, ,, Porters' Quay
> 12 ,, ,, ,, ,, ,, Custom House Quay
> 12 ,, ,, ,, ,, ,, Wool and Galley Quays.

Merchants found their work handled more quickly and efficiently by gangs than by teams combined *ad hoc*; wharfingers concluded special arrangements with favoured gangs; whether the Aldermen liked it or not, gangs had become a feature of waterside porterage. The Aldermen resigned themselves to the inevitable; instead of attempting to suppress gangs, they required them to consist of admitted Ticket Porters and regulated them to some extent. The latter endeavour was not completely successful; a combination of gangsmen and wharfingers proved invariably stronger than the rules devised to keep them in check.

Gangs maintained their own tacklehouses, weights and beams; on the quay or wharf where they held sway, they arrogated to themselves all the work, whether or not within their prerogative, and forcibly kept at bay all others, even admitted Ticket Porters. Although purporting to be freemen themselves, they employed foreigners in their service, claiming to be exempt from the rules prohibiting such employment. One of the gangsmen kept the gang's accounts and distributed the collective earnings. Gangsmen at Botolph's Wharf and Galley Quay acted not only as Porters, but also as warehousemen. To become a gangsman at one of the legal quays around the year 1800 cost a Ticket Porter £100; admission to the gang at Cox and Hammonds' Quays was priced at 100 guineas; at Ralph's and Young's Quays a gangsman in 1792 had even paid £200, although here the admission fee went to the employing wharfingers. Men often gained admission to a gang because their fathers or brothers had been members before them, but this did not dispense with entrance fees.

Gangsmen would not have paid such large amounts for the privilege of working hard, had not the perquisites been worth their while. Apart from lawful remuneration, there were considerable pickings. Colquhoun accuses gangs of downright plunder, but, looking upon all dock labour with a policeman's disenchanted eye, he did not carefully distinguish the authorized from the unauthorized. That gangsmen discharging sugar were allowed sweepings or molasses was common knowledge; a prohibition of this practice, passed by a general meeting of West India merchants in 1790, remained a dead letter. A wharfinger explained to a parliamentary committee ten years later that the allowance had become part of a gangsman's accepted wages and could not be abolished without compensation. Scrapings off warehouse floors came into the same category. 'Good money' or 'ready money', additional payments in respect of certain jobs, augmented agreed wage-rates; breakfasts and dinners were often supplied on the job so as to save time consumed by men leaving ships to obtain meals.

Colquhoun writing in 1800 counted 290 gangsmen employed by wharfingers, including those working in the coasting trade. They should all have been admitted Ticket Porters but, among gangs claiming compensation for loss of business through the opening of the docks, the investigating Commissioners discovered only one Ticket Porter among the five men forming the Wiggins' Quay Gang; of eight men making up the gang at Ralph's and Young's Quays just one-half were Ticket Porters, and one of the ten gangsmen at Porters', Page's, Bear and Sabbs Quays similarly lacked the necessary qualification. Only forty-five gangsmen figured among claimants under the Port of London compensation scheme between 1805 and 1809*. The smallest claim lodged by any individual gangsman was for £480 in respect of loss through the West India Docks (William Richards, claim No. 1020), the smallest award made to any gangsman £100 in respect of both the West India and London Docks (children of George Henbest, claims Nos. 611–613). The largest claim in respect of a whole gang came from the men (variously stated to be nine or ten) forming the gang at Porters, Page's, Bear and Sabbs Quays and amounted to £19,989 6s. 8d. No agreement being reached, it was submitted to a jury which returned a verdict for £2,237 18s. 6d. (claim No. 1133).[22]

(e) Demarcation Disputes

If organization furnished Tacklehouse and Ticket Porters with a battlefield, the most important issue at stake was prerogative. Which goods any one group of Porters could handle, and how exclusive their monopoly of such merchandise, were questions which determined the standard of living, if not the livelihood, of the contending parties. In these disputes the City authorities' power was absolute: inasmuch as Porters exercised rights derived from City privileges, neither they nor any outsider could contest the City's power to allocate such privileges as it chose. Yet even in this field custom sometimes modified City rule. For instance, the Common Council Act of 1597 gave any authorized Porter the right to uptown work, the carrying from one place to another within the City of miscellaneous burdens consisting of goods not allotted to a particular group of Porters—work done at a distance from the waterside. This would have left such labour open to many kinds of Porters, whereas it promptly became the exclusive right of a

* See pp. 144, 146 below

F

particular section of Ticket Porters, the Uptown Porters: the designation of Street and Corner Porters alone created a presumption in their favour.

The City authorities first defined the work of the Street Porters in the 1580s, assigning it according to two different criteria: it comprised on the one hand all carriage of iron, rope, cables and cordage, on the other hand that of pitch, tar, soap, ashes, clapboard, wainscots, fir poles, masts, deals, oars, chests, tables, flax and hemp, if imported from Dantzig or Melvyn (Elbing). The latter subsequently came to be described as East Country goods, though both their categories and ports of loading in due course were much diversified. Along with innholders, wharfingers and quay keepers, Street Porters were prohibited by the Common Council Act of 1597 from 'keeping or using any manner of triangle with beam, scales and weights or any other balances of any sort' to weigh merchandise, this being the prerogative of Master Weighers at the various beams and their porters. A Common Council Act of 1712 renewed the prohibition, alleging past infringements and stipulating a penalty of 20s. for future ones. As regards porterage, merchandise remained free to all unless it had been allocated. Only on this assumption can the Tacklehouse Porters' complaint be justified when they accused Street Porters of improperly handling all green woad for foreigners. The Aldermen did not think Street Porters were strictly entitled to this business but, for the sake of peace and quiet, recommended Tacklehouse Porters to relinquish it to the Street Porters. This was first done as a matter of compromise, but the Common Council Act of 1597 added green woad to the Street Porters' prerogative, except the weighing of it with which they were not allowed to concern themselves. By 1712 nobody remembered what green woad was; in listing the Ticket Porters' prerogative, the Common Council Act of that year spoke of 'all Wood, commonly called Green Wood',* thus enlarging the Ticket Porters' prerogative by a mere error in the deciphering of old handwriting.

Tacklehouse Porters had the handling of all merchandise of free merchants shipped or unshipped by cocquet or certificate, but were instructed in 1597 to allow Ticket Porters to do any surplus business

* See note 7.

which they themselves had not sufficient facilities to handle. The work allocated to the Tacklehouse Porters was obviously expected to employ them to, if not beyond, full capacity, whereas Ticket Porters served as a reservoir of unused or at least under-used resources. The preamble to the Common Council Act of 1608 bore out the latter assumption when it recited that Ticket Porters had been interfering with the handling of merchandise of free as well as unfree merchants. Instead of concentrating on this distinction, the Act barred Ticket Porters from the handling of any English merchants' goods, whether free or unfree, except in an emergency when Tacklehouse Porters could not cope with the volume of work. Thus, instead of dividing the field between Tacklehouse and Ticket Porters along the line of the City freedom, it introduced a new criterion—nationality. Far from helping to eliminate conflicts, it added to confusion. Eleven years later a new Common Council Act admitted 'that the said Act is therein so darkly penned that some doubt has arisen', especially in encouraging encroachments by Tacklehouse and Ticket Porters on the Aliens' Porters' prerogative. The new Act had to make it clear that neither Tacklehouse nor Ticket Porters were entitled to handle aliens' or denizens' goods. In vain did Ticket Porters plead with the City authorities to be allowed to deal with goods falling within their prerogative even if such commodities were assessed to cocquet duty.

Complaints against Ticket Porters meddling with the goods of merchant strangers were raised afresh half a century later, this time by Porters serving at the weighhouse in Cornhill; the Aldermen settled the complaints in committee. They could not have been without substance; in the course of a petition against the Tacklehouse Porters in 1673 Ticket Porters themselves admitted that of the merchants who employed them at the waterside some had been aliens or the sons of aliens. Having been naturalized, many had also become free of the City, whereupon the Tacklehouse Porters had usurped their work by virtue of their monopoly of the porterage of freemen's goods, much against the wishes of the merchants themselves—or so the Ticket Porters alleged. On a strict interpretation of the law, the Tacklehouse Porters had acted within their rights. The Aldermen could give the Ticket Porters no satisfaction.

Ticket Porters fared better when warding off unauthorized intruders. If these were not even freemen, an action brought in the City Chamberlain's name in the Lord Mayor's Court usually proved sufficient unless the foreigners were employed by a powerful corporation such as the East India Company. If that happened, more diplomatic procedure was followed: an Alderman who was also a member of the East India Company's Court would be requested to draw the Company's attention to its transgressions. Foreigners summoned for working as porters sometimes quickly obtained the City's freedom, in which case, though still not admitted Porters, they would not be punished very seriously for their misdemeanour. Especially in the early 1690s Ticket Porters suffered greatly from encroachments by watermen, coachmen, and basket women, particularly at Blackfriars, and petitioned the Court of Aldermen very urgently, the more so since one of their Governors was too busy with his other duties to defend the Ticket Porters' rights. Legal advice left no doubt that watermen were punishable as unadmitted porters if carrying burdens, but the position of coaches carrying boxes and bundles either inside or attached to their front and rear was more complicated: the practice could not be indicted if the owners accompanied their boxes, but only if the coach was used as a goods vehicle. The same rule applied to what Ticket Porters described as a horse-drawn sledge or small carriage whose driver collected from shopkeepers loads to be delivered in the neighbourhood —an early version of a district delivery van.

Lawyers disagreed about Porters or innkeepers employing apprentices on porterage work: according to one opinion, apprentices were entitled to carry their employers' goods, but not anybody else's; another held that if a man be qualified to take an apprentice he could employ him on any business lawful for the master to undertake. The problem became more serious towards the end of the eighteenth century; innkeepers and warehousemen, sometimes themselves admitted Ticket Porters, engaged foreigners to do their portering for them. Legal opinion justified such behaviour provided foreigners had been engaged for general services; it became illegal only if they had been hired specifically to perform porterage work. Nothing prevented Ticket Porters from claiming the labour by offering their services except fear that they would be beaten up by the foreigners concerned if encountered on the premises of innkeepers and warehousemen. Sometimes the Governor awarded damages against such employers, but they refused to comply with his verdict. Worse than that, the Court of Requests would not entertain Ticket Porters' suits, saying that their complaints did not come within its jurisdiction. Remedies in any case lay not against employers of unauthorized labour but merely against the employees themselves, who were rarely substantial or stationary enough to warrant prosecution. Where innkeepers and warehousemen had not joined the Brotherhood, Ticket Porters complained that they did not come under the authority of the Society's Governor and therefore could not be summoned before him—a view inconsistent with City legislation. More cogent was the financial difficulty: few Ticket Porters had the means of prosecuting in a Court of Record for the recovery of the penalty, which at best did not exceed 13s. 4d. The threat became more insidious in the 1790s when Parliament, in a bill introduced to regulate porterage rates for small packages carried out from different City inns and warehouses, planned to give inn and warehouse keepers unlimited powers to employ in this work whomever they wished. Timely intervention secured a clause in the Act safeguarding the rights of authorized Porters. Ticket Porters also complained of a combination between wharfingers, watermen and ship masters to accommodate on board coasting vessels men who unloaded freight and parcels when they landed, though this work belonged to the Ticket Porters.[23]

Demarcation of porterage duties broke down over 'catching burdens'. In a tariff fixed by the Aldermen in 1566 for the Fellowship Porters' work, some rates related to 'all light burdens called catching burdens'; these passed unchanged into the general regulations of Fellowship Porters in 1620 without making catching burdens their sole prerogative. When in 1635 Ticket Porters demanded the right of handling catching burdens, a meeting of Governors and Rulers of the Fellowship Porters on the one hand and of the Tacklehouse and Ticket Porters on the other reached agreement that either group could lawfully carry catching burdens. The dispute arose afresh in 1679 and the parties met again, read the minutes and re-affirmed the resolutions of the earlier conference, adding that any member of either Brotherhood could carry catching burdens to any part of the City. None of these meetings had sought to define catching burdens; the meaning of the expression remained obscure. When in 1694 a committee of Aldermen investigated mutual complaints from Fellowship and Ticket Porters, each alleging interference from the others in the labour of landing and carrying fruit, both sides claimed the work by virtue of their rights relative to catching burdens; the Aldermen found that nobody knew what catching burdens were. The definition, as propounded by the committee, was not very conclusive, describing as catching burdens 'all manner of fruit and garden stuff that are portable and come from western villages *amongst other things*★', and a bill for the better regulation of the Fellowship of Porters of Billingsgate, drafted in 1708 but never enacted, improved on it only very slightly when it described them as 'all fruit or garden stuff brought from the Eastern and Western villages in small boats or wherries which amongst other things are called catching burdens'.

(f) Prerogatives of Tacklehouse and Ticket Porters

When their respective spheres were first delineated, Tacklehouse Porters, in spite of much smaller numbers, had had the lion's share of the work falling to their Society. In the 1680s Ticket Porters could still claim that only one-third of the Society's work appertained to themselves, basing their claim on Customs entries purporting to show that in a year in which Ticket Porters dealt with 301 shiploads, 1,160 ships had been serviced by Tacklehouse Porters (the figures, however, take no account of possible variations in the size of cargoes). In 1707 Tacklehouse Porters stated that two-thirds of the work formerly done by them had now passed into the Ticket Porters' hands. Even if not literally accurate, the assertion had some substance. The development of overseas trade since the first allocation of work had brought into prominence some classes of goods and some countries of origin, thus shifting the emphasis and the workload. The overall change had favoured the Ticket Porters at the expense of the Tacklehouse Porters.

No one sector of imports illustrated this more clearly than that

★ My italics.

from the Caribbean islands; so few goods had come from the West Indies in the late sixteenth century that Tacklehouse Porters did not consider the business worth their while; it fell to the Ticket Porters by default. By the middle of the seventeenth century, however, trade with these islands had expanded substantially and the Tacklehouse Porters became interested. They were too late to obtain a share, and this, more than any other reverse, contributed to the deterioration of their relative position; the Caribbean trade furnished a precedent for the allocation of all American imports. At least, the Ticket Porters thus interpreted the verdict in their favour; they applied to goods from Virginia the ruling obtained on West Indies merchandise, sometimes forcibly depriving the Tacklehouse Porters of work, causing tumult and disturbances and even embezzling the goods, quite apart from taking for the handling of dry goods fees twice as high as those charged by Tacklehouse Porters for wet cargoes of greater bulk and hazard. On this occasion the Court of Aldermen gave both Virginia and West India merchants the choice of employing either Tacklehouse or Ticket Porters, provided that rates and prices were agreed between the parties.

But this was not the end, merely the beginning of further conflict. For in 1658 the Ticket Porters claimed all merchandise coming from or going to the plantations (a type of trade rapidly rising to prominence) on the ground that they alone had done this work for the past forty years or more, whereas the Tacklehouse Porters stood by the verdict of the previous year giving merchants an option whom to employ. The Court of Aldermen, quite unable to discover any consisten principle for the determination of demarcation disputes and anxious only to settle them somehow, allocated all English plantation goods to the Ticket Porters. So unsatisfactory was this verdict to the Tacklehouse Porters that Ticket Porters had to resort repeatedly to the Aldermen's authority to have it enforced; for the latter group it represented an important victory. The definition of an English plantation was next called in question when in the early eighteenth century Ticket Porters were interrupted in the discharge of a Hudson's Bay Company's ship by a Goldsmiths' Tacklehouse Porter claiming the right to this work because the freemen of the Company employed him in their service. Even the learned lawyer consulted in this instance could only suggest arbitration by the Governor of the Society of Tacklehouse and Ticket Porters.

Meanwhile another dispute had arisen. West Indies merchandise could be handled by either Tacklehouse or Ticket Porters, unless distinctly imported from English plantations; but who was entitled to carry and load it on re-exportation from London? Both the Society's Governor and the Court of Aldermen had given this right to the Tacklehouse Porters, probably by way of compensation for the loss of plantation goods, but as far as it concerned the re-export of plantation goods, the Ticket Porters had usurped the work. This was all the more serious for Tacklehouse Porters since many primary commodities from foreign countries, such as sugar from Brazil, indigo and tobacco from Cadiz, and cotton from Cyprus and Smyrna, were increasingly re-placed in the early eighteenth century by imports from English planta-tions, thus transferring more and more trade from the Tacklehouse Porters' sector to that of the Ticket Porters. Nothing could be done about English plantation goods as such, except those re-exported, when the right of either party to the work at the option of the employing merchant was re-affirmed.

New England and Newfoundland had been swallowed by the Ticket Porters under the omnibus claim to English plantations. Nor were they deterred when, in the later eighteenth century, New England settlers removed this justification by proclaiming their in-dependence. In 1793 Ticket Porters still insisted on their right to handle imports from the independent States of America, the province of Quebec and all existing and future British provinces and plantations. When the Common Council, in the course of a comprehensive re-allocation of prerogatives in 1798, defined the American territories, Ticket Porters were confirmed in their rights to goods from the United States, Hudson's Bay, Quebec, Canada, Nova Scotia, and the British plantations or colonies, present and future, in the West Indies, but all places north and south of the United States of America (Hud-son's Bay, Quebec, Canada and Nova Scotia only excepted) fell to the Tacklehouse Porters. This geographical delimitation, if not logical, sounded at least conclusive. Yet three years later the position of Guiana was in dispute, goods from Demarara (present-day Georgetown),

Berbice (present-day New Amsterdam) and Surinam being claimed by Tacklehouse Porters as being south of the United States and by Ticket Porters as British plantations. A subsidiary Act of 1801 had to add Guiana to the Ticket Porters' area.[24]

East Country goods had been the first type of merchandise subject to regional allocation, being made the Ticket Porters' prerogative in the 1580s and confirmed to them in 1608.* These rules had established the Ticket Porters' exclusive right, but that was not how Tacklehouse Porters read them: according to their interpretation, put forward half a century later, Ticket Porters were permitted but Tacklehouse Porters not forbidden to handle East Country goods. The Court of Aldermen rejected this highly controversial reading of the Act. Conflict broke out anew in 1685, this time on account of goods from Russia which the Ticket Porters claimed as part of the East Country, whereas 'a merchant of quality, formerly resident in Russia' gave expert evidence to the contrary. As Tacklehouse Porters asserted that they had always handled Russian goods, the Lord Mayor found in their favour.

This did not settle the question definitely. In 1716 the Ticket Porters complained that within the last two or three years the Muscovites had moved to Petersburg (present-day Leningrad) and that the Tacklehouse Porters had seized this opportunity of invading East Country work on the plea that it was Muscovy Company work, hence belonging to them. In this dilemma the Aldermen turned to Sir Benjamin Ayloffe, Bart., an old and eminent merchant trading to the East Countries, from whom they sought exact definitions of the geographical terms. Ayloffe's evidence, corroborated by two further East Country merchants, Sir Randolph Knipe and Charles Goodfellow, included all Baltic ports in East Country commerce and confirmed that Petersburg had lately been made a place of trade by the Czar. Elbing had not for many years sent any exports to England, but goods loaded at Dantzig, Königsberg and Riga did not come from their immediate hinterland, but from more distant countries such as Poland, Samogitia, Livonia and Russia; nevertheless, by virtue of being shipped from East Country ports they ranked as East Country goods. Moreover, Russian goods in particular

* See p. 66 above.

had formerly been exported to England through the port of Narva largely by members of the Muscovy Company; although these merchants were freemen of London, the Ticket Porters had always handled the goods. This was the merchandise exported now from Petersburg instead of Narva. This testimony ruined the Tacklehouse Porters' case; they had to admit that the only East Country goods with which they had regularly dealt came from a single port, Archangel. The admission formed the basis of the settlement imposed by the Court of Aldermen in 1716, giving the Tacklehouse Porters the imports from Archangel while confirming the Ticket Porters in their right to all other East Country goods. Though the Mercers' Tacklehouse Porters made one further attempt to claim merchandise from Petersburg, the decision ensured peace for most of the century, but it represented another Ticket Porters' victory at the Tacklehouse Porters' expense. In the 1790s, however, when re-allocation of prerogatives was impending, the Ticket Porters tried again to extend their area by analogy, this time by adding Sweden, Prussia and Denmark to the East Country. On this occasion the Common Council counterbalanced the Ticket Porters' gains in transatlantic territories by allocating in its Act of 1798 the East Countries, Russia, Hamburg, Bremen and Germany to the Tacklehouse Porters.

A grant of letters patent to George Penny, gent., of the lading and unlading of coasters' goods was mentioned in the Court of Aldermen in 1608 when that body appointed a committee to attend the hearing of the matter at the Lord Mayor's house. What sounds like royal interference with London privileges came to nothing; half a century later the handling of coastwise goods re-emerged as a bone of contention between Tacklehouse and Ticket Porters. At that time controversy centred on the discharge of tin and lead, claimed by Ticket Porters as coast goods, allegedly allocated to them by a Common Council Act, whereas Tacklehouse Porters purported to have handled tin and lead for the past forty years. As on other occasions, the Court of Aldermen tried to make tradition the basis of future regulation: Tacklehouse Porters were confirmed in their rights to tin and lead, Ticket Porters awarded all other coastwise goods. However, it was common knowledge by 1712 that Ticket Porters were still doing the tin work, contrary to this verdict; this was acknowledged by the Act which in that year threw it open to both groups of Porters.

Under the heading of coast goods, Ticket Porters also attempted to usurp the Channel Islands trade, which, however, in the same year was declared part of the prerogative of Tacklehouse as well as Ticket Porters. Meanwhile the question of coast goods had created confusion whenever goods from overseas were landed at some outport and transhipped to London, such merchandise being claimed under the heading of imports by Tacklehouse, as coast goods by Ticket Porters. On two occasions, in 1677 and 1696, the Aldermen found in the Ticket Porters' favour. The problem was complicated in wartime when enemy goods were prohibited: a Customs officer in 1712 discovered at Southwark some French walnut planks secretly imported, seized them, put them on a lighter and transferred them to Wool Quay; while the Drapers' Tacklehouse Porters were landing them as French goods, Ticket Porters claimed them as coastwise goods. In 1740 Tacklehouse Porters still contended that the term coast goods had been meant to apply to home-produced articles only; this was one of the points on which Ticket Porters would have been prepared to make concessions in return for fulfilment of certain of their own demands. The Act of 1798 finally classified goods in accordance with the port of loading, irrespective of intermediate landings.

Trade with France and Spain had always been a Tacklehouse Porters' stronghold. It had proved of great value during the seventeenth century when commercial relations with Spain were close and lucrative, but in the eighteenth suffered frequent interruptions through wars with France. Though Spain constituted a Tacklehouse Porters' area, Ticket Porters had through most of the seventeenth century handled Spanish iron, and when the Tacklehouse Porters asserted their rights in 1712, twenty-six merchants dealing in that commodity tried to retain the Ticket Porters' services. Otherwise controversy regarding France and Spain was directly attributable to wars; it turned on the definition of prize goods, determined according to the Tacklehouse Porters by the nationality of the ship. When the French ship *St. Joseph* was made a prize, Tacklehouse Porters laid claim to its cargo of arnotto indigo and sugar as prize goods, Ticket Porters as plantation goods. In the same way Tacklehouse Porters considered themselves entitled to handle a cargo of Irish beef because it was discharged from the French prize *Vancresson* and had been loaded at Le Havre. Ticket Porters were prepared to compromise, either on the basis of labour on prize ships being free to all or even by abandoning their claim, but only against reciprocal concessions. The question had not been settled in 1740 when the cargo of the Spanish prize ship *St. Joseph* was transferred to hoys, partly at Portsmouth, partly at Margate, and carried to London where Tacklehouse Porters discharged it while Ticket Porters claimed it as coastwise goods. Without laying down any general principle, the Aldermen decided this instance in the Tacklehouse Porters' favour, and in 1793 the Ticket Porters still treated the discharge of prize goods as a bargaining counter, claiming it merely for the purpose of sacrificing the claim in return for concessions. The war then breaking out once again reduced the Tacklehouse Porters' activities, above all by depriving them of the handling of French wines; but the prize goods question found its settlement at last by the classification of merchandise according to its port of loading.[25]

Goods from Ireland caused no controversy until in 1677 Ticket Porters accused four Tacklehouse Porters of retaining money due to them for work done on Irish goods—a claim based not on prerogative but on actual labour performed. Substantial contest over the right to Irish work started five years later, when the Ticket Porters alleged that they had handled these goods time out of mind (on another occasion, they moderated the statement to 'over forty years'), only to find that the Tacklehouse Porters were now petitioning the Governors for this work. Several traders with Ireland corroborated on oath the Ticket Porters' case, and their prerogative was finally established in 1698.

In exactly the same way the Ticket Porters in 1682 insisted on their ancient rights to Scottish goods while the Tacklehouse Porters sought to obtain the award from the Governors. No decision was made at the time, though the inroads on the Scottish business made by the Tacklehouse Porters working for the Haberdashers' Company were attributed by Ticket Porters to their own amiable disposition and disinclination to assert themselves! As soon as England and Scotland became united, they argued with admirable acumen that this constitutional change

turned Scottish into coastwise goods. Nor could the Court of Aldermen deny the cogency of this argument, in spite of testimonials from
twenty-eight London traders with Scotland that they preferred the
Tacklehouse Porters' services.

The Tacklehouse Porters thus being distinctly worsted in yet another
contest around 1700, the Aldermen must have hoped for opportunities
of putting some trade their way. This proved possible in connection
with the East India and South Seas Companies, though the history of
the latter enterprise renders it unlikely that much business resulted.
Several members of the Company of Goldsmiths were also shareholders
of both East India Companies existing in 1706 when they asked the
Court of Aldermen for the right to appoint Tacklehouse Porters to do
the East India work. The Act of 1712 accordingly allocated East India
porterage business to the Tacklehouse Porters, of whom however not
the Goldsmiths' but the Mercers' and Ironmongers' Tacklehouse
Porters were employed at the end of the century; the East India
Company then owned and occupied Lyons and Somers Quays between
London Bridge and Billingsgate. Work on behalf of the East India
Company came to an end when the East India Docks were opened in
the early nineteenth century. As regards South Sea trade, the Ticket
Porters claimed it as West Indies plantation trade, but never insisted
very strongly on the claim. They did not stand to lose a great deal
when the Act of 1712 allotted it to the Tacklehouse Porters.

Allocation of goods to one or other group of Porters narrowed the
area of conflict. Unless every type of merchandise from everywhere
became subject to specific regulation, a residual uncertainty was bound
to persist. In a tentative agreement arrived at in 1712, Tacklehouse
Porters were granted the right to unallocated goods, arrangements
confirmed by the Act later that year. No fundamental change in the
prerogatives of the two groups occurred during the eighteenth century;
conflicts centered on difficulties of interpreting existing rules. But by
the 1790s both groups of Porters had become dissatisfied with the
distribution of work. The Ticket Porters staked new claims on the
ground of simplicity: they demanded all goods coming from America
as well as from islands conquered or ceded now or in future—the latter
a promising item in an expanding Empire. Goods had hitherto been

allocated to Ticket Porters only on the basis of being of the 'growth, product or manufactory' of the designated area; this restriction gave rise to many disputes, and Ticket Porters wanted it removed. Tacklehouse Porters had stronger reasons for dissatisfaction with the way trade had developed during the eighteenth century: after the South Sea Bubble, commerce with the South Seas had shrunk to little importance; the Turkey, Levant and Mediterranean trades had been diverted into other channels and were not coming their way any more. Whenever French provinces and plantations had become British, their goods had passed from the Tacklehouse to the Ticket Porters' prerogative, whereas the independence of the United States had not involved the Ticket Porters in a loss of American merchandise.

The Common Council Act of 1798 made for greater clarity: it abolished the qualification of 'growth, product or manufactory', classified prize goods in accordance with the port of loading, and threw open to either group of Porters all exports, regardless of destination. Beyond that, while confirming Ticket Porters in their traditional areas, it strengthened the Tacklehouse Porters' position by reserving to them imports from Asia and Africa; wine and brandy, whatever their countries of origin, were for the first time explicitly allocated to the Tacklehouse Porters. This was a privilege at which Ticket Porters jibbed; in 1801 they tried to obtain the work of handling at least colonial wine and brandy, but remained unsuccessful.[26]

(g) Rates and Charges

Cost of living considerations were not absent from the Aldermen's minds when they ordered in 1595 that 'rates should be fixed for the carriage of burdens by porters and of loads by carmen from place to place in the City and liberties, taking into account the price of other things necessary at the present time'. Ten years later an elaborate scale of Uptown Ticket Porters' charges, varying both with the weight of the load and the distance of the journey, was fixed by the Court of Aldermen. The scale of 1605 endured for almost two centuries until replaced in 1799 by an even more elaborate and detailed list calculated on the same basis. The waterside Porters' remuneration adjusted itself more readily to the general price level than that of their Uptown brethren. When engaged by Tacklehouse Porters, waterside Ticket Porters were entitled under rules made in 1621 to 2*d*. an hour if employed for three hours or less. The daily rate amounted in winter (November to February inclusive) to 14*d*. and during other seasons to 16*d*., four or five hours counting as half a day. The cost of living had overtaken these charges by 1640; the hourly rate now rose to 3*d*., the day wage to 16*d*. in winter and 18*d*. at other times; a second increase five years later raised these rates to 4*d*., 20*d*. and 2*s*. respectively; moreover, even three hours now counted as half a day. Ticket Porters complained that Tacklehouse Porters tricked them by keeping them in attendance all day from a very early hour, sometimes until 10, 11, or midnight, seldom or never paying them a full day's wages, in the hope of wearying them and paving the way for the employment of foreigners. The unsatisfactory delimitation of how many hours constituted half a day's or a day's work caused many disputes. When Ticket Porters in 1712 suggested that they should receive 4*d*. an hour if employed for only one hour, but 2*d*. an hour if employed for two and three, and that four hours should count as half a day, the City's regulations entitling them to better terms must in practice have lapsed. The hourly rate was officially reduced to 3*d*. in 1798.

Ticket Porters employed by merchants direct worked at customary rates, so far as the City had not fixed their remuneration. A committee of Aldermen in 1675, in response to users' complaints, reviewed all Tacklehouse and Ticket Porters' rates; the request for reduction, apparently unfulfilled, was renewed in respect of the Ticket Porters in 1680. Such rates were notoriously sticky. Rice, for instance, was discharged at 4*d*. a barrel throughout the first quarter of the eighteenth century, though during that period barrels increased greatly in size. If Ticket Porters took exception to the growth of the physical burden, traders objected no less to a charge which in a falling market constituted an increasing proportion of the commodity's cost. Both sides eventually decided to abide by the existing rate, for they could not agree on any other. Sugar was paid per cask, three standard charges distinguishing casks weighing less than 8 cwt. from those weighing 8–12 cwt. and those exceeding 12 cwt. Heavy casks were in more general use in the 1790s when Ticket Porters asked for a rise, both on the ground of general living standards and because each load of sugar required a larger team of Porters possessing stronger tackle. The committee of West India merchants left charges unchanged for casks below 8 cwt., but paid for casks weighing 8–10 cwt. what had hitherto been the price for casks up to 12 cwt.; what had been the tariff for casks in excess of 12 cwt. now applied to casks weighing 10–16 cwt., and casks exceeding 16 cwt. were paid at a higher rate which had not existed before.

Tacklehouse Porters originally fixed their own remuneration by agreement with members of the Companies who employed them; such rates then became customary and difficult to change even though the cost of living or the nature of the work varied. Tacklehouse Porters complained of the low rates at which they were expected to carry liquid loads: they received no more than 16*d.* per ton for landing, loading, striking and laying down wine in cellars, however heavy the barrel or pipe; the corresponding remuneration for oil amounted to 18*d.* per ton, irrespective of the size of cask. On the other hand they earned very high rates of remuneration in the East India, Guinea, Turkish and Straights trades, or so it appeared to envious Ticket Porters.

In 1796 the Common Council decided to embody detailed rates for both Tacklehouse and Ticket Porters in an Act. It compiled an arbitrary table of rates which it advertised publicly to provoke comment and criticism. The advertisements drew no response. The Common Council then prepared to enact its proposals. This at last aroused protests: the West India merchants pointed to the recent increase in rates for sugar porterage and expressed anxiety lest any further rise in London costs diverted imports to the outports (a threat frequently employed by West India merchants towards the end of the eighteenth century); the East India Company let it be known that the Mercers' and Ironmongers' Tacklehouse Porters whom it employed had had a 20 per cent increase some years earlier and did not wish to be included in any contemplated change of rates; proprietors and lessees of the legal quays and warehouses drew attention to efforts made at this moment to convince the House of Commons and the public of the need for reducing costs in the Port of London. Dock schemes for the

Port were in the air, and wharfingers feared for their trade; concerned as they were with Porters' rates, they could not spare time for discussion till the parliamentary season had ended.

At last the Common Council could identify, and consult with, the parties affected by Porters' charges; the new table of rates emerging after a year's deliberations represented a compromise of all these interests. On thirteen foolscap pages, Tacklehouse Porters' rates were grouped under three headings, the first comprising wine, brandy, rum and geneva, the other two, alphabetically sub-divided by commodities, relating to merchandise from Holland, Hamburg, Bremen, Russia and all parts of the East Countries, and goods from the Mediterranean, Spain, Portugal, France and Africa. Four tables listed Ticket Porters' rates, according to ports of origin:

> British Plantations or Colonies in the West Indies.
> United States of America.
> Quebec, Nova Scotia, Hudson's Bay and Canada.
> Ireland.

Coastwise shipping rates received no mention in the Act of 1798.[27]

5

FELLOWSHIP PORTERS: GROUPING AND ORGANIZATION

(a) Corn, Salt and Coal Porters

THE City Corporation's prescriptive right to metage in the Port of London was confirmed by the charter of 11 Edward III, which, however, outlined it merely in general terms; it received fuller description in seventeenth-century charters as the right of measuring grain, salt, coal, fruit and all other merchandise sold by measure and coming to the Port of London. An unknown applicant in 1597 asked the Crown for a thirty-one years' monopoly of the measurage of all corn, grain, salt and coal transported or sold anywhere within the Realm. A scathing refusal branded the petition as a device for increasing costs all round. In describing measurage of commodities as part of the administration of corporate towns possessing sea or river ports, the refusal made particular reference to the grant to London of these rights which were worth as much as those for the remainder of England. The Crown saw no reason to deprive either London or other municipalities of the revenue.

Of commodities sold by measure, grain was the most important. After establishing a legal port in London, the Crown had enjoined the Constable of the Tower to arrest all ships landing corn at any place other than Queenhithe. This rule was illegal; by purchasing Queenhithe from the Crown in 1246, the City resolved the difficulty and opened the way for establishing or designating other wharves and landing-places. Short ordinances for corn porters are first encountered in the City Letter Books of 1277–78: porters were not allowed either to sell or to measure corn, nor even to touch it, until called by the owner. A much more comprehensive set of regulations emerged from the Inquisition held before the Court of Aldermen in 1300. By that time eight Corn Meters were stationed at Queenhithe, each of them accompanied by three Porters. Meters and Porters each had to have a horse; Porters in addition had to be equipped with five or seven sacks per man, Meters with a bushel, a half-bushel, a quarter, a strike, and a corn-dish. In the exercise of their calling, Meters were not to move beyond the Hanse Merchants' hall in Dowgate nor to work for strangers without permission from the Bailiff of Queenhithe. The joint fee for metage and porterage amounted to $\frac{3}{4}d.-1\frac{1}{4}d.$ per quarter, varying according to the distance of the destination. For over two centuries regulations are silent as regards corn porting. In 1519 six men undertook to carry wheat to the Bridgehouse Wharf granaries at 12d. per score of quarters and were accordingly appointed wheat porters and protected from interference.

The Inquisition of 1300 concerned itself with salt as well as corn. Salt could be sold only on Salt Wharf at Queenhithe; there alone were four Salt Meters stationed, each assisted by one Porter. Meters did not go into action until the Bailiff of Queenhithe had ascertained on oath from the vendor that a sale had been effected; to this transaction one party at least had to be an English merchant, as Salt Meters were not permitted to officiate between aliens. Meters had to have a bushel, to be filled with salt in two hauls, and a strike with which to level the surface of the bushel at the third haul; Porters required eight sacks each for carriage. Fees were fixed in the same manner as for corn, but in each instance $\frac{1}{4}d.$ higher. By the time the Lord Mayor swore eight Salt Meters in 1349, regulations had become far more detailed. Traders now had the choice between paying measuring fees only or an inclusive charge for metage and porterage, levied per sieve which contained 5 quarters and 6 bushels of large or 5 quarters of small salt. Meters were stationed at Billingsgate as well as at Queenhithe. At either place $2\frac{1}{2}d.$ represented the charge for measuring a sieve of large, 2d. for measuring a sieve of small salt. The inclusive fee applied only to the shortest of the distances listed in 1300, which ran as far as Westcheap, Horseshoe Bridge over Walbrook, Wolsiesgate in the Ropery, or St. Anthony's Church in Budge Row; the limits in 1349 were Bread Street and other distant parts of the City. For metage and porterage combined at the latter date merchants paid 8d. per sieve of large, 6d.

per sieve of small salt from Billingsgate and Wool Wharf, 6d. and 4d. respectively from Queenhithe. Comparison of charges from the latter landing-place over half a century suggests that the cost had slightly increased for large, but considerably fallen for small salt.

When a tax of 4d. per chaldron was imposed in 1330 on all coal entering the Port of London, official Coal Meters had to be appointed to ascertain the quantities discharged. Charters as well as prescriptive rights vested the appointment in the City of London, whose right remained unchallenged for two and a half centuries, but towards the end of the sixteenth century the Lord High Admiral contested it, and the conflict ended only in 1594 in the City's favour. At that time the largest item in a Coal Meter's expenses account consisted of sacks, the cost of which he had to defray himself; if Porters assisted him, they did not have to provide sacks of their own.

Porters acting with the City of London's Meters of measurable commodities combined in the Society of Billingsgate Porters, other-wise known as the Society or Fellowship of Corn, Salt and Coal Porters; they were briefly referred to as Fellowship or Billingsgate Porters. Corn, salt and coal did not constitute a comprehensive enumeration, but served as examples of measurable goods which came within the Billingsgate Porters' prerogative at an early date; to them were in due course added vegetables, fruit and fish. The City Corpora-tion believed the Society of Fellowship Porters to belong to the immemorial customs of the City, but no mention of the Fellowship occurs in City records before 1542, when a number of unadmitted persons were removed from it at the request of the duly authorized members. It is unlikely that an organization of Billingsgate Porters had emerged before the 1540s; not until the end of that decade did some-thing in the nature of regulations for their work reach the Court of Aldermen for confirmation. On this occasion the entry referred to 'the labourers and porters at Billingsgate', but it is unlikely that a hierarchic distinction was intended. Another committee of Aldermen considered and confirmed ordinances submitted by the Fellowship Porters in 1554. In 1559 the Billingsgate Porters had three Governors, drawn from their own ranks, and the duty of making rules for the Porters' good behaviour devolved upon the City Chamberlain.[28]

(b) Organization and Membership

Admission to the Fellowship of Billingsgate Porters was gained by nomination on the part of its Rulers and Assistants; no foreigner could fill a vacancy if a freeman applied for it. The Aldermen in 1566 had limited membership to 120 men, but the need for porterage services soon caused that figure to be exceeded. In 1620 the maximum was raised to 400, and less than half a century later a committee informed the Lord Mayor that the growing volume of work justified a further increase to at least 500. Within the next forty years the Fellowship claimed a membership of around 700. Especially the volume of British grain imports grew considerably during the later eighteenth century, augmenting the number of Fellowship Porters concerned with this commodity; in 1773 Porters of corn alone were alleged to consist of 1,300 men and they continued increasing in proportion to the growth in this trade.

On admission members took an oath: in addition to good behaviour and obedience to rules, they promised not to work with anybody who was not a brother member of the Fellowship—an early example of 'closed shop' practice. All Fellowship Porters in 1620 were presumed to be 'poor freemen by casualties decayed in their estates'. They had to furnish sureties for their honesty to the amount of £5 to the City Chamberlain to protect the property of merchants who employed them. In the course of the seventeenth century Porters neglected this duty, so that a committee of Aldermen investigating Fellowship records in 1678 discovered a large number of members who either had never furnished sureties or whose guarantors had died or become insolvent. The committee promptly suspended such Porters and recommended that in future sureties be called over once a year in order that insufficient or invalidated securities could be discovered and replaced. When sureties came up for review again a century later, the bonds furnished were not for £5, as before, but for £40, though the increase had no legal basis nor could anybody recall when it had come about; it had been in operation for over fifty years by 1757. Bonds were now given to the Fellowship Clerk, not to the City Chamberlain, and guaranteed the Fellowship against non-payment of quarterage as well as employers against dishonesty.

To exercise his trade, a member had to be properly equipped by carrying a sack and wearing a tally, a piece of leather with sixty holes and thongs which could be inserted into the holes, each thong so inserted representing a turn carried. The tally designated Fellowship Porters as essential workers and signified their freedom from impressment. The claim to exemption had been successfully asserted by the City before a Privy Council committee of trade in 1672, when war with the Dutch endangered London's coal supply, but at that period only Coal Porters obtained exemption. Towards the end of the eighteenth century several attempts to press Fellowship Porters for the Navy provoked retaliation in the form of indictments for assault and imprisonment against the naval men concerned by the City authorities. Membership was lost through absence from Fellowship labour for a year and a day unless excused by reason of sickness, suit for land or living or other extraordinary occasion, and through exclusion from the Fellowship for breaking the oath or failing to pay fees and fines imposed for disobedience to orders. Another disqualification was introduced in 1791 : no man who rowed himself in his own boat, in other words who was a waterman, could take labour as a Fellowship Porter.[29]

The Fellowship Porters' activities originally centred on Billingsgate. Therefore the choice of an *ex officio* Governor of the Society of Fellowship Porters fell naturally on the Alderman of the Ward of Billingsgate, with his Deputy as Deputy Governor. The Court of Aldermen reserved to itself power to make regulations for the Fellowship; it was to this Court that the Fellowship appealed for help against refractory members; the Court of Aldermen drafted new disciplinary regulations for consideration and enactment by the Common Council. But under its overriding jurisdiction the Alderman or Deputy of Billingsgate confirmed the Society's officers and rules, heard and decided complaints of misdemeanours, imposed fines and suspended members for non-payment. So heavy proved these duties that the Alderman and Deputy had to be relieved of them in 1654, when they were transferred to the Fellowship's Court of Rulers and Assistants, leaving merely a right of appeal to the Governor.

The Society's chief officers consisted originally of six Rulers, appointed by all past Rulers and present Assistants; in 1566 four (in another source three) of the Rulers had to be freemen, in 1620 all of them. Rulers remained in office for two years, so there were three vacancies annually to be filled. Tenure of office was burdensome, causing loss of earnings; refusal to accept election entailed a fine of 13s. 4d. Just like the office of Assistant in the Society of Tacklehouse and Ticket Porters,* that of Ruler in the Fellowship of Billingsgate Porters soon fell into abeyance. While the office was discontinued, the title devolved upon a different group of officers who had formerly been designated Assistants. Of these, the first twenty-four had been appointed by the Court of Aldermen; subsequent vacancies were filled through election by the membership. For this purpose a general meeting of members assembled on the morning of Midsummer Day and was fortified by hearing a sermon preached in the church at St. Mary-at-Hill. At that meeting all orders and enactments concerning the Fellowship were read over publicly to the assembled Porters. Only freemen qualified for the office of Assistant by 1620; the fine for refusing it was 3s. 4d.; once confirmed by the Governor or Deputy, Assistants held office until death or removal. Government vested in the Court of Rulers and Assistants, whose quorum of thirteen was reduced to nine in 1653 because Fellowship Porters were poor men, dependent on earning their living, unable to spare much time for Court meetings which took place at least once a month. When Rulers, as first established, had fallen into abeyance and the Assistants become known as Rulers, the Court came to be called simply the Court of Rulers; the erstwhile Rulers lingered on in the description of 'keymen' or six senior Rulers, serving in this capacity for two years in rotation, three being appointed to it annually. One of them acted as Upper Ruler, though no regulation sanctioned his appointment; he took the chair at Court meetings if neither Governor nor Deputy Governor attended. Some Rulers attempted to absent themselves from Court meetings because they preferred earning money as Porters, but the Court of Rulers laid down in 1797 that the Upper Ruler had no power to condone such absence.

The need for a disciplinary authority had been one of the main reasons for the establishment of the Fellowship. Disobedience to

* See p. 48 above.

Rulers, particularly during the allocation of work, brawling among themselves, going to law against other members without resorting first to the reconciliation methods available within the Fellowship, pilfering goods during the course of their employment, persuading purchasers to buy from one supplier rather than another, and charging in excess of authorized rates: these were Porters' practices which the Aldermen set themselves to stamp out. Punishment for pilfering followed the picturesque tradition of the sixteenth century: for the first offence a miscreant was carried upon a staff from the waterside to the Lord Mayor's gate where his misdeeds were openly proclaimed; a second offence involved expulsion. Fines only punished overcharging or demands for payment in respect of more turns or burdens than a Porter had carried, though the abortive bill of 1708 would have sanctioned up to three months' suspension from work for such offences. One of the chief causes for the frequently repeated injunction against Porters leaving work unfinished consisted of the custom of stopping in the middle of a job to go and drink at some distant public house.

(c) Administration and Funds

It is impossible to judge how well the Court of Rulers performed its disciplinary functions before the later eighteenth century, as its records, with the exception of one account book, perished in a fire in 1779. Though the Clerk transcribed from memory some of the minutes, rules and orders, records thus reconstructed do not reach back beyond 1764. At that stage the Court of Rulers had become a self-seeking body, as concerned with the personal welfare of Rulers as with the Fellowship's well-being. The decisive step occurred in 1767 when the Court recorded the following resolution:

Whereas many inconveniencys have heretofore happened touching and concerning the Nomination Election & Appointment of a New Assistant or Assistants (in the room of one or more dying going off by Fine or otherwise; and in Order to Assist the Upper Ruler and Assistants of the Court for the time being, And also for the better regulation and dispatch of the Business & Labour relating and concerning the Body of Fellowship Porters of Billingsgate London It is this Day unanimously Resolved and Agreed on by us whose Names or Marks are hereunder Wrote or Set, that from henceforth the present Rulers and Assistants do and shall during their Natural Lives, remain and be Rulers and Assistants, And in Case of the Death or Removal of any one or more of the said Rulers and Assistants, that then and in such case it is Agreed & Ordered that a General Court shall be summoned,

which would nominate a new Ruler for election. If the Clerk really remembered a resolution of this length twelve years after it had been recorded, his memory must have been phenomenal. Far more probably he reproduced in his own words the substance of the resolution which signified that the Court had become a select vestry enjoying life-tenure and nominating its own recruits; it had freed itself from democratic control. Self-discipline may have governed its decision that all courts be held at Fellowship Hall, not at a public house or tavern, but much thought was devoted to culinary details attending meetings, such as the substitution of cold roast beef for bread, butter and cheese until in 1782 the dinner on court days was replaced by a payment of 5s. to each Ruler. While dispensing with food, the Court continued to regale itself with wine, though it limited that drink in 1788 to one bottle, supplementing it by a bottle of brandy and (apparently unlimited) quantities of the beverage appropriately named porter. A feast held every Christmas was discontinued in 1789. As well as public meetings the Court held private ones, but no records of the latter survive, even if any were kept.[30]

Of other Fellowship officers, a Collector or Pennyman is first mentioned in the records for 1653, though the position had been created earlier. A Common Council committee reorganizing the Fellowship confirmed him in office, subject to annual appointment, and made him into a seventh Ruler for the purpose of collecting quarterage, assigning Porters to work, and managing the Fellowship's funds. He acted as the Fellowship's executive officer, accounted to the other Rulers for his financial transactions, and received a salary of 20d. a day. Though the rules provided for annual tenure, Henry Green-hill remained Pennyman throughout the period 1778-1782; he probably secured re-election once a year. He was eventually discovered, jointly with two of the Rulers, to have received 'enormous gratuities' from men who by their agency had been admitted to membership. The Court of Rulers had the grace to disapprove such practices and ordered the repayment of the gratuities, threatening to remove from office any further Rulers guilty of dishonesty. Six months later, owing to insufficient restitution on the part of Greenhill and one of the Rulers, both were expelled from the Fellowship. The Court of Rulers laid down in 1795 that, whenever the office of Pennyman fell vacant, the Upper Ruler should have the first refusal, provided a majority of Rulers considered him eligible; other Rulers should be invited in descending order of seniority to accept the position if the Upper Ruler did not.

A vacancy in the office of the Fellowship's Beadle was mentioned in 1782, the Upper Ruler eagerly vacating his high office in order to accept appointment to this humble function at the hands of his fellow Rulers. Four years later the Beadle's office again required filling; though the Upper Ruler on that occasion declined appointment, the Ruler next in seniority promptly accepted it. As Clerk, the Fellowship employed a lawyer acting in a part-time capacity; after election by the Rulers he was presented to the Alderman of Billingsgate for confirmation like other Fellowship officers. From an unknown figure the Court of Rulers in 1797 increased his salary to £20 p.a., but, like most lawyers under contract of employment, the Clerk in addition received his professional fees.

Fellowship members fell into two classes, designated Corn Porters on the one hand, Salt Porters or Quartermen on the other. Class signified seniority, not commodities handled; Corn Porters were the senior men and as such enjoyed privileges, including prior choice of jobs, of which corn work often proved the most lucrative; this accounts for their description as Corn Porters. They alone qualified to become Rulers. At each annual general meeting the six senior Quartermen were promoted Corn Porters. Priority of Corn Porters' choice of work weighed so heavily on the Quartermen that they petitioned the Court of Aldermen against it in 1698, complaining that Corn Porters had usurped work not only on heavy corn, but also on malt, which Quartermen regarded more particularly as their preserve; but the principle of Corn Porters' priority remained intact.

Fellowship Porters had their own meeting-place, which formed part of the *Blue Anchor* public house at 17, St. Mary-at-Hill, in the Ward of

Billingsgate. It burnt down in 1779. Of the hall then built by the Fellowship, independent of the public house, no trace remains today.

Fellowship revenues derived from a number of sources: admission and transfer fees, quarterage and fines. Admission was fixed in 1566 at 2s. 6d. for freemen and 5s. for foreigners, but of the former amount 6d., of the latter 1s., went to the City Chamberlain. A new member paid the Clerk 8d. for registering his sureties. Quarterage amounted to 8d. p.a., defrayed in quarterly instalments. Fees were substantially increased in the seventeenth century: by 1653 members paid 8s. 2d. entrance fee and 5s. 8d. quarterage, the latter composed of a weekly penny plus 4d. a quarter. Promotion to Corn Porters cost Quartermen a transfer fee of 4s. 2d. Members considered the level of fees excessive; in deference to their wishes, the Common Council after an investigation of Fellowship finances lowered the admission fee to 5s., the transfer fee to 2s. 6d., and the quarterage to 4s., abolishing the weekly penny. Fees underwent no further change for over a century, but members of the Court in 1767 exempted themselves from paying quarterage. In the later eighteenth century, when Fellowship members found employment good and profitable, the admission fee was twice increased, in 1778 by 1s. in favour of general funds, in 1785 by 2s. 6d. payable to the Upper Ruler. The propriety of the latter charge was open to grave doubt; eight years later the Court of Rulers sought to disarm criticism by allowing it to the Upper Ruler and Upper Ruler elect, but discontinuing it subsequently.

Under the 1566 regulations, retiring Rulers had had to submit, within a week of the general meeting, annual accounts to be audited by six Assistants and subsequently passed by the Governor or Deputy. When the Rulers of 1566 merged into the Assistants, this procedure fell into disuse; Porters complained in 1653 that no annual accounting took place. A committee investigating the financial position in that year found some extravagance; thereupon the Common Council limited the expenses of the Court of Rulers to 10s. per monthly meeting. The loss of the Fellowship's records prevents knowledge of the extent of its capital before 1779; in that year it held property insured at £200 as well as £800 in 3 per cent reduced Bank Annuities. By 1791 the securities in its portfolio had increased to a nominal value of

£1,500; the Fellowship's prosperity prior to the outbreak of the French wars is corroborated by its gross annual receipts on current account which between 1779 and 1791 increased from less than £300 to £730.

Porters by virtue of their work ran unusual risks in two respects: that of injury if they put a foot wrong or if the load slipped, and that of premature ageing because of the heavy physical strain involved. Poor public provision for incapacity made it desirable for the Fellowship to insure members against inability to work. Regulations endorsed by the Aldermen in 1566 had awarded 4d. a week to any member of three years' standing during incapacity from whatever cause; every working member had contributed to the insurance fund the weekly penny subsequently abolished.* How many pensioners were relieved, and to what extent, cannot be ascertained for the period before 1779; in the thirteen years following, for which accounts have survived, annual expenditure on relief varied from less than £34 in 1778–79 to over £109 in 1786–87. Superannuated members on the pension list at this period received £2 p.a., but retired Upper Rulers obtained another £2 from 1781 onwards, and their pension was doubled again to reach a total of £8 a year in 1785. Some pensioners in addition to money received an outfit of clothing. The Court of Rulers appointed twenty half-pensioners at £1 p.a. in 1788; five years later it substituted a coat and hat for their cash emoluments. On the death of a member or pensioner, provided his quarterage had not been in arrears by more than 4s., his widow or legal representative received a 5s. grant, but in 1791 pensioners' widows were declared ineligible for this payment.

(d) Porters and Meters

To enable City Meters to rely on the impartiality of Porters handling goods to be measured, Fellowship Porters had obtained exclusive privileges. Meters under the Common Council Act of 1620 were not to measure commodities unless assisted by Billingsgate Porters. In return for these obligations towards Fellowship Porters, Meters enjoyed powers of discipline and could have Porters suspended from work. Meters themselves, however, merely acted as supervisors, having purchased their places in order to pocket metage fees; the actual

* See p. 91 above.

measurers, known as Deputy Meters, were their employees. Only a member of the Fellowship of Porters could qualify for the function of Deputy Meter and thus climb a higher rung on the ladder. Corn Meters appointed in the fourteenth century had gone out of existence some time subsequently; when the Companies of Bakers and Brewers in 1570 complained of false measure employed in corn transactions, the Lord Mayor swore six* of the most senior and honest Corn Porters as Corn Meters. Corn imports into the Port of London continued to grow; the six Meters could not deal with them fast enough and obtained authority in 1596 to appoint assistants to help with the measuring, provided they assumed responsibility for their assistants' work and did not raise their fees. What had been inaugurated as a temporary relief measure grew into a permanent increase in Corn Meters, of whom there were ten by 1609, each with a Deputy. Abuses in the admeasurement of corn came to light in 1620: only two of the ten Corn Meters attended each week to supervise work, nor could Deputies always be found when required. Up to this time no Corn Meter had had more than one Deputy; this limitation was now removed. Each Corn Meter could appoint as many Deputies as he was prepared to supervise, provided he chose them from the ranks of Billingsgate Porters. Similarly, Sea Coal Meters, whenever in need of Deputies, asked the Fellowship Rulers for a list of applicants from which they made their choice. While becoming Deputy Meters, such men remained Billingsgate Porters; in 1714 the Fellowship's Deputy Governor suspended several Deputy Sea Coal Meters from duty, and when his action was queried, the Court of Aldermen confirmed it as *intra vires* the Fellowship Governor.†

The Act of 1620 protected Billingsgate Porters' privileges against other waterside workers, among whom bargemen, hoymen, and watermen received explicit mention; nothing but danger of loss or damage to commodities through foul weather, leakage or other urgent necessity could justify the employment of unauthorized workers. Such regulations were easier to pass than to enforce. Foreign porters labouring

---

* The text says sixteen. In view of what follows, this is likely to be an error on the part of the Repertory clerk.

† See p. 114 below.

in St. Katherine's, Shadwell, and other eastern suburbs had already in 1617 petitioned the Court of King's Bench for the right to work and form a fraternity. Though their petition failed, they continued in existence and crossed the Fellowship Porters' path again in 1682 before sinking into obscurity. A simple solution was found, after intervention by the Lord Privy Seal, to a collision with porters admitted by the Lieutenant of the Tower to work within the Tower Hamlets; the six men involved were absorbed in a body into the Fellowship of Porters in 1638. In the western part of their area, Billingsgate Porters collided in 1625 with the porters of the liberty of Westminster who unloaded commodities at Westminster Bridge (the name given in the seventeenth century to the landing pier at Westminster). Conflict flared up again in 1668 when a Fellowship Ruler was stationed at Westminster to ensure that members suffered no deprivation of rights.[31]

In the normal course of business, Meters or their Deputies knew of impending jobs before Porters did. The Common Council Act of 1620 therefore made it the duty of Meters to notify the nature and quantity of work involved to the Fellowship Rulers of whom two did duty during business hours, one at Billingsgate, another at Porters' Quay. The working day lasted from 4 a.m. to 8 p.m. in summer and from 6 a.m. to 6 p.m. in winter. Only danger to vessels and their cargoes or the arrival of fresh fish in Lent justified working on Sundays or exceeding normal working hours. Upon Rulers on duty fell the obligation to procure Porters in sufficient numbers to handle jobs, Meters and Deputy Meters being explicitly barred from finding Porters themselves. If Rulers did not supply Porters within two hours of a request reaching them, the applicant was free to employ any porters or labourers he could secure. Porters called upon by Rulers for a job had to accept it unless already engaged on other work; refusals led to fines for the first two offences, to dismissal for the third. Rulers had discretion how to man jobs, subject to two overriding considerations: they were to be impartial as between persons and to show favour to old, weak and infirm Fellowship members by allocating to them the less burdensome and strenuous work. Such discretion in favour of older weaker Porters became less necessary with the elaboration of rules which on the one hand entitled senior Porters to the first choice of jobs and on the other regulated in detail the handling of particular commodities.

All Porters in a team took regular turns in rotation. Once he had embarked upon a job, especially if it took him into the hold of a vessel, a Porter was not permitted to leave it unfinished without a Ruler's authority. No Porter was to carry two loads simultaneously while a fellow member stood by without work—a rule which received attention chiefly at times of poor employment. Rotation did not prevail in house or market labour, a type of work rarely undertaken by Billingsgate Porters, in which every man did as much of the job as chance allocated to him. The first and the last man in any team had particular functions: the first man at the end of the work had to help heave the last man away; the last man acted as paymaster, collecting porterage charges from the employer in bulk and distributing them among members of the team, until in the second half of the eighteenth century better arrangements for payment were made. Two regulations of 1797 served to facilitate such payment: Porters were not to change turns among themselves because it confused the counting, and the bills submitted in evidence of work performed had to show the Porter's name and the turns he had carried. Special regulations applied to the heaviest work of all, called backing work, the labour of carrying on men's backs commodities in sacks: such merchandise could be piled two or three sacks high, and the senior Corn Porter or the majority of Corn Porters present decided how many men should be employed on the job.

(e) Gangs

As in the case of Ticket Porters,* temporary association in teams in many instances gave way to permanent association in gangs. The City authorities regarded this development as undesirable; 'to refractorily associate themselves in gangs' was prohibited in 1668, when the Lord Mayor looked to the Rulers so to allocate the work as to avoid gang formation. Opposition to gangs proved as ineffective in the Fellowship as it had been in the Ticket Porters' instance. By the late seventeenth and early eighteenth centuries gangs of Billingsgate Porters operated at

* See pp. 62–65 above.

most of the legal quays, certainly at Fresh and Botolph's Wharves, Smart's, Dice, Wiggins', Wool or Chester, Porters' and Bear Quays. They competed for work beyond their action stations; the rivalry of gangs at the adjoining Bear and Porters' Quays led to legal proceedings which shed light on the organization of Fellowship Porters' gangs in the period. The Court of Chancery defined these gangs as partnerships at will. The Bear Quay Gang was alleged in 1718 to have operated from times immemorial, though the earliest admission could be traced only to 1694. It consisted of a dozen members, who took weekly turns at acting as 'housekeeper', the gangmaster who detailed members to their work. All members were obliged to turn out for work every day unless ill, unfit or excused by the housekeeper; unexcused absentees at the gang's choice forfeited 3s. a day or their share of the gang's earnings during their absence. The gang had a tacklehouse stocked with beams and other tackle; of this capital a new member had to purchase a share on admission. The Bear Quay Gang charged £55 in 1694, but £75 in 1715, and visualized raising its admission fee to £80. If dismissed from the gang for misdemeanour, a member received a mere £20 (later £30) for his share of the tackle; if he retired because of age and infirmity or in pursuance of a mutual agreement, his total proportion of tackle and other assets would be carefully ascertained and either paid out in the form of a lump sum or converted into a life annuity to ease his retirement.

The Court of Fellowship Rulers acquiesced in the situation by concluding in 1781 that, if it could not suppress gangs, it ought at least to control them. It took the gangs in hand by ruling that neither admissions to, nor resignations from, gangs be permitted without its approval—a regulation inappropriate to resignations. A Fruit or Chest Gang was first mentioned in 1778; though it had a gang house by 1781, its master, the gang's permanent housekeeper, had never been admitted to the gang by the Court of Rulers. The Court therefore placed an embargo on enlistment of further gangsmen until the gangmaster had himself complied with its regulations. From 1788 onwards Porters paid fines to the Fellowship for admission to gangs (ranging from 10s. 6d. to £1 2s.; admission to a coal or chest gang cost at least £1 1s.) and for resignation (1s.). The Rulers also organized the working of gangs; in 1789 they barred members of the Chest Gang from taking any other labour and consolidated the Puddledock and Whitefriars Gangs. Meters and other gangsmen were forbidden in 1801 to join the Greenwich (coal) Gang or break into its work. Thus by the beginning of the nineteenth century the Court of Rulers had come to look upon the regulation of gang work as one of its legitimate functions.[32]

6

FELLOWSHIP PORTERS: TYPES OF WORK

(a) Corn Work

DOWN to the eighteenth century, the most substantial sector of the Fellowship Porters' work covered the corn trade; by far the largest number of infringements of their prerogatives occurred in this field, excused mostly by complaints about their excessive rates. Corn regulations were unambiguous: whenever corn was moved from the waterside to any storage place on land, from a storage place on land to the waterside, or from one vessel to another, Billingsgate Porters alone were entitled to handle it; the same applied to the movement of corn from one storage place to another whenever it had changed hands. Certain exceptions to these general rules protected established interests: a freeman baker could employ his own or the miller's men to carry corn from his granary to the mill; a country carrier could send either a Fellowship or a Ticket Porter to fetch provisions to the inn where the carrier picked them up; foreign Porters of ten years' standing at Billingsgate were suffered to remain at work.

However much brewers and bakers had appreciated the establishment of impartial and reliable corn metage, they did not relish the corollary of Fellowship Porters' exclusive privileges; admonitions reminding them of their obligation not to employ unauthorized labour never ceased after 1573, and suppliers of the brewers' chief raw material, malt, joined them in attempts at evading the Billingsgate Porters' monopoly. Between the middle 1620s and 1707, dealers in various grains passed through the Court of Aldermen in monotonous succession at the rate of one every three years, offered some lame excuse for employing unauthorized porterage labour, and were made to pay the Fellowship Porters as though these had performed the work. Individual Porters found legal action for recovery of such charges troublesome and difficult because courts did not allow them to be witnesses in their own cases; the Fellowship therefore obtained permission to bring suits in the City Chamberlain's name. If a bold spirit resisted the summons to the Lord Mayor's Court by removing the case to the King's Bench, the City Solicitor pursued him thither.

When a grain vessel reached the Port of London, its master had to inform the Cocquet Office of the quantity and consignees of his cargo and supply a sample. These formalities completed, the Clerk of the Cocquet issued a permit to the master for the City Corn Meters to measure the merchandise. The master handed this permit to the clerk in the Corn Meters' office who notified a Deputy Meter; he in turn called for a team of Billingsgate Porters. A grain importer therefore had to deal with three parties, the Clerk of the Cocquet, the Meters and the Fellowship Porters, all entitled to fees for their services, all ready to inform one another of the arrival of consignments liable to such dues; a corn dealer wishing to avoid one usually attempted to elude all three, and when detected by the collector of one was subsequently mulcted of all three.

Many successful prosecutions notwithstanding, Fellowship Porters by 1707 had come to the conclusion that their Common Council Act had not been drafted with sufficient care to prevent many employers of unlicensed labour from slipping through its meshes. They petitioned for a new Act which would have increased penalties to £5 for the employer as well as the unauthorized interloper and to £10 for a Meter working unaccompanied by Billingsgate Porters. A bill was drafted and discussed in Common Council at great length from the middle of 1707 to the end of 1709. It had six readings in all; committees examined it after the second, third and fourth reading; full debates took place on a number of occasions. But in the end the bill was rejected.

The rejection strengthened the hands of those trying to dispense with the Fellowship Porters' services. A combination of wharfingers, bargemasters and corn dealers attempted systematically to elude the various City duties. At these opponents the Fellowship of Porters, by virtue of its right to sue in the City Chamberlain's name, struck a decisive blow by the action of *Fazakerly (City Chamberlain) v. Wiltshire*. In its nature the case did not differ from many that had gone before, nor was the matter in dispute particularly large: 300 quarters of malt had been carried from one barge into another by unauthorized labour, and the Fellowship demanded a penalty of £1. When sued in 1714, the owner of the malt removed the case by *Habeas Corpus* from the Lord Mayor's to the King's Bench Court—a move which had on many previous occasions deterred plaintiffs from continuing their actions. This time they sought instead by a *procedendo* to transfer the cause back to the Lord Mayor's Court. Owing to the intricacy of the issues involved, the Court of King's Bench did not surrender jurisdiction, but held hearings in 1716, 1717, and 1721, at the end of which all four judges pronounced in favour of the Billingsgate Porters. Spasmodic infringements continued: in 1733 the Lord Mayor was presented with a list of ten cargoes, adding up to 820 quarters of barley, 180 quarters of oats, and 90 quarters of malt, which had paid neither metage nor porterage dues; on most of them the City had also lost the cocquet duty. Similar practices were alleged in the 1740s. But the main battle regarding corn porterage was delayed by half a century or more in consequence of the Fellowship Porters' victory in *Fazakerly v. Wiltshire*.[33]

All Porters wanting corn work attended the Corn Office in Harp Lane. The Ruler on duty there allocated jobs in accordance with seniority; Corn Meters on their way to work called there for teams of Porters. Meters and Fellowship Porters were under an obligation to go anywhere within the Port of London at their own expense, however small the job. While senior men could refuse less remunerative labour, juniors were bound to accept it. At times of pressure, however, it became difficult for Rulers to man unpopular jobs; Fellowship Porters doing overboard work on malt had to be paid in excess of authorized rates in 1668 in order to induce them to do the work at all. A team made up at the office was deemed to have 'passed the bounds' when it had left Harp Lane or Cross Lane; while it remained in bounds, members were liable to displacement by their seniors who, after calling at the Corn Office, had caught up with the team. A team for a corn job consisted of seven men if working on board a vessel, or five in a granary. Larger numbers were permitted if the work consisted of backing labour or if a Ruler so directed; in 1801 an amendment to the rules allowed a Corn Porter to make the eighth man on a ship or the sixth in a granary. Whoever joined a team already complete 'cut into' the job —an offence punished by the Court of Rulers. When the team reached the place of work, the first Corn Porter to have joined it took the first turn. The Meter measured by means of the City bushel; as soon as he had finished, in the case of imports he proceeded to Custom House to certify the quantity measured so that corn duty could be levied. Porters wishing for further corn work on that day had to report back to the Corn Office.

A corn merchant's complaint in 1612 revealed that John Evans who had the title of 'Porter of the Bridgehouse', but in fact acted as clerk of works to that establishment, received from all vessels discharging corn within his domain one heaped peck for every lighter, one and a half for a hoy, and three for every larger vessel; in return he furnished food and drink to the Fellowship Porters employed with the Corn Meters. This arrangement raised at least suspicion as to the impartiality of the Porters; John Evans was restrained from continuing it. Porters purloining corn from the Bridgehouse granary were brought to the Court of Aldermen's notice in 1625. No great advantage accrues to pilferers of grain unless they operate on a sufficient scale to make the booty saleable. According to Colquhoun, Porters and other labourers in corn vessels in his day found no difficulty in amassing such loot, partly by direct plunder, partly in the guise of sweepings or old samples; he quotes instances of Porters of corn developing into substantial dealers in that commodity by purchasing their associates' ill-gotten gains.

Detailed rates for porterage labour were fixed by the Aldermen in 1566. The Common Council Act of 1620 re-enacted most of them, while slightly changing and elaborating the classification of corn. Heavy grain which included wheat, rye, peas, beans and barley, and later also cole, flax, and hemp seed, paid higher rates than light grains, consisting of malt, oats and beer corn. Four operations entailed different charges: a landing rate applied to the transfer of corn from vessels to shore or vice versa, a lower rate if grain was moved merely from vessel to vessel; charges for land carriage of corn depended on distance. Holdage of $\frac{1}{2}d$. a quarter had to be paid for corn which the Porters heaved out of a vessel's hold; Kentish and Essex hoys remained exempt from this charge. Pulling attributes the privilege of the men of Kent and Essex to gratitude for their supplying London with grain during the plague at considerable risk to their lives—a pleasant story, were it not that they enjoyed the exemption already in 1620, though it had not figured in the tariff of 1566. Rates of porterage for grain carried beyond standard distances became a matter for individual bargaining; in the absence of agreement the Alderman or Deputy of Billingsgate had the last word.

Corn porterage rates as laid down endured for a quarter of a century, but in the 1670s the Porters became dissatisfied with them, nor did corn merchants display great reluctance to see them raised. Landing rates for heavy and light grains were accordingly doubled in 1678, other rates remaining unaltered; to obviate difficulties of collection which arose from the rule that half the porterage rates were due from the seller and half from the purchaser of the merchandise, payment for transferring grain from one vessel to another became exclusively the seller's responsibility. At prevailing rates, Porters were entitled to 3d. per quarter for landing or loading malt. This trade, however, increased so much that Porters agreed with merchants and factors to work for less.

Disputes about remuneration below the official rate led to a distinction between 'up labour' and 'down labour', the former consisting of unloading malt and carrying it into granaries or lofts, the latter implying the reverse process. The basic fee for both labours was the same: $1\frac{1}{2}d$. per quarter for malt moved in sacks, 2d. if it was loose. 'Up labour' was, however, subject to several additions: firstly the $\frac{1}{2}d$. holdage charge; secondly, if a vessel did not lie at a quay or wharf, $\frac{1}{2}d$. a quarter for every ship across which the malt had to be carried; lastly, each pair of stairs up which the malt had to be transported added yet another $\frac{1}{2}d$. a quarter to porterage fees. Fellowship Porters successfully claimed the work, at a fee of 2d. a quarter, of shooting corn direct over the side of a barge into a lighter, though the bargemen would have been prepared to effect this transfer as part of their general duties without additional payment. It became increasingly the custom in the later eighteenth century not only to measure corn, but also to weigh it. This constituted a grievance to Billingsgate Porters, because transfer to and

from scales and weighbridges required a good deal of porting labour
for which no special remuneration was paid. Fellowship Porters were
not averse to bargaining about porterage rates with merchants who
provided them with large-scale employment, and special rates were
repeatedly sanctioned by the Court of Rulers.[34]

To leave it to whoever happened to be the last man in any Porters'
team to find the merchant responsible for payment, collect the money
from him and pay out all the members, may have served at a time
when a few well-known traders imported small quantities of corn. The
volume of eighteenth century business required more efficient methods
and led to the 'shift', an arrangement subsequently believed to date
back to times immemorial, but in fact begun in the early eighteenth
century. The 'Shifter' was a paymaster who in due course sought out
the merchants for whom Porters had worked and collected the porterage charges, but maintained an office where Porters could present their
own bills immediately on completion of work and receive prompt
payment. As Porters finished work at any time between 10 a.m. and
8 p.m., the office had to be open all day. It was the Shifter's function
to advance to the Porters their wages in cash—a task not rendered any
easier by the inefficiency of the Mint in the later eighteenth century,
which kept copper and silver coin in chronically short supply. Shifters
held their positions on lease from the Fellowship, deriving their revenue
from a deduction from each Porter's bill they paid, amounting to
$8\frac{1}{2}$ per cent of the turnover, that is 1d. in every shilling.

Of the three Corn Shifters, the senior and by far the most important
was the Shifter below Bridge who dealt with all corn discharged east of
London Bridge. The records do not reveal who first occupied the post;
a man not mentioned by name took it over in 1730, but failed within a
few years. He was succeeded by Thomas Brooks who held at a rent of
£40 a year, first for twenty-one years and later for further terms. At
his death two of his clerks carried on. The Fellowship put the lease out
to tender when it expired in 1785; Smiton, the then Shifter, and others
made offers, the best of which came from William Shone and Thomas
Ruston. These two accordingly obtained a twenty-one years' lease for
a down payment of £350 and an annual rent of £100, the enhanced
sums clearly reflecting the increase in trade. William Ruston, Thomas's

son, became principal manager of their office and took over Shone's share in 1799 or 1800. In due course, William Ruston was succeeded by a son who bore the same name. Until 1781 the shift office had been in St. Catherine's, but in that year the pool shift, that is the shift for ship's work, transferred to the Corn Office in Harp Lane, a more convenient location for Porters resorting there for corn work, whereas the granary shift remained at St. Catherine's. Shifters paid out at their offices or through public houses, the publicans welcoming the opportunity of acting as their agents in the expectation of seeing some of the money spent in the house. The Shifter above Bridge who dealt with corn porterage west of London Bridge handled a much smaller volume of business. He was often referred to as the Shifter at Queenhithe because he had his office at Brooke's Wharf. Nothing is known about him before the lease to a Mr. Bishop was renewed for one year in 1784 at the modest rental of £15. For a short period, a third Shifter existed for corn measured by the King's Meter into government stores, but he faded out quickly and was never again mentioned in the records.

(b) Salt and Coal Work

Salt and coal occupied fewer Billingsgate Porters than corn. The general monopoly of Fellowship Porters in respect of both commodities had been established in the early seventeenth century, exceptions being again made for foreign porters of ten years' standing and for an emergency. The only man summoned before the Court of Aldermen before 1800 on a charge of trying to cheat the Billingsgate Porters over salt dealt in wheat as well; when brought to book in 1631, he incurred higher charges in respect of wheat than of salt. Salt was exceedingly unpleasant to carry; not many competitors begrudged the Fellowship Porters the work. Monopoly was a temptation to slackness, of which their employers complained in 1641–42; a committee of Aldermen stationed a Ruler at Roomelands, a place at Billingsgate, from 6 to 8 a.m. and from 5 to 7 p.m. in summer, from 7 to 9 a.m. and from 4 to 6 p.m. in winter, with responsibility for the proper discharge of salt cargoes. For a working man who, apart from being a Ruler, had his living to earn and lost jobs by being on duty during the crucial hours of the morning, this constituted too heavy a burden; accordingly in 1653 it was added to the duties of the Pennyman who as the Fellow-ship's salaried employee had no need to go out on labouring jobs. Salt work required little regulation before the end of the eighteenth cen-tury. It ceased to be team work in 1793 and became gang work instead, being permanently allocated to men registered at the Salt Office in Love Lane, the *King's Head* public house, where Salt Meters applied for their gangs. Salt gangs varied in size: ten men each formed the gangs at Billingsgate, Cox's and Dice Quays, twelve at Griffin's and Yoxall's Wharf, thirty-one at the King's warehouse at Deptford. While the Meter remained at work, no member of a gang was allowed to leave an unfinished job without a Ruler's permission. A Mrs. Gregory acted as Salt Shifter at the Salt Office, deducting 1d. in every shilling for work attended by a Meter, $\frac{1}{2}d.$ if the work required no Meter.

Porterage rates for salt initially followed the same plan as for corn: a landing charge, the equivalent of the rate for the reverse operation, a charge for moving salt from vessel to vessel and another for merely shifting salt out of the hold; carriage of goods in excess of usual dis-tances to be subject to agreement. In order to avoid the vessel-to-vessel charge, salt traders moved ships so close that their sides touched, when the crew could heave the salt from boat to boat without carrying it. The Billingsgate Porters declared this practice illicit and demanded their rates, but a committee of Aldermen found against them in 1625. The Porters however had friends at court; the committee's report was suppressed and not even entered into the Court of Aldermen's Reper-tories; had not the salt traders preserved a copy of the decision favour-able to them, it would have disappeared without trace.

As it was, an increase in salt porterage rates in 1642, adding on an average 50 per cent to the 1620 rates, furnished the Aldermen with an opportunity to sit gracefully on the fence by neither depriving salt porters of work nor antagonizing salt traders: Porters obtained the full rate, now amounting to 10d. a weigh, for transferring salt from vessel to vessel if there was the length of a plank between them; for mere overboard heaving in contiguous boats, the Porters' right to work was recognized, but at only 2d. a weigh. They received retrospective compensation at this rate for salt which had in the recent past been so heaved by ships' crews. Eleven years later, 'in respect of the hardnes of

the times and for the better livelyhood of the said porters, and to in-
courage them with the more Cheerefulnesse to pay Quarteridge and
other dutyes for the supportacõn of the Government of their said
ffellowship', the Common Council, in agreement with a number of
salt traders, doubled that rate in response to considerable dissatisfaction
on the part of the porters of salt, a number of whom refused to work at
the rates fixed and had to be threatened with dismissal from the Fellowship. Their attitude was due to the rising cost of living, which reached
its zenith around the 1650s; nothing more is heard of higher rates for
well over a century, while general costs moved in the opposite direction. In 1776 and 1777, certain salt porterage rates were raised by the
Court of Fellowship Rulers—an act which was doubtless *ultra vires*, as
the Court of Rulers had no authority to exceed official rates, but in
practice sprang from an agreement reached with the salt merchants
affected.[35]

From the outset, Billingsgate Porters concerned with coal suffered
from competition. Richard Stukeley of Ratcliffe had a long dispute
with them in 1619, in which he accused them of being unpunctual and
unreliable; too few Porters presented themselves to unload his coal,
nor would they work in lighters, but only in ships, and they charged
arbitrary fees. Though the Porters promised to mend their ways,
Stukeley refused to abide by the settlement drawn up by the Court of
Aldermen and had to be committed to Newgate. At the Restoration
Grenadier Guards were granted the right of acting as coal heavers in
their spare time to supplement their pay. The award undoubtedly
conflicted with the Billingsgate Porters' privileges, but went unchallenged.

The City moved into action five years later on receiving complaints
about the practices of the Company of Woodmongers to which all
London coal merchants then belonged. Colliers from the Northumber-
land–Durham coalfield sailing down the east coast had originally
discharged at various quays and wharves, of which only some were
owned by woodmongers; if coal was unloaded at some general quay,
large consumers or at least retailers could purchase direct from the
vessel. Coal merchants now forced colliers to confine discharges to
their own wharves, where they pre-empted the coal, using City Meters

to ensure good measure. They appreciated this service in their capacity as purchasers, but not as sellers. Woodmongers sold coal in their own Company's chaldron sacks which were three to four bushels short of a genuine chaldron; hence a load of twenty chaldrons fetched the price of twenty-three or twenty-four. Woodmongers' carts had instructions to give City Coal Meters a wide berth and to bring back their loads unsold rather than to incur the risk of impartial measuring. This abuse necessitated legislation submitting coal retailers to local authority supervision; Common Council Acts of 1680 and 1694 compelled coal merchants to use Sea Coal Meters' approved chaldron sacks and to carry on each coal cart a bushel measure sealed by the City authorities.

Towards the end of the seventeenth century the City of London became insolvent and explored ways of raising additional revenue. One of these consisted of embodying the coal heavers of London in a fellowship which would pay the City an annuity of £500 for this privilege. While Sea Coal Meters had always been appointed,

> no sufficient Provision or care hath been taken of such who are employed in the discharge and unburtheninge or unloading of Ships or Vessels bringing Coles into the said River within the Liberties of the said City and delivering of the same by a measure commonly called a ffatt to the Buyers thereof But the Labourers concerned therein oftimes exact what price they please for the said Labour and at other times the Importers or Buyers of Coles have grievously vexed and oppressed the said Labourers in their Wages and obteining thereof,

a denunciation alike of Fellowship Porters and their employers, if it be true that neither observed the rates fixed for the work by the City authorities. Yet the Aldermen had a guilty conscience. When after deliberations lasting from November 1695 to July 1696 they eventually set up a fellowship of coal labourers with an office near Billingsgate to supply heaving labour at 16d. per chaldron for unloading, the grant to last for a mere three years in the first place, they provided that 'no Porter nor ffreeman of London nor Seaman belonging to such Shippe be excluded the said Worke who are capeable of performing the same as the occasion of the Coletrade shall require'. Rulers of the new fellowship were to be freemen of the City, an obligation not extended to members. The London coal heavers did not appreciate an honour

which, apart from administrative costs, threatened to siphon £500 a
year of their earnings into the City chamber; they appealed to the
Privy Council against it. No more did the masters of colliers approve
of a plan bound to increase their unloading costs. A strike of coal
heavers caused the organization to remain in suspense till the Privy
Council had ruled that the City could not incorporate men who did
not possess the freedom of London; so the fellowship of coal labourers
never came into existence.

However unwilling to become tributaries to City funds, coal
heavers had for long desired corporate organization. They had petitioned the Crown in 1681 for incorporation and an office to regularize
their employment. The petition was renewed in 1703 when events had
shown the Crown alone to possess powers of incorporating the coal
heavers. This time the City authorities opposed the move; if coal
heavers did not want incorporation on the City's terms, they were not
to be incorporated at all. Coal merchants formed their own society in
1731 and delivered a strong attack upon those Billingsgate Porters who
still worked in the coal trade. According to the society, woodmongers
had always employed their own men to unload coal until the Fellowship Porters had recently interfered and asserted their monopoly. That
the Act of 1620 had given Billingsgate Porters exclusive rights to carry
coal from colliers to shore dumps or houses, coal traders admitted, but
evaded the provision by discharging direct into carts; they further
accused Fellowship Porters of inability and negligence. The Common
Council brooded over this complaint from the middle of 1733 till late
in 1734 when it adjourned consideration *sine die*. Billingsgate Porters
still upon occasion cited a coal merchant before the Court of Aldermen
for denying them employment, but a majority of them appear to have
deserted this branch of Fellowship work.

By the time coal heavers sought the aid of the House of Commons
in 1758, Billingsgate Porters were not even mentioned. Contracts for
clearing coal vessels, originally concluded direct between masters of
colliers and coal heavers, had fallen into the hands of middlemen called
coal undertakers who had formed a society and opened an office
supplying gangs of coal heavers to ship masters. Heavers used a particular type of shovel. By prevailing upon the only two makers of such

shovels to sell their whole output to the Society of Coal Undertakers, the latter established ascendancy over the heavers, who could neither purchase new shovels nor have old ones mended but had to hire them from coal undertakers at 1s. a job. According to the length of life of a shovel, such rent amounted to a deduction of £1 or more per shipload, as compared to the shovel's market value of 3s. 6d. Undertakers did not relish the prospect of parliamentary enquiry; one of them for threatening a witness had to attend at the bar of the House on his bended knees. In due course Parliament established an office where all coal heavers could register their names for employment in rotation. Some fifty gangs took advantage of the arrangement. Labour could, however, still be engaged outside the office. Intent on retaining their power, undertakers decoyed heavers away from the office by promises of preferential employment to men not registering at the office, above all, employment in winter when work was scarce. They created a new category of workers whom they called basket men and paid at a rate of 2d. per score above the coal office wage. So well did coal undertakers succeed that the coal office had to close down for lack of heavers, whereupon undertakers promptly reverted to the old rate of wages, minus deductions varying from 1½d. to 3d. from the heavers' earnings of between 1s. and 2s. 6d. per score. Most coal undertakers kept public houses and forced heavers to patronize them on each day of employment. Heavers were expected to spend 6d. a day at the undertaker's establishment, a quart of beer not worth a penny costing them 4d.; those who objected to these conditions could not find work.

These abuses provoked another Act of Parliament in 1770, making it a punishable offence for coal undertakers to obtain rewards from coal heavers for procuring them employment or to be concerned in the victualling business; coal heavers' rates were subjected to the Court of Aldermen's supervision; prompt cash had to be paid to heavers' gangs on completion of work. The necessity for parliamentary interference illustrates the risk of abandoning corporate organization: had coal heavers continued to be Billingsgate Porters, the Fellowship could have conducted their collective defence against the coal undertakers' exactions. As it was, the few Fellowship Porters who still worked in the coal trade had to look to Parliament for protection. The need to prevent fraud in coal retail sales led to several Acts of Parliament establishing Land Coal Meters—at Westminster in 1746, between Tower Dock and Limehouse Hole in 1767, between Putney and Rotherhithe in 1786. But none of these Acts provided for Porters to assist the Meters in the manner in which Billingsgate Porters had worked with Sea Coal Meters.

The Coal Exchange in Lower Thames Street was established in 1768. Fellowship Porters must have worked there, for they held an annual feast there on the Thursday after Midsummer Day until their Court of Rulers abolished it in 1795. According to Colquhoun, the Port of London in 1800 employed twenty-five coal undertakers, 430 coal merchants and dealers, 800 coal heavers, 450 coal carters and 450 coal porters, but few of the last-mentioned would have been Fellowship Porters. Colquhoun suspected 600 of the 800 coal heavers of having experience of pilfering, often with the connivance of masters and mates of colliers, because vessels providing opportunities for pilfering obtained labour more easily and therefore achieved a quicker turnround; heavers disposed of pilfered coal at a special market held for this purpose at Execution Dock. The City of London purchased the Coal Exchange in 1803 and turned it into a free public coal market. Meters, heavers and whippers employed there, if unable to do a minimum daily quantum of work, were granted a fall-back wage, but nothing was said about Billingsgate Porters. An Act of 1807 made coal undertakers subject to licence, fixed the remuneration of undertakers, heavers and Meters' men (without demanding any qualification for such men), and explicitly permitted the employment of persons not free of the City in the London coal trade. It was almost the last nail in the coffin of those Fellowship Porters who had made a living out of the porterage of coal.

Distance and quantity alone governed the rates of coal porterage fixed by the Court of Aldermen in 1566. By the time the Common Council revised them in 1620, it drew finer distinctions. A landing rate applied to the carriage of coal over 15 ft. of plank and 18 ft. of shore and did not include the filling of sacks, for which other labour could be employed. Double that rate was paid for unloading coal at the Bridgehouse or at Broken Wharf, but in return for Porters either filling the sacks themselves or providing fillers at their own expense. An extra 1d. a chaldron became due for coal delivery into cellars or houses where Porters stacked it up in the storage space provided; if coal had to be carried upstairs, every pair of stairs added 2d. per chaldron to the charge. Owing to the fact that Billingsgate Porters were increasingly ousted from coal heaving work, disputes about rates rarely involved the Fellowship; when they did, it was usually a question of heaving coal out of lighters direct into carts drawn up at the dockside. For this work some Fellowship Porters in 1699 tried to obtain 8d. a chaldron, instead of the 4d. rate applying to a normal discharge; they justified the extra demand by taking credit for the distance which the coal sub-sequently travelled in the carts, though their own exertions were confined to shovelling it from the lighters into the carts. In view of such practices, it is perhaps not surprising that the coal merchants preferred to employ their own labour.[36]

The value of a Coal Meter's place in the City of London fluctuated over the course of time; a yearly rent of £90 was paid for it in 1594, rising to £200 in 1648 and falling to £80 in 1691. A Sea Coal Meter sold his place to his successor for £4,575 in 1743; twenty years later a similar sale still realized £4,430. Though James I renewed the grant of coal metage to the City of London in 1615, he reserved the right of placing nominees of his own in the lucrative offices of Sea Coal Meter, thus adding two to the existing ten in 1623. When Charles II forty years later appointed another six, he promised not to increase the number of Sea Coal Meters any further, and by the early eighteenth century it had fallen to fifteen, who took turns at attending the Coal Office to supervise the work.

Each of these Master Coal Meters had four Deputies; such sixty Deputies were classified into fifteen First-men, fifteen Second-men, fifteen Third-men, and fifteen Fourth-men. When vacancies occurred in this hierarchy, men from a lower class moved up in strict seniority without having to pay fees or gratuities. Deputies were the actual measurers of coal and had to attend each collier. Of the metage fee of 4d. per chaldron which originally they received on the spot, they retained 1d. (2d. per ton if coal was weighed instead of measured) for themselves, handing the balance over to the Master Coal Meters. Later, ship masters and undertakers paid metage dues to the clerk in the Coal Office, whose job it became to transmit to the Deputies their share. In accordance with seniority, a First-man went out on a job before a Second-man, and so on through the classes; when a senior man returned from a ship, he had a right to go out again before his junior. The Master Coal Meter in personal attendance in any one week could however confer priority upon all his own Deputies in disregard of seniority rules. Below the sixty Deputy Coal Meters in the hierarchy ranked thirty Supernumeraries or men at large, ordinary Fellowship Porters who could expect promotion to the lowest class of Deputy Meters as vacancies occurred, again in accordance with seniority. Supernumeraries obtained employment as measurers only if no Deputy Meter was available or on 'country voyages' out of the Port of London to places as far afield as Gravesend, which a Deputy Meter could refuse. If employed because no Deputy was available, Supernumeraries received the Deputy's full remuneration; if on a country voyage involving extra travelling and sometimes lodging expenses, they obtained not only the measurer's share of the metage, but another 10s., half from the Deputy who had refused the job, the other half from the coal undertaker. If a Deputy was sick or superannuated, his turns were worked for him by a Supernumerary, the fee being divided evenly between the two, and a dead Deputy's widow similarly received half the benefit of two or three or sometimes more ships' work handled by a Supernumerary. Any man working out of turn had to refund his earnings to the colleague whose turn it had been. The number of Deputy Sea Coal Meters and Supernumeraries combined limited to ninety the colliers which could discharge at any one time in the Port of London.

On board a collier a gang of sixteen coal heavers under a foreman shovelled the coal up from the hold by stages. On reaching deck it was filled into vats; the Deputy topped the vat and recorded the total quantity measured for the Coal Office; the coal duty was based on his certificate. A much improved technique of unloading coal came into use in 1786: of a gang reduced to nine men, four stood in the hold and shovelled the coal into baskets which another four whipped up by means of ropes running over a pulley; hence from coal heavers they became coal whippers. Their foreman was the basket man introduced by the coal undertakers,* whose function consisted of turning the full basket over into the vat. Coal heavers or whippers were rarely freemen, leaving Billingsgate Porters mainly to fill the role of Deputy Sea Coal Meters and Supernumeraries.

The conduct of the Coal Office in the early eighteenth century became corrupt. The fault lay partly with the clerk responsible for the office routine, who demanded gratuities from Deputies for permitting their promotion, fraudulently withheld some of the metage money due to Deputies, and allowed himself to be bribed by ship masters objecting to conscientious and meticulous Deputies into sending out of turn a Deputy of laxer standards.

But corruption in the Coal Office did not stop at the clerk. In the late seventeenth century, the share of metage money due to Deputy Coal Meters had become inadequate for their maintenance. Because they acted as Excise Officers in ascertaining coal duties, the government had allowed them additional remuneration which the Treasury paid over to the Master Coal Meters for onward transmission; that sum, proportionate to coal measured, amounted in 1712 to £120 per Deputy Coal Meter. Deputies being unlettered men, the Master Coal Meters had for many years concealed from them that the money was rightfully theirs. When that scheme miscarried, they discharged some of the more importunate Deputies and threatened further dismissals, maintaining their absolute right of hiring, firing, placing and suspending Deputies in the face of objections from the Court of Aldermen; to the most insistent Deputies they denied rights of seniority in work and promotion. Two Deputies were told that their superannuation rights would suffer unless they stopped pressing the Sea-Coal Meters for the money. One superannuated, bed-ridden and mentally deranged Deputy Coal Meter had his hand guided to sign a full discharge to the Master Meters for £120; they gave him 50s. for his pains. Deputy Sea Coal Meters eventually complained to the Court of Aldermen, which in 1714 initiated an enquiry, but found itself baulked by the Master Meters' refusal to co-operate or make their records available for inspection. As they had purchased their places, they remained a law unto themselves; the City held no coercive powers over them. Even in

* See p. 109 above.

I

order to ascertain the facts, the Aldermen had to rely on the testimony of retired Meters and other Coal Office veterans. The only force which the Aldermen could exert lay in their disciplinary power over Deputy Coal Meters who were Fellowship Porters; by suspending any Deputies who chose to obey their Masters rather than the Aldermen, the City eventually succeeded in introducing the necessary reforms.[37]

(c) Fruit, Vegetable and Fish Work

Though fruit and roots as measurable commodities belonged to the Billingsgate Porters' prerogative and were explicitly mentioned in this connection in the abortive Common Council bill of 1708, they did not play a large part until the later eighteenth century, the more so since Porters' privileges were limited by the rights of the Company of Fruiterers and their employees. Though the Fellowship Porters occasionally enforced their monopoly with regard to fruit, employment was not extensive, or else the Fruit Shifter leasing his office for twenty-one years in 1788 would have paid a higher annual rent than £25. Porters were not allowed to start on fruit work without prior notification to a Fruit Meter. Regulations in this branch of trade varied according to the nature of the commodities. Oranges and lemons were not measured at all, but counted by the chests and half-chests in which they were packed; this gave the Orange Gang which carried them the name of Chest Gang. Fellowship Porters delivered such fruit across the decks of ships lying between the fruit vessel and the wharf.

The Common Council had briefly in 1620 lumped together 'oysters, mussels, onions and carrots or any other burthen' when fixing a fee of 1d. a load for discharging such cargoes within the same wharf or quay, without bothering to delimit the volume or weight of the burden; at a time when jobs of this type were of little importance, such regulation was sufficient. Once unloaded, fruit and roots counted as 'catching burdens'* for purposes of further porterage; to them applied a rate classified similarly according to distance, but leaving the size of the burden out of account. This remained the state of remuneration in the fruit trade until 1800, when the Court of Rulers decreed that the price of labour for carrots be regulated in the same way as for

* See pp. 69–70 above.

potatoes—the latter fixed by unofficial agreement between the parties concerned.

Fish, above all shell fish, formed another sideline of the Billingsgate Porters; the measuring rather than the carrying of oysters became sufficiently profitable in the later seventeenth century for them to seek the Lord Mayor's intervention against unauthorized interlopers. Shell fish was measured on board ship. 1*d*. a burden had been the rate fixed in 1566 for carrying any kind of fish from a vessel to a horse or cart at the same wharf or quay. Some senior Porters exceeded it; as a punishment, their priority of choice was abolished, and Porters registered for the landing of mackerel, herrings, sprats and whitings in order of arrival. Now senior Porters suffered because their younger and stronger colleagues took on so much work that they found themselves deprived of employment in the fish trade. The rule had to be modified again: no Porter was permitted to carry more than two baskets at a time, so as to enable all Porters to share in the work. Fish labour was usually performed very early in the morning; salesmen paid porterage fees into a public house at Billingsgate before 9 a.m., and Porters shifted there later in the day. As regards oysters, the first Porter to register for the work was entitled to carry them from ship to shore and claim the landing fee, even though the proprietor could employ any Fellowship Porter of his choice to carry them thence to his own establishment. The Court of Rulers took the initiative in 1777 in setting at 5*d*. per bushel the price of landing oysters at Billingsgate and carrying them to the *Old Swan*; eight years later a differentiation was introduced in that oysters delivered from the waterside to carts in Thames Street continued to be paid at 5*d*. per bushel if carried in baskets, but 6*d*. if in the Porters' sacks, and the 1777 rate of 5*d*. was increased to 6*d*. in 1800. For landing oysters at Hungerford Market 3*d*. per bushel was charged if they had to be carried across one, 4*d*. if across a number of bottoms.[38]

II

THE ATTACK ON THE PORTERS'
MONOPOLY

1

GENERAL

O F the changes which the structure of the British economy in general and commerce passing through the Port of London in particular underwent between the middle sixteenth and the early nineteenth century, most noticeable was the quantitative growth: the greater volume of goods entering and leaving the Port of London, and the range of new articles which were involved in such commerce, at first tentatively as luxuries, then firmly establishing themselves as necessities. Typical examples occurred above all among imports, such as the India and China trades in tea and the whole of the West India commodities, headed by sugar. This expansion of the volume of merchandise required a corresponding increase and improvements in handling facilities; mechanical devices for lifting cargoes made their appearance in the shape of winches and cranes. Dissatisfaction became more and more vocal where accommodation lagged behind requirements, as in the limitation of space available for the discharge of dutiable commodities and in the risks involved when valuable cargo suffered delay on board ships anchored in the Pool of London or in lighters for lack of unloading space. Increasing pressure was put on the City of London Corporation by traders either to satisfy their demands for better and more spacious facilities or to relinquish its right to administer the Port of London.

It was by virtue of its duty of administering the Port of London that the City Corporation had originally ensured the availability of porterage services throughout the Port by providing and licensing Porters; their monopoly had been the corollary of the duty incumbent upon them to render services wherever required within the Port. In the course of 250 years the situation had changed. No fear now troubled any merchant that he might remain without labour to transport his goods. The Port of London abounded with hands stretched out to lift, with backs ready to bend to, any load which required moving. Competition for such work reduced the rates at which labourers offered themselves to considerably below those fixed for authorized City Porters. In easing the burden and speeding the task, mechanical devices made the old rates seem ever more inappropriate. In the circumstances, the claims of authorized Porters to the exclusive right to perform indispensable services rang more and more hollow in the ears of merchants overwhelmed with offers of alternative labour. Far from considering City Porters indispensable, they looked upon them as obnoxious; instead of appreciating, they resented the universality of their privileges within the Port. Time and economic thought had overtaken the Porters. For public authority to provide essential services under strict regulation had been a method appropriate to the sixteenth century. Three hundred years later, the most advanced opinion wanted services, essential or otherwise, to be regulated by the interplay of supply and demand, free from official interference; if merchants required commodities carried, landed, or loaded in the Port of London, their need would attract to the Port sufficient supplies of labour competing for the work. Traders were entitled to obtain the lowest rates at which men offered to do the job; to force merchants to pay a higher price to particular Porters meant curtailing their bargaining power, interfering with their rights.

Especially did this point of view prevail once dock construction began in the Port at the turn of the century. Within their own walls, Dock Companies exercised sovereign rule. They assumed liability for losses caused to the Customs revenue through smuggling or damage; hence they claimed absolute control over the men they employed. The West India Dock Company refused from the outset to employ City Porters or any men on other than its own terms. Not every dock company insisted on this principle right away, but all adopted it sooner or later. As the docks absorbed more and more of London's waterborne trade, progressively less remained within reach of the City Porters. Wharfingers outside the docks, themselves hard hit by loss of business to the docks, strained every nerve to survive in the competition mainly by lowering costs; one of the first cost items which they

AREA OF LONDON PORTERS' PRINCIPAL ACTIVITIES

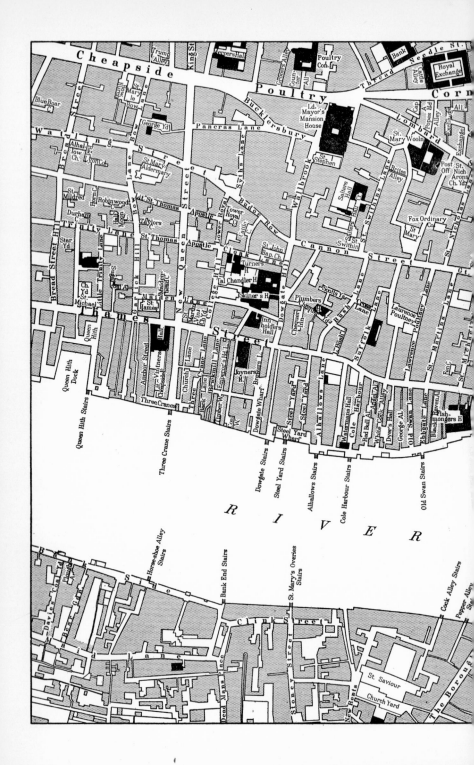

endeavoured to eliminate were the high charges made by authorized City Porters.

The situation could have been solved in two ways. By giving in to the new attitude towards the rendering of services, the City Corporation might have abandoned its licensing system for Porters in favour of unregulated competition. This was what many wharfingers and merchants wanted; it would have enabled those who regularly required porterage services to engage their own personnel who would do the work at a remuneration, at times, and in a manner fixed by the employers. The dock companies showed that this could be satisfactorily done by enterprises protected by their Acts of Parliament; others, less openly favoured by legislation, could achieve the same freedom only if the jurisdiction of the City of London over porterage services were removed. The City Corporation was reluctant to adopt this course because of the social problem with which it would find itself saddled. Porters' numbers having expanded in proportion to the increase in the Port's turnover, thousands of men made their living through licensed porterage and looked to the City Corporation as the guardian of their established expectations; had not the City, by deputing Aldermen to govern the principal Porters' organizations, sealed their existence with the stamp of its approval?

Nor was a less radical solution impossible. There were many merchants in the Port of London who required porterage services only occasionally and did not find it worth their while to employ their own labourers for the purpose. Such men hired Porters where and when the need arose. They had no objection at all to hiring licensed City Porters, provided these proved competitive in quality and price; indeed, a ubiquitous labour force on call constituted a considerable convenience, on one condition: it had to be efficient. No employer was prepared to put up with a licensing system which forced him to give work to older, slower, or more expensive Porters than he could hire elsewhere. By ruthless streamlining the City Corporation might around 1800 have effected the adaptation of its force of Porters to modern concepts of competitive business. The opportunity was missed. Just as the City Corporation resisted complete abolition of a licensed body of Porters, so did the Porters themselves resist change, partly for reasons of social justice, partly because monopoly and tradition had bred habits of supineness and comfort. This meant that they exposed themselves to crossfire: some of their enemies saw no virtue at all in a system of authorized Porters, others condemned the services provided as inefficient and expensive. A combined attack on both these grounds proved difficult to withstand.

The only authority capable of defending the Porters at all against these attacks was the City of London. But the City had itself become the butt of constant criticism: contemporary opinion considered it backward in economic thinking, narrow and selfish in its concern for its revenues, a bulwark of reaction. Its Port remained old-fashioned in handling facilities, falling behind the outports in modernization; every reform had to be wrested from an obstreperous and short-sighted administration by the clamour and blackmail of enlightened and progressive users. Moreover, the City Corporation did not enjoy an existence separate from the interests involved. Among its Common Councilmen and Aldermen were directors of dock companies, wharfingers and merchants, themselves parties in the conflict. Even its personnel had one foot in the other camp: the lawyer who held the appointment of City Remembrancer acted at the same time as secretary to the first dock company formed in the Port. Thus the City's power of resistance was weakened, both from without and within. Nor did anybody find it easy publicly to defend the Porters, a turbulent and ill-behaved body of men, as much the lowest grade of labour in the Port as they had ever been, oftentimes endangering the peace and intimidating and overcharging those members of the public too weak or inexperienced to assert their rights. From being a public service, licensed Porters had become a public nuisance. This was a view endorsed by the legal profession; here as everywhere else, liberal opinion opposed the Porters by interpreting restrictively their rights, by driving as many horses and coaches as possible through their monopolies. Increasingly deprived of any protection which faint-hearted City fathers unwillingly afforded, the authorized City Porters were doomed to slip in the course of the nineteenth century ever further down the slope to extinction.[39]

2

GEOGRAPHICAL ATTACK

THOUGH the jurisdiction of the Corporation of London for most purposes did not extend beyond the City and its Liberties, it included the whole Port of London for porterage.* The area of concentrated demand however was much smaller, limited uptown to the square mile of the City, along both banks of the River to a mile on either side of London Bridge. Most Porters were stationed within this area of concentrated demand, content to go to the periphery when called to particular jobs. Traders anxious to elude City Porters attempted to have their goods handled as far from the centre as possible, hoping thereby to escape attention; at worst, they disputed the City Corporation's right to control work in outlying areas. Porters at first defended their rights; subsequently they abandoned more and more outposts in order to concentrate the weight of their resistance on the area most vital to them. Thus it was reported in 1822 that for many years the Aliens' Porter had received no dues in respect of aliens' goods exported, because in practice he never obtained information of such exports in time to assert his rights, and that he had not troubled greatly to remedy this state of affairs because of the very small volume of trade involved. Far more serious was his failure to obtain his dues when aliens' goods were imported and discharged at the sufferance wharves located on the Southwark side of the River.

A threat to the Tacklehouse Porters arose in 1786 when the East India Company planned to lease a wharf outside the City limits hitherto occupied by the Board of Ordnance, in order to have it declared a legal quay and use it for all its own landing and shipping work. Tacklehouse Porters in that eventuality wanted an explicit extension of their rights to cover these premises. Nothing came of this forerunner of

* See p. 36 above.

the East India Docks, but six years later it was the turn of Ticket Porters to express anxiety at a scheme to build tobacco warehouses on a site occupied by Albion Mills. That danger past, the Excise Commissioners in 1795 mooted a plan to erect stores for coffee and coconuts outside the City limits. None of these projects endangered the legal title of City Porters to the work; they feared merely the difficulty of enforcing their rights. By 1811 the Society of Tacklehouse and Ticket Porters had been informed on good legal authority of the hopelessness of opposing in Parliament a bill transferring the landing of butter and cheese from the legal quays on the north to the sufferance wharves on the south side of the River; by the operation of the Act the Porters lost practically the whole of this work. They ceased to claim their rights at Southwark, except very occasionally and in the face of considerable resistance.

Fellowship Porters encountered the problem for the first time in 1798. Several bargemasters and others were in the habit of discharging malt at wharves far to the west and south of the Porters' usual area, at Scotland Yard and Millbank. City Meters measured the malt, but Fellowship Porters either encountered a refusal of work or, worse still, after being admitted to carry the malt, of payment on the plea that their rights of porterage did not extend westward from London Bridge. Undeterred by such refusal, Billingsgate Porters continued to offer their services until there was due to them on account of services partly performed, partly tendered, an amount exceeding £70. The City Solicitor, asked to take charge of the Porters' rights, hesitated and sought Counsel's opinion. Counsel made several points never hitherto raised: he doubted Fellowship Porters' exclusive rights to the discharge of up-country barges, that is barges coming downriver from the West country and unloading in Middlesex without ever entering the jurisdiction of the City of London; he was more positive in denying such exclusive rights where vessels had passed westward through the Pool and the Port of London in order to unload at some stairs or wharves in Middlesex. He upheld nothing but the claims of Billingsgate Porters who had, with the employers' consent, actually worked, instead of merely offering to work, to remuneration for work done. On enquiring, the City Solicitor could not discover any Fellowship

Porters performing the work with the employers' consent; hence no action was taken.

William Clay, a salt merchant who also engaged extensively in canal and waterworks promotion in London, in 1829 decided to elude the Billingsgate Porters by landing his salt in the basin of the Regents Canal, in which he had a substantial interest. There he neither employed City Porters nor paid City dues. The latter consideration prevailed upon the Fellowship Porters to suspend action, hoping the City would enforce metage payments at its own expense, thereby creating a precedent which Billingsgate Porters could follow, but already other firms in the salt trade were casting envious glances at Clay's advantage, resolving to follow suit unless the practice be stopped. The City's pursuit of its action was not nearly as energetic as the Fellowship had hoped; six years later the Billingsgate Porters were still endeavouring to ascertain from the Solicitor-General whether they had not the right of working in the Regents Canal Basin.

Coal merchants meanwhile had also discovered the dodge of settling at wharves in the basins of various canals and at Chelsea where they escaped City charges, above all those for metage until an Act of Parliament in 1831 abolished altogether all Land Coal Meters* and suspended for seven years the City of London's right to measure sea coal, ordering all coal to be sold by weight, not measure. Merchants promptly installed and licensed their own coal weighers, and the Act, when expiring in 1838, was renewed for another seven-year period. When a register of coal whippers was established in London by yet another Act of Parliament in 1843, it instructed the Registrar to enter all existing coal whippers and 'any other able-bodied Male Person whatever who shall be desirous of entering on the said employment', thus repealing any privilege Fellowship Porters had ever enjoyed in this work.[40]

* See p. 110 above.

3

THE WHARFINGERS' ATTACK

(a) Legal Quays

THROUGH such attacks on the periphery of their domain, authorized City Porters suffered losses, painful perhaps, but not vital. When on the other hand blows were aimed at their privileges in the centre of their area, the neighbourhood of London Bridge, they could surrender only at the price of their livelihood. Yet a succession of wharfingers in this part of the City had made it their ambition to free the trade of the Port from the impositions of the City Porters and pursued this aim ruthlessly. The first and perhaps the most obdurate of these wharfingers was Thomas Bolt, who in the late eighteenth century occupied premises at Fresh Wharf, Dice and Smart's Quays. He embarked on a long career of resistance to City Porters in 1791, when he refused Ticket Porters the handling of a quantity of hemp unless they took employment with him and worked on his own terms. Porters were not the only men aggrieved by Bolt. In defiance of rules made by the Court of Aldermen for keeping traffic moving in Billingsgate Dock, Bolt in his capacity as lessee of Smart's Quay (which forms one side of the dock) overcrowded the dock by keeping four vessels lying two abreast at his quay, besides seven or eight barges or lighters. This obstructed traffic and prevented several oyster boats from entering Billingsgate to sell their goods. Bolt threatened violence to their owners and to the Yeomen of the Waterside when they demanded the removal of his ships, and the oyster merchants had to sell their oysters outside the dock as best they could.

Legal tests of Bolt's attempt to escape all City privileges were initiated in 1793 when Bolt prevented the Aliens' Porter from landing at Fresh Wharf a cargo of raisins imported on behalf of an alien merchant. The Aliens' Porter, aware that Bolt's action formed part of a wider onslaught on City rights, sought the City authorities' advice and was told that no objection existed to his proceeding against Bolt at his own expense for the recovery of his dues. However, three years later the then Aliens' Porter died and his successor had to start the struggle afresh. Not only did Bolt in 1799 refuse the Aliens' Porter permission to work at his quays, but also, where they had done some work, he charged both the Aliens' and the Tacklehouse and Ticket Porters cranage, a new fee not hitherto known for the use of the crane installed at his wharf. William Stennett, the Aliens' Porter, resisted the charge, claiming that a wharfinger was entitled to wharfage, but that such wharfage comprised the use of all tackle available at the wharf, including cranes. The case of *Bolt* v. *Stennett* in 1800 went against Bolt, the judge deciding that the crane was necessary to the unloading on a wharf or quay which, being a public wharf, in this respect resembled a public highway which all persons could use on their lawful occasions. This however was a mere side issue.

The main question remained whether Bolt would allow authorized Porters to work on his premises. The City Recorder and the Common Serjeant had both been consulted on this point and had rather timidly suggested in the first instance suing not Bolt but those non-freemen whom he employed. Eventually the Corporation was brought to act, but on behalf of the Tacklehouse rather than the Ticket Porters, after Bolt had obstructed the Grocers' Porters in landing goods. Bolt held out till the last possible moment, but when the case came into open court allowed judgment to go against himself by default. This enabled him to claim that he had been compelled to allow Tacklehouse Porters to land goods, but not to carry them to store, and that the case had no bearing at all on Ticket Porters to whom as before he refused all access. So once again the General Purposes Committee of the Common Council investigated Bolt's liability to legal action, once again came to the conclusion that Bolt was in the wrong, but now found a different excuse for postponing action: an Act was pending for the purchase of the legal quays by the government; this rendered it inadvisable to sue the proprietor of a legal quay.

When at last the government did purchase the legal quays, a number of wharves were swept away to make a spacious promenade in front of the new Custom House. Dice Quay however remained, and Bolt's successor as wharfinger there in 1812 was Bent Reynolds, himself a suspended Ticket Porter and hence no lover of the Society of Tacklehouse and Ticket Porters to whose members he promptly refused all work, backed up in this refusal by the merchants whose goods he handled. The Lord Mayor tried to adjudicate at a meeting to which he called both parties, but Reynolds could not be moved, so that the matter had to be laid again before the Common Council. Tacklehouse and Ticket Porters were urged to come to some amicable arrangement, but amity was not a sentiment entertained by either side towards the other, and the substantial reduction of rates suggested by Reynolds and some fellow wharfingers was unhesitatingly turned down by a large majority vote of the Tacklehouse and Ticket Porters' Court. The ball passed back to the Common Council with a report that the parties' interests remained irreconcilable, but by 1815 conditions had changed: many legal quays had gone, followed by several wharfingers whose conduct had offered most provocation; Porters were now less anxious than they had been to bring the issue to court, and so the City had another respite from legal action.[41]

Edward Ogle, senior partner of the firm of J. & E. Ogle, substantial wharfingers occupying premises at Wiggins', Young's, and Ralph's Quays, in many instances acted as spokesman of the London wharfingers. When he found that Bolt had been successful in excluding the Ticket Porters from his wharves, he formed his own gangs by selling the right to work on his quays to selected Ticket Porters; in 1792 George Jacobs purchased such a vacancy at Ralph's and Young's Quays for the sum of £200.* This implied refusing access to City Porters who were not members of their gangs. In 1792 the City Solicitor proceeded against Ogles, but could not have achieved much as the Ticket Porters raised the same complaints again in 1798. By this time Ogles had changed their tactics: they now employed gangsmen on yearly engagements, both at the waterside and in their uptown warehouses. While at first careful to confine employment to Ticket Porters, they subsequently grew careless, so that in 1807 of five gangsmen at Wiggins' Quay only one was found to be duly admitted.

* See p. 64 above.

John Atkins was one of the Aldermen of the City of London qualifying as a Commissioner of Compensation for the losses caused by the establishment of docks in the Port; in this capacity he adjudicated on the claims of some of the gangsmen displaced by the West India and London Docks.* It was perhaps less surprising to the early nineteenth century than it is to us today to find that as a partner of J. & A. Atkins, warehouse keepers, he took advantage of the same proceedings to claim and obtain compensation for losses of his own. In addition he owned Atkins' Wharf, Rotherhithe, used for some time by the East India Company, and in 1819 barred the Mercers' and Ironmongers' Tacklehouse Porters from that wharf, thus impeding their work for the East India Company.

(b) Queenhithe

The Fellowship Porters' particular bugbear among wharfingers was Christopher Hill, a warehouse man and granary keeper at Winksworth's Wharf, part of Broken Wharf in Upper Thames Street, where he stored for sale malt brought downriver in West Country barges. Both the landing and carrying of such malt to the granary and its re-carrying, when sold, formed part of the Billingsgate Porters' privilege. Hill in 1822 employed unauthorized porters instead, and had several Fellowship Porters, including two of the Rulers, restrained by force from handling the malt. To crown injury by insult, Hill himself claimed full porterage dues from the sellers of the malt on the plea that he had rendered the appropriate services, while paying his employees at a much lower rate. This soon became general practice among wharfingers: though porterage was done far more cheaply than by the City Porters, this reduction in cost did not benefit the trade, but provided wharfingers with additional revenue equivalent to the difference between porterage rates charged to customers and wages paid to labour employed in the work. While the Court of Aldermen investigated the complaint against Hill, the latter not only continued using his own labour, but incited the corn trade in general to follow suit. The enquiry lasted an unconscionable time; when at last it emerged into open court, Hill refused to appear, in order to show that

* See p. 142 below.

K

he acknowledged neither the Court's jurisdiction nor the Billingsgate Porters' rights. Meanwhile he obstructed not only Porters but also City Meters. For a whole year, from September 1822 to September 1823, the Fellowship Rulers attended every meeting of the Court of Aldermen in the hope that that body would summon enough courage to arraign Hill, but were disappointed. No wonder that Hill spread news that the City Corporation did not dare prosecute him; accordingly more and more wharfingers requisitioned City Meters and Porters for unremuneratively small jobs, while refusing them access and facilities as soon as the volume of goods warranted the engagement of cheaper labour.

Associated with Christopher Hill in his crusade against the Billingsgate Porters was John Howell, wharfinger at Queenhithe, partner in the firm of Randalls, Howell & Co. His behaviour at his own wharf matched that of Hill, and the exasperated Porters, finding the Court of Aldermen reluctant to protect them effectively, took their complaint to the Coal and Corn Committee of the Common Council. Even their own Clerk had considerable misgivings about pursuing their rights, as he confided to the committee's chairman in a private letter. Howell explained his point of view: prior to engaging unauthorized labour, he had offered the Fellowship Porters the work of transferring malt from a barge to a wagon at $1\frac{1}{2}d$. a quarter, though he could get it done for considerably less, but as the authorized rate amounted to $2d$. a quarter, the Billingsgate Porters has refused his offer. The Coal and Corn Committee proved no more courageous than the Court of Aldermen. The principle of the Porters' privilege was not in doubt, but the committee sheltered behind the absence of exact description of this work or charge in any Common Council Act; this permitted the conclusion that such work was not specified by any Act, so that no infringement had been committed in refusing it to the Porters. Coupled with this verdict was a demand for a full, definite and specific table of rates drawn up by the Common Council.[42]

The success of the first Queenhithe wharfingers in defeating the claims of the City Porters proved a valuable precedent to their colleagues. The Society of Tacklehouse and Ticket Porters, faced with a similar refusal of work in 1828, decided to seek protection from the operation of the law rather than from the valour of the City authorities. The law, however, was unambiguous only with regard to intruders, but far less clear about the intruders' employers. Such employers were men of substance, well able to pay fines, whereas these could never be collected from casual labourers. The Society brought three unauthorized porters before the Lord Mayor's Court, where they were duly fined and in default of payment committed to prison. The Queenhithe wharfingers who had employed the men in defiance of by-laws now interceded with the Lord Mayor, who declined to interfere, whereupon they carried their petition to the Common Council. As usual, this body tried to pacify both sides by a compromise: on the one hand it ordered the three offenders to be released from custody and their fines to be remitted, on the other hand the legal costs in the action to be repaid to the Society of Tacklehouse and Ticket Porters from City funds.

The dispute led to a joint conference of Queenhithe wharfingers and officers of the Society with the General Purposes Committee of the Common Council on the Ticket Porters' right to work at Queenhithe. Robert Smith, himself a Tacklehouse Porter, but attending the conference in his capacity as a Queenhithe wharfinger, put their case: docks on the north and sufferance wharves on the south bank had made great inroads upon the business of the legal quays; in order to meet this competition, he, like others, had reduced porterage rates by between 40 and 70 per cent and had even exhibited at his premises a table of these new charges. Doubts having been raised whether as a Tacklehouse Porter he could legally do so, he had withdrawn the table for the moment. An opponent of far longer standing was John Blenkarne, who had himself been a Ticket Porter at Custom House until in 1813 he had snatched some labour to which a Tacklehouse Porter had been entitled. As soon as the Society's Court decided against Blenkarne, he had not only left the Society, but begun obstructing its members by refusing them access to any premises he controlled and by taking sides against them on every occasion; he could boast in 1828 that he had permitted no Ticket Porters to work at his wharf these fifteen years, that he would continue to bar them, and that no more than three Ticket Porters ever sought work at the legal quays. The General Purposes Committee was not impressed with Blenkarne's evidence, which in respect of the number of Ticket Porters seeking employment proved incorrect. The Queenhithe dispute concerned the discharge of coastwise goods which were never landed in the docks, whose hours of opening did not suit this particular type of trade; hence the argument of competition between legal quays and docks did not apply to such goods, and the Society of Tacklehouse and Ticket Porters re-asserted its full rights, covering not only legal quays, but the whole Port of London, and asked for the Corporation's support, implying that in return for such support it might agree to lower its charges so as to enable wharfingers in other respects to compete with the docks. Rulers tried meanwhile to ascertain whether in fact wharfingers had reduced their charges for landing coastwise goods, but a number of wharfingers objected to this form of industrial espionage, above all Samuel Barber who was not only a wharfinger at Chamberlain's Wharf, but also Drapers' Tacklehouse Porter and a Ruler of the Society of Tacklehouse and Ticket Porters. The Common Council on this occasion came down on the side of the Ticket Porters and threatened with proceedings any wharfingers who would in future seek to obstruct their employment.

The Rulers triumphantly made the round of refractory wharfingers and showed them the Common Council resolution, whereupon most wharfingers denied any intention of depriving Ticket Porters of their labour; only Robert Smith persisted in his refusal of co-operation and had to be threatened with legal action. The future showed that he was not really less amenable, but merely more honest than others; in spite of alleged compliance, wharfingers succeeded in withdrawing more and more work from the Ticket Porters. Typical was the case of Mason, a wharfinger at Brooke's Wharf, who in 1829 employed three non-freemen whom the Society of Tacklehouse and Ticket Porters summoned before the Chamberlain. When they refused to obey the summons, the case was laid before the Common Serjeant, Thomas Denman (the later Lord Denman), who pronounced the right of the Ticket Porters to be clear and advised them to enforce it, but not in the Lord Mayor's Court. Mason himself contended that his wharf was private property and that nobody had a right to enter it, unless hired by him. Legal proceedings in a court higher than the Lord Mayor's being expensive, the Society wanted the City authorities to conduct the litigation, whereas the Common Council in complete disregard of the Common Serjeant's advice pointed to the Ticket Porters' powers of proceedings in the Lord Mayor's Court, thus making interference by the City Corporation unnecessary. The Society found a good test case in 1830 when two watermen on board a barge unloaded 233 bundles of paper at Mason's wharf. The Common Serjeant advised proceedings in the Mayor's Court, assuming that defendants would apply to the King's Bench for a prohibition, thus enabling the legality to be argued in the higher court; instead of which the City Chamberlain in whose name the suit was brought died in the following year, putting a premature end to the action. Wharfingers sometimes pretended to object to Ticket Porters using wharf tackle. In order to remove this cause of complaint, Ticket Porters purchased large quantities of rope of their own, only to find that the wharfingers would not admit them to the wharves, whatever their equipment.[43]

Robert Smith at Queenhithe opposed with impartial vigour Billingsgate as well as Ticket Porters. Fellowship Porters first encountered his resistance in 1828. They approached the Common Council, where the wharfingers' untiring spokesman, Deputy Routh, did his best to defeat or at least delay all moves by Porters. Robert Smith did not obey the Common Council's summons to appear, but merely claimed by letter the right of doing labour at his own premises by his own servants and tackle—a claim pronounced by the City Solicitor to lack legal basis. Prosecution in this instance was successful, as Robert Smith in 1833 was still complaining about the Billingsgate Porters' charges, thus proving that he had not succeeded in disembarrassing himself of their services.

The firm of Cap & Chuck, of Ware, Hertfordshire, sent barges of malt to London where it had them unloaded by unauthorized labour. A party of Fellowship Porters led by a Ruler in 1831 discovered one of their barges in the process of discharge at Mill Stairs, St. Saviour's Dock, and offered their own services. The barge foreman did not prevent them from doing the work, but warned them that they would not be paid for it, which proved correct. In this instance the City's law officers were instructed to proceed against the firm at the Fellowship's expense. The agreement of the City authorities was always easier to obtain if enforcement was not directed against a London man or firm.

William Stennett, when Aliens' Porter, had suffered a good deal from the action of wharfingers who obstructed him in his rights; it was he who had fought and won the case against Bolt in 1800.* On his ceasing to be Aliens' Porter,† his son set up as a wharfinger at St. Botolph's Wharf, and in 1836 when 163 casks of olive oil from Marseilles arrived at his wharf, he not only refused to permit the Mercers' Tacklehouse Porter to unload the consignment, but threatened to give him into custody if he did not leave the premises. Tacklehouse Porters occupied a stronger position than Ticket Porters; with the support of the Mercers' Company assured to him, the Tacklehouse Porter could take Stennett to court.

Sometimes the best settlement was a private compromise. Samuel Barber, a wharfinger who had figured in other conflicts with authorized Porters,‡ in 1838 tried to deprive Billingsgate Porters of the work of unloading apples. After many conferences, the parties agreed that, where the Fellowship Porters had the overboard labour, the landing could be done by the wharfinger's men, whereas the Billingsgate Porters were entitled to the landing work where no overboard labour was involved.

(c) Challenge to the City Corporation

More and more, wharfingers inclined to challenge not only the Porters' claim to the labour, but also the City Corporation's right to legislate in this field. Of this nature was the action started in the Court of Exchequer by Combe, Delafield & Co. in 1838 for a discovery of the City Corporation's title to porterage of corn and grain landed within the Port of London. On this occasion the City Corporation could not withdraw from the contest. The action suffered interminable delays: one of the Fellowship Rulers named as co-defendant in the suit died, and in some way or other the case continued to occupy the courts for ten years. In 1848 the City Corporation raised a counterclaim, and the dispute was eventually carried to the House of Lords, where the City abandoned it upon advice received that success was unlikely. The

* See p. 127 above.   † See p. 147 below.   ‡ See p. 132 above.

publicity given to the inability of the Billingsgate Porters to enforce rights which for centuries had undoubtedly been theirs constituted the most disastrous defeat yet sustained and encouraged all who still used Fellowship labour to make themselves independent.

John Ismay Nicholson and Frederick Besley, for instance, wharfingers at Somers and Lyons' Quays, complained to the Common Council that Orange Porters charged them 2½d. for the porterage of boxes of oranges or lemons from the quays to their warehouse in George Lane, whereas other warehousemen on the opposite side of the street had the same work performed for them at 2d. per box. After vainly trying to persuade the Orange Porters to abate the halfpenny, complainants had engaged unauthorized labour, whereupon the Fellowship of Porters threatened proceedings. After looking to the Common Council for permission to employ whom they liked, Nicholson and Besley suddenly withdrew their petition and declined to give evidence; they had discovered that courts of law were more likely to favour their cause than those of the City Corporation.

Bellamy, wharfinger at Gordon's Wharf, Rotherhithe, refused the Billingsgate Porters in 1874 the discharge of a cargo of barley at his wharf. The Society's lawyers asked the City Corporation either to take proceedings against Bellamy or to allow the Society to do so in the City's name; the Common Council sanctioned the latter method, provided the Society indemnified the Corporation in terms acceptable to the City Solicitor. Although the Society agreed to this condition, action was successfully prevented by the City Solicitor's refusal to outline any terms of indemnification which would be acceptable to him. Similarly, when I. H. & G. Scovell, of Cotton's Wharf, who had always allowed the Fellowship Porters to discharge large quantities of fruit and roots at their premises, suddenly in 1875 changed their policy and decided to supply their own labour, the City law officers stultified the Fellowship's attempt to assert its rights by drawing attention to the Combe Delafield case; the Corporation accordingly refused permission for action to be taken in its name. This was the last occasion on which Billingsgate Porters attempted to assert their rights in the courts before hydraulic cranes made their claims altogether nugatory.[44]

4

THE COMING OF DOCKS

(a) West India Docks

AGITATION for more and better facilities for the handling of cargoes in the Port of London led towards the end of the eighteenth century to the erection of wet docks in various parts of the Port. The first of these, the West India Docks, received statutory sanction in 1799. While a House of Commons Committee was discussing the bill, the Rulers of the Tacklehouse and Ticket Porters spotted the intention of the City Corporation to renounce its right of regulating porterage services within the docks which would in future enjoy the status of legal quays. 'Intention' was perhaps too strong a word for the City Corporation's policy. Its representatives had tried in vain to persuade the House of Commons Committee to leave its ancient privilege of appointing and licensing porters and harbour masters intact; faced with a *fait accompli*, the Common Council, for lack of a quorum, lost a resolution reasserting the City's rights. Even had it been passed, the resolution would have been a futile gesture of protest. Porterage rights were among those which the Select Committee had determined to vest in the directors of the West India Dock Company. Those who made their livelihood as Porters now 'have not the consolation of seeing among the proposed compensations to sufferers themselves expressly included in such consideration', but the omission was repaired during the passage of the bill. The Act in its final form mentioned among those likely to sustain damage 'any Owners or Occupiers of the same legal Quays and Sufferance Wharfs, Warehouses, Docks and other Tenements and Hereditaments, or any Tackle House Porters, Ticket Porters, or Free Carmen, of the City of London' and provided for compensation.

Practically all the goods drawn into the West India Docks belonged

to the prerogative of the Tacklehouse and Ticket Porters; Fellowship
Porters were so little concerned in them that they never even troubled
to petition Parliament against the bill, hence they did not figure among
parties entitled to compensation. On the other hand, a party concerned
in the West India trade and not expressly provided for was the Aliens'
Porter, who had failed to assert his rights in time; though he subsequently claimed that he had demanded entry soon after the opening
of the West India Import Dock in August 1802 in order to exercise his
office, this claim failed to withstand close investigation, and Stennett
eventually did not tender his services at the West India Docks until
1822. Meanwhile the Tacklehouse and Ticket Porters had grown
impatient. The West India Docks had been opened to imports (which
concerned Porters far more than exports) in 1802; Porters promptly
lost much business; the Act stipulated for compensation, but at the
same time did not allow registration of claims and adjudication to
begin until three years after the docks had opened. In 1803, Tacklehouse
and Ticket Porters sought the Common Council's view how best to
proceed during this interval, but were merely told that their application was premature, and when in the following year the Ticket Porters
ceased beating about the bush and stated plainly that they were poor
men, unable to afford waiting three years for their compensation, the
Common Council managed to avoid an answer by burying the petition
in the files of the City Lands Committee. Not until 1825 did the
Billingsgate Porters put the willingness of the West India Dock
Company to admit them to the test. They then established what they
must in practice have known, that the West India Dock Company
would have no dealings with them; the Company's Secretary obliged
by an official letter testifying to his firm's refusal to admit their privilege. In 1829 the Corporation of London sold the City Canal to the West
India Dock Company, which turned it into the South West India Dock.
So far as the Fellowship Porters had enjoyed rights of work on the banks
of this canal, it meant a further loss of rights without compensation.

(b) London and East India Docks

A site at Wapping had been favoured by dock promoters even before
the Isle of Dogs; in the late 1790s both projects had been engaged in a

race to secure parliamentary approval. Though the West India Docks gained statutory sanction first, the London Docks followed suit within twelve months. Being situated much closer to the centre of activities, they constituted a much more dangerous threat to the various Porters. In early 1796, Registers and Rulers of the Society of Tacklehouse and Ticket Porters on behalf of the latter, Masters of the Tackle Houses of the twelve superior Companies of the City of London and the Company of Vintners on behalf of their Wine Tackle Porters separately petitioned the House of Commons against the London Docks bill. On the bill's reintroduction in another session twelve months later the City Corporation weighed in with no less than two petitions, followed by the Fishmongers' and Goldsmiths' Companies on behalf of their Tacklehouse Porters. In 1798, 1799, and 1800, as regularly as the swallow follows spring, a petition from the City Corporation followed the re-appearance of the bill. Nor did this opposition remain without effect. Anxious to buy off the City Corporation, the promoters of the London Docks offered to acknowledge City privileges in the docks if it ceased resistance to the bill. Agreement might well have been reached on this basis, but for the refusal of the House of Commons on principle to give statutory endorsement to the City's rights and privileges in the docks. So the London Docks Act passed in 1800, with a compensation clause identical with that contained in the West India Docks Act, again mentioning explicitly Tacklehouse and Ticket Porters; this compensation received confirmation by another Act which three years later legalized the establishment of bonded warehouses in docks designated by the Customs authorities.

As in the case of the West India Docks, the party not considered at all was the Aliens' Porter. William Stennett took no action to safeguard his or the City's rights until some time after the London Docks had opened for business. Early in 1806 he appeared at the gate, accompanied by several witnesses, to demand entry, showing his deputation from the City Corporation and specifying the alien cargoes which he wished to work. He had given the London Dock Company notice in writing of his intention to establish a test case and was ceremoniously refused admission, first by the gatekeeper, then by the docks superintendent in person. Legal advice had been in this event to seek a remedy in the law courts; only if it failed should the City Corporation resort to the compensation procedure outlined in the Acts. Stennett accordingly sued Beeston Long, Treasurer of the London Dock Company, in the King's Bench Division; the case came before Lord Ellenborough and a special jury who gave adequate expression to the law as well as to their feelings by finding for the petitioner and awarding him damages in the sum of 1s. A court verdict cannot be justified by feelings alone; legal reasons have to be adduced. So the hoary fallacy regarding geographical limitations of the City privileges was disinterred: the London Docks were situated in Middlesex, outside the City liberties, and while the Court admitted that the Aliens' Porter's rights extended to sufferance wharves even though outside City limits, the London Docks did not occupy the site of a sufferance wharf. The Aliens' Porter subsequently compiled figures for the purpose of calculating his real loss. For aliens' goods landed in the Port of London 1797–1804

	£	s.	d.
gross receipts had amounted to . . .	13,006	4	7
on which after deducting 25 per cent for expenses	3,251	11	1
had remained a profit of	£9,754	13	6

After the opening of the London Docks, of the aliens' goods landed in the Port for the period 1805–1810

	landed by Aliens' Porter			discharged in London Docks		
	£	s.	d.	£	s.	d.
gross receipts were . . .	2,304	8	6	10,380	1	11
25 per cent expenses deducted .	576	2	1	2,595	0	4
profit remaining . . .	£1,728	6	5	£7,785	1	7

so that more than 80 per cent of his business had been lost through the London Docks.

Like the Aliens' Porter, the Fellowship Porters did not go into action until the London Docks had started operations. In March 1805 their

Clerk drew the Company's attention to the Billingsgate Porters' exclusive rights to the landing of fruit and nuts, whether inside the docks or out. Even more important was the discharge of corn. The London Dock Company did not challenge the City's rights of metage; Deputy Corn Meters were admitted to vessels lying in the London Docks. But although such Deputy Corn Meters had instructions not to exercise their functions, except when assisted by Fellowship Porters, the Company refused to admit such Porters, and the Deputy Corn Meters worked with the Company's own employees. Not only did such behaviour run counter to the oath of office taken by Deputy Corn Meters, not only did it expose them to fines of 20s. for each offence under the Common Council Act of 1620, but in the eyes of the Billingsgate Porters it created a dangerous precedent: if the London Dock Company successfully separated the operations of the Meters from those of the Porters, others were bound to follow suit. The City Corporation agreed with these views. Owing to the fact that Fellowship Porters did not figure among parties mentioned by the London Docks Act as entitled to compensation, loss of business was likely to be unrequited. The City brought an action against the Treasurer of the London Dock Company in 1807, but dropped it for reasons never divulged to the Billingsgate Porters, though to the outside observer they are obvious enough: in the same King's Bench Division which had dealt with the Aliens' Porter's claim, the City could expect to obtain another 1s. worth of damages. Highly dissatisfied with the Corporation's conduct, the Fellowship Rulers approached the London Dock Company direct with a view to securing compensation: there was at least a suggestion in the air that such compensation would have benefited the Rulers personally, not the Fellowship at large, and the London Dock Company broke off negotiations on realizing that it was dealing with a claim not for general compensation which would satisfy once for all the body of Billingsgate Porters but merely for a privileged minority. Whether this interpretation be true or not, certain it is that one of the Rulers, James Hollamby, registered his personal claim for compensation and that the Court of Rulers entered a protest against such conduct as likely to prejudice the Fellowship's general rights.

The East India Docks were authorized in 1803. An amending Act passed three years later contained provisions unlike any that had appeared in previous legislation, authorizing 'the said East India Dock Company, or their Directors, to hire or employ, from Time to Time, such and so many Labourers and Workmen, for the purpose of landing, loading, or unloading, receiving and shipping off any Goods, Wares, Merchandize, Stores, and other Articles, Matters and Things, that may be imported or brought, carried or conveyed into the said Docks and Basons . . . .' For the first time the engagement of unlicensed dock porterage labour was expressly authorized. The Acts contained the usual compensation clauses, mentioning the City Corporation and the Tacklehouse and Ticket Porters. Billingsgate Porters had no claim to compensation, but were not greatly affected as they had never handled much of the East India trade.[45]

(c) The Compensation Scheme

The West India Docks Act had appointed Commissioners to manage the award of compensation to parties injured by the establishment of the Docks. Claims, when lodged, had to be examined by the Commissioners within one year, compensation to be determined for preference by agreement, but in the absence of agreement by jury verdict. The precedent of the West India Docks served in the London Docks Act; the latter measure re-enacted previous legislation in appointing the same body of Compensation Commissioners to manage compensation in respect of the London Docks. This course was followed once again for the East India Docks—not immediately, as perhaps it had been hoped in this instance to dispense with such elaborate procedure; but an amending Act of 1806 copied the compensation provisions of the two previous Acts, adding to the responsibilities of the Compensation Commissioners already in existence.

The Commissioners divided claimants into five classes, only two of which concerned Porters: the Corporation of London and its appointees, the City Companies, Tacklehouse and Ticket Porters formed class 2 whose demands totalled £313,051 19s. 3¼d., whereas class 4 contained alongside lightermen and their foremen, lumpers and watchmen, also gangsmen, and claimed £426,737 1s. 8½d. These huge amounts were drastically pruned by the Compensation Commissioners. Class

4 claimants received a little more than one-fifth of their aggregate demand, a proportion generally observed in the satisfaction of compensation claims under the scheme; but class 2 obtained only £27,250, just over one-twelfth of the sum demanded. This reduction was effected in two ways: partly by totally disallowing claims, partly by scaling down those admitted.

Although the total number of claims amounted to 1,376, this enables no direct calculation of the number of claimants. On the one hand, some claims emanated not from individuals but from groups; to that extent there were more claimants than claims. On the other hand, many claimants lodged more than one claim, either in different capacities (a man might claim as an individual Ticket Porter, but also as a member of a gang, or face losses in his callings both as a Ticket Porter and as a warehouseman) or for different docks. Sometimes a man died before his claim was settled; if his widow pursued it, hers counted as a separate claim.

The appointment of Compensation Commissioners suffered from the difficulty inherent in all matters of this nature: desirable as it would have been to exclude all interested parties, this would have barred everybody with adequate knowledge and understanding of the problems involved. Accordingly, among the people designated as Commissioners, Aldermen of London concerned with the business of the port preponderated; two at least were active wharfingers pursuing compensation claims of their own.* Among others adjudging on the demands of various persons connected with the Fellowship Porters was Alderman Harvey Christian Combe, who in 1810 became Governor of the Society of Tacklehouse and Ticket Porters.

Tacklehouse and Ticket Porters, fortified by special mention of their title to compensation, were not slow in staking claims. Twenty-six Tacklehouse Porters put forward fourteen demands, totalling £51,450 14s. 3¼d., and were awarded £11,620 — 23 per cent of their claims, a higher proportion than most groups of claimants. In one of their earliest reports the Commissioners dealing with class 2 claims laid down the principle that Tacklehouse Porters were entitled to compensation for loss, based on a comparison of profits for

* See p. 129 above.

three years before with three years after the opening of the docks concerned.

Apart from the Tacklehouse Porters themselves, claims were also registered by the Companies appointing them, amounting to

£	s.	d.		
8,000	0	0	from the	Grocers
8,200	0	0	,, ,,	Salters
10,790	16	8	,, ,,	Clothworkers
12,200	0	0	,, ,,	Goldsmiths
13,106	13	4	,, ,,	Fishmongers
14,471	15	0	,, ,,	Haberdashers
16,312	7	10	,, ,,	Vintners
24,186	0	0	,, ,,	Ironmongers
32,220	0	0	,, ,,	Merchant Taylors
no specified sum			,, ,,	Skinners.

These demands presented the Commissioners with a difficult problem. Counsel made an oracular pronouncement to the effect that 'the several Companies are entitled to some compensation for their loss or diminution of their patronage in the appointment of the Tackle House Porters, as the Porters' gains are affected, but that Counsel can state no satisfactory principle for ascertaining such compensation'. This total lack of legal guidance accompanied a recommendation to disallow entirely the claim of one of the Companies in order to provide a test case for the decision of a jury, and the Grocers were chosen for this honour, as being first on the list. *Mandamus* was, however, in due course refused to the Grocers, access to a jury thus being barred, and this procedure then applied to all other Companies, whose claims were disallowed in bulk. In their final report the Compensation Commissioners stated the principle which had emerged from this practice: 'The Claims arising from consequential or secondary causes, which were not only extremely large, but were very assiduously and earnestly pressed upon the consideration of the Commissioners, were in all instances invariably rejected, as not coming within the scope and meaning of the Acts.'

After the Grocers' defeat, most other Companies accepted their loss with resignation. An amusing memorial was submitted by the Salters' Company at a time when compensation still appeared a possibility: the Company questioned the justification of attempts to ascertain the losses of individual claimants, suggesting instead an aggregation of losses of all Companies entitled to have Tacklehouse Porters, followed by rateable division of the total compensation—one may guess that the Salters' Tacklehouse Porters did not do a great deal of business. The claim of the Vintners' Company, which did not appoint Tacklehouse but Wine Tackle Porters, entailed lengthy proceedings. The Commissioners asked for accounts to substantiate the Company's claim; the Company's Clerk in 1809 refused to render such accounts. He persisted in his refusal over two years, in spite of the Commissioners' insistence that without inspection of accounts they could not deal with the claim. When the Company's reluctance to disclose its records had at last been overcome in 1812, the reason for it became obvious: annual profits derived from the Wine Tackle Porters' work had risen, not fallen, since the West India and London Docks had been established. The Vintners' claim fared no better than those of the other City Companies.

Individual Ticket Porters' claims can best be summarized in tabular form (see p. 145).

Most claimants capitalized their annual losses at ten years' purchase, though occasionally a more modest applicant was satisfied with eight years. The Commissioners on the other hand made awards on a basis of slightly above two years' purchase which were usually accepted by the claimants. Claims from Uptown Porters were disallowed on the ground that compensation was not designed to cover the work of carrying packages between warehouses in the City and the legal quays. No compensation accrued to any Porters appointed after the passage of the relevant Act, as they were deemed to have known of their impending loss of business, nor to Porters in arrears with quarterage or suspended from the Society of Tacklehouse and Ticket Porters, as in that condition they were not entitled to work.

Forty-five Porters presented claims amounting to £57,574 13s. 4d., not in their individual capacity, but as gangsmen working at the legal quays, and were awarded £7,787 18s. 6d., or just over one-seventh of

Number of claimants	Amounts claimed (£)	awarded (£)	Number of recipients	Number of claims disallowed	Reason for disallowance
7	45	—	—	7	Uptown
13	60	30	1	12	Uptown
13	90	30	1	12	Uptown
4	100	40	2	—	—
		25	2	—	—
11	120	40	1	9	Uptown
				1	No quarterage paid
8	150	50	7	—	—
		40	1	—	—
9	180	55	6	2	Not admitted before opening of Docks
		20	1		
15	210	65	11	4	One at least not admitted till 1799
36	240	75	24	8	Not admitted in time to suffer losses
		30	2		
		20	2		
20	270	100	1	9	?
		80	9		
		30	1		
18	300	100	2	—	—
		90	13		
		30	3		
69	330	100	66	1	Suspended as a Ticket Porter
		30	2		
32	Odd amounts totalling £19,328 18s. 5d.	Total of £975	13	19	Some not admitted in time, some do no personal labour, some prove no loss

their total demands. The largest claim came from Samuel Sollis's gang, nine men working at Porters', Page's, Bear and Sabbs Quays who asked for £19,989 6s. 8d. and were offered £2,250. Being dissatisfied with this offer, they took the claim to a jury from which they obtained £2,237 18s. 6d. One of the gang, William Miller, had demanded a jury verdict for himself alone, but this the Commissioners refused. Another gangsman was disqualified by the Commissioners because he was not an admitted Ticket Porter, yet engaged in work which only Ticket Porters were entitled to do. The Commissioners' strict insistence on membership of the Society of Tacklehouse and Ticket Porters defeated many compensation claims from gangsmen.[46]

Knowing the weakness of their position, Billingsgate Porters pursued compensation only half-heartedly. The first demand made in connection with Fellowship Porters' employment came from T. O. Powis, the Fruit Shifter, who calculated his own loss from the denial of the Billingsgate Porters' right to work in the London Docks at £20 per year on the remainder of his twenty-one year lease and therefore claimed 125 guineas. James Hollamby, one of the Rulers, followed with a claim which originally he hoped to keep secret from the Fellowship, such claim to be pursued only if the Fellowship's collective claim failed. Hollamby mentioned no particular amount, nor did the Fellowship's collective claim when it arrived, no more than a claim from William Ruston, their Corn Shifter. All these claims related to the London Docks. Before they had been pursued to any length, the Fellowship's Clerk wrote to the Commissioners that the Fellowship abandoned its claim to compensation, having decided to insist on members' rights to work in the London Docks. In the circumstances the Commissioners found it unnecessary to adjudicate on any of these claims.

If the Billingsgate Porters' claims caused the Compensation Commissioners neither headache nor money, the opposite was true with regard to the Aliens' Porter. An initial difficulty consisted of the duality of claims: one from the City of London in which the office of Aliens' Porter vested, another from William Stennett as the City's lessee and deputy as Aliens' Porter. William Stennett, who was a warehousekeeper as well as the penultimate Aliens' Porter, had taken a seven-year lease of the office from 1803. He had warned the City of the losses to be expected, both from the establishment of the docks and from the Treasury's intention to purchase the legal quays and turn some of them to other purposes, thus driving even more of the business to the docks. Indeed, the City Solicitor doubted whether an Aliens' Porter still had any legal existence after the passage of the London Docks Act. In view of this uncertainty, Stennett's lease when it expired in 1810 was renewed for one year only, and on this short-term basis Stennett continued as Aliens' Porter for another ten years; in 1820 there were even suggestions to confine the extension to six or three months. In his capacity as Aliens' Porter, Stennett had claimed compensation for loss of business amounting to almost £7,000. But the Compensation Commissioners pointed to the many renewals of Stennett's lease long after the passing of the Docks Acts, when he must have been well aware of the risk involved, yet had been the highest bidder at a public auction. They therefore refused to consider his claim for compensation at all.

In December 1820 Stennett died, but a son of the same name carried on. Twice more the Aliens' Porter's lease was extended for twelve months, though by 1821 the City inserted the right to give six months' notice, but in 1822 even this arrangement appeared too permanent, and the Common Council rejected by a large majority a proposal to renew the lease for another year, extending it by a mere three months. However, the business which had suffered very badly till about 1816 had recovered again, and Stennett held the Aliens' Porter's office until 1833 when it still yielded to the City more than £600. In that year an Act of Parliament empowered the Treasury to purchase these rights from the City at a price representing 12⅔ years' average net proceeds. Writing half a century later, Mayhew attributed the disappearance of the Aliens' Porter to the expiry of the East India Company's charter in 1834; but the two events were not interconnected, though both sprang from an attitude of mind which looked upon charges discriminating against unauthorized traders as a disgraceful survival from a barbarous past.

The City Law Officers doubted the Aliens' Porter's title to exercise his office in the West India Docks, though they affirmed it for the

London Docks, but in any case the City Corporation registered claims for compensation in respect of both. In each instance it reserved the right to bring an action against the dock company concerned for the enforcement of the Aliens' Porter's functions; if the suit succeeded, the compensation claim would lapse. The legal position was exceedingly obscure: the Prime Minister and the Chancellor of the Exchequer held a conference with the City Corporation in which they disclaimed any intention on the Government's part to deprive the City Corporation of its rights through the Docks Acts, but advised a private Act of Parliament as the best way of undoing any harm that might have been done. Accordingly the City petitioned the Privy Council for such an Act, but the Solicitor-General rejected the petition as *ultra vires* the Crown.

All this had stayed compensation proceedings, and in September 1811 Timothy Tyrrell, Clerk to the Compensation Commissioners, put it to the City Solicitor that compensation proceedings were expected to finish in November and that all pending claims should be either prosecuted or dropped. The City sought another legal opinion, which was discouraging and pointed to the failure of claims in respect of the office of City Gauger. Thereupon the City relapsed into inactivity and had to be stirred by a new warning, described as final, in December 1813. The City then asked for extension of time until 25 March 1814 to prepare the accounts required to substantiate its compensation claims as Aliens' Porter, Packer's Porter, Corn Porter and Coal Meter. Requests for extension continued at three-monthly intervals until 1815, when it was granted time until the Commissioners' next general meeting; by that time its own remained the last claim pending. However, not until four years later was that claim at last presented in a monetary form, amounting to £29,750 15s. 3d. with interest. The Compensation Commissioners countered this by a very simple calculation: before the passing of the Docks Acts, the Corporation had let the office of Aliens' Porter to Stennett at £205 p.a., since the passing of the Acts at £105 p.a. The difference of £100 represented the annual loss suffered by the City which the Commissioners capitalized at twenty years' purchase by an offer of £2,000. The Corporation declared it completely inadequate and unacceptable and demanded arbitration by a jury. The Commissioners were prepared to proceed to such arbitration; delay ensued because William Stennett died in the middle of preparations for the case and his executor procrastinated. Eventually the Chancellor of the Exchequer intervened again and called a conference to which both the City Corporation and the Compensation Commissioners sent representatives. Even after the conference it took another nine months before the City agreed to accept the Commissioners' offer of £2,000. When at last this claim had been settled in 1823, the Compensation Commissioners could conclude their labours. Their first meeting had taken place on 1 August 1799; a quarter of a century later, they met for the last time on 17 June 1824 to sign the report to the Treasury recording their proceedings.[47]

(d) The later Docks

The coming of the earlier docks had been a blow to Porters, but at least they—or those most closely concerned—had been entitled to compensation for loss of earnings. Subsequent dock projects handled the Porters' interests more roughly. A Select Committee of the House of Commons in 1810 dismissed representations on behalf of the Society of Tacklehouse and Ticket Porters against the Commercial Docks bill by declaring that the intended docks did not form part of the City of London and would not be considered as legal quays, but as sufferance wharves—both points of complete irrelevance to the Porters' rights. The Commercial Docks Act of 1810 took no account of the Tacklehouse and Ticket Porters' claims, but—like the East Country Docks Act of the following year—explicitly reserved the rights of measurage and porterage of the City of London, its Deputies, Meters and Fellowship Porters (otherwise Billingsgate Porters). Indeed, the Company's treatment of Fellowship Porters over a lengthy period was most considerate. In 1826 William Allan, the Company's Secretary, assured the Fellowship Rulers that 'The Directors desire me to assure you that all necessary facility shall be cheerfully afforded to the Porters of the Fellowship whenever they may have occasion to work at the Commercial Dock', and in the following year the Company even offered to build in the Commercial Docks an office for Meters and Porters if they so desired. Protestations of assistance to the Porters on the part of the Company's employees formed the subject of another letter by the Secretary in 1828. The honeymoon of the Billingsgate Porters and the Commercial Dock Company lasted forty years. In 1852 the Commercial Dock Company bought up the East Country Docks. Fellowship Porters did not anticipate any danger to their employment, but from that date onwards encountered the same refusal of admittance which had already become customary in other docks.

Two dock bills reached the House of Commons in 1825: one for the South London Docks—an abortive project—the other for the St. Katherine's Dock. Apprehending further inroads on their privileges, both bodies of Porters petitioned against both Acts, whereas the Corporation adopted an attitude of neutrality. As a matter of policy, Billingsgate Porters endeavoured to have inserted in all wet-dock bills a clause protecting their rights. The parliamentary agent for the St. Katherine's Dock bill, soon to become Secretary to the St. Katherine's Dock Company, succeeded by means of a trick in preventing this clause from being adopted, so that Fellowship Porters' rights received no recognition at all in the Act. Originally the Dock was not destined for grain, but a considerable corn trade gradually established itself there, all of which the Billingsgate Porters lost. The General Steam Navigation Company opened a steam-packet wharf within the St. Katherine's Dock, to which it transferred the discharge of potatoes and other measurable goods in 1849. This stimulated the Fellowship Porters once again to assert their claims, but the Wharf Superintendent rejected their demands out of hand; not only had Billingsgate Porters never before been admitted to St. Katherine's Dock, not only had they never demanded their rights at Brunswick Wharf, Blackwall, whence goods had only recently been diverted, but his main argument was that the exercise of such rights for very obvious and substantial reasons would not only be quite incompatible with satisfactory working at St. Katherine's Wharf, but would altogether inhibit the discharge of business. If an argument in such general terms sufficed to defeat the Porters' rights, there was indeed no hope left.

Though the Act establishing the first of the mid-century London docks, the Victoria Dock, contained a clause protecting the rights of the Corporation of London in respect of metage and porterage, little meaning attached to this any more as far as Porters were concerned. A dissentient minority among the Fellowship Porters still clamoured for legal action against dock companies refusing access to members in 1847, but the Court of Rulers by that time admitted the hopelessness of this claim. From the late 1840s the dock companies did as they liked. The repeal of the Corn Laws in 1846 had opened the floodgates. Dock companies employed Irish labourers at 2s. 6d. a day to work the corn with the City Deputy Corn Meters, while charging the corn trade porterage rates fixed for City Porters and pocketing the difference. The constant passage of steam vessels threatened to damage any corn ships trying to discharge in the Pool; practically the whole of the corn trade was driven to the docks, even when the companies there raised porterage charges above those of the Billingsgate Porters outside. Business was lost on the north bank earlier than on the south bank, but by 1860 the situation of the Porters was equally bad on both sides of the River, and the City Corporation refused to concern itself with it. The bulk of the trade moved down-river where newer and larger docks had been constructed; City Porters did not even attempt to assert their rights there and were reduced to accepting employment as dock labourers on the dock companies' terms, in complete disregard of any privileges that might have been theirs.[48]

5

THE INNHOLDERS' ATTACK

EORGANIZATION of Port of London facilities at the beginning of the nineteenth century drew attention to Porters' privileges at the waterside. Wherever new techniques for dealing with old problems were introduced, opportunity for reform arose; many of those anxious to modernize and streamline the cargo-handling services of the Port of London looked upon the loosening of the City Porters' stranglehold as one of the essential ingredients of reform. Waterside Porters, forming a target for merchants, wharfingers and dock promoters, occupied a more spectacular position than their uptown colleagues who around 1800 encountered only a few opponents. The most regular employment fell to Uptown Porters stationed in the various markets where goods for sale were unloaded and carried to salesmen's stands in the early morning; goods sold had to be transported to the purchasers' premises or vehicles. Uptown Ticket Porters in doing this work met with opposition chiefly from innholders. The large-scale traffic required to keep London supplied with food brought much business to London inns; country wagons and carts called with merchandise for the London produce markets. Innholders acted as agents for the suppliers, undertaking responsibility for the dispatch and sale of goods in the market and the remittance of the proceeds in the form of either money or purchases of whatever country suppliers required from London. Innholders developed ancillary services necessary to ply this profitable trade, especially the delivery of merchandise to salesmen in the markets by their own employees and often in their own carts. It was at this point that innholders found themselves obstructed by the privileges of the Uptown Ticket Porters.

Legally, the Ticket Porters' market privileges were ill-defined. Two innkeepers who in 1805 employed Ticket Porters for work in Newgate

Market and then withheld the money owed to them, escaped without punishment because the City's Law Officers regarded prosecution as too difficult. This at least was the reason officially advanced; lawyers being foremost in the fight to see the City Porters' privileges abolished, this obviously perverse opinion constituted merely one blow in the battle. The underlying plan became clearer five years later when the Society of the Inner Temple arranged a test case against the Uptown Porters. A foreigner, George Wagner, accepted from a member of the public in Fleet Street a letter for delivery, complete with porterage fee. Two Ticket Porters claimed the job as their prerogative; one of them sued Wagner in the Lord Mayor's Court. The Society of the Inner Temple thereupon financed Wagner to remove the case from the Lord Mayor's Court to that of King's Bench, in an attempt to have the privilege disproved once for all.

These had been preliminary skirmishes. The real battle was joined on 11 June 1819, when thirty-seven London innholders presented a petition to the Common Council to have the Ticket Porters' privileges set aside. They explained that their principal trade consisted in the accommodation of public transport and in the receipt, custody and delivery of goods conveyed to and from London. Many of them were themselves public transport contractors owning coaches and wagons; all required establishments in expensive central situations in the City and employed large numbers of servants. In the pursuit of this business innholders complained of interruption by Ticket Porters who claimed as their privilege the most profitable section of the whole trade, the delivery of goods within London, while refusing to perform any other part of the duties appertaining thereto and making no contribution to the capital or expenses entailed in maintaining the trade. To the innholders, neither the exertions nor the skill of the Ticket Porters appeared commensurate with their duties; the regulations under which they demanded the work, doubtfully expressed, had been enacted at a time before the trade of innholder had assumed its modern connotation.

Before the General Purposes Committee of the Common Council, a number of innholders substantiated these claims by oral evidence. Joseph Hearne, proprietor of the *King's Arms*, Snow Hill, talked of the many wagonloads of meat and butter which reached him every week and which in his capacity as carrier and innholder—he owned the Aylesbury and Winslow (Bucks.) wagons—he was responsible for delivering safely and expeditiously to Newgate Market. In his eighteen to twenty years as an innholder he had always effected his own deliveries, though on one occasion, when importuned by Ticket Porters, he had permitted them to deliver a wagonload in Newgate Market. The experience had not been encouraging : they had delivered all the merchandise addressed to stands within the market, but had refused to deal with some items consigned to destinations like Holborn, Clare Market and Westminster. His trouble with Ticket Porters was confined to Newgate Market; he also delivered poultry at Leadenhall Market by his own employees, but never encountered any obstruction there. The owner of the *Rose Inn*, Fleet Market, John Blomfield, a member of the Fellowship of Carmen, used his own licensed cart to deliver at Newgate Market meat sent up from the country in hampers and packs. He had been interrupted by Ticket Porters who charged as much for pitching meat out of his cart as he charged for carting and pitching combined.

Similar was the experience of the innholder of the *Three Cups*, Aldersgate Street. When Ticket Porters interrupted his meat deliveries in Newgate Market two years before, he declared himself willing to employ them instead of his own servants if they would work at his terms, but they refused to do any work other than pitching. They ran from wagon to wagon, picking and choosing their work instead of completing one job first; this meant that often wagons were held up for want of Porters to do the unloading, nor did he consider Ticket Porters competent to do the heavy work. In contrast, his own workers engaged on a weekly contract, in addition to unloading, collected empties and reloaded the wagons at no extra charge; they were under agreement to complete the job by 8 a.m., which Ticket Porters would never have done. A number of innholders and salesmen in Newgate Market gave further evidence to the effect that, for periods varying from twenty to sixty-six years, innholders had always used their own labour to unload their wagons in the market and that, when it came to reloading, Ticket Porters had either refused outright to do it or proved incompetent if they attempted it. In a separate memorial, ten salesmen from Newgate Market strongly supported the innholders. They argued that meat delivered by an innholder's single wagon at the Market had often been consigned from various parts of the country. The innholder alone knew both consignor and consignee and had prior information of merchandise arriving. Market hours were extremely short, putting a premium on prompt and correct delivery of so perishable an article as meat; empty hampers and covering cloths had to be quickly collected. Employment of Ticket Porters would cause delay affecting both quality and price of meat; hampers and cloths would not be collected and returned to carriers. Whereas in the case of wrong delivery responsibility now clearly attached to the innholder in charge, it would be impossible to discover the Ticket Porters responsible if they were allowed to handle the goods.

Evidence adduced by the Ticket Porters did not disprove any of these arguments. A stand for Ticket Porters existed at Newgate Market. Fifteen to twenty men were stationed there, their hours of work at this time of the year (this part of the hearing took place in midsummer) being from 1 to 7 a.m. One of the Ticket Porters present had worked in Newgate Market in 1779 and remembered proceeding in the Lord Mayor's Court against a master wagoner and his servant for doing Ticket Porters' work in the Market and winning his case. At that time, six to eight Ticket Porters attended Newgate Market. Strong opposition from wagoners and innholders dated mostly from recent years. In Leadenhall Market eight to ten Ticket Porters had worked from the 1780s, the earliest date remembered by anybody. A witness who had tried to work there as an inn porter in 1785 and had been prevented from doing so, gave evidence that he had been constrained to take up his freedom and membership of the Society of Tacklehouse and Ticket Porters. Ticket Porters' services had never caused any dispute at Leadenhall; salesmen were well satisfied and always paid full rates. No trouble had occurred until about 1814 or 1815, and in 1818 the Society's Court had deputed two Rulers to attend the Market and try to settle differences which had arisen. A good many country wagons did not go to inns at all but drove direct to markets where they had to be unloaded. Ticket Porters engaged in this work were employed neither by the wagoner nor by the salesman but by the distant supplier of the goods which they handled. Innholders and wagoners behaved antisocially in employing non-freemen and even aliens in the porterage of goods to the various markets and causing a great deal of obstruction to the public by unloading and reloading country wagons in the streets.

Opinions were strongly divided in the Select Committee, so much so that the innholders' application for permission to deliver all their goods by their own servants failed only as the result of the chairman's casting vote. On the other hand, the Committee deprecated any tightening of regulations in order to ease the Ticket Porters' task in enforcing their privileges, but considered existing powers of the Governor and Rulers quite adequate for this purpose. The Ticket Porters would have liked at least a public proclamation of their rights, but none was forthcoming.

Once the question of the markets had been raised, Uptown Ticket Porters found themselves exposed to obstruction in a number of places, often by innholders, but not always. Foreigners plying as porters in Bridge Street interfered with the work of Ticket Porters at the southern end of Fleet Market; in this case, the Alderman of the Ward was requested to instruct street keepers to deal with the nuisance. T. H. Giles, an innkeeper who had not taken part in the petition of 1819, interrupted Ticket Porters working at Newgate Market by insisting on the employment of his own labour in unloading meat. The Ticket Porters concerned summoned the meat salesman to the Court of Requests, but the Commissioners declined to adjudicate, on the ground that the matter was too important. Giles in turn began an action in the Court of King's Bench against the Newgate Ticket Porters. Five years after having proclaimed on the innholders' earlier petition, the Common Council's General Purposes Committee faced the same issue again and referred it to the City Solicitor, who recommended prosecuting one of the unauthorized porters working in the market; he did not advise the Corporation to defend the action brought by Giles. As the porters sued would be poor men unable to pay any fine which might be imposed, whereas Giles was a substantial innholder, this amounted to denial of a legal remedy. At Leadenhall Market, where much better relationships existed than at Newgate, a report in 1826 that salesmen were employing non-freemen led to an investigation by a committee of the Court of the Tacklehouse and Ticket Porters. It declared the complaint groundless, yet at the same time recommended the dispatch of some strong Porters to Leadenhall Market—an indication that there must have been some cause for dissatisfaction.[49]

6

THE ALL-OUT ATTACK

(a) Markets

I N outlying parts of the Port, on the wharves, in the docks and in the markets—everywhere the City Porters' privileges suffered attack. Everywhere they lost ground, neither immediately nor completely, but steadily. The City Corporation defended them reluctantly, shamefacedly, dilatorily, yet did not completely abandon them. But the City fathers consisted of elected members. Porters did not belong to the social class seeking election to the Common Council or the Court of Aldermen, whereas it was from men such as their opponents—wharfingers, dock directors, innholders, corn merchants— that City representatives were pre-eminently recruited. Hence the power to complete the Porters' defeat rested within the City parliament. On this battlefield all the enemies of the City Porters eventually met.

The Society of Tacklehouse and Ticket Porters in 1831 rashly applied to the Common Council for aid in defraying the legal expenses of establishing its members' rights. The General Purposes Committee recommended a £50 donation, but the question could not be put for lack of a quorum. When reopened on the following day, the report was referred back for reconsideration, accompanied by a mandate to examine and report how far the privileges claimed by Tacklehouse, Ticket and Billingsgate Porters were injurious to the trade of the City of London. Unmistakably a new wind blew in the Common Council; its chill struck, above all, the Fellowship Porters who had done nothing at that moment to draw attention to themselves, but now asked to be represented at the enquiry and submitted a list of witnesses they wished to call. They were very conscious of the fact that their privileges mostly derived from Common Council Acts two hundred years old, carelessly drafted and obscurely worded, forming a very insecure basis for litigation and protected by fines reflecting a much higher value of money in the past. However, in this enquiry the Billingsgate Porters took a back seat; it was the doom of the Society of Tacklehouse and Ticket Porters which was being sealed.

The main attack on the Ticket Porters, being delivered partly by meat salesmen, partly by innkeepers, concentrated once again on their activities at Newgate Market. Much of the evidence recapitulated assertions from the 1819 enquiry: innkeepers claimed that, so far as they transferred in their yards to a single innholder's cart loads of meat received from three or four country wagons, they acted as a clearing-house, reduced congestion, and contributed to the efficient functioning of deliveries. By the employment of their own staff they speeded up the process of pitching merchandise, reloading and removing wagons from markets. So far as country suppliers of meat required goods from town, only innkeepers could be trusted with buying, storing and dispatching them. As Ticket Porters claimed payment in proportion to the quantity of goods handled, they tried to pitch as much merchandise as possible; in their feverish haste they unloaded badly and damaged the goods, increasing the total price by 33 per cent as a consequence of such negligence. Because they received no remuneration for returning empty hampers, Ticket Porters did not bother to do so; the Deputy conducting the case against the Ticket Porters, in his capacity as a meat salesman, had learnt from a policeman at 11 o'clock on a Saturday that a hamper belonging to him and worth 15s. had been found in the middle of Newgate Street; a Ticket Porter had collected it from his premises at 6 o'clock. Ticket Porters were paid better for delivering meat open than packed; thus, particularly when business was slack, Ticket Porters surreptitiously untied hampers and delivered the meat loose in order to earn the higher rates. They proved more competent in pitching individual carcasses than packed meat. Pitching-pay for meat being better than for vegetables and fruit, Ticket Porters either kept gardeners' carts waiting while dealing with the meat, or did not bother to unload greenstuffs at all, but employed Irish labourers to do it on their behalf, paying them a very small wage out of the 2s. 6d. a wagon or 1s. 6d. a cart demanded by themselves. Gardeners could see no reason, if Irish labour were used to unload their goods, why they should not employ such labour direct.

Salesmen admitted that Ticket Porters had their uses where merchandise was not consigned to an innkeeper, but direct to the market as part of a mixed load of goods. The driver of the wagon recognized a Ticket Porter as a person authorized to unload the goods by virtue of the ticket he wore, when otherwise a crook might easily gain access. But the method suggested by the Ticket Porters—of sending goods, accompanied by way-bills specifying various recipients, direct to the market in the charge of wagoners—would not work because wagoners, few of whom could read, could not decipher way-bills and instruct Ticket Porters to whom to deliver, nor would the consignor be protected against dishonest wagoners. Meat purchasers usually brought their own carts to market, employing labourers to carry their meat first to the scale to be weighed, then to their carts. There were many bad characters among such labourers; witnesses considered that this work might well be done by Ticket Porters. This indeed was the practice of some buyers who, however, insisted on always being served by the same Ticket Porters and not by whichever Ticket Porters happened to be available.

Ticket Porters' evidence concentrated on Leadenhall Market, where conditions favoured them. There, unloading by Ticket Porters of wagons coming direct from the country was the rule, and salesmen declared themselves satisfied with this procedure. About twelve Ticket Porters attended every morning from 3.30 to 7 a.m. More would come if there were more work to do, but although unloading in inn-yards and delivery by innholders' servants had started only recently and in a minority of cases, this encroachment by the innkeepers had left insufficient employment even for these twelve. When inn porters were resorted to, wagons often had to stand in the market for an hour before they arrived; the horses had to be taken out, thus increasing congestion. Leadenhall Market salesmen disliked it on account of this delay as well as the need to resist the higher charges, on an average double those of Ticket Porters, and finally because of the greater strength and fitness of the Ticket Porters, of whom only one or two on account of age fell below standard. Ticket Porters were in attendance from midnight onwards, if necessary, and unloaded so quickly that there was no need to uncouple the horses. The main business of the market was done between 5 and 7 a.m., and unless unloading had been completed by 5 o'clock, it interfered with selling. Mixed loads presented no difficulty to Ticket Porters, if labelled properly; if labels were lost or defaced, neither a Ticket Porter nor an innkeeper, but only the wagoner could sort out the load, and if his memory failed him, the consignment was sold and the money handed to the wagoner to pay over to whoever claimed it at the other end. Ticket Porters in Leadenhall Market neither returned, nor were expected to return, empties; this was done in the afternoon by salesmen's or innholders' employees; Leadenhall Market had ample space, so the empties were not in anybody's way. Salesmen considered the Ticket Porters' charges reasonable, but had to admit that innkeepers did not like the preference given to Ticket Porters and therefore to the best of their ability diverted business from Leadenhall to Newgate Market. On the strength of this evidence, the General Purposes Committee preferred Leadenhall to Newgate Market conditions and pronounced decisively in favour of the Ticket Porters against the innholders, merely suggesting a reduced table of porterage rates to satisfy Newgate Market objectors.[50]

That the innholders manifested disgust at this outcome of their efforts had to be expected. In a petition placed before the Common Council in 1834 they tried to enlist support for 'freedom of trade in the City', rallying sixty-six salesmen to their plea. On the other side, thirty-two salesmen signed a certificate of support for the Ticket Porters' case. The General Purposes Committee remained unshaken, repeating its previous recommendations and adding the suggestion of a £50 cash contribution to the legal expenses of the Society of Tacklehouse and Ticket Porters; the Common Council disagreed with this view. Where this resistance on the part of the Common Council centred, became obvious two years later when Bush, proprietor of the *Vine Inn*, Bishopsgate, not only refused the Ticket Porters work at Leadenhall Market, but had two of them taken into custody for demanding the labour. The Leadenhall Market Ticket Porters complained to the Court of Aldermen against Bush in a petition which in the Repertories reads like all other petitions, but of which the first draft was less conventional. A passage scored out and omitted in the final version ran:

> . . . and your Petitioners are exceedingly sorry to be obliged to state that the Innkeeper above alluded to is encouraged in his persecution of your Petitioners by The Lord Mayor who has declared the whole body of Ticket Porters to be a nuisance and threatened them with imprisonment for persisting in their labour in order to obtain a livelihood for their wives and children.
>
> That your Petitioners are exceedingly sorry if any Ticket Porter has offended His Lordship which His Lordship has stated to be the case but they humbly submit that such ought not to be a ground for His Lordship's exercising his high power and authority to the detriment of the whole body.

This explanatory passage did not eventually appear in the official petition; records do not reveal in which way His Lordship eventually exercised his high power and authority, but the Court of Aldermen refused to act, referring the Ticket Porters to their legal remedies. The verdict went against them at the London Sessions, the Recorder suggesting that as the Ticket Porters laboured under the impression that they had rights, their case might well be met by granting them compensation for loss of employment. The Court of the Tacklehouse and Ticket Porters' Society took up this suggestion in a resolution which, after deeply regretting the Common Council's refusal to confirm the views of its General Purposes Committee, asked the Corporation either to support Ticket Porters in the exercise of their just rights and privileges or to compensate them for the loss sustained by the prejudice created against their services. But the powers that be had no wish to adopt either course. Only once more, in 1851, did the Ticket Porters complain to the Common Council about interruption by innkeepers. That petition was read, but no order was made thereon.

(b) Steam-packet Landing-places

Another battlefront had emerged at the landing-places of steam-packet services. In 1831 the Margate and Gravesend Steam Packet Company complained that at Fresh Wharf, London Bridge, Ticket Porters daily forced their way violently on to steamboats, practising incivilities and impositions against passengers; the writer of the letter, the Company's Secretary and Agent, had a day or two earlier been struck with great violence and nearly forced into the water by a Ticket Porter in a hurry to board the boat. The Packet Company suggested that in future only a limited number of Ticket Porters be authorized to work on steam-packet wharves, such Porters not to board vessels unless hired or called by a passenger, to leave them promptly when requested, and to be removable for transgressions. As one of the Ticket Porters' old enemies, John Blenkarne,* was partner in the Packet Company, the evidence could not be expected to be biased in their favour, but cast the worst possible light on their behaviour. Many of them, drunk and using foul language, fought each other for the right to carry ashore passengers' luggage and to call cabs. The authorized charge was 2d. per package, but if a passenger had a large number of packages and chose to carry some himself, the Porters nevertheless charged for all of them; if passengers looked as though they did not know the proper fees, they were usually overcharged—a safe practice since passengers would have to prosecute at their own expense and remain at hand in London until the case came on. Ticket Porters had been angered by a reduction in their rates decreed by the Rulers, largely at the request of Jackson, who as Merchant Taylors' Tacklehouse Porter was himself a Ruler, but also a wharfinger at Fresh Wharf; they sabotaged the new charges. Another of their tricks consisted of preventing coaches from approaching the landing-stage so as to discourage passengers from handling their own luggage and to carry invalid passengers all the way from the packet to the coach. These abuses could easily be obviated, as was disclosed by the practice in St. Katherine's Dock. Twelve Ticket Porters only were admitted within the gates, hand-picked by the Dock Company's Secretary and liable to dismissal for misconduct. They worked at the steam-packet landing-stage and paid all their takings into a common fund, thus removing any Porter's temptation to cut out his colleagues in an endeavour to increase his own earnings.

At Custom House Stairs the problem had arisen in an acute form as early as 1808 when a Fellowship Porter, carrying a passenger's trunk off a packet, had been set upon by several Ticket Porters claiming the

* See p. 131 above.

work, and subsequently beaten and arrested by a City police officer on a charge of breach of the peace. The Alderman trying the case dismissed the charge, but in order to prevent further scuffles temporarily found in the Ticket Porters' favour. The decision held good for fifteen years. In 1823, Billingsgate Porters again claimed a share in the work on the plea that it formed part of 'catching burdens' open to both groups of Porters.* Ticket Porters, on the contrary, contended that it came under the description of 'burthen labour' allocated to them alone, of which the allowance in their rates for landing and carrying baggage, trunks or bundles constituted abundant evidence. This view carried the day; a committee of Aldermen investigating the rival claims awarded the work exclusively to the Ticket Porters. No further trouble arose at Custom House Stairs until 1851 when inconvenience and annoyance was experienced 'owing to the intrusion of parties calling themselves Ticket Porters', persons of abusive and boisterous conduct who made exorbitant charges for the conveyance into and from the baggage warehouse of packages of passengers arriving from foreign parts, many of them in poor circumstances.

The employment of Ticket Porters in the service of passengers at steam-packet wharves was one of the matters investigated by the Common Council's General Purposes Committee in 1832–33, which reached the conclusion that it afforded the best security to passengers landing and embarking at such wharves, but suggested an official scale of charges as well as the grant to wharfingers of disciplinary powers over the Ticket Porters employed at their premises, including rights of suspension for improper conduct. This recommendation hung fire for ten years. In 1843 the Secretary of the General Steam Navigation Company drew the attention of the Court of Registers and Rulers to it; only then did the Court agree to wharfingers' exercising such powers in future over Ticket Porters at their wharves.[51]

(c) Sufferance Wharves

Meanwhile much cargo work originally handled at the legal quays had sought other outlets. Wharfingers, prominent among them the Ticket Porters' enemy, John Blenkarne, unhesitatingly attributed the loss of

* See pp. 69–70 above.

the Irish trade to the Ticket Porters and to no other cause: in 1822 the law had permitted Irish imports to be discharged at the sufferance wharves on the south bank, and there they had gone and stayed, in spite of the great inconvenience arising from the overcrowding of sufferance wharves and the fact that nine-tenths of the goods eventually had to be carted across London Bridge at great expense in time, wear and tear, to be sold on the north bank. Many warehouses on the City side stood vacant, ready to receive Irish imports which in former days London had sent to customers as far afield as Maldon or Yarmouth; now these places imported their own, and London had lost the business. Irish trade formerly handled in Thames Street had gone to the St. Katherine's Dock when it opened in 1828. Similarly the American trade had been drawn to one or other of the docks, and the legal quays saw it no more. Wharfingers insisted that it was the character of the Ticket Porters, not their charges, which had driven the trade away, and that they would not employ Ticket Porters even if their services were available free of charge.

The evidence suggested to the General Purposes Committee of the Common Council that causes other than Ticket Porters bore responsibility for the loss of most of this trade. In order to encourage its return to the quays and wharves within the City, the Committee proposed to increase the number of Ticket Porters available; to permit wharfingers and merchants to employ either Tacklehouse or Ticket Porters at their option in the handling of coastwise, Irish or North American goods; to grant wharfingers control over Ticket Porters in the same manner as had been proposed for steam-packet wharves; and to bring into force a scale of reduced charges submitted by the Society of Tacklehouse and Ticket Porters. The principle followed by the General Purposes Committee was embodied in the words:

that it is not expedient for the Corporation to protect any labour which does not promote the public interest; that the employment of Tackle House, Ticket and Fellowship Porters under judicious arrangements and with such reasonable charges as will afford a fair remuneration is productive of great general benefit, by affording sufficient security to merchants, traders and the public in removing with facility, care and dispatch their goods, wares and merchandizes.

This was a view of the Porters' usefulness more favourable than prevailed generally in the 1830s; after reconsidering it once or twice, the Common Council accepted this part of the report early in 1834. The Royal Commission on Municipal Corporations in England and Wales three years later came to a different conclusion: it refused to believe that the City Corporation's privilege of porterage for hire possessed the virtues claimed for it; the advantage derived by the public from a responsible body furnishing surety for losses occasioned by the misconduct of Porters could be put beyond dispute only if such Porters obtained employment in free competition with others not so regulated; the price of labour was bound to be enhanced by the emoluments of several officers which had to be defrayed out of it, as well as by pensions and gratuities afforded to decayed Porters. That merchants enjoyed guarantees against frauds in measuring and delivery did not impress the Commissioners, since they had received no complaints from ports where such protection did not exist. It was in keeping with this view that a judge in the City of London Court in 1885 ruled all Acts of the Common Council constituting and governing the Society of Billingsgate Porters and all acts of the Fellowship Rulers null and void, because *ultra vires*. That indeed had been the view proclaimed by the Porters' enemies for almost a century. But even in 1885 the judge's decision was reversed by the Court of Queen's Bench. As late as 1891 the City of London Court admitted, though with regret, a Billingsgate Porter's right to claim his work.[52]

III
THE DECLINE

1

GENERAL

(a) Outliers and Full-time Porters

To everybody except themselves, the City Porters had by the early nineteenth century become an embarrassment. A few among them had moved to better-paid and more profitable occupations. After having risen to these heights, some kicked away the ladder leading back to their humble origin by cutting their links with Porters' organizations—invariably so where conflict with the fellowship's hierarchy had inaugurated the excursion into new fields. Porters had no worse enemies than former colleagues who knew their organizations and weaknesses from within and brought personal experience to bear on exposing the hollowness of their claims. Severing connection with the Porters represented a move up the social scale; nobody with ambitions to rise in the world could afford to be looked upon as a mere Porter.

Even among the more affluent, membership of one of the Porters' organizations was not unknown. Some employers of Porters treated it as a convenience: disciplinary action could be taken more easily from within than from without the Porters' organization; by citing a refractory Porter before the Rulers, they brought the fellowship's self-governing machinery into play. This consideration would have enlisted a good many members if it had been more effective, but contractors were disappointed in their hopes of successful action by the Rulers in ensuring better porterage services. A few employers, actuated by no utilitarian motives, maintained a titular membership merely by contributing to the Porters' funds as a form of charity. Yet others remained members as a precaution. Though they had attained prosperity by engaging in different occupations and had outgrown the need for carrying burdens on their backs, they could never foresee in an uncertain world whether their luck would hold, and it was as well not to burn their boats. To continue paying regular subscriptions to one of the Porters' fellowships cost very little while earnings were good. If such members suddenly fell on evil days, no question arose as to their right to resume porterage work. More than that, fellowships were organized to favour members of longer standing; by paying a lifetime's contributions, but taking up activities only late, a man graduated to the more worthwhile and easier jobs without having first to pass through the onerous and ill-paid ones. Fellowships further made some provision for superannuation; a member of many years' standing might even qualify for such support in his old age without being put to the proof of how long he had actually laboured as a Porter. To such men, membership represented a cheap form of social insurance; while they hoped the occasion for claiming their rights would not arise, the existence of the rights diminished their material insecurity.

Between the Porter looking entirely to fellowship labour for his support and the man who had left porterage but kept his foot in the door against the economic blizzard which might drive him back to the shelter of privileged employment, there were many with at least a foothold in some other trade, but compelled or tempted seasonally to resume porterage. So far as it corresponded to the periodic changes in demand for porterage services, this influx and withdrawal of 'outliers' was of considerable benefit to an occupation which always experienced extreme difficulties in matching supply with demand; apart from seasonal peaks which were expected and could be provided for by organization, porterage demand suffered from sudden and unforeseen fluctuations, and no labour force geared to peak demand could hope to find employment all the year round. A group of occupationally mobile outliers, ready to swell the ranks of Porters when needed, yet able in slack periods to move into alternative work, could have acted as an ideal regulator of labour supply. But it is unlikely that many outliers found themselves so favourably circumstanced. What determined their movements into and out of portering was the demand, not for porterage services, but for the output of their alternative occupations. No reason exists to assume that fluctuations in such trades would dovetail at all with fluctuations in porterage employment; on the contrary, in all probability both were geared to the general movement of the business cycle, causing outliers to seek porterage jobs while their trade was depressed, when unemployment prevailed even among full-time Porters, and to withdraw to their chief occupations just as business revived in the porterage line.

In maintaining their membership and making their labour available at times and for reasons no longer connected with the provision of porterage services in London, outliers tended to amplify fluctuations in employment; they also caused a conflict of interest which baffled Rulers. In small organizations it would have been easy from personal knowledge to identify working and inactive Porters. With a membership numbering thousands, of whom a sizable proportion had ceased to work as Porters at all or confined their porterage activities to certain seasons of the year, two groups of members with different and often divergent interests arose: working Porters, anxious to be sure of employment, mistrusted seniority which might give outliers an advantage over them; nor should outliers be entitled to work only when it suited them, but be liable to obey a summons to work whenever labour fell short of requirements. This demand was solidly anchored in the rules and regulations of their organizations, but any effective enforcement would have proved unacceptable to outliers, not only to those who in season expected to follow their better-paid and less irksome trades, but even more to those who maintained membership without any intention of ever working at porterage at all. Labouring Porters also wanted superannuation benefits reserved to men who had worn themselves out in portering, instead of being bestowed indiscriminately on members proving the longest record of contributions. Such distinctions presupposed the identification of outliers for the purpose of subjecting them to different regulations. Outliers, on the other hand, resented discrimination and did not look upon themselves as members of a different kind. To have established without their co-operation when they had last worked at porterage, or how much time every year they passed in porterage as distinct from their other employment, would have required a far stronger and more efficient administration than the fellowships possessed; not only were existing instruments blunt and inaccurate, but it was to the outliers'

advantage that they should remain so. To the extent to which a decision
between the conflicting interests depended on the Court of Rulers, both
groups strongly contested elections to that Court. Whatever other part
outliers played or did not play in the fellowships, they could be relied
upon to put up candidates for rulership. So far as election could be
swayed by the disbursement of funds to influence voters, outliers
were in a stronger position than working Porters to provide their
candidates with substantial support. Whether a labouring Porter or not,
once a man had been elected a Ruler, he found himself more and more
engulfed in administrative duties. Well might he struggle to earn his
living by porterage in the intervals of exercising rulership functions,
but only by neglecting the latter could he find time, hence he had to be
paid for administrative duties if these were not to remain unfulfilled.
From whichever faction he had originally been drawn, a Ruler in
office became in fact an outlier, a man personally more concerned with
rights of seniority and standing in the fellowship than with the livelihood afforded to the organization's backbone, the labouring Porter.

(b) Supersedure of Porters

The great majority of members of course remained labouring Porters.
Indeed, their traditional way of life and work changed remarkably
little. In retrospect it is easy to see that they would eventually be
displaced by mechanical handling devices, that transport development
cast them for the part played by the handloom weavers in the industrial
revolution. Even in the early nineteenth century this was by no means
clear to contemporaries; they saw in the displacement of Porters an
infringement of old monopolies, a delivery from ancient privileges
which had outlived their usefulness, but not the inevitable supersedure
by technical progress. The process appeared to be arbitrary, fostered by
entrepreneurs who had hitherto availed themselves of the Porters'
services, but had now decided, in the pursuit of the free and competitive
economy which they had been taught to consider most advantageous
to themselves, to employ what labour they liked and to ride roughshod
over the Porters' rights. Though in the long run a misconception, this
interpretation drew support, at least for waterside Porters, from the
technical backwardness of the Port of London. Throughout the

nineteenth century, those outports which had not dropped out of the race altogether on account of inability to accommodate the ever-larger vessels constructed, modernized their facilities more quickly and effectively than London. The French wars with their opportunities for entrepôt trade inaugurated a dock boom in London which had spent itself with the coming of peace in 1815; very little technical innovation took place between then and the middle of the century when the second wave of dock-building started, but considerably further down-river. A certain amount of steam equipment was introduced at the same time, but the real conversion of the Port to its modern shape and method had to await the coming of the Port of London Authority in the twentieth century, well after the Porters' demise as such. The technical backwardness of the nineteenth-century Porter of London matched that of the Port of London, so that the former did not appear out of place in the latter; astonishingly little change of technique took place in the Porters' activities throughout the seven centuries of their known existence, and of such change more occurred in the last fifty years than in all the previous period. Were it possible to measure the productivity of Porters thoughout these ages, it would be found not to have increased significantly.

In the absence of substantial increase in productivity, Porters could establish no convincing case for improved real earnings, but remained a depressed occupation right up to the end. Those who felt that by acquiring special skill they could claim to have improved their product-ivity, contracted out by forming a crafts union representing their separate interest; hence the Amalgamated Society of Stevedores. Porterage, the residual unskilled occupation, continued to attract floating labour coming to London and looking for ways of earning a living. Who were these newcomers who swelled the ranks of regular Port workers? It is difficult to know. The number of Catholic churches in dockland suggests Ireland as one of the countries of origin; the name of an occasional Porter who has penetrated into one of the fellowships hints at German immigration; but for every one who may thus be attributed to a particular section, there are ten without any marks of identification, still the flotsam borne into London on the tide of economic change throughout the country as it had been in the sixteenth century. But then the City of London had by its intervention stabilized the labour market and discharged its police functions; it had introduced a licensing system by compelling Porters to take up the City's freedom and join the appropriate organizations; this had enabled it to sweep out the remainder by employing ward constables in giving effect to vagrancy legislation. Times and economic opinion had changed: no longer was such interference suffered, nor could the City of London make of its freedom a prize for which working men found it worth their while to contend.

One power was left: Porters' organizations, being the City's creations, could be kept closed to newcomers; membership could be maintained at a fixed level or even reduced. This, however, did not in the circumstances of the nineteenth century exclude competitors; it merely diverted them. Even by the late eighteenth century the larger wharfingers had made attempts to have their porterage work done by casual labour, engaged on contractual terms unrelated to the status of Porter. When the docks opened in the nineteenth century, they used the authority of Parliament and their special position of responsibility for the Customs revenue to legalize the exemption which wharfingers had merely usurped; compensation to authorized City Porters they might be willing to pay, but employ them they would not. Steam-packet wharves and innholders in and near the City markets joined in this game of beggar-the-Porter which, by the time an entirely new method of goods transport appeared in the shape of railways, the Porters had all but lost. Parliamentary policy banished railway termini to the more outlying parts of London, areas in which Porters had rarely found much employment; here not even tradition spoke in their favour, as in the markets and at the waterside. Hence railway companies had no difficulty at all in reserving porterage work to their own staff. All these employers made use of City Porters much as mechanized cotton mills made use of handloom weavers: if after running their own establishments to capacity they had any surplus work, they were not averse to giving this out to the representatives of the older industrial order; similarly, they welcomed the Porters' assistance during industrial disputes with their regular staff—casting Porters in the rôle of strike-breakers did not endear them to their unionized competitors and hardly augured well for their future. But just as handloom weavers could less and less eke out a livelihood on the small surplus of orders left when the power looms had taken their fill, so Porters found the scope of their activities more and more circumscribed; in other words, they were being starved out of existence.

Like handloom weavers, the Porters were an unconscionable time a-dying, partly because the carrying of burdens, requiring nothing but brawn, continued to attract men who had failed in more skilled trades long after it had ceased to offer any real prospects, partly because newcomers to the occupation while young and strong were more likely to make ends meet than older men weakened by a working life of physical strain. So far as Porters' organizations still retained any control, they exercised it in an attempt to alleviate their older members' lot. This exposed them to twofold protests: younger Porters saw positions of influence and better-paid work reserved for senior men; the older Porters, in spite of the preference enjoyed, found themselves less and less able to make a living. Thus, not only had Porters to contend with powerful enemies from without, but also the last decades of their corporate existence were marred by violent internal dissensions. However pathetic the maintenance of privileged corporations reduced to purposelessness by economic development, it was bound to be futile. That recognition took a century to dawn upon the Porters themselves, a whole century before they realized that the Port of London would be a great deal better without them.

2

TACKLEHOUSE AND TICKET PORTERS

(a) Waterside Work

Not many sectors of work continued to be contested between the Tacklehouse and Ticket Porters. The old question of transhipped goods arose once more in 1812 over a cargo of clover seed loaded at Ostend, landed at Ramsgate, thence dispatched to London in a different vessel; the Ticket Porters made a last attempt to claim this cargo as coastwise goods, but it was allocated to the Tacklehouse Porters. A consignment of oil from Newfoundland in 1822 raised the question whether Newfoundland formed part of Hudson's Bay, Quebec, Canada or Nova Scotia; this being denied, the imports belonged to the Tacklehouse Porters as coming from territory north of the United States. Waterside Ticket Porters, seeking relief after much loss of work, met with refusal on the ground that they had received under the Docks Acts the compensation due to them.

They had periodically suffered from the intrusion of watermen into their work; in 1819, watermen again performed certain labour belonging to the Ticket Porters, but declared themselves willing to give up the labour if so instructed by high authority. The Society's Court asked the Lord Mayor to intervene, but he declined. The records do not indicate how the contest was settled, but in 1827 Ticket Porters at the Custom House petitioned the Court of Rulers not to admit any watermen to their Society—a petition ordered to lie on the table. On that occasion watermen at Tower Stairs had forcibly seized and carried the luggage of intending steamboat passengers arriving in coaches at Tower Hill and Thames Street, defying the Ticket Porters' privileges; a fight had ensued in which the watermen prevailed by force of numbers. The law, as represented by a Middlesex magistrate, had taken the watermen's side in indicting a Ticket Porter for assault. Had it been a

London magistrate, the Ticket Porters' chances would have been poor, but against a Middlesex intruder the City's Police Committee promptly instructed the City Solicitor to defend the Ticket Porter. In the end both sides refrained from prosecution, but this did not forever still the fights between watermen and Ticket Porters at Tower Stairs. Soon after the Metropolitan Police had come into existence, one of its members in 1830 witnessed a brawl there and took a Ticket Porter into custody. The Society of Tacklehouse and Ticket Porters thereupon acquainted the Commissioners of Police officially with their members' right to demand work at Tower Stairs. Scuffle-hunters, unauthorized men always on the look-out for porters' jobs, caused the Society to renew its complaints to the Police Commissioners ten years later.

The Society of Tacklehouse and Ticket Porters made only occasional attempts to regulate the methods of work of its waterside members. In 1810 its Court expressed regret that nobody but the Governor personally could give permission to a Ticket Porter to leave ship's work; in 1833 it suggested that on each wharf one Porter should be authorized to control the others and wield disciplinary powers. No action resulted from either of these proposals and the Society did not pursue them. When the landing of herrings became a seasonal and profitable job at Billingsgate Stairs, occasionally and exceptionally at Fresh Wharf Steam Packet Station, the Society granted permission to Ticket Porters to take regular turns at the work; it did the same for red herring, pickled and dried fish work at the Custom House in 1840.

Complaints resulted that Ticket Porters not only charged for the job six-and-a-half times the rate at which it was done by non-freemen, but that they were too lazy to carry barrels of herring in a sling between two Porters, but rolled them along the ground, damaging the contents and injuring passers-by. At steamboat landing-places, Porters sometimes wrested luggage forcibly from passengers' servants; in 1817 the Society cautioned all Porters by publishing in *The Times* punitive proceedings taken against a member guilty of such conduct. When the more delicate female passengers objected to Porters smoking, the practice was forbidden in 1829. In order to prevent Porters from fighting for jobs at steamboat landing-places, the Society's Court made steamboat passenger

N

work at Custom House into turn labour in 1832, but continued to allow all Porters to join in cargo work. Porters anxious to increase their earnings tied small packages together and carried a number of them simultaneously; if the cord broke, pieces of luggage dropped to the ground and were damaged; such labour-saving was explicitly prohibited in 1836. At the Custom House each Porter could take on as many packages as he could carry without tying them up, the work to be performed in turn, and no Porter carrying luggage to a coach was to leave until its doors had been closed in order to prevent annoyance from scuffle-hunters. Except on the legal quays, Ticket Porters rarely worked in gangs, but for the purpose of better discipline the St. Katherine's Wharf had introduced the pooling of receipts among its Porter force and a voluntary arrangement to the same effect prevailed at the Custom House, also among the fish carriers who paid a commission to a publican to advance their earnings to them promptly.

Ticket Porters at the waterside often faced the accusation of demanding far more money than their work was worth, but as wharfingers and others usually refused to employ Ticket Porters, whatever the level of charges, no revision of the waterside rates fixed for Ticket Porters took place, apart from the voluntary reduction enacted by the Court of Rulers for passenger luggage at steam-packet wharves.* At Billingsgate in 1829 the volume of work in carrying barrels of red herrings to fish merchants' premises justified the Court of Rulers in voluntarily reducing charges below the rates fixed by the Common Council. Having volunteered reductions both for steam-packet and herring work, the Society did not propose to tamper again with these rates when invited by the Common Council in 1833 to submit a scale of prices for labour adapted to the contemporary price level, but expressed readiness to reduce rates for landing goods in the Irish trade. Nothing in the end was done to put these proposals into practice.[53]

(b) Uptown Work

Uptown Porters wore white aprons as the uniform of their trade. In addition they should have displayed their tickets. To counter the activities of impostors and intruders, the Society in 1838 altered the

---

* See p. 163 above.

badge to a metal shield showing the City arms on one side, the wearer's Christian and surnames and number, date of admission and stand on the other; but the public took its cue from the aprons, so that non-freemen wearing white aprons were often mistaken for Ticket Porters. It was impossible to forbid anybody to wear a white apron; the Society could only circularize known customers and draw attention by public notices to the deception practised. Occasionally the Society still succeeded in having intruders fined in the Lord Mayor's Court and thrown into a debtors' prison for inability to pay the fines imposed. When a new officer at the Post Office prevented Ticket Porters from being admitted to carry the luggage of arriving passengers, the Post-master-General could still be prevailed upon to promise that all Ticket Porters displaying their badges openly should be admitted. But the Uptown Porters also suffered from large-scale attempts to supplant them. A firm of solicitors on behalf of clients in 1825 approached the Society of Tacklehouse and Ticket Porters for a licence to establish a parcel delivery service in town, an application referred to the City authorities as the original holders of the privilege. The project, like many mooted in the boom of 1824–25, came to nothing. Far more serious was the founding of the Corps of Commissionaires, well organized and disciplined by Captain Edward Walter to render services of an efficiency which the Ticket Porters had long ceased to equal. Almost with its dying breath the Court of the Society of Tacklehouse and Ticket Porters objected in 1861 to the Corps extending its sphere of activity to the City, but in vain.

The Society's functions regarding Uptown Porters were more positive because it had to keep the pitching-blocks in good condition. The block at Smithfield required repair in 1810; a new block to replace one removed from Bull Head Court, Newgate Street, in 1815 was erected alongside the wall of Newgate Gaol and removed to the back of the pump at the end of the coach stand in the Old Bailey in 1827; the assistance of the Court of Aldermen had to be invoked in 1818 against the refusal of the St. Benet's, Fenchurch Street, church-wardens to allow the re-erection of a pitching-block removed from that church during repairs; in 1823 the Society's Court set up a committee to survey and report on all its pitching-blocks, as a result of which repairs were carried out to blocks at St. Paul's, London Bridge, Royal Exchange, and the southern end of Fleet Market. If an Uptown Porter wished to change his stand, he had to obtain the Court's permission and pay a 5s. fee. As work shrank in the 1820s, the Court was flooded with requests from the various stands not to increase the number of Porters stationed there: the first came from the Lad Lane stand in 1821 and caused the Court to ask for a comprehensive list of stands and Ticket Porters* and to appoint a committee to report on the number appropriate for each stand. A standstill order operated pending this report, but as nothing further happened, Aldgate stand in 1822 asked for and obtained an embargo on further admissions. Similar requests came in 1823 from the stands in Temple Gate, Exchange South, Doctors' Commons and Gracechurch Street (the latter repeated in 1829), in 1824 from Broad Street, in 1826 from Exchange South East and in 1827 from Newgate Market; only in the last case was the request complied with. On the other hand occasional requests reached the Society for the stationing of Porters in new locations; in 1828 two inhabitants of Gracechurch Street suggested that four of the eight Porters plying in that street should transfer their station from the *Spread Eagle* to the *Cross Keys*, and in 1835 the inhabitants of George Yard, Lombard Street, not only improved the entrance to their Yard, but provided seats in the archway to induce the Society to station two or three Porters there. In 1840 the Society opened its last new stand in the Minories near the terminus of the Blackwall Railway.

In Newgate Market the Society of Tacklehouse and Ticket Porters faced the dilemma that certain meat traders would employ only their regular Ticket Porters,† whereas the other Ticket Porters wanted the work distributed for the general benefit by making it turn labour and asserted that this had been the original practice. After fourteen years of procrastination the Court eventually agreed in 1842; by that time little labour was left for Ticket Porters in the Market. A proposal that the Court of Rulers should in each market appoint one Ticket Porter as foreman to control and discipline the others came to nothing.

A detailed table of rates for uptown work formed part of the

---

* See pp. 56–59 above.   † See p. 160 above.

Common Council Act of 1823. It standardized loads by weight: under 56 lb., from 56 lb. to 1 cwt., and from 1 to 1½ cwt. For each weight the charge varied according to distance, the minimum relating to a quarter of a mile, the next stage to a distance of between one-quarter and half a mile, and then going up in jumps of half a mile each; every half-mile above two miles added 6d. to the charge for the lightest, 9d. for the medium, and 1s. for the heaviest load. If, however, the load weighed less than 14 lb. and the Porter combined it with an equally small return load—a provision designed for letters and messages—he could charge only half the rate for the return load. Fifty-two Ticket Porters in a petition to their Court of Rulers expressed their dissatisfaction with the standard rate of 9d. for the porterage of a burden not exceeding 56 lb. for a distance of between half a mile and a mile, which they considered ought to be raised to 1s.; they would have liked all loads and distances above this standard to be subject to individual bargaining, and also a 1s. per hour waiting fee for Porters. Overcharging for services remained in the class of serious offences for which the penalty amounted to 20s.

The Common Council Act of 1823 also confined Ticket Porters stationed at a stand to a radius of six yards from this stand, stipulating a fine of 5s. for contravention. Many Ticket Porters declared this rule impossible to observe, but it arose out of a conflict which raged around the Ticket Porters' stand at Doctors' Commons for half a century. Doctors' Commons, a site in the City, had been purchased in 1567 by a number of ecclesiastical and civil lawyers who lived and practised there. In 1768 they became incorporated as the 'College of Doctors of Law exercent in the Ecclesiastical and Admiralty Courts'. Five courts of law formed part of the complex of buildings, including the Prerogative Court concerned with wills disposing of estate exceeding £5, if left either within more than one diocese or in the diocese of Canterbury. To obtain probate of such a will, members of the public had to resort to Doctors' Commons. Their route of approach led from St. Paul's Churchyard into Dean's Court, whence a low archway gave access to Doctors' Commons.

A stand for Ticket Porters existed in St. Paul's Churchyard, near Dean's Court, from the middle eighteenth century onwards. Strangers looking for Doctors' Commons and in search of somebody to direct them afforded these Ticket Porters an opportunity of enquiring whether they wanted to prove or inspect a will or to consult a proctor (as these lawyers were called). Proctors complained that Porters importuned members of the public who refused to divulge their business, or, even worse, that one or two unscrupulous lawyers had bribed Ticket Porters to entice clients; all a Porter had to do was to assert that a certain Proctor did not exist, had given up his practice or had died, and to suggest a substitute who would give attention to the caller's business. A number of lawyers complained to the Society of Tacklehouse and Ticket Porters and to the magistrates in 1806, alleging that this practice had been going on for six years, and two of the offending Porters had their tickets withdrawn. The proctors installed a lodge in the Dean's Court archway and stationed a keeper there to give information to the public regarding proctors' offices and courts at Doctors' Commons.

In 1813 three new Ticket Porters joined the stand in St. Paul's Churchyard. Instead of plying for business at their stand, they loitered in the archway, hoping to earn tips by giving information which the lodge-keeper supplied free of charge. These Porters incurred the wrath not only of the lodge-keeper but also of Thomas Wilson, who kept a bookshop opening into the archway and accused them of constantly parading in front of his premises. Investigation revealed that once again the Porters had been tempted by some of the shadier members of the legal profession, whereupon the Porters were merely admonished to keep away from the archway, instead of being confined to the stand in front of the *Tobit's Dog* public house as the proctors asked. Balked of their objective, the lawyers organized a petition by inhabitants of Castle Baynard Ward against the Ticket Porters' stand in Dean's Court to the Common Council, which, however, did not act upon it. The inhabitants of Castle Baynard, prominent among them Wilson the bookseller and Brickwood the most insistent of the proctors, returned to the onslaught in 1820. Of the three Ticket Porters who had indulged in objectionable practices in the archway in 1813, two continued loitering there, accompanied by two newcomers; instead of taking lawful employment at their stands, they worried the public at Dean's

Court with impertinent enquiries. This time the Society confined the offending Ticket Porters to their stand; three of them who disobeyed the Society's instructions were suspended, but carried on undismayed during suspension and were accordingly dismissed from the Society in 1823. They then promised to reform their ways and succeeded in obtaining reinstatement.

For a time they lay low, but after ten years they passed to the offensive by complaining to the Society of Tacklehouse and Ticket Porters of malicious and vindictive persecution on the part of the lodge-keeper and the Wilsons, father and son: if any member of the public spoke to the Ticket Porters, they would immediately shout: 'Mind your pockets! be on your guard!' They had repeatedly summoned the Ticket Porters before the magistrates, but never obtained a conviction, nor was it sensible to require Ticket Porters to stand in the narrow lane at St. Paul's Churchyard where they could not help obstructing the public thoroughfare, whereas Dean's Court was out of the way; hence they asked for protection against further insults and rescission of the order regarding the stand. Wilson the bookseller promptly put in a counter-petition, and the Court of Rulers maintained the *status quo*. This did not satisfy the inhabitants of Doctors' Commons; twenty of them, including of course Wilson and Brickwood, pleaded with the Court of Aldermen later in 1834, accusing all twelve Ticket Porters at the stand of patrolling the archway like sentinels and intimidating the public into answering their questions:

> many of these Men are sometimes in a state of Intoxication and will when interfered with and requested to withdraw from the Door of any resident they choose to fix themselves at, refuse to leave it and set the Inhabitant at defiance using at the same time abusive and deriding language and by the means aforesaid they obstruct hinder and impede the free passage of the public Street.

It was around 1830 that Charles Dickens frequented Doctors' Commons, as usual observing and taking in the whole situation. This is how Sam Weller in the *Pickwick Papers* describes Doctors' Commons to Jingle:

> Paul's Churchyard, sir; low archway on the carriage side, bookseller's at one corner, hot-el on the other, and two porters in the middle as touts for

licences. . . . Two coves in white aprons—touches their hats when you walk in—'Licence, sir, licence?' Queer sort, them, and their mas'rs too, sir— Old Bailey Proctors,—and no mistake.

Here it all is, the archway in Dean's Court, Wilson's bookshop, and the Porters with their suspicious practices who, according to the enraged inhabitants, would not even accept such Porters' work as came their way, finding the misdirection of the public more profitable. Police aid was therefore sought to remove these City Porters to their proper stand.

The lawyers' particular enemy, William Little, one of the Ticket Porters dismissed from the Society for bad behaviour at Doctors' Commons but subsequently readmitted, in 1836 countercharged the proctors' protagonist Brickwood with using the lodge-keeper for the purpose of diverting clients from other proctors to himself. Moreover, the lodge-keeper gave information about proctors and proctors only, so that callers enquiring after other members of the legal profession had to apply to the Ticket Porters for information. The man at the lodge, not to be outdone by a Ticket Porter, accused Little of keeping a common brothel, whereupon Little brought a libel action. Meanwhile the *Tobit's Dog* public house in front of which Ticket Porters had always had their stand had been demolished. Brickwood, fearing the Society would now officially station the Ticket Porters in the archway, declared in ringing tones that

> we in Deans Court and its vicinity (complainants through a long period of years of the misconduct of these Individuals) are extremely anxious to exonerate ourselves from this Infliction of evil, convinced from long suffering experience that a more disreputable and grievous Nuisance could hardly be visited upon us or upon any persons valuing the Blessings of tranquility and exemption from the most annoying disturbances.

To warn the public, the lodge-keeper displayed under the archway at Dean's Court a large notice reproducing the order of the Court of Rulers which prohibited Ticket Porters from standing there. The Ticket Porters still argued that this was the only suitable spot for them to occupy, annexing testimonials from thirty inhabitants of Castle Baynard Ward who knew them to be men of good conduct, and asked that they be allowed to stand in Dean's Court. This could hardly have been the common opinion: a memorial from ninety-two inhabitants of St. Paul's Churchyard attributed the removal of the *Tobit's Dog* purely to a desire to dislocate the Ticket Porters and asked for nothing less than their complete departure.

Unmoved by all this clamour, the Society of Tacklehouse and Ticket Porters persisted in its order to the Ticket Porters to keep to their stand, but they would not obey, and within three years Brickwood and another proctor were again on the warpath. A conference between Brickwood and some of the Society's Rulers agreed upon a trial period of one month, during which the list of proctors displayed inside the lodge would be transferred to the outside, while the Porters remained at their erstwhile stand. If no incident occurred during this month, the lodge-keeper would remove from the archway the notice containing the caution against the Ticket Porters standing there. The Society's Clerk requested the removal of the board when the month was up, but whether the proctors agreed to do so is not on record. After this incident the conflict faded from the pages of the Porters' documents, but in 1852 the Clerk of the Society of Tacklehouse and Ticket Porters charged 3s. 4d. for his trouble in making an appointment with, and attending, Mr. Alderman Wilson respecting the stand at Dean's Yard and pointing out to him the Society's right to have men there and that, if any public inconvenience arose, it was due not to them, but to those who interfered with the labour. Would it be fanciful to suspect Mr. Alderman Wilson of being the son of that bookseller who had spent many years trying to have the Porters removed from outside his shop? A new Probate Court was established elsewhere in 1857, when an Act empowered the College of Doctors of Law exercent in the Ecclesiastical and Admiralty Court to sell and liquidate its estate and surrender its charter of incorporation. That was the end of Doctors' Commons as an institution. Ten years later the buildings were pulled down, though the low archway at the corner of Dean's Court remained standing until 1894. Faraday House, Queen Victoria Street, now covers the site of Doctors' Commons.[54]

(c) Reduction in Numbers

To the end the incongruous marriage of Tacklehouse and Ticket Porters determined the Society's organizational structure, though

Tacklehouse Porters gradually withdrew from effective participation. They had always belonged to a social and economic class superior to that of the Ticket Porters, being entrepreneurs and not labourers; it was not unusual for them to blossom out into wharfingers or steamboat operators, with interests antagonistic to those of the Ticket Porters, and into Common Councilmen entitled to pass judgment on the Society's affairs. When Tacklehouse and Ticket Porters had originally been joined in the same organization, this class difference had been considered an advantage: Tacklehouse Porters would exercise a moderating influence on the unruly Ticket Porter element, would by their standing ensure respect and consideration for the Society's just demands.* While not welcoming the association, Tacklehouse Porters had at least tolerated it. Now that it positively embarrassed them, they preferred to sever connections. Summoned to a meeting of the Court of Rulers of which he was a member, Samuel Jackson, Merchant Taylors' Tacklehouse Porter, in 1836 replied by a short note: 'Gentlemen, In reference to your notice of this day, I beg to inform you that it will not be convenient to attend also that you will consider me in future *not* in any way connected with the Society.' Not being steamboat proprietors like Jackson,† other Tacklehouse Porters were less abrupt or discourteous. In 1841 the Society asked for Common Council consent to the admission not only of two named men as Tacklehouse Porters to the Companies of Fishmongers and Clothworkers, but also of any other Tacklehouse Porters whom the twelve principal Companies might from time to time appoint. The Common Council approved the two men specifically mentioned, while refusing blanket authority for future candidates. Having taken note of the Common Council's attitude, the Fishmongers' Company did not proceed with the appointment of their nominee; it was no longer worth their while having a Tacklehouse Porter. The Clothworkers on the other hand went ahead and two years later made a second nomination, the last Tacklehouse Porter to join the Society.

The Common Council Act of 1823 limited the Society's total membership to five hundred. Such a limitation would never have been imposed, had not the actual number already fallen below this figure.

---

* See pp. 14, 15, 47 above.　　　　† See p. 163 above.

Moreover, sudden contractions in membership took place whenever the Court enforced the rule of removing from the registers members in arrears with their quarterage by more than two years; in 1837 this reduced the number of Ticket Porters at one blow by fifty. No more than approximately two hundred Ticket Porters sought their living at the legal quays in 1833 when the City authorities at last decided to come to grips with the licensed Porters' problem. The only satisfactory method of meeting the demands of merchants and others for the abolition of these irksome privileges, without breaking faith with those who relied on them for their livelihood, consisted in the reduction of the number of persons privileged, which natural wastage would effect, not quickly, but certainly. This meant making new admissions to the Porters' organizations dependent upon Common Council consent. The Registers and Rulers of the Society of Tacklehouse and Ticket Porters demurred, pointing out that the right to appoint Tacklehouse Porters could not be taken away without the concurrence of the twelve principal Companies, and that gradual diminution of the Ticket Porters' number would force the trade to resort to unauthorized labour, thus extinguishing the privilege of the remaining Ticket Porters and giving a monopoly of market work to half a dozen innkeepers of considerable wealth. Not even the Porters themselves found this argument very convincing; in case it should not commend itself to the Common Council, they asked for compensation out of Corporation funds for those affected.

At its first reading, the bill was described as a measure for gradually reducing the number of Porters; it passed in 1835 under the more neutral title of an Act in relation to the admission of members into the Societies or Fellowships of Porters. The preamble recited the expediency of restraining such admission, which under section 1 required the authority of the Common Council, while section 2 provided that all persons thus admitted must sign a renunciation of all claims or vested interests in their places or offices and all titles to compensation if they lost part or the whole of their functions or emoluments; section 3 ensured that the Act did not confer upon existing or future members of the Societies any rights or claims which they did not already possess. A meeting of the Court of Registers and Rulers to consider the effect of this Act upon members was held for once not at the Guildhall but in the *Bridge House* tavern, Queen Street, and its minutes were not entered in the regular minute-book but preserved only in draft form. The Act spelt gradual extinction for the Society. In the markets, innkeepers would now seize the whole of the business once it had become impossible to enforce Ticket Porters' rights and privileges, because not enough of them remained available to serve the needs of trade; Uptown Porters could henceforth make a living only in so far as they became regular employees of merchants, bankers and warehousemen. In the circumstances, the Court considered it neither just nor feasible to continue subjecting Ticket Porters to quarterage payments, regulations and orders; already the Society's funds were inadequate to meet its obligations to pensioners, owing largely to the expense incurred in upholding its privileges in the Lord Mayor's Court. The Registers and Rulers demanded early relief from responsibilities which they could no longer adequately discharge.

It was not long before the limitation on Ticket Porters' numbers made itself felt in practice. One of the few trades where Ticket Porters in season still enjoyed full employment was in the discharge of dried and pickled herring at the Custom House. Merchant factors complained in 1837 of an inadequacy of labour in this trade and threatened to establish a gang of men under their own superintendence unless more Ticket Porters became available. The Society's application to the Common Council to authorize the admission of twenty-five new Ticket Porters constituted a test case. Investigation found the shortage to be seasonal. The Common Council's General Purposes Committee proposed to remedy it by admitting Billingsgate Porters to share the work with Ticket Porters, but though a bill to this effect obtained a second reading in the Common Council, it was eventually defeated. The Ticket Porters passed a vote of thanks to the Common Council for this decision, but renewed their petition for twenty-five new members in 1840. The Common Council remained firm. A petition in 1841 which would have added fifty new Ticket Porters was not even presented, as only two Rulers could be induced to sign it; the others pointed out that several steamboat services had just been diverted from London Bridge and Custom House wharves to Blackwall and Southampton, thus diminishing Ticket Porters' opportunities. The last such application, this time for twenty members, remained lying on the Common Council's table in 1849. The only successful applicant for membership of the Society in the 1840s laid stress less on the need for porterage labour than on his own deserving and distressed condition; but when others imitated him, the Common Council closed even this avenue to membership. At the last enquiry into the number of Ticket Porters in 1853, enough of them were found for work in slack periods, though the number did not suffice to deal with spells of busy trade; this applied above all in fish-carrying work, which employed twenty of them, supplemented by outside labour during the season. According to one of the Ticket Porters engaged in this occupation, Ticket Porters by this time had ceased to interfere with merchants employing their own labour in unloading herrings brought by railway; but far from doing that, dealers of their own free will continued to ask for Ticket Porters' services.[55]

(d) Organization and Funds

While members were still freely admitted to the Society in 1812, admission fees were increased. The following scale applied:

| | Tacklehouse Porters if giving security to | | Ticket Porters obtaining freedom by | | |
	the Governor	their own Companies	servitude or apprenticeship	patrimony	redemption
	£ s. d.	£ s. d.	£ s. d.	£ s. d.	£ s. d.
Court . . .	10 6	10 6	12 6	15 0	1 1 0
Clerk . . .	10 6	5 0	6 6	8 0	10 6
Bond Stamp .	1 1 0	—	1 1 0	1 1 0	1 1 0
Beadles . .	—	—	3 0	4 0	6 0
Governor . .	—	—	3 0	3 6	6 0
Total . .	£2 2 0	15 6	£2 6 0	£2 11 6	£3 4 6

Fees were also payable to the beadle of 1s. whenever a Porter required a new badge, and to the Clerk of 6d. on removal from stand to stand and of 2s. when new guarantors had to be added to a security bond. Court fees rose further in 1818, when the scale became:

| | Tacklehouse Porters if giving security to | | Ticket Porters obtaining freedom by | | |
| | the Governor | their own Companies | servitude or apprenticeship | patrimony | redemption |
	£ s. d.	£ s. d.	£ s. d.	£ s. d.	£ s. d.
Court . . .	1 1 0	1 1 0	1 1 0	1 5 0	1 10 0
Clerk . . .	10 6	5 0	6 6	8 0	10 6
Bond stamp . .	1 17 0	—	1 17 0	1 17 0	1 17 0
Beadles . .	—	—	3 0	4 0	6 0
Governor . .	—	—	3 0	3 6	6 0
Total . .	£3 8 6	£1 6 0	£3 10 6	£3 17 6	£4 9 6

Apart from official admission charges, Ticket Porters sought to extort money from a newcomer for an entertainment, £10 10s. being demanded in 1820 from a man who joined the stand in Bartholomew Lane. The Governor put this down firmly, fined the Porters who had exacted the amount and had a proclamation against such practices printed and displayed. Ticket Porters at St. Michael's Alley nevertheless demanded the same from a newcomer five years later, and the Governor did nothing more drastic than repeat the prohibition and make the miscreants pay the expenses of the summons.

Once admitted, members were liable to quarterage, which up to the beginning of the nineteenth century amounted to 1s. a quarter. The Society had great difficulty in obtaining regular payments. In 1810 the Court disqualified from voting in internal elections members whose contributions were in arrears exceeding one year. The Society decided to double quarterage in 1822, a group of members wanting to devote the increase to a separate legal fund. The higher rates received sanction by the Common Council Act of 1823, which also laid down a table of forfeits for members in arrears with their quarterage for 5 quarters amounting to 1s., 6 quarters amounting to 2s., 8 quarters rendering themselves liable to expulsion. After 1835 a member so expelled, even though willing to wipe out his arrears, could not gain readmission without the Common Council's authority any more than a new member; hence he had to petition the Common Council as well as the Society in order to regain membership.

Centuries back, the Society had undertaken to indemnify employers who suffered damage through a member's misconduct. For many years the Society had not been reminded of that obligation, but in 1836 it received a complaint from John Yeldham, driver of the Maldon and Burnham coach. A bill for £21, accepted by some Essex merchant, had matured. As it had been payable at Barclays Bank in Lombard Street, Yeldham had come up to town carrying cash to pay for it. He did not go to Lombard Street himself, but entrusted the money, £20 10s. in gold and 10s. in silver, to Samuel Brady, a Ticket Porter. This was the last that anybody ever heard of Brady. The demand for damages came as a shock to the Society of Tacklehouse and Ticket Porters. Brady had been a Ticket Porter for over twenty years; in all this time the Society had not checked on his guarantors. When it did, it found one of them dead, the other, a journeyman cork-cutter in Whitechapel, seventy-two years of age, ill and dependent on his family. In the circumstances the Society tried to back out of its obligation to indemnify Yeldham, who addressed himself to the Common Council. This was at a time when the Common Council, in spite of strong recommendations from its General Purposes Committee, refused to support the Ticket Porters' attempts to maintain their privileges or to make a £50 contribution to their legal expenses.* The Society did not miss its opportunity of holding the Common Council's unfavourable attitude responsible for its inability to meet this obligation. Having delivered its blow, the Court protested its ardent desire to show respect and gratitude to the General Purposes Committee and made other arrangements to reimburse Yeldham—a voluntary levy on all members which raised £5 from the Rulers, £10 from Waterside Porters, £4 from individual Porters contributing 2s. 6d. each, £2 from the Porters stationed at Doctors' Commons, so that £21 could be handed over to Yeldham.

The supreme authority within the Society remained the Governor, an Alderman elected to this office by his brethren. Among those who

* See p. 161 above.

discharged this function were Harvey Christian Combe, M.P., a prominent brewer who had been one of the Compensation Commissioners under the dock scheme* and whose firm, Combe, Delafield & Co., eventually took the Fellowship Porters to the bar of the House of Lords to break their privileges,† Sir Matthew Wood, M.P., the champion of George IV's unfortunate queen, who directed the Society's government with care and distinction for a quarter of a century, and Sir John Humphery, M.P., who brought Hay's Wharf to the peak of prosperity towards the middle of the century, but whose period of office as Governor saw the Society of Tacklehouse and Ticket Porters into its grave. The Governor drew from the Society emoluments only to the extent of admission fees indicated in the tables above; none of the Governors accepted these fees, but all returned them to the Society's pension funds. The Governor had power to summon before him or the Court of Rulers any offender against the Society's rules and regulations and to punish him by a fine not exceeding 20s. or suspension not exceeding three months for any one offence. With the consent of the Court of Rulers, he also appointed and fixed the pay of the Society's officers and servants, though within limits authorized by the Common Council, and expelled members for repeated or persistent offences, working during suspension, or non-payment of fines for twenty-eight days. The validity of rules, orders and regulations which he made in conjunction with the Court of Rulers depended on the Court of Aldermen's approval.

As before, the Society's Court consisted of twelve Rulers, including two Registers, sitting under the Governor's chairmanship if he attended; seven members formed a quorum. Monthly meetings were held, except in November. In the absence of the Governor the Court had no authority to hear and decide complaints. This constituted a grievance; after 1810, Rulers never ceased to demand powers of dealing with complaints without requiring the Governor's presence. A number of Ticket Porters strongly opposed this power being granted to their Rulers, if it entitled them to suspend members or fine them more than 5s., but the Common Council Act of 1823 gave the Court power to summon members, hear disputes, fine offenders up to 20s. or

---

* See p. 142 above.   † See p. 134 above.

suspend them for up to three months. Opinions about the efficiency with which the Court functioned varied considerably. A steam-packet operator alleged in the 1830s that the Court would receive complaints only from members of the Society and that, in order to bring to the Rulers' notice misconduct among their members, he himself had to join the Society. He did not consider this remedy very efficacious, as the Court of Rulers did not usually furnish much redress for complaints because it had little control over members. This evidence was contradicted by Thomas Garrard, a Ruler for forty-six years, who claimed that anybody could complain to the Court of Rulers about members, that the Court investigated all complaints and suspended or fined Porters if the complaint was substantiated; he instanced cases of Porters being fined for swearing or smoking at work.

An application by several Ticket Porters in 1810 disclosed that new Rulers on the Ticket side had lately been co-opted instead of being elected by the whole Ticket membership, as required by the Common Council Act of 1798. The more democratic form of election was thereupon restored. The only financial advantage officially accruing to Rulers and Registers was exemption from quarterage during their period of office. A unanimous resolution of the Court of Registers and Rulers in 1812 to increase the Rulers' allowance per meeting from 3s. 6d. to 5s. a person indicates that unofficial emoluments had crept in. Later in the year the particular meetings qualifying for the allowance were specified. The Common Council Act of 1823 took no account of such payments, but disqualified from rulership recipients of alms and pensions, with the exception of service pensions. In 1834 the financial situation of the Society deteriorated to such an extent that a Ruler proposed reducing Rulers' fees to 3s. 6d. There was an equal number of votes for and against the proposal, but four years later it was carried unanimously. In tune with the remuneration of the Rulers, Registers who up to 1812 had received 5s. per meeting were on that occasion raised to 7s. 6d. and reduced back to 5s. in 1838. Another economy measure taken as early as 1818 consisted in the reduction of the annual gratuities given to the Society's beadles from £2 2s. to £1 1s.

The Society's financial activities remained on a small scale. An average of £100 annually passed through the Registers' hands, less in the

o

last quarter of the eighteenth century, more during the period from 1824 to 1832 when herring work paid Ticket Porters well. In 1826 there was a cash balance amounting to £57 worth investing in long annuities. Permanent and rapid decline set in after 1833, making the annual amount fall, less than two decades later, below £20. The stringency was aggravated by fraud on the part of one of the Society's Registers who committed suicide in 1839, leaving a letter admitting his defalcations which the Rulers computed at over £24—a paltry enough sum, but important at a time when the Society's funds had fallen to a low level.

These funds, after defraying current expenses, served to support pensioners. Between 1798 and 1812 the Society laid out an average £12 a year for relief and charity. Superannuated Ticket Porters on the pension list received £1 p.a., widows 10s.; the number of individuals relieved must have remained very small. In 1812, rates of relief were doubled for widows and increased by 50 per cent for men; from 1813 to 1819 annual relief expenditure ran at the rate of £21. It then dropped back to £15 until 1836; after that date financial stringency left a mere £5 a year to be devoted to this purpose. Where so few could obtain relief and so many needed it, importance attached to the selection of pensioners. One of them was struck off the list in 1813 because he resided two hundred miles from London and had not collected his money for over eighteen months; five years later a vacancy created by a pensioner's death was not filled. From 1819, with a view to economy, men and women pensioners were reduced to six each by a process of natural wastage. In its Act of 1823 the Common Council enjoined a selection of pensioners strictly and solely according to seniority, without devoting any thought to the extent to which this represented a test of need.

Finance represented one among several indications that the Society was drawing to its close. Tacklehouse Porters were not the only rats anxious to put distance between themselves and the sinking ship. Having ceased to count himself a member of the Society in 1828, a Ticket Porter ten years later informed the Court that he considered the Ticket Porter's job as a calling to starvation. At some time in the 1830s the Rulers and Clerk forewent a year's remuneration in order to tide the Society over its financial difficulties. The six Rulers elected on the Ticket side in 1840 were recruited from two stands only, five from the Custom House, the sixth from Leadenhall Market. Not only did Rulers cease to draw emoluments for holding office; in 1844 they were called upon to pay 10s. each in order to defray the Court's expenses. In that year they gave up keeping their minute-book, though they continued meeting with fair regularity at monthly intervals until 1853; after that year Courts met irregularly at something like quarterly intervals, more frequently in summer than in winter. The account book, which contains many further blank pages, showed annual accounts entered by the Registers up to 1851.

When in 1858 the House of Commons in the course of a bill reforming the City of London Corporation considered abolishing Tacklehouse and Ticket Porters, the Society rallied once more to draft a petition for compensation, signed by the Governor, two Registers, four Rulers and the Clerk. The bill failed, but a ginger group of ten Ticket Porters thought this an opportunity for reviving the Society as an active body and recovering its privileges by legal action. On a loose sheet, a Court of Rulers and Registers in 1862 recorded the exclusion from membership of a Ticket Porter who had refused to comply with regulations. For the first year in all its existence, no Court meeting took place in 1866; in the three following years it met only once. A Ticket Porter still dared to threaten a market salesman at Billingsgate with legal action to enforce his right to labour in 1870, but the last receipt for the rent of Guildhall for Court meetings refers to two occasions in 1871. The end of the Society as a corporate body also signified the end of Ticket Porters as such. Only seven years later, when a body of eminent people addressed the Common Council on abuses inherent in the methods of paying Porters, they confused Ticket with Fellowship Porters and hazarded the unlikely guess that Tacklehouse Porters had undergone a metamorphosis turning them into Deputy Corn Meters. A writer describing porterage services in the metropolitan fruit and vegetable markets in 1896 went into some detail both about past and present. He obviously had never even heard of Ticket Porters.[56]

(e) *Wine Tackle Porters*

The only Porters still carrying a name reminiscent of the old Society are the Wine Tackle Porters, that body of men with whom the Vintners' Company in the eighteenth century had replaced its Tackle-house Porters. At the beginning of the nineteenth century, it employed fifteen Master and seventeen Assistant or Servant Wine Tackle Porters. Masters wore distinguishing silver badges numbered 1–15. Up to 1802, porterage fees were pooled and divided weekly into sixteen equal parts, each Master Porter receiving one share. The sixteenth share went into a fund from which the Vintners' Company paid twice a year the general expenses of the wine porterage business and gave a dinner attended by the two senior Master Porters 'in white frock dresses, but this custom was consider'd a bad one inasmuch as the Company expended a considerable sum to entertain two men who felt themselves in a Society they were unaccustom'd to and consequently under a restraint they dislik'd.' Nothing demonstrated more clearly the difference between these Master Tackle Porters, uncomfortable in the company of their social superiors, and the older form of Tackle-house Porters, free of the City and members of their own Companies, well-accustomed to the society of liverymen and dignitaries before they could aspire to become Tacklehouse Porters. So the half-yearly dinner was abolished and the Master Porters allowed £5 instead. At the same time the burden of expenses was redistributed, leaving the Vintners' Company to bear $\frac{17}{32}$ and the Master Porters $\frac{1}{32}$ each. While the Master Porters' remuneration varied with the total porterage earned, Servant Porters received fixed wages of 13*s*. a week plus some trifling perquisites. They were appointed by the Master Porters and presented to the Vintners' Company's Court for approval.

Four of the Master Porters had by 1819 grown too old and infirm to perform active duties though they still drew their remuneration. The remainder as well as the Servants were allocated to a number of tacklehouses. There is in the Vintners' Company's possession a wooden board showing two Porters in top hats, supporting the Company's arms; large letters underneath pronounce:

VINTNERS' COMPANY TACKLE HOUSE.

Of such tacklehouses, the following existed:

	Masters	Servants
London Docks	1	—
Botolph Lane, Eastcheap	2	2
Three Cranes' Wharf, Queen Street . .	1	2
French Ordinary Court, Crutched Friars .	1	4
Bishopsgate Street	1	3
Tower Street	1	1
Fleet Street	2	2
Snow Hill, Old Bailey	2	3
	11	17

Additional tacklehouses, not permanently manned, had been established further west at Holborn, Greek Street, Well Street, Swallow Street, Charing Cross (Strand) and Beaufort Buildings. When the Servant Porters' wages proved inadequate, the Vintners' Company rearranged duties and remunerations. According to a plan approved in 1820, the number of Masters was reduced to thirteen, all of them fit and efficient, the number of Servants increased to eighteen, and a third category created, that of labourers appointed by the Masters, of whom there were thirteen, succeeding the Servants by promotion when vacancies occurred. The City was divided into eight 'walks' named after the manned tacklehouses, to which twelve of the Masters were assigned. A Master personally supervised all work done within his walk, unless more than one job went on simultaneously; if damage or accidents occurred on his walk, he was held responsible. The thirteenth Master acted as clerk or housekeeper, staying at the central office and keeping the porterage accounts. Though Servants and labourers worked under the Masters' direction, they were liable to lose a week's wages if they caused losses or accidents through negligence or carelessness; if a Master Porter was ill or unable to attend to duty, the Senior Servant took his place until he returned. Incidental expenses became a first charge on porterage revenue, together with fixed weekly salaries amounting to 5s. for the four senior Masters, 30s. for the senior Servant, 18s. each for the next four Servants and 16s. each for the remaining Servants and labourers. After these deductions, net revenue was divided into sixteen shares, one to each Master Porter, one to the Vintners' Company, and two to a new Superannuation Fund—subsequently renamed Wine Porters' Fund—for aged and infirm Master Porters and their widows, invested in $3\frac{1}{2}$ per cent stock and distributed at the discretion of the Vintners' Court.

Like all Porters, the Wine Tackle Porters in the course of the nineteenth century suffered from a shrinkage of business, but unlike other Porters they were backed by a strong and benevolent Company to which they could turn for support. When stringency asserted itself in 1832, the Vintners' Company made over its own sixteenth share of net receipts to the Wine Porters' Fund to cure a deficit there, though at the same time it cancelled the weekly salary of the four senior Master Porters, replacing it by a single 4s. allowance to the housekeeper only. A similar crisis was met in 1848 by doing away with the Master Porter acting as housekeeper, appointing the Vintners' Company's Accountant as bookkeeper, and appropriating the upper part of one of the tacklehouses as his counting house and residence. Shrinkage of business forced the gradual closure of tacklehouses: when the entrance to the London Docks underwent extensive alterations, the tacklehouse at the gate disappeared in 1844; the landlords of the Bishopsgate tacklehouse gave notice in 1883, when it was known that the railway company might any day require the premises of the Botolph Lane tacklehouse, so the Wine Tackle Porters rented another cellar in that lane, plus a room close by in Botolph Alley for a counting house. This was not given up until 1910, at the same time as the tacklehouse at Snow Hill; French Ordinary Court, Crutched Friars, followed seven years later.

Tackle Porters performed much of their work at public houses. At these places the Porters often demanded drink money and sometimes rioted when met with a refusal. The Court of the Vintners' Company asked its customers not to supply intoxicants to Porters, and disciplined offending Porters if reported; Servants known to be drunk on duty were not recommended for promotion to Masters,

Masters in the same position were reduced in rank to Servants. There was good reason for strictness on the Company's part. Not only did careless and incompetent work lead to considerable damage, but the lives and safety of the Porters themselves were in jeopardy. A pipe of port weighs the best part of a ton; no other wine comes in containers quite as heavy, but in each case very great weights have to be manipulated. Accidents occurred frequently, resulting sometimes in death, more often in loss of limb or in severe rupture. The number of Wine Porters dying in their thirties and forties exceeded the national average.

Around 1880 a new economy drive began by temporarily not filling a vacancy for a Master Porter, in view of the fact that earnings for the period 1878–82 had fallen a quarter below the earnings of 1873–77. Reorganization in 1883 reduced the number of Master Porters from twelve to eight and transferred to them perquisites paid for providing and fixing posts and sockets for wine merchants which had hitherto gone to the Servants. From eight the number of Master Porters fell to six in 1894, while the number of Servants was allowed to shrink to four. In 1910 the Vintners' Company took what appeared to be the logical step of banning the appointment of further Master Tackle Porters. But it was not as logical as it sounded. Wine Porters' services were still in demand which the reduction of manpower during the first World War did nothing to abate. Not that the Vintners' Company cherished any illusions about the manner in which its customers took advantage of its facilities: '. . . the Vintners' Wine Porters' assistance is generally required when it is a difficult matter, and when it is an easy one, firms use their own gear', reported a Court in 1916. By the end of the war the Wine Porters' accounts were deemed satisfactory, and the Company was reluctant to discontinue a tradition of porterage services rendered over more than four centuries.* What had become redundant was the distinction in rank among Wine Porters; after the last Servant had been promoted Master Porter in 1919, labourers and Servants became terms merely to signify a probationary period in the Company's service before the man in question advanced to permanent employment as a Master Porter. The number had fallen to three, at times of labour shortage in and just after the second World

* See p. 38 above.

War even to two, but as any single job of work may require three strong men, the Company has endeavoured to make the number up to three whenever it has been able to find suitable men. Thus it is that the three Tackle Porters in the employ of the Vintners' Company form the last, if somewhat tenuous, living link with the Society of Tacklehouse and Ticket Porters.[57]

3

FELLOWSHIP PORTERS: COMMON WORKING REGULATIONS AND REMUNERATION

(a) General Working Conditions

UNLIKE the Society of Tacklehouse and Ticket Porters, the Fellowship of Porters regulated the working methods of its members in great detail. This difference was due to more Billingsgate than Ticket Porters working in teams formed and changed from day to day and from job to job. In making up teams, seniority had to be weighed against priority in applying for work and the employers' desire for quick and efficient services; where teams could not go into action until preparatory work had been done, there had to be rules as to who was to do it. This necessitated a labyrinth of working regulations, many differing according to the commodities handled, but a few common to the work as a whole, such as the obligation to wear a Fellowship badge when on duty. No Porter could assert his seniority over others unless he displayed his badge. A Porter enabling a stranger to exercise Fellowship privileges by lending him his badge was dismissed from the Fellowship. To disobey a Ruler's warning for a job counted as serious insubordination; a fine or suspension followed the first offence, double that penalty the second and dismissal the third. On the other hand, Porters refusing to continue work after hours were usually cautioned but not punished. A bad habit common among Porters consisted of leaving one job unfinished to take up another where they expected to earn more; no Porter was allowed to abandon work once started, except with a Ruler's permission. This applied especially to potatoes, owing to pressure of work in this branch of trade; Porters engaged in the morning could not quit until the Meter had left the job and the way had been broken, both clear indications that work had stopped for the day.

Neither age nor activity, only the date of admission determined seniority. After twenty-six or twenty-seven years as a Quarterman, a member was appointed by the Court of Rulers to the Onion Bill, a category of Porters usually able to secure the easiest and most remunerative employment which took place on board vessels in the River. Unlike Quartermen, members of the Onion Bill never had to carry sacks, unless on their way to work in which sacks were required. The Court of Rulers kept the Onion Bill within reasonable proportions, limiting it after 1835 to 100 members. From the Onion Bill, Corn Porters, the most senior grade, were recruited; 300 to 400 men usually enjoyed this privilege, most of them after more than thirty years in the Fellowship. Corn Porters alone were eligible as Rulers.

The amount of strain on Porters varied with the work. Only young and fit men were capable of backing labour—goods in sacks which Porters had to hoist on their backs and carry. To be prepared for such jobs, all Quartermen going on duty carried sacks; those who neglected to provide themselves with such equipment could be refused work. This became a grievance with Porters, especially if the job turned out to require no backing; after 1843 even Quartermen did not have to carry sacks unless going to work which necessitated their use. Owing to the different weights of identical volumes of commodities, malt and nuts made heavier loads than potatoes. No more than six Corn Porters became members of any team engaged in backing work; neither they nor members of the Onion Bill were compelled to take part in the actual backing, though they decided the number of men making up the team beyond a minimum of six. On no account were Fellowship pensioners allowed to take any share in backing work. Sometimes a barrow was required in conjunction with such jobs; if so, upon the senior man in the team devolved responsibility for returning it to the Corn Office.[58]

Of the common rules, the most important concerned the regulation of turn labour. It pivoted on a number of offices maintained under the supervision of individual Rulers for the supply of Porters. Anybody who needed Porters resorted to these offices; any Porter who wanted turn labour attended at the office of his choice at the appropriate hour. Not even the time could be left to individual ascertainment; in 1835

the Court of Rulers determined the clocks which governed the time at
the Tower Street, Horselydown, *Cock and Lion* and Queenhithe
offices; the Custom House clock was added two years later to regulate
hours of labour at Billingsgate Market. In several offices the Fellowship
eventually provided its own clocks, but where men turned out
overnight for work next morning, an outside clock still had to rule, a
purpose served mainly by the church clock in Seething Lane. Men
wishing to 'go on berth' had to be at the office when the clock struck.
To go on berth two hours before work actually began, proved a waste
of time; one hour, introduced in 1838, sufficed. As the clock struck,
men put their names on the slate in the office according to seniority, an
act which entitled them to accept work in that order; any Porter
trying to obtain a job without having gone through this process was
deemed to 'run on the job', for which he risked forfeiture of his
remuneration and possibly suspension. Not only did a Porter have to
start from the office, but from the appropriate office: Tower Street
supplied Porters for work afloat and below Bridge, Queenhithe for
work above Bridge, Horselydown for work on the South Bank; a
Porter going from Horselydown to work above Bridge would have
forfeited the job, and a Meter at Horselydown going to work afloat
had to collect his team of Porters at Tower Street. Meters were liable
to punishment in their capacity as Billingsgate Porters if they omitted
to notify a job and indicate its nature at the correct Porters' office, but
found themselves teams of Porters in an irregular manner. For Corn
Porters another method of obtaining work existed; they could join
a team already in action which, though adequately manned, could do
with another man. This was described as 'going heaver and goer'. A
Corn Porter could go heaver and goer on any day on which he had
first sought work regularly at one of the offices by putting his name on
the slate, but had failed to obtain a job.

The list on the office slate ruled the allocation of jobs for that day;
a Porter whose name did not appear on the slate could find a job only
when all those on the list had been employed. But this principle was
weakened by rules regarding bounds. Every one of the offices constituted the focus of a geographical area. Until a team of Porters
setting out on its way to work had passed the bounds of this area, it was

liable to be joined by a senior Porter who had caught up with it after calling at the office. If the team was at full strength, a senior Porter by joining it displaced its most junior member, who had then to return to the office and try his luck afresh. Once the team passed out of bounds, it was considered complete; no Porter, whatever his seniority, could displace any member. This system was apt to cause dissatisfaction and heartburning. Perhaps for that reason the Court of Rulers changed the bounds at frequent intervals, often several times a year. Not only when offices moved did new bounds have to be fixed, but bounds were often being widened or narrowed; sometimes they merely included that part of the street in which the office was situated, to the inter-section with the nearest crossroads, at other times they required detailed delimitation in all four directions.

If a Meter with a team left the office for a job, but delayed going off the bounds, the team remained liable to interruption as long as they lingered inside the bounds. In this contingency a team could leave the bounds and wait for the Meter outside so as to guard against late-comers. Similarly a Meter going out to work with a team might change his mind and return to the Meters' office to send another Meter. Porters with him, having forfeited their turns by leaving the bounds, safeguarded their rights by returning to their own office and putting their names on a separate section of the slate as waiting for this particular job. If on arrival at the waterside they did not find the expected vessel ready for work, a Meter and his team would return to their respective offices. On being informed that work could now begin, the Meter would announce the job once again at the Porters' office; the team which had turned out with him in the first instance was still entitled to accompany him, but Corn Porters who had meanwhile put their names on the slate could cut in. If, on the other hand, a Meter had gone out on a job with four Porters and found on arrival that a larger team was required, the senior Porter returned to the Porters' office for additional men. In completing such a team, Porters who had already been at the office when the Meter first set out had preference over others. Thus the procedure of turn labour protected senior Porters by ensuring them prior consideration if they went on berth at the right time.

The system of turn labour served two purposes: by making it impossible to know which Porter would turn out for which job, it prevented collusion between a Porter and buyer or seller of a commodity and guaranteed strict impartiality; the precedence enjoyed by seniority ensured to the older and feebler Porters a share of work. To direct the heaviest work to the strongest shoulders, the Rulers in 1838 made a temporary order confining all Porters of fewer than five years' standing to potato and backing labour, except with a Ruler's special permission; those breaking this regulation could be cut out during any stage of the job by any Porter of longer standing. On the other hand, a system exclusively favouring older Porters would have left the younger unable to earn their livelihood in slack times. To hold the balance between providing protection for senior and opportunities for junior members, the Rulers kept certain categories of goods as 'open work' to which turn labour did not apply, but where employment went to the firstcomers. Up to 1818 potatoes, malt and oysters were treated in this manner, though potato work subsequently became turn labour.

Though seniority determined Porters' rights to jobs in turn labour, they did not always go to work in that order. Some jobs were more onerous and less lucrative than others, either because their distance from the office involved time and outlay on travelling or because of the small quantity to be dealt with; some jobs combined both disadvantages. Porters had the right of refusing a job without losing their turns, thus retaining first choice of all subsequent jobs offered. Employment declined by senior Porters was then offered to their juniors. Porters had to be available for any job which required manning; if none of the Porters present was willing to go, the Ruler on duty had to find other men to perform the labour. It seemed fair to assign small and unprofitable jobs to the younger men in the knowledge that advancing seniority would put them in the way of more remunerative labour; meanwhile they could not be allowed to endanger the livelihood of men grown old in Fellowship work. At least, it seemed fair to Porters. Not so to merchants who felt no obligation towards older Fellowship members, but required their work done as fast as possible and therefore wanted young Porters and looked upon a system giving preference to old men as rank bad management. Especially did they resent seniors choosing the largest jobs, well knowing that they were too infirm to carry them through, thus necessitating the summoning of relief teams half-way through the work, with consequent delays. That Porters preferred large to small jobs and that older Porters were entitled to assert that preference, was of course generally known. Meters and merchants wanting young and vigorous Porters who worked speedily and effectively, often understated the quantities to be worked when informing the Porters' offices of impending jobs, in the hope of making the job sound unprofitable so that the older men would refuse it in favour of a team of junior men.

When unprofitable jobs were seen to be impending, Porters, far from going on berth at the office, disappeared altogether from view. Rulers or others responsible for work being manned had to seek them out, even if it meant leaving the office and tracking them down to their hideouts, if necessary to their homes, to warn them for work. One of the disadvantages of holding office as Ruler consisted of the time lost in this search for Porters to undertake unprofitable duties. Only too often did no Ruler attend at an office. In that case, his function devolved upon the senior Porter on the spot, who did not lose his own turn by going off bounds to find and warn junior Porters for work. When a man had accepted a job, he was wiped off the slate for the day; but if a Corn Porter had been compelled to undertake a small job, his name remained on the slate so that on returning he still had first choice of jobs offered at that office during the day. To stop Porters from drifting out of the office as the prospect of small jobs loomed up, every Porter seeing such jobs materialize was not only entitled but was required to detain at the office his successor on the slate until all jobs so far notified had been manned. To refuse unprofitable jobs did not constitute an absolute right, but remained subject to the overriding necessity of manpower being available to deal with all work offered.

Porters had to go properly with the Meter from the office; clandestinely meeting a Meter out of bounds or avoiding detection by going in a boat by a roundabout route to the vessel to be worked were offences for which Porters forfeited their earnings. Nor were Porters allowed to take freelance work or payment direct from the trade; it had to be assigned to them by the Ruler in charge, in the case of gangs by their foreman. A Porter obtaining work irregularly, even if he did not steal another man's job, did so at his own risk; if the labour either did not become available or was not paid for, the Fellowship afforded him no redress. Action could be taken against Porters who followed a Meter through the bounds and then left him or, after having accompanied him to the place of work, refused to assist in measuring. Discipline had to be enforced if the Fellowship was to retain and defend its privileges; merchants avidly sought for excuses to have the work done by cheaper unauthorized labour. Both the owners of the premises at, and of goods on, which Billingsgate Porters worked had to be empowered to suspend such Porters for insubordinate behaviour or other forms of misconduct; Porters aggrieved by such disciplinary measures could appeal to the Common Council. One form of misconduct from the Fellowship's point of view consisted of not doing work personally, but hiring another man, not a Billingsgate Porter, to perform it at a wage lower than that claimed by the member. The Fellowship put a stop to this practice in 1868, except for instances sanctioned by a Ruler. Not tying sacks carefully and properly could lead to suspension; if offenders could not be identified, the whole team was held responsible. Smoking or having a lighted pipe during working hours was generally forbidden, but particularly at wharves or in any ship or vessel. Residents objected to Porters keeping their tallies by means of marks chalked on doorposts; brewers resented Porters doing the same on their premises. Misconduct or bad language on board ship implicated the whole team unless the responsible party was disclosed.

The system of turn labour had the subsidiary advantage of affording opportunities to reward Porters for meritorious conduct. The Fellowship was anxious to detect work clandestinely done by interlopers; any Porter discovering and reporting such work in progress was entitled to a turn in the job, when claimed by the Fellowship, irrespective of his normal eligibility, and the same applied to a Porter who gave notice to the Meters' office of goods unloaded in an attempt to evade not only the City's porterage, but also the metage dues.[59]

Work afloat followed its own rules. In busy times a team working a vessel consisted of no more than five men, if hands were wanted for discharging other vessels (the rule originated in 1801 when wartime requirements caused a labour shortage); all team members above five counted as heavers and goers and could be drafted to other vessels, regardless of seniority, in order to enable further teams to be formed. When labour was plentiful, as in 1821, seven men were allowed for overboard work, which consisted of shooting cargo from the vessel into sacks in another craft, usually a lighter. At such times any team on board a vessel comprising fewer than seven Quartermen could be joined by any Porter to complete that number, subject to the ban on the employment of watermen and lightermen in porterage work which formed part of the general rules. The favourite place for work in a team afloat was in the boat's nose; a regulation reserved this to Porters suffering from physical handicaps. As no more than one man in every team could occupy this preferred place, of several contenders for the privilege only the senior was allowed to join the team. Making and breaking the way presented problems wherever a vessel could only be reached by erecting gang-planks from the shore or via another vessel; as no remuneration was given for doing it, each Porter preferred to leave the job to his team mates. As many men as necessary, in order of seniority, were obliged to do the work. How many men this implied had to be decided on the spot, together with many other disciplinary measures. It fell to the senior Porter aboard to make these decisions; provided he could establish his seniority, his juniors had to accept his orders.

Wharfingers in the 1830s alleged that of all labour in the Port of London, Billingsgate Porters alone made an additional charge for landing goods from ships beyond the third tier; indeed, resentment had grown to such proportions that Fellowship Porters did not dare to make this imposition, but simply refused to work cargoes from ships beyond the third tier, while claiming them as their privilege once they reached the third tier. According to Robert Smith, an old enemy of City Porters,* wharfingers had to provide their own labour to carry goods from the fifth, sixth, and seventh to the third tier where they were taken over and landed by Billingsgate Porters. No remedy was devised for this complaint.

* See pp. 131–133 above.

Regulations had to be framed for relieving Porters who tired before a job had been completed. Porters working afloat after 6 p.m. could not go ashore before the end of the job unless they provided a relief man, but remained responsible for any further work required until the Meter himself had left the vessel. Teams had to apply for relief to the Fellowship office of the area within which the job was situated. Porters sent out to relieve teams at work were subject to the same seniority rules as governed ordinary regulations for employment: if they relieved colleagues without being appointed by a Ruler to the job, they were treated as running on the job. Not so, however, where a majority of a team had determined that they needed an additional man; such a team could take on a senior Porter applying for work without reference to the office. No Porter who had been relieved was eligible for other work on the same day, but he could turn out for jobs as usual on the morrow. It was not always practicable to send back for relief. At least within a team afloat, internal relief arrangements provided for Porters exchanging jobs in order of seniority, the most senior Porter taking a spell in the most junior's place, the second in seniority moving into the most senior's berth, and so on throughout the team.

A number of Porters worked not in temporary teams but in permanent gangs. Originally the Fellowship had levied a fine on any Porter joining a gang, but this was abolished in 1805 or 1806. To join the Bell Gang in 1808 a Porter had to pay the gangsmen a general fee of £5 5s. and another £2 2s. towards their equipment of barrows and shovels. The Court of Rulers kept the membership records of gangs; changes in gang personnel had to be notified to Fellowship Hall. Many gangs were formed in the first half of the nineteenth century; the Court of Rulers enumerated a number of Porters, from four to sixteen, to constitute a gang, such as the Bow Creek Gang for 'promiscuous labour' in 1822, the gang for carrot labour at the sign of the *Marquis of Granby* and the *Punchbowl*, St. Katherine Street, in 1827, and a gang for wheat and peas at the King's Victualling Office, Deptford, in 1829. Other gangs formed for seeds at Old Swan Stairs (1834) and for fruit, one at Puddledock and two at the legal quays (1838), one at Hungerford Market and one for apples in particular at Brewers' Quay (1848). In 1866 the Fellowship prohibited the practice of individual

P

Porters' belonging to more than one gang, though this was unlikely to have been a frequent occurrence.[60]

(b) Manner and Rates of Payment

To prove the amount of work done and obtain payment, Porters had to make out bills and hand them to paymasters or Shifters dealing with the commodity handled. Considering the prevailing illiteracy, the writing of such bills proved a formidable undertaking. To avoid error and confusions, bills became ever more detailed and elaborate: after

SPECIMEN BILL SUBMITTED BY A PORTER TO THE CORN SHIFTER

Friday	Augt. 16–1850
Grenaway	
only 26	278
27c $1\frac{3}{4}$	3.11$\frac{1}{4}$
out $1\frac{1}{2}$	4
	3. 7$\frac{1}{4}$
Chas R. Brown	
1830	

Notes: Entries in italics added by Shifter's office.

Grenaway is the name of the employer for whom the work was done.

Chas. R. Brown is the Porter's own name; he ought to have stated his Christian names in full.

1830 is the year of Brown's admission to the Fellowship.

4*d*. is the shift deduction.

1816, one or two colleagues working on the same job had to endorse each bill as proof that it represented genuine labour; Porters had to indicate the year of their admission and their Christian names at full length; a Porter making out a bill on behalf of an illiterate colleague had to endorse it; separate bills were required for jobs done with different Meters. The Shifter paid bills promptly on presentation. Sometimes Porters submitted bills for fictitious work or added turns not carried. If the Shifter subsequently discovered such a bill to be bad, he advertised for the Porter concerned to come and repay its value. Porters did not hurry to accept this invitation and had to be threatened with punishment for failing to take up a bad bill within a fortnight. For a serious fraud with regard to a bill, a Porter could be dismissed from the Fellowship. Porters obtaining by deceit work belonging to other Fellowship members had their bills stopped. In spite of all its complications, the shift system had the inestimable advantage of securing to Porters payment immediately upon completion of work. When it had ceased to exist in the Port of London, it continued for coal and salt heavers in the Port of Liverpool in the 1890s, their need for prompt payment admitting of no practicable alternative.

To defray expenses, Shifters made deductions from each bill cashed, in most instances 1*d.* in every shilling. Often they employed as agents the licensees of public houses, who shifted bills on the Shifters' behalf. Such establishments were known as 'wet offices'. Publicans performed this service without any remuneration, though one of them in one month in 1852 shifted 7,000 bills—evidence that their services in that capacity met with appreciation. On at least one occasion, the Fellowship Rulers asked for a public house to be made into a wet office to show recognition to a licensee who had made available his premises for the assembly of Porters going on berth for work.

This method of paying Billingsgate Porters came under heavy attack in 1878 from a number of 'Noblemen, Citizens and other Gentlemen', including the Duke of Westminster, Lords Ebury and Enfield, Sir Ughtred Kay Shuttleworth, Messrs. Samuel Morley, W. Cowper Temple and Thos. Hughes, who considered the shift deduction as completely unjustified. Sickness and unemployment benefits, even to Fellowship members, appeared to them insignificant and out of all proportion to the contributions exacted; where deductions were levied on non-members of the Fellowship, no benefits at all accrued to contributors. Not only Shifters, but the Fellowship in general were indicted because the bills of all Billingsgate Porters could most readily be redeemed at public houses; indeed, men employed as assistants in certain gangs could not cash theirs anywhere else. Publicans expected men to spend money on these occasions and subjected to delays and vexations those who refused to comply with this custom. That this salvo, fired at the Common Council in the form of a petition, had its origin in complaints from the sufferers, is borne out by the support it received from 337 Fellowship Porters who argued that, though a shift office existed at Fellowship Hall, it opened only for an inconveniently short period each day, thus forcing many members to do their shifting at public houses, nor did it shift at all for non-members. This view was not shared by the Court of Rulers or even by the Common Council's General Purposes Committee which investigated the complaint. Both pointed out that the work in question belonged to the exclusive prerogative of the Billingsgate Porters. If at periods of pressure they agreed to share the privilege with non-members, $1d.$ in the shilling constituted a licence fee paid for the right to participate in work not normally open to them, their contribution to the fund maintained by the Fellowship for making good losses occurring from time to time. Shifting in public houses had been sanctioned by long usage and found to work satisfactorily; any abuses brought to the notice of the Court of Rulers would be dealt with in summary fashion. The General Purposes Committee did not adopt so complacent an attitude towards the latter practice, but pointed out that during its lengthy investigations of the charges and replies Parliament had passed an Act which anyhow rendered payment of wages in public houses illegal.[61]

Rates of porterage usually changed piecemeal, as dissatisfaction of employers or Porters in any branch of the trade caused a reconsideration. In each instance, past Common Council enactments had laid down an appropriate charge, and changes can conveniently be dealt with under the various commodities concerned. In the middle 1820s, however, complaints from the grain trade caused a more general review by a Common Council committee which found many porterage rates, as enacted a century or more ago, out of date; the basis of computation had changed, and what Porters now charged often did not represent what some Common Council in the remote past had laid down. So the committee compiled its own table of rates for grain, somewhere half-way between what employers suggested and the Fellowship demanded, with most grain rates $\frac{1}{2}d$. a quarter higher below than above London Bridge. Separate rates followed for coal, fruit and roots, nuts of various kinds (with special tariffs for small nuts, walnuts, and chestnuts as well as apples, pears, onions and all other measurable fruit or roots not before specified), tarrace (a volcanic earth used for making cement), salt and shellfish. The committee's considerable labours deserved a better reception than the Common Council's decision to postpone consideration. Not till twenty months later did it resume its debate on the scale of rates.

It took another year for a final version to emerge. By this time Billingsgate Porters were willing to reduce prices for fruit which paid well and gave younger members adequate employment, but saw no justification for lower corn rates, all the more since current charges constantly secured employment to Fellowship Porters in areas outside the City jurisdiction where employers could not be coerced into giving them the work. A comprehensive tariff enacted in 1827 covered five and a half pages of print. Overboard rates for grain varied according to five criteria: whether the grain consisted of heavy or light seeds, whether it came out of Essex, Kentish or other vessels (home counties craft paying less), whether delivered from West-country, Ware or other vessels into craft without previous metering, whether malt was delivered in sacks or had to be shot, and whether discharge took place above or below London Bridge (above remaining cheaper). Landing charges used two of the same criteria: heavy or light grains, above or below London Bridge; beyond that, they varied according to distance and level, each thirty yards and each flight of stairs adding $\frac{1}{2}d$. per quarter, as did every three tiers of vessels after the initial three. Coal porterage remained proportional to distance, whereas fruit and roots were subdivided according to their nature, distance carried, distance of vessel from shore, size and weight of containers used and whether backing labour was required. Salt porterage varied with distance, a factor of little importance when it came to shellfish which was transported only within Billingsgate Market. The only people who voiced strong objections to this Act were potato merchants aggrieved by an increase in porterage rates, who threatened to employ non-freemen rather than pay enhanced charges; the Court of Rulers poured oil on troubled waters by enjoining Porters to continue working at the old rates. In 1848 the existing tariff was thrown into the melting pot once more by an instruction from the Common Council to its General Purpose Committee to review it, but nothing came of this.[62]

4

FELLOWSHIP PORTERS: TYPES OF WORK

(a) Corn Work in General

WHILE struggling to free themselves from the obligation of employing Billingsgate Porters, members of the corn trade nevertheless on occasions eagerly turned to them. Moving with the times, their regular labour now and then entered into combination and struck for higher wages. When that happened, employers remembered with relief the ever-ready Fellowship Porters whose prompt availability in 1801 and 1810 broke strikes of labourers working in granaries. Employers suffering from labour disputes were only too pleased to make use of Billingsgate Porters even in fields where the latter claimed no privilege, as happened in 1834 when Fellowship members worked at rates declared unacceptable by trade unions. However great the assistance which merchants and Billingsgate Porters rendered to each other in periods of industrial dispute, at most times their interests were diametrically opposed.

This became most clearly apparent when the atmosphere turned unfavourable to privilege: the trade cycle assuming a downward swing after 1815, owing partly to post-war recession, partly to the deflationary policy of a government bent on re-establishing the value of sterling, prices fell. Specific porterage charges represented an increasing proportion of the total cost of agricultural commodities falling in price and imposed a growing burden on trade. A petition of 1822 signed by corn and malt dealers from such widely differing places as Ipswich, Reading, Henley-on-Thames and Great Marlow pointed this out to the Common Council. The combination must be suspect, but the gravamen of their charges was clear. In addition to levying excessive rates, Fellowship Porters were accused of standing by and being paid for doing nothing when measuring took place. If a barge carrying a mixed load arrived at Scotland Yard and found the wharf so fully occupied that it preferred continuing its journey eastward to discharge flour and timber at the Grand Junction or some other City wharf before returning to Scotland Yard to unload grain, Billingsgate Porters demanded porterage on the complete cargo, even that part of it which they had never touched. Some West country grain sellers, having no need to travel so far downriver, avoided these charges by unloading at Westminster or elsewhere west of the City limits; Hertfordshire barges passed right through the City westwards. The complainants cited as special grievance the Porters' claim to second labour on grain on which they had already enjoyed the first labour, but which after a period in granary had to be remeasured or merely returned to the distant owner, if it could not be sold at a profit in London. Voluminous calculations accompanied these complaints to show how much more cheaply porterage was performed in the out-ports.

In their reply to this onslaught Fellowship Porters explained that only a small part of the grain water-borne to the Port of London was delivered from vessel to shore, a job claimed as Fellowship privilege. Most corn was measured on board before being transferred to craft and carried to buyers or lodged in granaries. Billingsgate Porters demanded the labour of measuring and transferring to the craft, but not the carriage from craft to shore. When grain was transported on land, Fellowship Porters claimed a right, not by virtue of their privilege but merely as freemen entitled to employment in preference to non-freemen—a doubtful argument, this; however, granary keepers had wrested this work from them by designating it second labour and performing it by their own men. A much reduced table of rates, submitted to the Common Council by an unidentified source, would not in the Rulers' view benefit either the corn trade or the public at large, but drive men out of corn porterage work. Vessels did not arrive at regular intervals; a labour force excessive for the require-ments of a slack week might a fortnight later prove quite inadequate to cope with the unloading of a whole fleet, immobilizing Meters for lack of Fellowship Porters. At the level of charges at present prevailing a team of Porters having to go as far as Limehouse to work ten quarters of oats lost money; if the quantity amounted to twenty, they broke even, on thirty to fifty they made a small gain. Of corn sold in the Port of London, the largest part changed hands in quantities of less than fifty quarters.

Handling malt gave rise to two distinct charges, one for overboard work, the other for landing, but where malt was not carried any distance, it was customary to charge overboard work only; if it had to be moved some distance, the overboard charge was allowed for in the landing charge, which depended on distance carried but could not for that reason be described as second labour, as complainants had done. Prices of labour, according to the Porters, were basically contractual: not only had they been determined by collective bargaining before enactment by the Common Council, but where jobs deviated from the standard pattern, individual agreement among the parties replaced the enacted charge. When the difficulty of a job came to be assessed, more depended upon ease of access to the shore on landing and to warehouse premises on delivery than upon distance of carriage; no table of rates based on distance alone could do justice to the work. Complainants claimed to speak on behalf of the corn trade above London Bridge, a very small fraction of the whole, whereas no objections had been raised by the large corn merchants east of London Bridge who paid higher rates and represented the vast majority of the trade. The Fellowship suspected the curiously mixed authorship of the petition, which had only one feature in common: contact with certain wharfingers who at this time by an all-out attack on the City Porters' privileges endeavoured to rid themselves of authorized labour so as to perform the work themselves henceforth, charging official rates to their customers, but paying much lower wages to their staff.*

A full-scale investigation by the Common Council's Coal and Corn Committee alone could disentangle claims and counter-claims. For purposes of comparison, accounts of grain delivery charges at Liverpool and Newcastle were obtained. The former port granted no privileges to any particular class of workers; in both places porterage charges proved to be much in excess of those prevailing in London. This defeated part of the complaint. To deprive Porters of second

* See p. 129 above.

labour meant identifying, perhaps long after the event, cargoes which Porters had already worked once—an almost impossible task. Expert witnesses from the corn trade admitted that firms established outside City limits sometimes engaged unauthorized men for second labour, never however when a City Meter was employed, nor did there exist any strong objection to the Billingsgate Porters performing both labours. Neither corn factors nor brewers in general considered the rates charged by the Fellowship Porters excessive; while they might earn rather well at times of great pressure of business, at that moment they could obtain no more than a bare subsistence.

On the basis of these findings, the committee proposed neither to deprive Billingsgate Porters of second labour nor to abate charges for the first, but to make some reduction in the rates for second labour and forbid strictly any variation of rates once enacted by the Fellowship's Court of Rulers. Charges should be exhaustively ascertained, clarified, embodied in a table differentiated according to commodities and publicized. But already the wharfingers had influential friends at court. The Common Council did not accept the committee's report, but referred it back for reconsideration.

Deliberations in the Common Council may have given the committee more guidance on the direction its reconsideration should take than the bare minutes suggest. It organized a small-scale public opinion poll by asking forty users of Fellowship labour—brewers, wharfingers, corn factors, granary keepers, and coal merchants—for acceptable porterage rates. The response did not suggest that Fellowship charges constituted a highly explosive preoccupation in the City of London. Of the forty, nine took the trouble to reply: one firm to declare its satisfaction with existing rates, eight others to disclaim any obligation to use Fellowship labour, hence any interest in its remuneration. This was also the attitude adopted by a number of representative wharfingers and malt factors whom the committee consulted. Of corn traders operating east of London Bridge and disbursing thousands of pounds a year for porterage, not a single one stirred. Disconcerted by so little response, the committee then wrote to the first signatory in each place subscribing the joint petition from Ipswich, Reading, Henley-on-Thames and Great Marlow, requesting copies of actual charges made by Billingsgate Porters. The reaction to this invitation was even more surprising: two signatories replied, the first to say that he never supplied any goods to London at all, but had been prevailed upon by neighbours to sign a petition which would afford general relief to agriculture through reduction or removal of superfluous charges; the second transmitted accounts for metage and porterage, not in London, but at Ipswich, Liverpool and Newcastle. The petition which had set the investigation on foot and tried to deprive Fellowship Porters of their work stood exposed as a pure machination of intriguing wharfingers.[63]

The Common Council Act of 1801 had limited the Fellowship's grain privilege to 'first labour', which consisted of all carriage of grain from vessels in the Port of London either to the shore or to any other vessel, unless such grain had already been handled by the Billingsgate Porters. When a corn cargo reached the Port of London, the consignee gave a delivery order on the vessel's captain to a lighterman, granary keeper, or, if the merchandise had already been sold, to the purchaser. The recipient of the order was obliged to have the grain measured by an authorized Meter; all Acts of Parliament which in the 1820s modified the corn duties took care to leave this City privilege intact. The order was therefore lodged at the office maintained by the Board of Corn Meters.

The Corn Meters in Trust were ten Common Councilmen elected to this office by their fellow members, usually just after having completed a four-year period of service on the Common Council Committee of Control over Coal and Corn Meters, a committee comprising sixteen Aldermen and thirty Common Councilmen. They remained Corn Meters in Trust for a further four years unless they lost their seats on the Council. Their description misrepresented their function; they did not themselves engage in measuring, but merely in the superintendence of 152 Deputy Corn Meters who were Fellowship Porters and did the actual work. Corn Meters in Trust met as a Board at least once a week. They had power to suspend or reduce in rank a Deputy Corn Meter, but for more drastic action the sanction of their parent body, the Committee of Control over Coal and Corn Meters, was required. The eighteen senior Deputy Corn Meters were known as

Placed Men. They allocated the work among the Deputy Corn Meters on a principle akin to that of the Porters' offices, precluding prior knowledge of which Meter would be sent to which job. Deputy Corn Meters drew their remuneration daily from the Placed Men for the day's work; the Placed Men themselves settled up once a month with the Corn Shifter. For corn brought down-river and discharged above London Bridge, Deputy Corn Meters delivered their accounts to the clerk at Brooke's Wharf, who collected the metage and accounted to the Corn Meters in Trust. The Deputy Corn Meters' returns of work performed determined not only the City metage, but also the national Customs duty, hence they were of national importance. A Deputy Meter, when assigned to a job, called at the appropriate Porters' office and collected a team of Porters.

Once attached to a Meter, Porters were entitled to hold all work which this Meter did during his tour of duty, provided they had followed him by the correct route without attempting unauthorized shortcuts. Even if some of the work led them out of the area served by their office, the fact that the Meter in charge could deal with the job legitimized the team in doing likewise. So wide a franchise was unsatisfactory at periods when many Porters suffered from lack of employment. In 1868 the Rulers limited to thirty quarters the amount of grain a team could handle on board any vessel for which it had not turned out. A job could not always be done in one day. If the Meter was entitled to hold it for the following day, the Porters working with him at the end of the first day could equally retain their hold on the work by asking the Ruler at the office to allocate it to them or, if no Ruler was in attendance, leaving their names at Fellowship Hall on the evening of the first day. In doing so, they assumed not only the right but also the duty to complete the job. Much difficulty arose over attempts to register for grain work on the previous evening. As a general rule neither Meter nor Porters could be designated until the morning when work began; an exception had to be made, however, for jobs which started before the usual working time. The Fellowship limited such exceptions: Porters taking their turns on the eve for an early-morning job, even if Corn Porters, took seniority as Quartermen only; unless they started operations at least half an hour before normal working time began, they were treated as running on the job.

Having completed his team, the Meter started out, carrying a shovel, a strike and a bushel; these implements of work being heavy, it became in 1878 the duty of the youngest Porter in the team to carry them, as well as to ensure that they were returned to the office promptly after completion of the job and not left at the place of work or in a public house. On board ship the Meter and three Porters descended into the hold. One Porter held open the sack while the other two forced the bushel into the grain. The Meter topped up the bushel with the shovel, one of the two Porters levelling the grain in the bushel with the strike. It was then emptied into the open sack and the Meter marked the tally in chalk on his shovel. While at Liverpool such hand-bushellers of grain qualified as specialists among Porters, in London all Billingsgate Porters took their turn according to seniority. The remaining Porters stayed on deck and hoisted the full sacks out of the hold, swung them across and lowered them straight into barges. Working with a team of eight Porters, a Meter would dispose of an average of fifty quarters of corn per hour; if a special effort was called for, the hourly throughput could be stepped up to seventy quarters. Of the Porters, those in the hot and dusty air of the hold tired quickly. After a two-hour spell, Porters in the hold therefore exchanged places with those on deck; not so the Meter, who had to remain in the hold throughout.

In the course of the nineteenth century, steam hoists were installed in many flour-mills situated along the waterside to raise the grain straight from the barge. Such grain was sold by weight, not measure; hence these mills required the services neither of a Meter nor of Fellowship Porters. Duty continued to be assessed on the basis of measure, but measure as ascertained by deeming each sack of grain to contain four bushels. Much to the millers' disgust, metage and porterage charges continued to be levied in these circumstances, but Billingsgate Porters compromised by reducing their charges by 1d. a quarter and assisting in the operation of the steam hoists. Where grain was brought alongside the mill by railway, on the other hand, they could not claim the discharging work at all.

The law of the land required that corn be re-measured on sale out of granary. The buyer therefore applied for a Meter who collected his team of three or more Porters in the usual manner; upper limits in the manning scale for granary teams were set at six Corn Porters or four Quartermen. The actual work consisted only of filling and striking the bushel and emptying its contents into sacks. Carrying out the sacks and delivering the goods formed no part of Fellowship labour; it could be done by the granary keeper's own employees.

The working of Corn Meters without Fellowship assistants withdrew more and more corn work from the Porters. It was this practice which a group of Porters met to discuss in August 1830 at a public house on Tower Hill. Expecting little help from the Rulers, they appealed over their heads to the membership to attend a general meeting at the *Paul's Head* tavern. Faced with a strong faction within the Fellowship, the Rulers stated a case for the opinion of the Common Serjeant, Sir Thomas (later Lord) Denman, who declared it to be beyond doubt that Corn Meters ought not to work unless accompanied by Billingsgate Porters. The Common Pleader concurred. In a petition to the Common Council, 1,334 Fellowship Porters embodied this view, but though the Council ordered a committee to investigate, it seemed far more interested in the processes leading to the drafting of the petition than in the substance of the controversy. The only body empowered to give direct instructions to the Deputy Corn Meters, the Board of Corn Meters in Trust, refused to act upon Counsel's opinion, but left its Meters free to go to work with or without Billingsgate Porters at the customer's option.

The Metage on Grain (Port of London) Act, 1872, abolished all compulsory measuring of grain. The City Corporation tried to continue metage on a voluntary basis, whereas the Fellowship of Porters adapted its regulations to work performed without any Meter or weigher. In neither instance was the experiment successful; so after a year's trial the City Solicitor dismissed the 152 Deputy Corn Meters with a gratuity of £15 each, reminding them that, as Billingsgate Porters, they were entitled to all work reserved to the Fellowship— if they could find any.[64]

Grain work provided very irregular employment. Corn often arrived in convoys of ships. In order to discharge quickly, a large

number of Fellowship Porters had to hold themselves in readiness—
far more than could find employment while few or no ships were in
port. Peak demand for porterage services greatly exceeded regular demand—a complaint regarding dockwork echoed throughout the century
and fully documented early in the next century in Lord Beveridge's
book on *Unemployment*. The nearest approach in the earlier nineteenth
century to Lord Beveridge's statistics are some figures supplied to the
Common Council in 1824 on the authority of William Ruston, the
Corn Shifter below Bridge, according to which upward of 700 Porters
held themselves ready, taking one day with another, for corn work
below Bridge, this figure being capable of indefinite increase if there
was an unusual rush of work. Actual daily employment fluctuated
between 300 and 800, so that on an average 100 to 300 men a day found
themselves without a job. Rulers who manned corn work at peak
seasons had to resist the temptation of denuding other Fellowship
employments which did not always dovetail to the extent of being able
to spare Porters just as the corn work required them. On the other hand,
the grain trade depended greatly on the weather. If it started to rain
while a Meter with a team of Porters was on his way to a cargo, the
owner of the grain could prohibit work for fear that the merchandise
might be damaged by damp. If that happened, neither Meter nor
Porters received any compensation for their trouble.

From the middle seventeenth to the later eighteenth century, the
general level of prices did not vary much. As a result, Fellowship
Porters suffered no great hardship through continuing to work at rates
settled in 1678. Towards the end of the eighteenth century, however,
the cost of living rose, first spasmodically and during the French war
rapidly. Porters employed on waterside work also suffered from the
dislocation of the flow of imports which naval warfare entailed. Grain
Porters asked for an increase of $\frac{1}{2}d.$ a quarter and $\frac{1}{4}d.$ a sack on all
grains. The rise in the cost of living constituted their main argument;
they also complained of the growing strain of discharging cargoes now
that the corn trade employed larger vessels with deeper holds; to unload a given quantity of grain in such conditions often required three or
four additional men, spreading stationary rewards over an increased
number of earners. Porters sometimes had to travel to distant parts of

the Port, Limehouse or Deptford for instance, to deal with small quantities of grain, particularly if carried in foreign vessels which were not allowed higher upriver than Limehouse Reach where, before the days of docks, Porters worked in the appalling confusion and congestion prevailing in the Lower Pool. The shutting of continental ports, the uncertainty of ship arrivals in wartime, hard frost and other causes beyond their control added to the Porters' hazards; sometimes ships could not be worked because no gang-planks reached them, even via another ship, or no lighters or barges were available. The argument for an increase in rates was strong; a Common Council committee recommended it after investigation, provided the work performed was first labour and the cargoes were discharged east of London Bridge. With these reservations the increase passed the Council and entered into force in 1801.

Subsequent increases in rates often took the guise of special arrangements made between the Rulers and individual customers, such as a table of rates agreed with John & John Field, seedsmen, in 1804, in which charges differed according to the delivery of the seeds to the shop, the shop cellar, the warehouses in Thames Street (where the porterage rose with the storeys) or Pudding Lane; different basic rates applied to clover seed, peas and other heavy seeds, and light seeds. In the following year, Queenhithe factors agreed to increases in the price for canting and stacking malt, introducing in addition an extra $\frac{1}{2}d$. a quarter for the first pair of stairs plus another $\frac{1}{2}d$. for the next two pairs—an unauthorized increase in rates made by the Rulers and not discovered by the Common Council until almost twenty years later when it had to be withdrawn forthwith, but by that time the general price level had completely changed.

Prices continued rising throughout the first decade of the nineteenth century. Like all fixed-income recipients, Billingsgate Porters could not adjust their rewards quickly to the cost of living and suffered from the widening gap between their earnings and their expenditure. In 1810 they asked the Common Council for another $\frac{1}{2}d$. a quarter or $\frac{1}{4}d$. a sack for all grain work, pointing out that since the last increase, rates of labour and the cost of living had risen and rendered it difficult for them to make ends meet. Indeed, members could find more profitable work elsewhere and did not present themselves for Fellowship labour, reducing the Court of Rulers to printing notices and advertising in the newspapers the penalties to which Porters exposed themselves by neglecting their employment. The Common Council could hardly refuse, nor were corn factors averse to paying enhanced rates, provided sufficient labour became available. The amounts asked for were enacted in full within three months. This enabled the Court to enlist large numbers of recruits to the Fellowship, welcome in time of war. But when peace returned a few years later, the Fellowship found itself crowded with members for whom it could not procure sufficient work.*

A Porter entitled to corn work, the most remunerative of the Fellowship's activities, prepared to turn out in all weathers, go wherever required within the Port of London (albeit his fares exceeded his earnings) and stay until the job was done, in 1824 earned approximately 3s. a day. This calculation excluded from computation all those who had failed on any one day to find employment. It made insufficient allowance for the large number of unremunerative jobs, small quantities of grain handled at a very large distance from the Porters' point of departure. In the busiest year they had known, 1827, Corn Porters succeeded in earning £1 5s. 3d. a week (gross of fares). Ruston compiled a detailed table of porterage for 1827: (see p. 226). He gave no indication of the intervals between the arrival of these boats or period over which they discharged, why the ratio of staffing to volume of cargo varied from one man per 1·7 quarters to one man per 33 quarters discharged; above all, of the working time for which the amounts set out in the end column represented the reward.

Grain metage and porterage combined amounted in the 1850s to a five per cent *ad valorem* tax which flour did not bear, thus putting London millers at a five per cent disadvantage *vis-à-vis* country competitors. The Court of Rulers, when faced with this complaint, reduced the price of corn labour by one-third, bringing it back exactly to what it had been in 1801, much to the satisfaction of the Corn Shifter below Bridge, in spite of the loss of income he suffered from the proportionate fall in the shift deduction. Applying only below Bridge, this reduction

* See p. 258 below.

Q

Ship's Name	Name of Captain	Port of departure	Number of Porters	Quantity discharged (qrs.)	Gross earnings	Waterage deducted	Net earnings	
							Total	per Porter
					£ s. d.	£ s. d.	£ s. d.	s. d.
Earl Clancarty	Boxer	Rotterdam	65	521	5 19 3	1 1 8	4 17 7	1 6
Cowan	Eschelby	Danzig	32	1052	14 1 5	10 8	13 10 9	8 5
Susannah	Carpenter	Petersburgh	75	1423	16 6 1	1 5 0	15 1 1	4 0
Bee	Snow	Maldon	60	212	2 8 7	10 0	1 18 7	0 7½
Elizabeth	Byford	Boston	72	604	6 18 5	12 0	6 6 5	1 9
Little Hermitage	Beaumont	Colchester	18	267	2 11 0	3 0	2 8 0	2 8
Union	Loft	Leigh	6	60	13 9	1 0	12 9	2 1½
Resolution	Raven	Maldon	6	10	2 3½	1 0	1 3½	0 2½
Traveller	Howes	Hamburg	102	907	10 7 10	1 14 0	8 13 10	1 8¼
Aurora	Schroder	Pillau	42	1029	11 15 10	14 0	11 1 10	5 4
Aurora	Hazewinkel	Groningen	72	624	7 3 0	1 4 0	5 19 0	1 7
Susan	Dales	Riga	66	1516	20 5 6	1 2 0	19 3 6	5 9

for the first time in the nineteenth century brought corn porterage charges above and below Bridge to parity. Among the body of Billingsgate Porters, a dissident group strongly disapproved the reduction, alleging that it had been decided upon at the Shifter's behest, chiefly to appease the Common Council at a time when the privileges of the Fellowship as a whole had come under review.*65

(b) Malt Work

Special rules applied to malt work done at breweries which was paid for directly by the employers, not by the Corn Shifter. Brewers insisted on settling porterage charges at a place where their beverage was on tap and expected some of the earnings to return to them at once in exchange for liquid refreshment. Long after most other owners and dealers of grain had struggled free from the Billingsgate Porters, brewers employed them in the transport of malt. An industry in which

* See p. 290 below.

capital outlay looms much larger than labour cost employs a small permanent staff, relative to the total size of establishments, hence is more willing to use outside contractors, nor do wages play a large part in its cost structure. Fellowship Porters in the nineteenth century carried malt in sixteen establishments, including most of the large London brewers (except Whitbreads), though such places as Pott's Vinegar Yard, the Deptford Victualling Yard, Junction and Irongate Wharves should not perhaps feature in this list. Nothing illustrates more clearly the loss of business suffered by the Porters than that by 1892 the number of breweries employing Billingsgate Porters should have dropped to three, of which one was just being equipped with machinery to supersede manual porterage. In this trade most establishments prescribed exactly the manning scale, thus limiting the size of Fellowship teams working on their premises. This left little for the Court of Rulers to regulate, except such turn labour rules as that every barge carrying malt should count as a fresh job, that all Porters working in breweries had to be prepared to do backing work, to stay on till the job was finished and not to make out their bills until the barge was clear. Porters pitching sacks in brew-houses or leaving them in unauthorized places were liable to suspension from malt work. Sometimes brewers admitted fewer turns than Porters claimed. Originally the deficiency had fallen on the last man in the team; the Court of Rulers considered it more equitable that all men still working in the last round, beginning at the most junior, were to bear a turn's loss each until the deficiency had been made up.

Of all the Porters' employers in the malt trade, the largest were Barclay & Perkins, of Stoney Lane and Bankside, who at certain times found work for more Billingsgate Porters than the rest of the trade; at the zenith they kept 140 men busy. The awe which such large employers inspired justified a deputation of Rulers to wait upon the firm if any difference arose. In 1867, sixty Billingsgate Porters still found work at this brewery, but by 1892 the number had dropped to twenty-five. The second-largest employer in this trade, the City of London Brewery, gave work to sixty Fellowship Porters at the best time; when the Court of Rulers detailed instructions for labour there in 1868, a team of twenty Porters dealt with the malt received by wagon, but could recruit another twenty Porters if a barge arrived while wagon work was still in progress, and vice versa. Two of the Rulers waited on the managing director of this brewery to arrange for a standard price for all porterage work, whatever its nature. Employment in 1892 had declined here to four Porters only. Courage & Donaldson, of Horselydown, made use of thirty Porters in 1828, paying them at the *Anchor* tap, one of their houses. Work in their lofts being the most arduous, the team was split into three groups, the ten junior men working the first fifty quarters in the lofts, the ten senior to them the next fifty quarters, the senior men the following fifty quarters, and so on, rotating every fifty quarters. A year later the manning scale was reduced to twenty Porters. In 1832 the team shrank to fifteen men whenever the malt arrived loose instead of in sacks. Porters were not allowed, as in other breweries, to assemble for work on the premises, as this caused inconvenience, but had to go as a team from the Corn Office when work was ready. By 1863 much of the malt reached this brewery by wagons, and teams for wagon work were reduced to ten men. Further reductions took place in 1869 when the barge team shrank to twelve, the wagon team to eight men; the firm had by this time installed mechanical tackle which the two senior men had to operate; those who could not do this had to relinquish the job altogether in favour of the two next in order of seniority.

Reid & Co., of Whitefriars, also paid Porters at their public house, originally at the legal rate of porterage, amounting to 2*d.* a quarter, expecting Porters to consume a pint of beer. This was known as the pint shift. Reids subsequently agreed to pay 2½*d.* a quarter, provided Porters drank a pot of beer; the pint shift turned into a pot shift. From eight in 1839, the team employed by them increased to twenty Porters, but contracted again to twelve in 1881. Hoares and Calverts were the other two breweries with sufficient malt work to have at one time teams of forty Porters effecting deliveries at their premises.[66]

(c) Corn Shift

Porters of corn other than malt looked for payment to their two Corn Shifters, of whom by far the more important was William Ruston, the

Corn Shifter below Bridge.* He combined his duties with the discharge of other functions in the corn trade which he kept secret; he derived an income from furnishing certain returns, based on Customs statistics. Whatever his means, he had obtained the office of Corn Shifter below Bridge in the face of considerable competition. Up to 1801 the annual rent had been £100. However, in 1801 porterage charges in the corn trade were raised,† and as the Corn Shifter received 1d. out of every shilling of porterage collected, his emoluments automatically increased. The Common Council offset these higher revenues by raising the rent by £50 a year. When a new twenty-one-year lease was granted in 1807, the annual rent rose to £250. Many Porters suspected that, official payments apart, Ruston found ways and means of showing financial appreciation to the Fellowship Rulers.

The Corn Shifter's task below Bridge was complex. Half the porterage fees, often very small sums, were owed by more than 2,000 corn buyers, many of them resident in the country and coming to town at infrequent intervals. When they disputed the accounts rendered, lengthy arguments ensued about trifling differences. Although the sellers of the corn were usually Londoners and therefore easier to reach, the fact that porterage was due partly from sellers, partly from buyers, did not ease the Corn Shifter's task. The annual average collected by Ruston between 1820 and 1826 was computed by him as £34,692—the Rulers' accounts yield a somewhat different result, but of a similar order of magnitude—and rapidly increasing; corresponding figures amounted to £46,842 in 1829 and £44,586 in 1830. Roughly one-twelfth of these sums represented the Shifter's gross revenue, his precise deduction amounting to

$\frac{1}{4}d.$ from amounts of 1d. to 4d.

$\frac{1}{2}d.$ „ „ „ $4\frac{1}{4}d.$ to 8d.

$\frac{3}{4}d.$ „ „ „ $8\frac{1}{4}d.$ to 10d.

1d. „ „ „ $10\frac{1}{4}d.$ to 1s. 2d.

and so on in proportion. On the basis of more than 200,000 Porters' bills a year, every 3s. 6d. of this revenue represented a separate unit of

---

* See pp. 103–104 above.   † See p. 224 above.

collection. Classifying debts outstanding on shift account in 1827 (£10,500) in order of magnitude, Ruston pointed out that

One-fifth	consisted of debtors to the amount of						less than 5s.	each
One-fifth	,,	,,	,,	,,	,,	,,	5s. to 20s.	,,
One-fifth	,,	,,	,,	,,	,,	,,	£1 to £5	,,
One-fifth	,,	,,	,,	,,	,,	,,	£5 to £50	,,
One-fifth	,,	,,	,,	,,	,,	,,	over £50	,,

On account of the large number of both debtors and creditors, Ruston had to employ four clerks; his current expenses (including legal costs and bad debts) amounted to £1,360 a year, of which £500 represented his own remuneration. In addition to porterage, Ruston at no extra expense to the City Corporation also collected metage, lastage and fillage dues on corn, raising his total annual collection above £50,000.

When Ruston's lease as Corn Shifter below Bridge expired in 1828, it was not renewed, the Fellowship having decided in future to carry on the shift on its own account.* Legally this implied a fundamental change; to practical arrangements it made hardly any difference. The Common Council was firmly convinced that only one person could possibly manage the corn shift below Bridge; that man was William Ruston. Instead of leasing the office of Corn Shifter below Bridge, Ruston now held it by appointment to the Fellowship. In other words, the capital to carry on the shift was to be found by the Fellowship and administered on its behalf by Ruston, who gave security for it in the amount of £10,000, but in effect Ruston began by advancing it to the Fellowship, though £5,000 was raised later in the year to reduce its indebtedness to Ruston. Subsequently Ruston asserted that even the £7,000 provided did not suffice to carry on the shift; sometimes he required £10,000 to £11,000 for the purpose. At all times therefore the capital employed in the corn shift represented partly Fellowship stock, partly Ruston's own contribution. This however presupposed the inclusion in the total amount of metage and those other Corporation dues which he also collected.

Under the new arrangement, Ruston as an employee of the Fellowship of Porters had to have a salary. The Fellowship Rulers proposed

* See p. 281 below.

3½ per cent on the amount collected. Their calculation seemed eminently reasonable: on the assumption that Ruston continued to defray all expenses hitherto borne in his capacity as lessee and that £39,000 was the annual amount collected, 3½ per cent yielded £1,365, precisely the current expenses computed by Ruston himself, including his own remuneration of £500 p.a. However persuasive the arithmetic, Ruston immediately informed the Rulers that he considered the percentage inadequate. The Common Council's Coal and Corn Committee thought Ruston's claim too high, that of the Court of Rulers too low, so split the difference in fixing the Corn Shifter's proportion at 4½ per cent, yielding for the next decade or two annual gross revenue in the range of £1,500 to £2,300. Ruston was highly satisfied with this percentage, the more so as, according to the Court of Rulers, he had at one time protested his willingness to do the work for 4 per cent. The Court of Rulers, on the other hand, objected to this excessive deduction from Fellowship revenues, achieved largely by the doubtful statistics supplied. Scrutinizing accounts submitted by Ruston in 1829, the Rulers pointed to an amount of £32, described as losses on bills paid, which consisted of under-payments erroneously accepted by Ruston's clerks in full discharge; £73, disguised as loss in taking stock, represented in fact an overestimate of outstanding debts; £38 excess of office expenses had arisen from an increase in turnover not allowed for in the estimates; of £290 bad debts, approximately £90 did not concern the Fellowship, but was owed to the Placed Men for metage; £100 doubtful debts represented nothing more than Ruston's estimate and included one-third due for metage which inured to the City Corporation, not to the Fellowship of Porters. Yet all these figures had been adduced to persuade Common Councilmen that Ruston required the full 4½ per cent deduction to make ends meet. A gift of two punchbowls to the Court of Rulers after a suitable interval might suggest that Ruston thought it wise to propitiate a body which had eventually acquiesced in the diversion to his pockets of substantial revenues.

For the payment of Porters' bills, Ruston maintained four offices. The chief one, known as the 'dry office', was his own house where Porters could present bills from 9 or 9.30 a.m. to 6 p.m. The other three were wet. He undertook to bear the loss due to bad debts. However, Billingsgate Porters continued to allege during Ruston's period of office that he failed to live up to his obligation, but deducted from the Porters' pay any bills which merchants had not settled, even if payment was refused three years after services had been rendered. To this charge Ruston returned a qualified denial: if the Porter had done the work and charged correctly for it, no loss fell on him. From complaints referred to the Fellowship Court of Rulers it becomes evident, however, that on at least one occasion Ruston had to be prodded by the Court into an effort to recover money for a job done. Ruston on his side stressed the volume of bad bills presented to him, which he could make Porters take back only by rigorously stopping current payments to them:* in 1841 his portfolio contained over 10,000 of them. Porters failing to collect their bad bills at his summons could be punished by the Court of Rulers, but experience had taught him that this procedure was not effective—notwithstanding the occasional dismissal from the Fellowship of Porters submitting bills for work they had not done. The other duties incumbent upon Ruston in his capacity as Corn Shifter were to account monthly to the Fellowship Rulers and annually to the Common Council and to employ in shift duties only Billingsgate Porters. On the latter obligation he defaulted recklessly; of his four clerks only one had taken up membership of the Fellowship. As collector of other Corporation dues, Ruston also superintended Deputy Corn Meters and settled monthly with the Placed Men.†

The Corn Shifter at Queenhithe, who dealt with porterage earned above Bridge, conducted business on a smaller scale altogether. Richard Hopkins held the office in 1818, but assigned the lease in 1827 to John Eayres, a Porter who had for some time managed the shift on Hopkins' behalf. The annual rent paid for the lease of the Queenhithe shift amounted to a mere £31 10s. Eayres's lease expired in 1829, only one year after Ruston's, and the Fellowship similarly took this shift into its own hands, appointing Eayres to manage it, which he did for thirty years. This being a much smaller concern than the shift below Bridge, Eayres's deduction had to be fixed at 6 per cent as against

* See p. 211 above.　　　　† See p. 220 above.

Ruston's 4½; yet Eayres's annual gross revenue never exceeded £30 to £40, and no controversy arose over his percentage. Like Ruston, Eayres had to defray his own office and legal expenses and bear the risk of bad debts, but if these resulted from faulty bills, he summoned the Porters concerned before the Court of Rulers and made them refund the money. He also accounted once a month to the Rulers and once a year to the Common Council and gave security, amounting to £1,000, for the capital employed in his shift. How small this capital was, emerges from a request by the Rulers in 1842 to Ruston to advance to Eayres £100 to meet a temporary emergency. All Eayres's bills were shifted in public houses.

On Eayres's death in 1859 the Fellowship amalgamated the corn shifts above and below Bridge in William Ruston's hands, though Ruston, who had been Corn Shifter for well over half a century, could hardly attend personally to his duties any more on account of advancing years. Of the amalgamated corn porterage rates collected, the Shifter continued to deduct his twelfth, paying out of this sum in the first instance his office expenses, which in 1859 amounted to £547 17s. 6d. and were not in future to exceed that sum without Common Council consent. After further deducting the Shifter's remuneration of £200 a year, the balance remaining was added to general Fellowship revenues. By 1866 the working capital, then £4,550, and the expenses allowance had become greatly in excess of requirements, owing to the fall in turnover; £250 in that year proved adequate to defray the costs of the shift office. Two years later, Ruston was pensioned off at the age of eighty-two, the corn shift and the City Corporation each contributing £100 a year to a life rent for him. In view of his age and length of service, the Common Council refrained from the usual valedictory scrutiny of the discharge of Ruston's duties; not so the Fellowship Rulers, who, true to tradition, dragged a dispute with him into the Court of Chancery.

The disappearance of the powerful and venerable though somewhat suspect figure of William Ruston necessitated new arrangements for what was patently a dying concern. These largely prompted the Common Council Act of 1868 which regulated corn shifting for the last part of the Fellowship's existence. Much quarrelling preceded the passage of the measure: members of the corn and fruit trades as well as some Billingsgate Porters petitioned in favour of the bill, while other Porters opposed it; amendments to refer the bill back for reconsideration, to adjourn further consideration till the next court and to let the General Purposes Committee deal with the several petitions received, all had to be defeated before progress could be made. Collection of porterage accounts now became the duty of the Clerk of the Corn Meters in Trust, who remitted to the Fellowship Rulers weekly the money received to the nearest £100 and monthly the exact balances while rendering monthly accounts audited by the Corn Meters in Trust. Out of the shift revenue, the first £300 paid for the additional labour and expenses incurred by this collection. Porters' bills were shifted at Fellowship Hall. Monthly porterage accounts, as rendered by the Clerk, survive for the period from 1880 to 1894. They show very considerable variations: in a good month (June 1882), £1,788 might be earned, in a bad month (July 1884) as little as £43. A monthly average of £600 in the early 1880s dwindled to little more than £100 by the middle 1890s.[67]

(d) Salt Work

The handling of salt is disagreeable to health and ruinous to clothes. Only a small group of junior Porters, the most poorly paid and ill-used of the Fellowship, concerned themselves with this commodity. Originally salt work constituted turn labour, the first ten men on berth being entitled to hold a vessel throughout its discharge. The team increased from ten to fifteen in 1818, the Porters' turn being in as soon as they left the recognized meeting place for salt work, a public house in Love Lane, with the Meter. In 1829 salt work became gang labour; Salt Porters constituted themselves in three permanent gangs of fifteen men each. Porters wishing to join these gangs put their names down and were appointed to vacancies in accordance with seniority. Most of the work arose in conjunction with Salt Meters. Of these, four existed until the 1830s; theirs were offices of profit purchased from the City Corporation. But in the 1830s, salt metage was reorganized, largely owing to the shrinkage of business; a salaried official of the

Corporation combined part-time work as sole surviving Salt Meter with similar unexacting functions as first Serjeant of the City Chamber, Yeoman of the Waterside and Clerk of Billingsgate Market. Like his four predecessors, he did not personally undertake metage, but acted through Deputy Salt Meters who were Fellowship Porters and worked at porterage when there was no salt to measure. Metage on salt amounted to 1s. per ton, of which 8d. went to the Salt Meter, 4d. to the City Corporation.

Just as for corn, payment for salt porting was effected by means of a salt shift for which Bernard Steers, the Salt Shifter, paid an annual rent of £30 to the Fellowship, maintaining his office at the *Cock* in Love Lane. His lease expired a little later than that of the Corn Shifters, at the end of 1830, and the Fellowship in pursuit of its new policy took over the salt shift, but appointed Steers's son, Robert, Salt Shifter on its behalf and allowed him to retain the last annual rent payment of £30 due from his father by way of working capital, on which he paid interest of 5 per cent. His own commission amounted to $3\frac{1}{2}$ per cent of gross revenue collected—£212 p.a. at the time he took it over, but falling rapidly, owing to tariff reform and the substitution of rail for water transport, until in 1852 the annual percentage accounted for less than £4, having averaged £25 for much of the intervening period. He gave security to the Fellowship in the amount of £1,000. When Steers in 1856 vacated his office, either by resignation or death, the volume of business did not warrant the appointment of a successor. His surviving functions were added to the Pennyman's duties, who discharged them at no extra reward.

Salt merchants had a grievance regarding porterage arrangements. Billingsgate Porters did not obtrude their services upon soap and glass producers, who used salt for manufacturing purposes; presumably because cargoes of salt reached these industries unobserved, they could be unloaded by unqualified labourers at cheap rates. Yet salt merchants invariably had to use Fellowship Porters and pay the full charges. These had been raised by $\frac{1}{4}d.$ per cwt. in 1810 to compensate the rise in the cost of living. When that tendency was reversed, salt merchants became more insistent and submitted substantial complaints about Billingsgate Porters to the Common Council in 1834. The Fellowship met trouble half-way by volunteering a scale of charges, amended mostly by extending standard distances, as comparison shows:

Salt porterage per cwt.

	Old rate	Revised rate
Delivery out of vessel into craft or other vessel alongside	$1\frac{1}{4}d.$	$\frac{3}{4}d.$
Landing on wharf and delivery into carts or wagons standing opposite the wharf, if distance		
does not exceed 80 yards	$1\frac{1}{2}d.$	
„ „ „ 110 „ and one flight of stairs		$1\frac{1}{4}d.$
between 80 and 120 yards	$1\frac{3}{4}d.$	
„ 110 „ 200 „		$1\frac{1}{2}d.$
„ 120 „ 220 „	$2\frac{1}{4}d.$	
„ 200 „ 300 „		$1\frac{3}{4}d.$
„ 220 „ 300 „	$2\frac{1}{2}d.$	
For every additional 80 yards	$\frac{1}{4}d.$	
„ „ „ 50 „		$\frac{1}{4}d.$
„ „ flight of stairs after the first		

and this was accepted.

Salt being an unpleasant commodity to handle, it took longer for Fellowship Porters' privileges in this field to be challenged. When they became a subject of dispute, this was chiefly due to the restless salt merchant William Clay, subsequently a baronet, member of Parliament for the Tower Hamlets and magistrate for Middlesex and Westminster, who had already started discharging goods in canal basins and thus evading the City rights.* His firm, Clay & Newman, had refineries in the North and transported salt in 40-lb. squares to London in barges. On entering the Port of London the cargoes were measured by City Salt Meters. This infuriated Clay who was carrying his own property to his own warehouses and could see no purpose in having it measured. Squares of high-quality refined salt were liable to

* See p. 125 above.

breakage and soiling; by not exercising a sufficient degree of care, Salt Meters often dirtied or chipped them. Once the Salt Meters had done their worst, Billingsgate Porters took over, exercising their right of discharging these salt cargoes at the firm's City warehouses. According to Clay their charges, three times the current value of labour services, represented between 15 and 30 per cent of the cost of salt at the works. Clay intervened personally with the Court of Rulers; subsequently his firm, supported by other salt merchants, petitioned the Common Council. No satisfaction resulted from either approach, but Porters found it so hard to obtain from salt merchants money for work done that seven resigned from salt gangs rather than continue doing battle for their remuneration. Eventually a test case was taken to the Court of King's Bench, which found for the Porters.

(e) Coal Work

In the coal trade Billingsgate Porters had almost lost their foothold. Gangs of coal whippers, each working under a basket man, discharged coal ships. Such gangs were employed by licensed coal undertakers, persons paid by the shipowners at piece rates and forbidden to engage directly or indirectly in the victualling trade. The law was easily evaded: fathers, mothers, sons, daughters, relatives and friends of publicans obtained licences as coal undertakers and favoured the publicans' customers when choosing whipping labour. Even Fellowship Porters had no illusions of winning back their complete privileges from the coal whippers, but argued that none of the Acts regulating employment in the coal trade counted among the whippers the gang foreman or basket man whose business it was to fill the vat. While employed by coal undertakers paid by shipowners, he was not impartial as between buyer and seller, nor had he given bond for true performance as had Billingsgate Porters. He ought to be treated as an assistant in measuring rather than as a labourer in whipping; in other words, all gangs of coal whippers should work under a Fellowship foreman. Twice the Billingsgate Porters put this audacious demand to the Court of Aldermen which shelved it. When they made a third attempt in 1817, supported by thirty-seven coal merchants, their own Court of Rulers rejected the argument. Not within living memory had the coal whipping work been claimed by Fellowship Porters, who were under an obligation to work only alongside other Fellowship Porters, hence could not labour with coal whippers. As for claiming the easy task of the basket man while leaving to the whippers labour so severe and heavy that few Billingsgate Porters either could or would undertake it, the Rulers feared for the safety of life or limb of any Porter who possessed the temerity to act on such a ruling. The Common Council had no difficulty in rejecting the petition; the date being 1818, it could draw attention to the many ex-service men who had sacrificed pensions to rely on coal whipping for a livelihood. Eight Fellowship Porters made a final bid for exclusive coal work in 1822, only to be told on the City Solicitor's authority that, whatever their rights, they could not in practice be enforced.

A parliamentary enquiry in 1827 elicited that whippers were paid 1s. a chaldron, affording them in full employment a daily wage of 7s. to 8s. They worked in gangs of five, of whom three shovelled the coal, the other two holding open the sacks and stowing them when full; for the stowage they received 3d. per chaldron from the carmen. Most of the coal work remaining to Fellowship Porters was performed by permanent gangs. Coal work continued to be turn labour at Greenwich, where in 1811 the Court of Rulers limited the manning scale to six, except for jobs where the men themselves agreed to the employment of additional hands. Nevertheless, by 1824 the Rulers spoke of 'constant men' in the Greenwich coal work who could make application to the Tower Street Office for additional help in dealing with coal-ships, and if 'constant men' resigned, the extra men received first consideration in the filling of vacancies. In other words, Greenwich coal work had become gang labour in practice, even though the decree forming a Greenwich Gang of twelve men did not set the seal of official approval on existing arrangements until 1835. This was only one of a number of gangs in coal work. Where a coal barge made fast outside the area of any gang, it either discharged the coal in bulk, in which case the Porters beginning the work were entitled to clear the whole cargo, even if this took a number of days, or it unloaded limited quantities only, when Porters held work for the day and had to go on berth afresh on the morrow—a rule extended to all coal work in 1855.[68]

(f) Fruit Work in General and Fruit Shift

Fruit, roots, and vegetables constituted a very wide field of work for Fellowship Porters in which conditions varied according to the type of greenstuffs handled. A few rules applied to all: Porters going off to fruit work had to leave evidence that they had done so, or else their turns would not be in, and a few offices were common to all fruit work: the *White Hart*, Botolph Lane, for work above, the *Coopers' Arms*, Thames Street, for work below Billingsgate, the *Pitt's Head*, Broad Street, Ratcliffe, for work in the Stone Stairs district. Common also was the institution of the four Fruit Meters who dealt with potatoes and roots as well as fruit. They purchased their offices from the City Corporation without the right of alienation; one at least had paid a price of £3,960 for it. The emoluments warranted the outlay. Each Meter drew £10 p.a. from the City Corporation plus 1d. of the metage fee paid on every bushel measured on his behalf. Between them the four Fruit Meters in 1833 earned a gross revenue of £5,618; deducting expenses of £1,444, they were left with net earnings of £4,174. Fruit Meters were Billingsgate Porters, but neither engaged in porterage nor performed measuring duties themselves. The latter work was done by one or other of the thirty-six Deputy Fruit Meters, the principal Fruit Meters confining themselves to supervision and paying Deputy Fruit Meters for their measuring labour. Deputy Fruit Meters had to be Fellowship Porters of long standing; the only two men appointed to the office without previously having belonged to the Fellowship had to be subsequently discharged for dishonesty. Deputy Fruit Meters worked as Porters when there was no measuring of fruit to do.

With the exception of the porterage of oranges and lemons, work was paid for by the Fruit Shifter, a position occupied from 1804 to 1825 by Thomas Owen Powis, who resided at Canterbury Square, Southwark, and shifted all bills there, permitting no payment elsewhere. He held the shift on a lease for which he paid £25 p.a., less than any of the other Shifters. When that lease expired in 1825, merchants in various branches of the greenstuffs trade were trying to have porterage rates reduced, and collection of the dues encountered considerable difficulties. The appointment of Fruit Shifter rested with the Common Council which did not move very quickly. As an interim solution the Court of Rulers made one of their own members, James Hollamby, Fruit Shifter, voting him a salary of £3 a week and starting him off in an office in Tooley Street, rented at £30 p.a., with stationery and equipment purchased at a cost of £7. The Clerk to the Fellowship considered the appointment illegal and invalid, because *ultra vires*. Hollamby and his fellow Rulers were less concerned to bridge the gap left by the Common Council's dilatoriness than to prove the fitness of the Fellowship and its personnel to manage the shift without outside help. The success of the experiment might have established a precedent for other shifts. Hollamby secured an undertaking from the Fruit Meters that they would furnish him with daily accounts of deliveries from vessels on behalf of the various merchants. It was the breach of this undertaking more than any other single cause which doomed the experiment to failure. John Hurles, one of the four Fruit Meters, not only made no returns to Hollamby, but refused him access to his account books and prevented Deputy Fruit Meters from giving him any information. In law Hurles was liable to produce his books for inspection when called upon, but took refuge in the fact that he had purchased his situation, which in his eyes signified that he could not be compelled to make his records available. Hollamby's failure to conduct the fruit shift in the face of the Fruit Meters' opposition became obvious within two months. Indeed, he failed rather disastrously. How much the Fellowship lost through Hollamby's short tenure of office cannot be ascertained with any precision: the Fellowship Clerk, a hostile witness, put the cost at £200 to £230, but attributed it as much to Hollamby's personal incompetence as to sabotage on the Fruit Meters' part. This interpretation acquires verisimilitude from the unusual volume of bad Porters' bills discovered in the shift during Hollamby's two months; many Billingsgate Porters assumed that he was unlikely to detect faulty bills. A pressure group among the Fellowship Porters, no friendlier to Hollamby than the Clerk, estimated the loss at £500. Hollamby tried to have himself exonerated by the Court of Rulers from the accusation of incompetence, but his motion was negatived. The Rulers found that Hollamby's bookkeeping confused the fruit shift with the Fellowship's general accounts, so that neither could be subsequently verified with any accuracy.

John Hurles had good reasons, other than the dignity of an independent Fruit Meter, for sabotaging the Hollamby experiment. Fruit and roots—potatoes above all—were a growing branch of Fellowship labour, showing promise of good profits. Hurles himself wanted to become Fruit Shifter, and by frustrating the Fellowship's attempt to manage the shift without outside help, he forced its hand. As soon as the Fellowship realized the financial disaster in which Hollamby's tenure of office had involved it, the Rulers asked Powis, their erstwhile Shifter, to resume the shift at an enhanced rental of £75 p.a., collecting as many arrears of the Hollamby period as could be recovered. But Powis was an old man, and six years later Hurles himself received his appointment as Fruit Shifter at the Common Council's hands. Owing to the increase in fruit work, he offered a rental of £100 for the first year and of £110 p.a. thereafter, but it was at an annual rent of £157 10s. that the lease was eventually granted, the rental not to be raised for ten years and to be reduced in proportion to any fall in Porters' rates which might take place. This clause had to be invoked in 1835 when the revenues of the fruit shift fell by about one-sixth as a result of lowering porterage charges,* and the rental was accordingly reduced to £130 a year. Hurles admitted before the Royal Commission on Municipal Corporations to a net profit of £50 a year, but in addition enjoyed an income in his capacity as Fruit Meter.

Hurles's duties were those usual among Shifters: he gave security to the Fellowship for £2,000, advanced the capital required, maintained a shift office and took responsibility for bad debts—the latter much attenuated in practice: if a merchant proved unable to pay, the loss did not fall on Hurles alone, but on all four Fruit Meters *pro rata*. If Porters had made out wrong or incomplete bills, they bore the loss themselves, provided the Shifter returned the bill within the week; where a collective bill for a whole team contained an excessive number of turns, the surplus was deducted from the team member shown to have the largest number of turns. Nor did Hurles need to maintain an

* See p. 245 below.

R

establishment on the north bank; Porters working there sent a representative to Hurles's office daily to collect their pay. Hurles did not permit the shifting of bills to be delayed by more than three days. In the 1860s full-time Shifters were abandoned in most branches of Fellowship labour. In pursuit of this simplification the Fellowship asked the Common Council to enquire into the necessity for filling the Fruit Shifter's office, and after examination the Common Council agreed that this function could be satisfactorily combined with that of the Fruit Meter (the sole survivor of the former four Fruit Meters) on Hurles's resignation. Nut and potato bills were shifted by 1878 at the City Meters' Office in Tooley Street, but the work was practically at an end and required hardly any further arrangements for payment.

(g) Potato Work

One of the substantial branches of the vegetable, root and fruit work consisted of potato labour. The delivery of each potato ship was to be attended by a Ruler—a measure designed to keep merchants satisfied in a branch of trade which provided much employment as well as to check abuses. Potatoes, being commodities ready for consumption, lent themselves to theft; Rulers could dismiss Porters for purloining them. Their handy size also rendered potatoes suitable missiles for pelting opponents, a practice frowned upon by the Court of Rulers.

In 1818 the Fellowship reluctantly decided that times had become too hard to leave potato work the prerogative of young members; in the interest of the senior Porters it had to be made into turn labour, and the *Admiral Duncan's Head* in Tooley Street was appointed the office where Meters would seek Porters. In spite of this general rule, a particular employer could still stipulate that his own potato work should be open labour for the six senior men presenting themselves at 6 a.m. all the year round. But for the bulk of the work, the change in the average age of men affected the manning scale: during open labour ten men had formed a team; as soon as the work fell into the hands of senior men, the Rulers doubled that figure, though they reduced it again to fifteen in the course of the same year. This process continued in times of good employment: in 1828, potato teams were restricted to ten, except when working in warehouses, but in the following year went back to fifteen; in 1834 the figure was set at twelve. Potato work assumed ever larger proportions so that a very drastic reduction in manning took place in 1836, teams consisting of eight men for landing, only five for overboard work, though the Ruler in attendance could at his discretion exceed these figures. Apparently the discretion needed to be almost invariably exercised, for while the Ruler or senior man remained entitled to keep a team of five men at work, the full team in the same year was increased to a complement of twelve. However, with a view to manning other potato labour proceeding simultaneously, the foreman of any team could send to another job any members considered supernumerary in reverse order of seniority. Similarly a Meter requiring labour for a potato vessel and finding another manned by more than eight Porters could requisition the surplus for his own ship. Potato merchants exercised strong pressure to have their jobs adequately manned; hence constant warning on the part of Rulers to Porters who had joined a team not to abandon work until the end of the day.

It became necessary during the potato season to draw into this labour non-members who, as supernumerary Porters, were put at the disposal of Rulers at Tooley Street to man potato work. Potato transport in steamboats increased pressure; though unloading teams consisted of only eight men, Rulers on the spot could increase numbers to expedite delivery. In 1867 teams once again shrank to five men, team leaders being charged with applying to the Porters' office for additional labour if the manning proved inadequate. No Porter could be relieved by supernumeraries after 4 p.m. On the other hand, any Porter finishing a potato job acquired the right to make up any team to a total of seven men. Potatoes were rarely landed on the north bank, but here a more generous manning scale prevailed: potatoes or nuts landed in boxes, barrels or packages between London Bridge and Billingsgate could be handled by twenty men to each hatchway, plus ten additional men for every extra winch or runner used at a hatchway. By 1873 even three men turning out with a Meter before breakfast were allowed to hold a potato job for the day, if the Ruler on duty considered them adequate for the work.

In relation to the effort involved, potato work was less well paid than other branches of Fellowship labour. This explains not only the difficulties experienced at frequent intervals in the nineteenth century in manning it, but also the dodges to which Porters committed to potato labour often resorted. At all times it proved difficult to persuade Porters to make the way and otherwise perform duties incumbent upon the team as a whole before taking their indivual turns. Some Porters tried to leave one potato team in order to go as heavers and goers to another where prospects appeared rosier; to render them liable to be cut out by newcomers to any team which they had improperly left hardly seemed adequate punishment. Refusal to take turns at fetching sacks and carts from warehouses entailed penalties.

When potato work was at its height in the later 1840s, a dispute arose between the Fellowship and its employers. Potatoes were weighed as well as measured. Landing and weighing formed a single process, potatoes being carried off the vessel to the scale. But in winter 1845 the Porters, standing on the letter of the law, refused to continue work after 6 p.m. This annoyed merchants whose ships remained ready to discharge up to 8 p.m. They therefore decided to occupy the time up to 6 p.m. with the discharge of potatoes, requiring Porters to return next day for the weighing, without however paying porterage in excess of the amount previously given for the combined operation. This increased not only Porters' working time, but also their risk: they received no payment for potatoes subsequently found to be damaged to the degree of being unsaleable; delay in weighing gave disease more time to spread among potatoes. The Court of Rulers therefore took the matter up with the employers and agreed that, if weighing was undertaken on the day of landing, arrangements should continue unchanged; if left to the next day, two Porters should be detailed for this work at a remuneration paid partly by the Fellowship, partly by the Fruit Meters. For two seasons this compromise held good; from the 1848–49 season onwards the expense fell wholly on Fellowship funds. In order to make sure that the work was not shirked, no member of the team was allowed to leave until those entrusted with the weighing, for which remuneration was apparently not very generous, had been designated.

Working in a sellers' market for porterage labour, the Court of Rulers right at the beginning of the century felt strong enough to increase rates in particular branches of work on its own account without obtaining Common Council sanction. Potatoes above all could bear higher rates, and the Court agreed with the potato merchants on a scale starting at $1\frac{1}{2}d$. per sack for the first eighty yards, adding a farthing each for the next thirty, twenty-five and twenty yards respectively, such labour including the discharge of potatoes from the vessel, carriage over a distance measured from the wharf to the warehouse door or cart and loading into carts or other appropriate receptacles. Every pair of stairs added $\frac{1}{4}d$. per sack to the porterage; the same addition rewarded the carriage of the goods from the fourth or fifth tiers of vessels, twice that amount from the sixth or seventh. Another $\frac{1}{4}d$. per sack was added to the basic scale in 1810 to compensate the rising cost of living in the preceding decade. Certain potato merchants, in order to secure for themselves sufficient labour at periods of peak employment in potato porterage, offered fees above the fixed charges. In order to disguise this, the arrangement took the form of agreeing with the Rulers on a standard sum per sack to be paid for every operation, instead of differing charges applying to different types of work. Times having changed by 1834, potato salesmen demanded abolition of the extra $\frac{1}{4}d$. porterage on each sack of potatoes, increase of the standard distance from eighty to ninety yards and inclusion of the fourth and fifth tiers of vessels in the basic charge. The Porters yielded quickly and allowed the changes to be enacted. Nothing was heard again of rates for forty years until in 1875 Southwark potato salesmen and factors informed the Common Council of the unwillingness of Billingsgate Porters to work at official prices, a complaint referred to the City Solicitor. Discussion between the parties ensued, leading to a slightly improved scale of rates for Fellowship labour.[69]

(h) Orange Gang

In 1826, Billingsgate Porters, aided by the superintendent of Billingsgate Market, established their right to land herrings there. Analogously, when pads of fish arrived by van at Custom House from east-coast ports, Fellowship Porters contested the Ticket Porters' right to carry the goods to the salesmen; the conflict led to open battle, both forces directed by their respective Rulers, but fought on the Fellowship's part by forty men against a mere twenty Ticket Porters and won by the bigger battalions. Both sides referred the dispute to their Courts of Rulers, but the Ticket Porters, with the right on their side, took it to the Court of Aldermen. However, the eventual solution owed nothing to that body, but represented a compromise arranged between the two organizations of Porters concerned. Fish work was not the only field in which they had crossed swords. Billingsgate Porters had in the late eighteenth century found their way into orange work and formed the Orange Gang,* even though Mediterranean goods belonged to the Tacklehouse Porters, being measured not by the bushel but by the chests and half-chests in which they were packed. Pineapples and onions similarly arrived in chests or boxes and, if landed between Billingsgate and London Bridge, formed part of the Orange Gang's work. The Tacklehouse Porters had long ceased to claim what was theirs by right; the compromise consisted of a renunciation of the Tacklehouse Porters' claim to orange work in return for a guarantee from the Fellowship Porters to yield the fish-pad work to Ticket Porters—a settlement very favourable to the Billingsgate Porters, who reaped a reward for giving up what had never been theirs.

The work done by the Orange Gang became the most substantial and enduring form of fruit and vegetable labour. Its season varied over the course of the century; in the early part the Gang found little employment from June to September when members were permitted to engage in other branches of Fellowship labour; as soon as orange work began, no Orange Porter could take any other labour, nor was there much temptation. Fruit picked in various Mediterranean areas began to arrive from September onwards, but did not reach maximum quantities until the end of the year and continued undiminished until May. As ships became faster and growers perfected new varieties of early-ripening citrus fruit, the season was extended backwards in the year.

In season the Orange Gang worked harder than the remainder of the Fellowship Porters, employment being more regular and resulting in

* See p. 96 above.

higher earnings. Rates of pay of Orange Gang members, unlike those of other Billingsgate Porters, were not determined by the Common Council, but by a committee of fruit merchants and brokers, and resulted in members earning approximately 8*d*. an hour. In 1830 the Orange Porters complained of a change in Customs procedure; duty now being assessed on Mediterranean fruit by the chest, merchants greatly increased the capacity of chests, the Porters quoting examples of

	Old weight (cwt.)	New weight (cwt.)	Porterage (d.)
Seville oranges	$1\frac{3}{4}$—2	3	4+1
Oporto oranges	$1\frac{3}{4}$—2	$2\frac{1}{2}$+	4+1
Lisbon oranges	$2\frac{1}{4}$	$2\frac{1}{2}$—3	5+2
Malaga oranges	3	3—$3\frac{1}{2}$	4+2
St. Michael's oranges . . .	1	2	2+$\frac{1}{2}$
Jars of grapes	28–30 lb.	90 lb.	2 for 2 jars

the first column of porterage representing the basic fee for carrying the load 230 yards, the second the addition for ladders, stairs and greater distances. In spite of having to carry these much heavier loads, which led to broken limbs and other injuries as well as to many fatal accidents —Orange Porters claimed one-third of their number killed within the last twelve years from accidents and lung disease due to overstrain— rates of porterage had not changed. For comparable loads Ticket Porters received almost double the remuneration earned by Orange Porters. Oranges had formerly been stored near wharves on ground or first floors, but had now to be carried three or four storeys high into warehouses far from the waterside; it required skill as well as strength to convey fruit 'from the Ships decks at Cox Quay Fresh Wharf and Botolph Wharf to the Warehouses of the different Merchants and Brokers . . . some as far as Philpot Lane frequently across four or five vessels at the Wharf and at low water up a two Story ladder of 45 Steps to the Wharf and often up three pairs of stairs or down into Cellars at the Warehouses.'

Orange Porters had hitherto contented themselves with inadequate remuneration because, when merchants bought entire cargoes of oranges, sometimes two or three shiploads in a single transaction, and had them carried direct from ship to shop, Porters had been paid as though they had transported the fruit first from ship to warehouse and then from warehouse to shop, but now oranges were auctioned at the warehouses. Merchants had also employed Orange Porters to load fruit from their shops either on coastal vessels or vans for provincial sale, but wherever the law permitted, non-freemen now did the work. Faced with this complaint, a committee of orange merchants and brokers engaged in protracted negotiations with the Porters, from which no increase in rates resulted; on the contrary, some dealers even threatened reductions, though a few privately expressed sympathy with the Porters' grievance. Porters' rates had become a very contentious issue in the Common Council, which with relief accepted the Coal and Corn Committee's advice that 'the arrangements made with regard to the payment of the orange porters being what they are, no interference be attempted'.

Whatever their grievance, members of the Orange Gang earned more than most Fellowship Porters; hence to join the Gang a member paid £10 for the privilege of admission. The Gang itself disposed of another source of income by hiring out at the rate of 2d. a day knots and hats required in fruit porterage work, some of them to non-members temporarily employed in the labour. Orange Porters did not participate in the financial arrangements made for other Billingsgate Porters in the greenstuffs trade, with the exception of onion work for which they submitted bills to the Fruit Shifter's office in the usual manner. Methods of paying for the bulk of their work were a forerunner of present procedure. The Orange Gang employed a clerk who would nowadays be called a tally clerk. Standing by while work was in progress, he handed each Porter a small metal disk known as a tally every time he passed him. The tally signified a load carried. As remuneration varied according to the distance the load had to be moved, tallies represented amounts differing in value from ¾d. to 3d. In the evening, Porters returned to the clerk the tallies collected in the course of the day and received the equivalent in cash. Instead of suffering a shift deduction of 1d. in every shilling, members of the Orange Gang received the full value of their bills, but paid 1s. 6d. a week each towards the remuneration of the clerk, who combined the functions of tallying and shifting without great strain: the main employers being three or four large fruit merchants and importers established in Pudding Lane, he could in twenty minutes on a Saturday collect the Orange Gang's weekly earnings by means of a round of visits to a few offices.

Throughout the early nineteenth century thirty to forty men constituted the Orange Gang—a figure adjudged inadequate by representatives of the fruit trade, certainly at the height of the season. The Gang's position was a curious mixture of submission to, and independence of, the Court of Rulers of the Billingsgate Porters. On the one hand every place in the Gang had to be filled by the Court's choosing one of two Fellowship Porters nominated for the vacancy; on one occasion in 1865 the whole Orange Gang was newly constituted by the Court in this manner, and Rulers took disciplinary measures against the Gang if it objected to members newly appointed by the Court. On the other hand, once constituted, the Gang led an existence independent of the Fellowship Rulers, neither shifting for the bulk of its employment with the Shifter appointed by the Fellowship nor observing regulations of work determined by the Court of Rulers; its own foreman made most of the working rules applying to Orange Porters and conforming with the requirements of fruit trade employers.

To cope with peak demand at the height of the season, the Gang employed assistants. Such men were engaged on a day-to-day basis, sometimes at a daily wage, by Orange Porters acting as sub-contractors. Orange Porters considered it reasonable to assign to such assistants the heaviest chests, carrying the lighter ones themselves; hence the employment was not greatly sought after. Towards the middle of the century, fruit traders complained that the Orange Gang engaged most of the assistants straight from gaol or similar circles. Such assistants could be, but rarely were themselves Billingsgate Porters, the Orange Gang claiming a right to give employment to whomsoever it chose, even if this entailed preferring a non-member to a Fellowship Porter. The device of restricting regular and profitable employment to a small body of men antagonized the fruit trade, and in 1870 the Court of Rulers increased the number of the Orange Gang to fifty, at the same time forming a supernumerary Gang of twenty-five men who worked as ordinary Fellowship Porters from June to November, but became Orange Porters during the six months' main season from December to May. Selection of supernumeraries followed the methods adopted for the main Gang: the Orange Gang, in the first half of November, submitted fifty nominations of which the Court of Rulers chose one-half. In 1872 the Orange Gang tried to have the supernumerary Gang doubled for the season, but this the Court of Fellowship Rulers refused to do. As numbers still proved inadequate, the Court had to agree in 1875 to the main Gang being increased from fifty to seventy members. By 1877, however, the Orange Gang was petitioning to have the strength reduced to the erstwhile fifty, a request granted after some delay.

Not only did the Orange Gang have its own clerk; if in need of legal advice or representation, it briefed its own solicitor, who was not the Clerk of the Fellowship of Porters; it had a permanent foreman from at least 1830 onwards and maintained a separate capital fund and banking account. This capital, fed by subscriptions, fines, entrance and hiring fees, swelled by voluntary contributions from the fruit trade and drained by current expenditure connected with the work, operated as a sick and superannuation fund for Orange Porters; members claimed that no more dangerous collective employment than theirs existed in London. On a member's death the fund paid £12, a smaller amount on the death of a member's wife. In two years for which accounts of the fund have survived, 1877 and 1878, the Gang paid out in sick benefits £326 and £257 respectively, as well as £84 and £109 in pensions and £22 and £6 in respect of deaths—sums which compare favourably with the scale of grants made by the Fellowship as a whole.* Perhaps this generosity was excessive, for four years after these accounts had been rendered, the Gang went bankrupt and had to borrow £300 from a firm in the fruit trade in order to re-establish its finances.

The Orange Gang's bankruptcy in 1881–82 coincided with the entry into the fruit trade of Sir Henry A. Isaacs, head of H. Isaacs & Sons, the largest importers and brokers of citrus fruit. Sir Henry became an

---

* See p. 269 below.

Alderman of London and in 1889–90 served as Lord Mayor. He made a Fellowship Porter, E. Williams, his sub-contractor for all porterage work. The firm of Keeling & Hunt, standing second in importance in the trade, appears to have been a branch of Isaacs' operating under a different name; as soon as Williams became porterage contractor for H. Isaacs & Sons, he discharged the same duties for Keeling & Hunt. The other two firms employing Orange Porters, Knill & Grant and Jno. & Jas. Adams & Co., were of lesser importance. By virtue of his capacity as porterage contractor to the two largest employers, Williams now became clerk and paymaster to the Gang and established complete ascendancy over all Orange Porters. Williams himself kept a public house in Botolph Alley; he also possessed a fine country house with stables, luxuries attributed by *The Star* evening paper to the ill-gotten deductions from Orange Porters' earnings. Employers paid Williams 2d. for each chest of oranges carried from ship to wagon on land; he passed on to the Porters only 1d. in the form of a tally, and tallies issued by him could be changed only by one person and in one place: by E. Williams in his public house in Botolph Alley. Here he redeemed 1s. worth of tallies for 11d.; substantially he had reverted to the former shift deduction. He insisted, moreover, on Porters purchasing beer or tobacco when redeeming tallies; on Saturday, when work ended at 2 p.m., he kept Porters hanging about till 7 or 8 p.m., waiting to be paid, giving them credit for anything consumed on the premises until paytime. Williams succeeded in extracting further minor tributes, such as 6d. a week from each member for the use of a gang room in which to keep hats and coats, as well as 1d. a day for the hire of boards on which to carry the chests. In vain did Porters appeal to Alderman Isaacs against these practices; that circumspect dignitary closed his eyes by retorting that his firm's porterage arrangements rested entirely in the hands of his sub-contractor E. Williams.

Thus it came about that Williams held undisputed sway until the London dock strike of 1889. Tom Mann, the dockers' leader, personally called a meeting of Orange Porters at the *Mitre* tavern in Fish Street Hill and organized their campaign. Even though not at the height of the fruit season, the fight proved unexpectedly easy. An ultimatum addressed to H. Isaacs & Sons and Keeling & Hunt was delivered at 8 a.m. on 12 September, Williams having previously intimated unwillingness to mend his ways. Three hours later the two firms capitulated and informed the Porters that they had dispensed with Williams's services. A reporter from the *City Press* received an assurance that neither firm had the slightest inkling of the practices in which Williams had indulged; they pleaded complete ignorance of his blatant contravention of the 1883 Act prohibiting payment in public houses. In a courteous letter published under the heading 'Peace with Honour' in the *City Press* of 14 September, the foreman of the Orange Porters' Society expressed the Gang's thanks to Alderman Isaacs, the two firms and the *City Press* itself for the quick settlement of its grievances. Though the Fellowship of Billingsgate Porters in 1889 paid out £32 in strike money, it seems unlikely that much of that amount was required to dislodge Williams.

The new lease of life acquired by the Orange Gang as a result of the dock strike proved short. Orange Porters had suffered from the sweating practices in which Williams had indulged; the 'scurfs', outside labour employed by the Orange Gang, resented the sweating to which they were subjected. Not that scurfs on piece-rates were paid less than Gang members; sweating took the traditional form of Orange Porters carrying the lighter burdens and leaving the heavier ones to the scurfs, payment being made on a load basis irrespective of weight. This was a period when unskilled labourers no longer resigned themselves to whatever terms their employers exacted. Between 700 and 800 scurfs under contract to the Orange Gang in 1891 formed themselves into a branch of Ben Tillett's Tea Coopers' and General Labourers' Union and withdrew their labour from all jobs in which Orange Gang members had a hand. Unloading of fruit came to a standstill, highly perishable cargoes deteriorated in the holds of ships tied up at the wharves. Fruit traders insisted on having their work done; if no labour was forthcoming to discharge fruit at the wharves, ships would have to be moved into the docks. While not primarily concerned with the merits of the dispute, merchants attributed it to the monopoly of a labour force now neither young nor vigorous nor even numerous enough to cope with the work without outside assistance; hence they ranged themselves among the Gang's opponents. Negotiations followed in which the Fellowship sought to save for its members the last substantial branch of porterage work furnishing regular employment. Being informed that at least 400 Billingsgate Porters stood ready to take up work in this trade, the Fellowship proposed expanding the Orange Gang to 200 permanent members and re-establishing the jurisdiction of the Rulers, who would elect Gang officials and supervise members' suspensions and dismissals.

Implementation of this reorganization, accompanied by an agreement with the Union, might have saved the Orange Gang. Indeed, for a short period the scheme worked: Orange Porters resumed employment, calling on members of the Union for any additional labour required and ceasing to monopolize the lightest loads. But the Fellowship had been deluded about the number of potential Orange Porters. Only sixty-seven members came forward for enrolment; even of those the majority were doubtful whether they could perform such heavy work. Moreover, old Gang members resented a reorganization which deprived them of the chance of picking and choosing their work and threatened them with the resumption of shift deductions; so they withheld tools from Porters joining the Gang, started squabbles and brought work to a standstill by disorders. This being the state of the Orange Gang, the Tea Coopers' and General Labourers' Union found it easy to administer the *coup de grâce*.[70]

(i) Fish Work

The Fellowship of Porters derived its distinctive name from Billingsgate,* a dock and market increasingly devoted to the fish trade. It was not unusual for fish salesmen in that market to be Fellowship Porters themselves and to give employment to fellow members; the Court of Rulers acquiesced in these arrangements, while insisting that such members had to register themselves as salesmen at Fellowship Hall and remained disqualified from taking porterage employment at Billingsgate Market until one month after giving official notice of withdrawal from the position of salesman there. Nor would it tolerate a scheme by two of these salesmen in 1807 who had the shrewd idea of getting themselves elected Rulers so as to secure authority over other Porters

* See p. 84 above.

and thereby the best labour for clearing their own fish cargoes, while assigning inferior labour to their competitors. Mussels, if sold by measure on board a vessel lying in Billingsgate Dock, formed part of the Porters' prerogative; if, however, they were landed and sold, Porters could not insist on their being measured on board ship before unloading. Sprat boats could not open for sale before market hours; every boat counted as a separate job every day. Porters could not go into business on their own account by purchasing boatloads of sprats for re-sale without risking suspension from Billingsgate. For a short while, carrying pads of fish from wagons to the market fell under the Rulers' jurisdiction. However, the agreement with the Ticket Porters which secured orange work for the Fellowship Porters* brought pad work to an early end.

The most substantial employment in the fish trade arose from oysters. Though a small trade was done at Hungerford Market, most oyster vessels came to Billingsgate. Oysters required measuring, for which purpose there existed a staff of eighteen Day and three Night Deputy Oyster Meters. The Principal Oyster Meters for whom these men deputized were City Corporation officials, namely the Yeomen of the Waterside of whom the Clerk of Billingsgate Market was one. Their function consisted merely of providing the measures, and even that devolved upon the City Corporation after 1826. Deputy Oyster Meters had to be members of the Fellowship of Porters, but their membership was a formality, as they could afford to purchase their situations at a price averaging £1,500; on one occasion a Deputy Oyster Meter's place changed hands at £2,000. Most of the purchase price went to the previous holder; the City chamber benefited only to the extent of £40 per alienation. Deputy Oyster Meters exercised mere superintendence over measurage; though the right of measuring, shovelling, unloading and delivering all oysters brought in any boat for sale along the Thames to the Port of London was theirs, they never exercised it in person. At least two of these Meters in evidence admitted that they had never measured oysters in their lives. However, their presence on board the boat was necessary for the lawful sale of oysters at Billingsgate Market during the hours of 8 a.m. to noon and 2 p.m.

* See pp. 245–246 above.

to 6 p.m. for Day, 6 to 8 a.m. and 6 p.m. to dusk for Night Deputy
Oyster Meters. The latter had been an afterthought. Like other fish,
oysters could originally only be sold after the market had opened at
8 a.m.—too late for dispatch to inland destinations that day. For this
reason, by the early nineteenth century, practically all boats opened
before the market bell rang; Night Deputy Oyster Meters enabled
them to do so lawfully. The additional cost entailed was a small price
to pay for the advantage of catching the morning transport.

The duty to provide sufficient men for metage to be adequately
performed fell upon Deputy Oyster Meters; through them the City
Corporation also discharged its obligation to provide measuring
implements. For these unexacting services, Day Deputy Oyster Meters
had received 6s. per boat plus their dinner in those late eighteenth
century days when a standard oyster boat had taken two days to
deliver. In the nineteenth century boats became larger and new payment arrangements were agreed with oyster proprietors. The oyster
bushel contains double the quantity of an ordinary bushel. For the
first five score oyster bushels measured, Day Meters received 5s. a
score, for all further quantities 4s. a score. In addition they drew from
the Corporation $\frac{1}{2}d$. per bushel, 13d. for each boat entered, and 2d. a
day groundage. Day Meters pooled their revenues; Night Deputy
Oyster Meters received 4s. a boat from the oyster salesmen and retained their individual earnings. The City Corporation took the view
that, as Deputy Oyster Meters were paid for measuring oysters, they
ought to measure oysters or, if unwilling to soil their hands, at least
to pay out of their own pockets men to do the work—a view not
shared by the Deputy Oyster Meters who resisted it energetically till
at least 1850.

The men who actually measured the oysters were holdsmen, Fellowship Porters working in the holds of oyster vessels. Not receiving
remuneration from Deputy Oyster Meters, they demanded payment
for their work from the purchasers of the oysters. Purchasers
sometimes refused, knowing full well that a metage fee had already
been levied, and at least one oyster salesman was reduced to paying
holdsmen out of his own pocket, realizing how essential it was for
trade to keep holdsmen satisfied. But holdsmen had their own methods

of securing remuneration; if inadequately rewarded, they gave very bad measure, and buyers who systematically withheld payment of holdsmen received such short measure that they soon discovered the expediency of remunerating men on whose judgment depended the quantity purchased. Holdsmen had nothing to fear from Deputy Meters who in the early days had at least appointed them, but now neither appointed nor rewarded nor even supervised them, never descending into the hold. Finding the effort of appointing holdsmen too much for them, they had deputed this function to Cornelius Thompson, the senior Day Deputy Oyster Meter, who appointed holdsmen on behalf of all Meters. Each boat required two holdsmen, one to represent the purchaser, another the seller; salesmen could appoint any Billingsgate Porter of their choice as a permanent second holdsman in their service. Holdsmen in their turn could employ assistants, provided they were Fellowship Porters. The payment due to holdsmen amounted to 1d. a peck, that is 8d. an oyster bushel. It was difficult to designate it correctly, as a metage fee had already been paid. Lawyers overcame the terminological hurdle by describing it as 'a mere gratuity'. Through a strange historical accident, there existed two oyster vessels at Billingsgate where these rules did not apply; holdsmen in these vessels, Billingsgate Porters like the rest, did justice impartially between buyers and sellers, because they received remuneration for their work from the City Corporation. However, this example failed to contaminate anybody else.

In all instances where oysters were unloaded from a vessel or sold, the work belonged to the Fellowship Porters, but where discharge took place from a wagon or cart for the purpose not of sale but of storage, the owner could employ whom he liked, and Fellowship Porters had no right to interfere. Holdsmen's employment remained completely distinct from the labour of carrying the oysters to the shore, so much so that any Porter descending into the hold lost his place in the team of oyster carriers. Oysters could be landed only at the upper or northern end of Billingsgate, where the extension of the market made landing facilities and approach space for boats more and more inadequate. A salesman to whom a whole boatload of oysters had been consigned could choose his own labour from among Billingsgate Porters; oyster labour remained open labour. Special early morning work started at 4 a.m., but men wanting a day's or half a day's job started at 5.30 a.m. and 1.30 p.m. in order of seniority.

The first man on berth the oyster boat nearest the landing stairs had to make the way by putting shore planks down, on pain of losing his place to any other team member making way in collaboration with the holdsmen. Men had to do their own carrying, not to employ others, least of all non-members. To make turns equivalent, Porters worked in rotation, no man beginning a new turn until his senior in the team had carried a bushel or as many pecks or half-pecks as added up to the same porterage fee. Men absenting themselves for more than a quarter of an hour while the boat was open for work went to the bottom of the team. If work had not been completed by midday, Porters returning from dinner held their positions in the team on condition of being prepared to carry fractional turns, amounting to less than a bushel, if necessary to clear the vessel. In order to allow a certain amount of rotation among those seeking work in the oyster trade, no Porter occupying first place in a team was eligible for oyster work on the subsequent day. As always in team labour, the last man in each team collected the dues and paid his mates.

Records do not show how and when Billingsgate Porters lost their fish-carrying privileges. Modern descriptions of Billingsgate Market are replete with Porters depicted as wearing leather hats with hard flat tops on which fish boxes rest. These men are licensed by the City Corporation's Markets Committee to act as Porters at Billingsgate, but they are not Billingsgate Porters in the sense in which this term had been understood from the sixteenth century to the nineteenth.[71]

S

5

FELLOWSHIP PORTERS: DECAY OF THE FELLOWSHIP

(a) Strength of Fellowship

THE nineteenth century saw both the greatest expansion and the final contraction of the Fellowship of Billingsgate Porters. Beginning the century with approximately 2,000 members, it grew to 2,300–2,400 within the first five years, when over 1,000 worked in grain alone and the Rulers could not provide sufficient labour for the discharge of corn vessels, leading the corn trade to address a collective complaint to the Fellowship. A considerable influx in the second decade, consequent upon an increase in porterage rates,* eased the labour shortage, but also owed much to the return after 1815 of ex-servicemen seeking employment in a crowded labour market. In 1817 the Fellowship passed the 2,500 mark, and as numbers continued rising in spite of diminishing employment, a Common Council Act of 1822 set an upper limit of 3,000, at which figure membership remained for a decade. In the early 1830s admissions fell below a hundred a year, not enough to counterbalance losses from death or retirement. This was due to policy, not lack of candidates; pressure to join remained heavy, and individual applicants spent three years on a waiting list which contained 400 names. In 1819 the Deputy Governor had imposed a twelve months' stop on new admissions; this policy was resumed by the Common Council in 1835 when it made increases in membership of either the Society of Tacklehouse and Ticket or the Fellowship of Billingsgate Porters dependent on its own express permission†—the first step on the road designed to lead to the euthanasia of these inconvenient bodies.

The Fellowship had no intention to submit meekly to mercy-killing,

* See p. 225 above.   † See p. 187 above.

especially as the immediate events leading up to the Act had concerned Ticket, not Billingsgate, Porters. Rulers protested that at a time when annual wastage of members exceeded new admissions, Meters were being delayed for lack of Porters to accompany them, and that further reductions in Porters' numbers would lay the City Corporation open to compensation claims from merchants damaged by delay, particularly in the small and unprofitable jobs which accounted for so large a proportion of their work. To reinforce its argument, the Fellowship within three months of the Act's passage sought authority to admit a hundred new members. The purpose of their proceeding remained fresh in the minds of Common Councilmen; even a motion to permit fifty new members was promptly rejected. When the General Purposes Committee after enquiry recurred to this recommendation, its report was referred back for further consideration, especially to allow representations from salt merchants, a section of the trade determined to free itself from the Billingsgate Porters. The committee persisted in its recommendation, which was then disagreed with.

So far the Common Council had shown admirable firmness of purpose. Had it had the strength of mind to persevere, its porterage troubles might have ended half a century before they did. But from 1837 onwards over Billingsgate, though not over Ticket Porters, it prevaricated. Early in that year the Fellowship prevailed upon water-side potato salesmen in Southwark to ask for the admission of a hundred additional Porters, and the request was granted. This opened a breach which the Fellowship quickly exploited. Potato salesmen now con-demned in more general terms the policy pursued: either limitation of numbers should cease or regulations should provide for periodical admission to the Fellowship so as to maintain an adequate labour force. Had the Council bowed to this demand, the Fellowship would have survived for ever after—an ambition cherished by the Court of Rulers. The Common Council avoided the trap by refusing all general authority for admissions, but permitted another hundred members to be recruited, and when later in 1838 the Court of Rulers asked for yet another hundred members, the Common Council weakly complied. So great was pressure of potato work that season that early in 1839 the Governor of the Fellowship appointed supernumerary Porters, men not admitted to the Fellowship, but treated like members during temporary employment in potato labour. Meanwhile the Fellowship persisted in whittling away the Common Council's determination: in January 1839 it sought and obtained authority to enrol another 200 members, repeating this performance in October 1840 and in December 1841, every time at the height of the potato season, though on the last occasion the resolution met with some opposition.

The total number of members still stood close to the permitted maximum of 3,000; but while over 2,800 men were carried on the Fellowship's books, only 1,600 or so engaged in regular Fellowship labour. It was the dead weight of something like 1,200 non-working members, the outliers,* which swelled the Fellowship out of all proportion to needs. With new admissions barred and old members retiring from work all the time, the proportion of outliers to working members steadily increased; at the same time the Fellowship sought no further admissions for eight years, during which total membership dropped to roughly 2,400. Then in 1849 the Fellowship returned to the assault, supported by sundry of their employers, and asked for another 200 members. Even within the Fellowship a ginger group of young men opposed this application on the ground that they suffered from having too many rather than too few members, reducing junior Porters to unemployment. But potato merchants complained of labour shortage, and as the Common Council stood firm, Porters were allowed to nominate four supernumeraries to participate on equal terms in potato work, though without prospects of permanent membership. This was the last attempt to keep up the Fellowship's strength. By 1855 the working part had fallen to 700–800 members and continued its rapid decline. The Governor and Deputy Governor, without authority from the Common Council, sanctioned individual admissions down to 1890 to enable Meters and Shifters to belong to the Fellowship. Occasionally a working Porter slipped into the Fellowship alongside such outliers, but no more than one or two at the time, not enough to make any material difference to total working strength. Corn work declined up to 1862, experiencing a brief revival thereafter, but resumed the downward trend after a few years. From 1,500 in the

* See pp. 170–172 above.

middle 1860s, membership fell below 1,000 in 1880 and was halved again before the end of the decade: 1892 is the last complete year for which it can be calculated from the quarterage books; dues were paid by 168 members. By that time, however, a large number of Porters looked upon quarterage payments as a waste of their precarious funds.[72]

Senior Porters at most times made a tolerable living, whereas in periods of slack trade many juniors had to seek other employment for eight months out of every year. By the third quarter of the century conditions had deteriorated: up to the age of thirty-one, the average Fellowship Porter earned a mere 10s. to 15s. a week, increasing his earnings to from 15s. to 25s. thereafter. That only men of the lowest possible standing, both financially and morally, sought employment for such small rewards was taken for granted not only by disaffected outsiders but even by their own Rulers; one of them, John Henry Liquorish, alleged in 1817 that the great majority were of fraudulent disposition, and three years later the Rulers in a printed petition accused a past Deputy Governor of using the Fellowship as a receptacle for characters whom no master would employ. This explains habitual insubordination among men who defied orders and resisted all disciplinary measures not only at the time but also by casting their votes at the next election against Rulers who had attempted to enforce discipline. The truth of this picture of Billingsgate Porters is substantiated by the frequent reiteration of such incidents; its onesidedness is suggested by evidence regarding many members who concluded a career as working Porters by becoming respectable tradesmen.

Why admission fees to the Fellowship rose from 8s. 6d. in the later eighteenth century, records do not reveal; £5 5s. became the customary charge, endorsed by the Court of Rulers in 1867 and confirmed in the following year by an Act of Common Council. Of this sum, 5s. reimbursed the Court of Rulers for enquiries made into the applicant's record. New members now furnished a single bond of £40 for good and faithful discharge of their duties. On promotion to Corn Porter, a member paid 4s. 6d.—a fee charged at least from 1836 onwards, though the City by-law authorized only 2s. 6d. Quarterage, in spite of the price level changes of a century and a half, remained at 4s. a year. When in 1812 the Rulers became much concerned about arrears, they decided to bar from work any member not paid up for the current quarter. Unable presumably to give effect to this rule, they essayed the lesser sanction of allowing such members to be cut out by their juniors not so in arrears. Penalties for owing quarterage were formalized in 1822 when the Common Council Act provided for delay up to

18 months a fine of 1s.

2 years „ „ „ 2s.

2½ „ „ „ „ 3s.

3 „ „ „ „ 3s. plus loss of three years' seniority

4 „ the penalty of dismissal.

About thirty Porters a year suffered loss of membership on these grounds. The procedure was elaborate. In April and May the Fellowship inserted advertisements in the *Morning Herald* and the *Morning Advertiser or Publican's Paper*, calling upon members in arrears to pay their quarterage on pain of dismissal. Names of defaulters for at least two years were posted up at the Corn Office for the next six months, showing the date on which they would lose membership, failing payment of arrears. From the days when Porters took seriously their duty of attending daily at the Corn Office, this counted as personal notice. It was queried in 1816 by John Hudson, who had been admitted a Fellowship Porter in 1792, but impressed into the Navy in 1794, though he had arranged for a friend to pay his quarterage. The Rulers remained unaware of Hudson's service in the Navy, of which they had never had notice. When the friend died, Hudson's quarterage payments came to an end. Not having been seen for four years, he was presumed dead in 1798, an entry to that effect being made in the Fellowship register, and when he returned in 1808 and made application to pay up his arrears and resume membership on the old basis, the Fellowship refused to accept his arrears and reinstate him, offering him merely a fresh admission. This meant loss of sixteen years' seniority; instead of pursuing the matter, he worked as a cooper until 1816, when depression forced him once again to seek employment as a Porter. Only after investigation by the Court of Aldermen did the Rulers decide to reinstate Hudson on payment of his quarterage arrears.[73]

(b) Administration and Finance

The Fellowship continued to be controlled by the Alderman of Billingsgate as Governor and the Deputy of that ward as Deputy Governor. Both had powers to suspend for one month or dismiss from the Fellowship members who did not obey rules and regulations, though they used dismissal sparingly, involving on the average no more than one Porter a year. The Governor rarely attended meetings of the Court of Rulers, leaving this duty to the Deputy Governor, who made an appearance whenever anything beyond routine business was transacted, especially new admissions or the hearing of offences involving dismissal, but did not participate in work such as deciding on petitions for relief. On an average he would attend four or five of the twelve meetings a year. Like Rulers, he received an annual allowance of £24, later increased to £36. This emolument did not add to the attractions of his office, but constituted a fund from which he was expected to dispense charity to needy Porters. A good and at the same time wealthy Deputy Governor like Benjamin Bower did not draw this allowance, but added it to general Fellowship funds. The allowance remained customary until 1868 when a Common Council Act formalized its payment.

At all times the Fellowship had a part-time Clerk, a lawyer attending two days a month. Up to 1821 he received an annual salary of £100, but in addition presented bills of fees, averaging £55 p.a., in respect of legal business transacted on the Fellowship's behalf. His salary was increased to £150 in 1822. Apart from attending Court meetings and representing the Fellowship in proceedings before higher bodies, the Clerk acted as returning officer in Rulers' elections. Evidence of strained relations within the Fellowship is provided by a regulation of 1868 that any Porter waiting on the Clerk without authority of the Rulers would in future be liable to punishment. It is not clear whether this served to protect the Clerk or the Rulers. The Fellowship also had a Beadle who summoned Rulers and prepared lists of causes for court meetings and handed them to the Upper Ruler before sittings, gave public notice of the times of sittings, served summonses, prepared the court room, attended the sessions and cleared up afterwards, delivered messages and letters, posted up rules and orders when directed by the Court, presented himself twice weekly at Fellowship Hall in order to relieve the Pennyman or run any errands required by the latter, and attended Fellowship elections. All this amounted only to a part-time job, the office of Beadle usually going to Rulers or past Rulers as a reward for services rendered. Like Rulers, the Beadle from 1822 onwards received a salary of £36 a year; the Court of Rulers further allowed him a coat every other year. On being appointed Beadle, a Ruler had to vacate his office, nor could a Beadle stand for election as Ruler. If the Beadle died, the Upper Ruler discharged his duties until a new Beadle could be appointed on the next quarter day.

The only full-time officer among Rulers was the Pennyman, who acted as Treasurer and attended at Fellowship Hall on working days, in summer from 6 a.m. to noon and from 3 to 7 p.m., in winter from 8 a.m. to noon and from 3 to 6 p.m., until in 1868 his attendance was made to begin in the morning and end in the evening an hour earlier. In addition to his pay as a Ruler, the Pennyman received under the Common Council Act of 1822 a salary of £60 p.a. Pennymen were to be elected by the whole membership, but in fact the Court of Rulers chose them from among themselves until 1850, when official procedure was observed for the first time. From the seventeenth century onwards the remaining Rulers had been working Porters receiving £24 a year in order to compensate them for the loss of work entailed by their duties of supervising and ruling the Fellowship. On days of court meetings they enjoyed a free dinner; if in addition to court sessions they lost entire days through attending to Fellowship business, this entitled them to 5s. a day. An Act of 1822 improved these rates: the annual allowance became £36, the compensation for days wholly occupied in Fellowship business 7s., but where a Ruler on duty found the work beyond his capacity and called in a fellow Ruler to assist, no allowance became payable to the second Ruler though he was in duty bound to obey the call.

Officially the number of Rulers had been twenty-four until the Common Council Act of 1822 reduced it to twelve, with a quorum of seven.* In the absence of Governor and Deputy Governor the chair

* See p. 280 below.

at monthly court meetings was taken by the Upper Ruler, who until 1822 was elected for the year by the Court of Rulers as constituted on Midsummer Day; after that date Rulers took monthly turns at acting as Upper Ruler. Discipline imposed a fine of 2s. 6d. on any Ruler for interrupting another in debate without the chairman's permission. Monthly meetings were calculated to occupy one day, but the large number of disputes and complaints to be heard, coupled with the indisciplined and refractory behaviour of Porters, often doubled their length; fifteen to twenty causes represented an average day's work. At its meeting of 10 April 1862, the Court of Rulers managed to deal with twenty-two causes involving 132 Porters. Even on a normal day, twenty to a hundred Porters might be required to appear; this was possible only because a large number of parties could be relied upon either to disobey summonses or to present themselves in a state of inebriety, which made effective argument impossible. To secure proper attendance, any Porter indicted before the Court of Rulers was suspended from work until he had paid 1s. to a Ruler—a vexatious regulation which reached heights of absurdity when in 1832 everybody concerned in a complaint, whether as plaintiff, defendant or witness, was put under the same obligation. The rule did not survive twelve months, being replaced by an order to plaintiffs and defendants to pay into court 1s. in respect of each witness they proposed to call—a measure subserving the purpose of expedition rather than justice.[74]

The Fellowship's capital had grown to £5,600 by 1810. Within the next twelve years it increased to £8,000, much of it absorbed in the Fellowship's advance of £7,000 to the Corn Shifter below Bridge.* In those days the Fellowship went from strength to strength: in addition to the money held by the Shifter, it had £2,000 in 3½% reduced and £700 in new 3½% Annuities during the period from 1832 to 1835; this took no account of the Fellowship's hall, furniture, books, pictures and plate, which in 1836 were insured for £1,500. The capital stock continued to increase up to 1841, standing in the Fellowship's books at a value of £11,000, at which figure it remained till 1848. Then it gradually declined, dropping to £10,000 in the 1860s, about £8,000 in 1870 and below £5,000 at the end of the 1880s. The

* See p. 230 above.

Common Council Act of 1822 established the Governor, Deputy Governor and three Rulers named by them as trustees to hold the capital stock. Annual Fellowship revenue, derived from admission fees, quarterage payments and fines, in the best years around 1840 amounted to more than £5,000; more usually it remained around £3,000, a figure it did not attain again after 1847 until the late 1860s when the amalgamation of shift and general revenues deprived the figures of significance. Quarterage accounts for the 1880s show annual receipts from this source to have been over £220 at the beginning of the decade as against an amount varying between £125 and £150 at the end. The Fellowship in 1831 opened a banking account with Esdaile & Co., cheques requiring the signature of three Rulers and the Clerk; the stoppage of that banking house in 1837 led to the transfer of the account to the London Joint Stock Banking Company.

The main purpose of Fellowship funds after defraying current costs consisted of provision for old or infirm Porters—the final stage of a system of organization which in all phases attempted to ease the lot of men who had lost the vigour without which a hard and strenuous occupation became impossible. The number of claimants to relief within the Fellowship at all times exceeded funds available, so controversy centred on the choice of pensioners. While assistance from outside sources disqualified, the Court of Rulers otherwise used its discretion with due regard to character and conduct, favouring candidates marked out by age, infirmity and poverty rather than seniority in the Fellowship. Under these rules, the number of pensioners rose in 1818 from twenty-four to forty-four, all of whom received clothing, but the original twenty-four also £2 each a year. Selection on merit was replaced in 1819 by a strict seniority rule without reference to need. Another sixteen were added to the clothing pensioners in 1826; moreover, when a money pensioner died, a clothing pensioner was appointed in his place. The number of clothing pensioners went up again by twenty-five in 1828 and to a hundred in the next year, while another 100 men qualified for the £2 a year grant. For the first time the Fellowship relieved a substantial proportion of the men likely to be in need of assistance out of a total membership of 3,000. A year later, frightened at its own generosity, the Court of

Rulers voted to reduce the number of pensioners from 200 to 150 by appointing one new clothing pensioner instead of every two money pensioners deceased until there were no more money pensioners left. In 1833 the total number was once again increased to 200, this time all clothing pensioners. By 1836 the absurdity of a strict seniority system had become obvious; a distinction was drawn between regular followers of Fellowship labour entitled to receive clothing, and former outliers who had acquired a right to some benefit by virtue of seniority.

Ten years later new Rulers quietly changed the policy to one of awarding pensions only to men who had worn themselves out in Fellowship labour. The case which caused this conversion concerned a Ruler who, after twenty years of Court membership, lost an election, whereupon he promptly applied for and received a life pension of £18 a year, notwithstanding the fact that he owned considerable property. The Court of Rulers was evenly divided on the award, but, with the seniority rule still in operation, the Governor gave a casting vote in the applicant's favour. The number of members relieved must have fallen severely, as the Court in 1846 ordered its increase to forty. What relation such orders bear to actual numbers must remain doubtful, in view of an 1847 entry showing only thirteen pensioners, then increased by another six. The Common Council Act of 1868 recognized the change which had taken place in selection by restoring to the Court of Rulers discretion, subject to confirmation by Governor or Deputy Governor, to award relief without regard to seniority, but instructing it to give preference to Porters who had ceased Fellowship labour within two years of the application for relief on account of age, accident or infirmity. Silence thereafter covers the number of pensioners until 1893, when only four remained, ranging in age from 74 to 81 and in awards from £20 to £10 a year.

The relative merits of clothing and money grants as a suitable form of relief occupied many Courts of Rulers and occasioned frequent changes of policy. In 1815 a narrow majority of the Court carried a motion to grant no new money pensions, but to devote funds available through the termination of existing ones to the increase of clothes pensions—a motion rescinded nine months later when the majority on the Court had changed and the mixed system of clothing for all and money for some continued. Money pensions were again to be abolished in 1826; a grant of 2s. 6d. in 1828 from Fellowship funds to all pensioners remained, replacing a gratuity hitherto given by the Deputy Governor. In 1830 pure money pensions were converted to clothing pensions with money additions: fifty senior pensioners had £1, the others 10s. each, but senior pensioners compelled to enter the workhouse received £3 instead of clothes. In 1831 these rates became more generous: in addition to clothes, senior pensioners received £2 each, the next fifty men £1 each, Corn Porters entering the workhouse £4 a year. A reorganization of relief was made in 1835: the fifty senior pensioners hitherto in receipt of clothing were not to have any at midsummer, but £2 each instead, the other fifty not hitherto clothed to receive clothing at midsummer instead of money at Christmas. The Court appropriated to permanent pensions an annual sum of £350; no pure money pension was to exceed £1 a month, and permanent pensions could be awarded only to men who had ceased all Fellowship work. The following year's economies in Fellowship expenditure led to discontinuance of the winter clothes issue, though at Christmas in the next two years clothes pensioners received 10s. each instead. Subsequently pensions were standardized at £13 a year and raised to £18 in 1847.

Apart from permanent pensions to disabled Porters, relief included a number of non-recurrent grants, such as 5s. to widows and dependants of deceased Porters, occasionally supplemented by contributions to funeral expenses; many Porters, however, belonged to benefit societies which defrayed funeral costs. The scale of death benefits established in 1829 took account of seniority, awarding 10s. in respect of a man of less than ten years' standing, £1 if his standing amounted to less, £2 if to more than twenty-one years, the last two sums being increased to £2 and £3 two years later; £5 was expended on the funeral of past Rulers. Benefits suffered deductions in respect of quarterage and other debts outstanding and were withheld altogether if a member had paid no quarterage for three years or more. The Court retained discretion as to the award of benefits. As important as death grants were those made to members suddenly struck by illness or accident. These led to so many impositions that the Court in 1830 voted to abolish such payments altogether, as it despaired of its ability to distinguish genuine from fraudulent applications. Total cessation of accident benefits would have entailed great hardship; in fact the Court continued paying £1 in respect of accidents wherever a Ruler had verified the circumstances. In 1835 relief became limited to applicants who had been admitted to hospital, had broken a limb or produced medical certificates of at least a week's inability to work. Accident relief was stopped once again in 1848, this time for financial reasons. The Fellowship paid an annual subscription to the City of London Truss Society for the benefit of members, beginning at £2 2s. in 1823, increased to £4 4s. in 1830, and for the year of 1845 to £12 12s.; on one occasion it donated £2 2s. to the Billingsgate Ward Charity Schools. In all, the Fellowship disbursed on relief never less than £900 in any year between 1831 and 1846, the highest amount for any one year being £1,275 for 1831–32; it had been considerably less for the few years before 1831 for which accounts survive, and after 1846 it rapidly fell to approximately £600 by 1852, less than £200 at the end of that decade, and an average of only £50 in the 1860s. It was raised to £350 in some years in the middle 1870s, even exceeding £400 in the early 1880s, but then dropped irretrievably to just over £100 around 1890 before tailing off completely.

When the Bishop of London instigated a public fund for the suffering poor in the particularly cold winter of 1854–55, the City chamber contributed £1,000, out of which it donated £100 for the relief of Billingsgate Porters. Another £1,000 was put at the disposal of the Coal, Corn and Finance Committee to relieve suffering in the winter of 1860–61, but although coal whippers and Fellowship Porters received special mention, a motion earmarking £200 for the Billingsgate Porters did not pass.

Applicants for pensions unable to obtain satisfaction from the Court of Rulers sometimes threw themselves on the Common Council's mercy. John Kilbey, a Billingsgate Porter totally disabled through an accident sustained during porterage labour, asked for such intervention in 1835 which resulted in the Rulers granting him a 10s. a week allowance. They did so reluctantly; as soon as the Common Council could be expected to have forgotten about Kilbey, they reduced his pension from £26 to £12. However, if the Common Council had lost sight of Kilbey's allowance, Kilbey himself had not; he approached once more the Common Council which accused the Rulers of breach of faith as well as of an act of unfeeling injustice, indicating its desire for the restoration of Kilbey's original award. Less lucky was Zachariah Rye, member of a ginger group attacking the Court of Rulers between 1818 and 1825,* but old and worn-out by 1842. He had no illusions about the affection entertained for him by the Court of Rulers, so hoped for greater success from an appeal to the Common Council, which, however, concluded that he had made out no case calling for interference. When he tried again eleven years later, the vote on whether to refer his petition to the General Purposes Committee or leave it to lie on the table resulted in a deadlock, broken by the Lord Mayor's casting vote in favour of the second alternative.

Even at periods of relative affluence the Fellowship could not satisfy all genuine applications for relief. Not unnaturally, Billingsgate Porters' thoughts turned to self-help. A general meeting in 1834 demanded superannuation arrangements; out of it the Fellowship Porters' Accident and Superannuation Society was born. Unfortunately no records of this organization survive; it met at the *Bull's Head*, Bull Court, Tooley Street (which suggests that it catered principally for the fruit and vegetable section) and survived until at least 1846. A Fellowship Porters' Provident and Benevolent Institution came into existence in 1837, devoted to the building of twenty-four almshouses and a chapel at Spring Grove, Westow Hill, Norwood, and the payment of superannuation and accident benefits on a mutual insurance basis. Members subscribed 2d. per week; pensions were based on seniority in the Fellowship, not in the Provident Institution. The Court of Rulers allowed contributions to be received at Fellowship Hall. In 1841 the Institution, then in financial difficulties, appealed to the Common Council for a donation. The Common Council granted £200, a generous gesture, but hedged around by conditions: the first half of the sum to be paid when twelve, the second half when sixteen of the almshouses had been completed. It is unlikely that the Institution ever saw the £200. It approached the Court of Rulers for financial help in

* See p. 272 below.

1842, but that body received several counter-petitions and concluded that it could not give away funds belonging to the whole Fellowship in order to assist members of one section. In the Rulers' view, no superannuation fund could succeed unless it commanded prior approval from at least a large majority of members and was managed by the Court of Rulers, which required statutory power to levy compulsory contributions from members proportionate to their seniority. To test members' views, the Court asked Porters willing to contribute 1s. a month towards such a fund to put their names down at Fellowship Hall.

The danger of being superseded by a compulsory scheme worried the Provident and Benevolent Institution. It had completed its church, of which Prince Albert had laid the foundation stone, and eight of its almshouses, occupied by pensioners; it had disbursed in five years £416 10s. on account of pensions, £36 4s. on account of accidents, and £1 to the widow of a deceased member. It agreed with the establishment of a compulsory fund, provided its contributors could transfer to it and obtain credit for the payments already made. A pressure group among Billingsgate Porters strongly favouring compulsory superannuation insurance opposed all claims of the Provident and Benevolent Institution on the grounds that it had wasted its funds: instead of adding to places of worship in an area already well supplied and of building houses on a gravel pit remote from families and friends of potential pensioners, it would have done far better to distribute all its funds in the form of pensions. That the foundation stone of the church had engraved upon it the names of the Institution's managers symbolized the regrettable spirit of personal aggrandisement animating the enterprise. Apart from misinvestment, the critics alleged mismanagement: too high a price had been paid for a plot which could never be made to accommodate more than twenty-four houses; the builder, having obtained the order by jobbery, had put up poor houses, some of which, though less than five years old, already required repair. The Institution's expenses exceeded its income, and the general body of Porters had lost faith in it. There must have been substance in this criticism as the Institution fades out thereafter without further trace. A committee of Rulers after enquiring into various suggested superannuation schemes recurred to a fund under the Court's management which would clothe thirty men and pay pensions of £30 to thirty and of £20 to another forty, as well as disburse £100 a year for accidents and £320 for death benefits, provided contributions proportionate to seniority were compulsorily exacted. The feasibility of this rosy vision was never put to the test.[75]

(c) The Period of Ginger Groups

When an organization decays, defeat by outside interests is invariably aggravated by internal dissension. Scapegoats have to be found on whom to fasten responsibility for successive failures. The greater internal disunity, the deeper the inroads made by enemies of the organization. In the Fellowship of Porters, the obvious choice for a scapegoat was the Court of Rulers, partly because it laid itself open to attack, partly because it conducted the Fellowship's day-to-day affairs. At all times during the nineteenth century a ginger group of Billingsgate Porters controverted and opposed the Court of Rulers for its vacillating and spineless policy. Members of such a pressure group would sometimes, after several years of agitation, secure election to the Court of Rulers, gaining insight into the distribution of power between the Fellowship Porters and those on whom they depended: the City authorities, the wharfingers and other employers and the Shifters. Like most former poachers turned gamekeepers, they would moderate both their language and their claims; in fact from irresponsible agitators they turned into responsible Rulers. But that was merely a signal for a new ginger group to arise and turn the fire of its invective upon the Court of Rulers as now constituted.

A well-phrased and lucid petition to the Court of Aldermen in 1817, followed up by another to the Common Council, represented the opening blows in this campaign. Three Porters, Zachariah Rye, James Hollamby and John Christey, formed the nucleus of a ginger group meeting regularly at the *Anchor Tavern*, St. Mary-at-Hill, around which dissatisfaction of approximately 400 Porters crystallized. Complaints placed before the Aldermen cover eleven folios of the Repertories, the Court having deferred consideration of previous representations on the ground that chapter and verse had not been given. The indictment fell under five heads. Under that of financial mismanagement, the pressure group charged the Rulers with claiming disposal of the Fellowship's capital. It was admitted that the Fellowship's income had greatly increased in the last thirty years, yet it could have been raised even further. Above all, the shifts—the assets yielding the largest revenue—had been let much too cheaply. In this context a comparison covering the last thirty years of rents paid by Shifters with proceeds of the shift deduction of 1*d*. in every shilling was suggested. By-laws had fixed admission fees at 5*s*.; the Court of Rulers without authority had raised the charge to £5. Rulers did not give sufficient security for proper application of Fellowship revenue to the relief of needy members. That relief was described as quite inadequate and not proportionate to the Fellowship's income, aggregating a bare £200 a year. Rulers had broken old by-laws and regulations by indulging in unnecessary and improvident expenditure and not appropriating the proceeds of fines in the manner laid down by the Common Council.

The second head of the accusation alleged general negligence: Rulers had failed to protect Fellowship rights and privileges, above all against non-free intruders and in the London Docks, at Scotland Yard and various other places, creating a precedent for general disregard and abolition of the prerogative. This was attributed to a large extent to the Rulers' failure within living memory to attend daily at their duty stations, especially the Corn Offices, in order to appoint Porters to jobs. Nor did they hold annual general meetings at which Acts and orders governing the Fellowship were read out to the membership, accounts submitted and adopted and needy members relieved, as laid down in the regulations. Under a third head, the Court of Rulers was charged with becoming a law unto itself. When regulations made by the City Corporation a century or more ago became obsolete, they were replaced by orders and customs of the Rulers' own making, less advantageous to Porters, though more convenient to Rulers, because they established their independence of both the Fellowship at large and the City Corporation. In former days Rulers in rotation had served as Upper Rulers; having passed the chair, they had retired from rulership and created a vacancy in the court. Now Rulers held office for life instead of submitting to annual re-election and reserved to themselves the right of nominating candidates for election to

T

rulerships. By its constitution the Court of Rulers comprised thirty-one members; at most it now numbered twenty-four and at the moment of complaining only twenty, though this had not made additional funds available for relief purposes.

The inadequacy of earnings within the reach of junior men formed a fourth head of indictment: if a team of seven Porters accompanied a Corn Meter to a small job, fees had to be divided among seven claimants. Nor did Porters attain seniority quickly enough. In 1620 six Quartermen per year had been made Corn Porters out of a total membership of 400. While in the intervening two centuries the membership had grown to 2,500, the number promoted annually had not increased in proportion, but only to twenty-four; indeed, for some years only twenty men had obtained such advancement before the figure reverted to twenty-four, and only pressure of current criticism had now raised it to twenty-eight, a number still representing a restrictive monopoly of men already so appointed. Quartermen now could hardly expect to become Corn Porters until they had served thirty-one to thirty-three years in the Fellowship; many would never become Corn Porters at all. Finally, Rulers were charged with corruption: every one who had served a turn as Upper Ruler received a life pension of £20 per year from William Ruston.

With this resounding indictment the ginger group submitted recommendations for reform. A re-definition of the Rulers' duties by the Court of Aldermen was needed. Relief should be allotted strictly by seniority and vary in amount proportionate to the member's contributions to the shift. Shifts themselves represented a waste of potential revenue, owing to the inadequacy of the annual rents paid by the Shifters. Though somebody had to remunerate Porters and collect porterage from customers, the work depended on the accuracy of returns furnished by various Meters; clerks in the Fellowship's own employ could discharge these functions, which would require a capital of no more than £6,000—an amount the Fellowship could find from its own resources. In order to keep a financial check on operations, the pressure group suggested the appointment of a court of elders, consisting of twenty-one of the most senior Billingsgate Porters retired from labour and charged with auditing the Rulers' accounts at regular intervals, at least once a year, and holding surplus funds. To bring the number of Corn Porters into proportion to total membership, thirty-seven men annually should be promoted to that rank, and the whole body of Fellowship Porters should once a year nominate and elect candidates to the Court of Rulers.[76]

The reaction to this onslaught was immediate. A notice went up by authority of the Rulers at the Tower Street Office, reading as follows:

Brothers,

A Petition has been presented to the Lord Mayor & Court of Aldermen signed by 406 Fellowship Porters complaining of various grievances & stating it to be the Petition of the *Fellowship* whereas that number is scarcely more than a Seventh Part of the Fellowship; of course they cannot speak to the Sentiments of the Majority.

'A Counter Petition to the Above now lyes at the Hall for the signature of all Porters who feel themselves satisfied in being protected in their *Seniority* and with the present system of governing the *Fellowship* as a very *serious* attempt is being made to equalize the work, that the Junior Men may have the *Senior Mens Work*, *Young Porters* become *Rulers* over *Old Men*, And *Old Men* deprived of their Privileges they now enjoy—may soon feel the effects of not actively exerting themselves in *Counteracting* the designs of a few Artful and Self Interested Men.

'The Petition will lay at the Hall a few days Longer.

The Court of Rulers branded the authors of the original petition as a few of the most discontented Porters, chiefly of recent standing, who aimed at fomenting discord and dissatisfaction and at raising prejudices against, and undermining the powers of, the Rulers. William Ruston, Corn Shifter below Bridge, took the view that the petition chiefly represented the attitude of young Porters of but a few years' standing, hence not yet in a position to earn much; many of its signatures had been obtained from outliers, small shopkeepers not working at Fellowship labour and in better financial circumstances than Billingsgate Porters. On the other hand, support came from a group of potato merchants who certified to the Coal and Corn Committee that their business had frequently suffered delay through the Rulers' failure to attend at their duty stations.

Nothing but a point-by-point refutation of the indictment could clear the Court of Rulers of the many accusations levelled at it, and on this the Rulers embarked. While maintaining, not very accurately, their claim to the disposal of the Fellowship capital by virtue of Common Council Act, they proudly pointed to its increase from £150 in 1787 to £6,000 at present, an increase attributed to their own prudent and economical management, which included the suppression of a very expensive annual dinner. Relief payments, far from falling below what the Fellowship could afford, now maintained forty-four superannuated members, twenty more than at the earlier date, quite apart from non-recurrent relief grants; further additions to the pension list were under contemplation. They denied misappropriation of fines and justified the allowance of 7s. to any Ruler occupied in Fellowship business for a whole day, other than that of the court meeting. Ignorant Billingsgate Porters constantly demanded legal action to assert exclusive privileges here, there and everywhere in a world where courts of law looked disapprovingly upon vague traditional rights curtailing or excluding the freedom of others. Actions of this type had been fought and lost in the past, one at least in spite of all the City Solicitor's exertions; Rulers had been advised by Counsel to resort to litigation as little as possible and to rely rather on custom and courtesy for retaining as much employment as possible at various wharves. It was through great exertions in both Houses of Parliament, instigated by Rulers, that the Porters' rights in the Commercial and East Country Docks had been safeguarded by the Acts constituting them; the unsuccessful attempts to provide similar protection in the London Docks had been in the City Solicitor's hands.*

On attendance at duty stations Rulers were more evasive, claiming on the one hand that the Pennyman gave constant service at Fellowship Hall, at least one other Ruler, sometimes as many as six or eight, at the Tower Street Corn Office, three at Queenhithe where one was permanently stationed, and one at Horselydown; on the other hand they admitted that an annual remuneration of £24 did not enable them to live and that they attended at various stations largely in order to take their turns at Fellowship labour, though they allocated Porters to jobs until they joined their own teams. The Tower Street Office where

* See pp. 139, 140, 149, 150 above.

Corn Meters sought their Porters required constant attendance from 4 a.m. to 8 p.m. in summer, from 6 to 6 in winter, a burden bearing very heavily on Rulers, some of whom would have resigned, had not the Court latterly granted them 7s. a day for loss of labour due to this duty. Apart from office duties, Rulers lost the second Wednesday of every month through attendance at court meetings. To read publicly all Acts and orders relative to Fellowship Porters would probably require twenty-four hours, even assuming a place could be found for assembly of upward of 2,500 members. So far from the Court of Rulers striving to free itself from control by the City Corporation, the Deputy of Billingsgate Ward in his capacity as Deputy Governor attended monthly court meetings whenever they transacted business more important than the settlement of internal disputes. The Common Council Act of 1620 had provided for twenty-four Rulers from whom, not in addition to whom, six Keymen and a Pennyman were to be appointed;* were the Court to consist of thirty-one members, Fellowship Hall would not contain its meetings. The present number of nineteen appearing fully adequate to discharge Rulers' duties, the Court had postponed filling five vacancies, thereby saving on Rulers' remunerations. Life tenure of rulership had been observed time out of mind, not instituted by any living Rulers; the same applied to the nomination of candidates for rulership by the Court. Were nominations thrown open to the Fellowship at large, it would be swamped by unsuitable candidates, forcing the Deputy Governor frequently to resort to the veto in order to prevent their election. To give a genuine choice to voters, the Court of Rulers never nominated less than three candidates for any vacancy. The Rulers had no objection to a closer definition of their power and authority if this appeared desirable to the City Corporation.

Sensing lack of sympathy in the Court of Aldermen, the ginger group redoubled its efforts to win support from the Common Council. To a body of newcomers among Fellowship members it appeared a grievance that, whereas twelve Porters per month had been admitted to the Fellowship on the average of the years from 1793 to 1815, the present Deputy Governor had limited the number to six at a time when

* See pp. 86–87 above.

great pressure existed to join the Fellowship. When accused of deriving support from outliers, the pressure group argued that Rulers could command any outlier, however profitable his main employment, to undertake Fellowship labour if such attendance were required.[77]

Out of this welter of charges and counter-charges, of insinuations refuted and irregularities half-admitted, the Coal and Corn Committee of the Common Council tried to crystallize the facts. On the financial side it recorded satisfaction with the ability displayed by successive Courts of Rulers in increasing the Fellowship capital. Far from discovering improper expenditure of funds, the committee described the expenses incurred as just, moderate and appropriate, and the amount of relief afforded as commensurate with means. On shifts the committee's first thoughts amounted to no more than limiting leases to fourteen years, but reconsideration commended the more radical proposal of transferring shifts to the Fellowship while leaving the appointment of the actual managers—still entitled Shifters, in spite of the legal change—in the hands of the Common Council, which also was to supervise the annual audit of the Fellowship's capital and income accounts and to receive a list of pensions and pensioners; no distribution of capital should take place without Common Council consent. Current surpluses were to be applied to increasing the capital stock from £6,000 to £10,000, and once that goal had been reached, to the augmentation of either numbers or allowances of pensioners who in future would be selected exclusively by seniority without consideration of age, infirmity or poverty. The expenses allowance of £6 a year for Rulers' courts, fixed in 1653,* had become ridiculously inadequate and should be replaced by a figure of £150. On constitutional matters the committee looked upon an annual public recital of Acts and orders as impractical and proposed the issue of a book of rules handed to members upon admission. Nomination to all offices, hitherto in practice a Rulers' prerogative, should be extended to the membership at large, all Porters of twenty-one years' standing to qualify for rulership, whether Corn Porters or not. In pronouncing upon the allegation that the initial onslaught on the Court of Rulers had been vexatious and ill-judged, the committee did not venture

* See p. 91 above.

beyond the view that 'although the Petitioners seem to have gone in some respects upon erroneous statements, yet there were sufficient grounds to warrant them in presenting their said Petition, and that the result of the investigation of the same will tend to public benefit'.

This faint praise goaded the ginger group to further exertions. While the Common Council was incubating a bill to give effect to the committee's proposals, amendments could be offered. The pressure group criticized the intended measure as generally too favourable to customs introduced by the Court of Rulers without sanction from the Corporation, too little concerned with the protection of ordinary Fellowship members. Future Shifters should be compelled to join the Fellowship, thus becoming amenable to its rules and regulations. Meters should be under an obligation to make their books available for inspection by Shifters. Annual income and expenditure accounts should be exhibited at Fellowship Hall for all members to see. Until the Fellowship's capital stock had reached £10,000, annual expenditure should be limited, the total to £1,000, that on administration to £700. Frequent delays in filling vacancies proved that twenty-four was too large a Court of Rulers; requirements could be met by half that number, if three would give daily attendance in the Corn Offices at Tower Street, Queenhithe and Horselydown at 7s. a day, as hitherto. Rulers should hold office for two years, six Rulers a year vacating their position. The Pennyman, to be elected like the rest of the Rulers from among candidates nominated by the whole membership, had hitherto received in accordance with the Council by-law 20d. a day, amounting in a full year to £29 13s. 4d. This allowance had become inadequate for full-time service and should be increased to £74. The number of Quartermen to be promoted to Corn Porters per year should correspond to one-eightieth of total membership. Not only Acts and orders promulgated by the City Corporation, but also orders of the Court of Rulers should be printed and distributed. Such proposals were not unduly controversial, but at the same time the ginger group pointed out that the Court of Rulers was using the interval between the committee's report and the expected Act to foil future reforms by filling gaps in its ranks through co-option so as to present a *fait accompli* of twenty-four life Rulers by the time the Act was passed. Moreover it was disposing of vacancies for pensioners as from midsummer next to men of its own choosing who had supported the Rulers in the current controversy. The warning led to a standstill order from the Common Council preventing all further appointments to the Court of Rulers, pending the Common Council Act.

On its side, the Court of Rulers presented amendments of its own. Its number having during the proceedings fallen to fifteen and remaining fixed at that figure, it proposed to abide permanently by that number. It strongly deprecated any change in the nominations for rulership. To confine eligibility to Corn Porters secured the selection of men best acquainted with the work and of the longest standing in the Fellowship; nomination by Rulers left the choice to men familiar with the character and ability of candidates. Fifty or a hundred candidates for every vacancy might be the result of throwing nomination open to the membership at large, quite apart from the impossibility of finding a room big enough for all members to assemble for purposes of nominating and electing. Ordinary Porters would nominate ignorant, improper and unfit candidates as well as outliers not regularly engaged in Fellowship labour, and the Deputy Governor would be hard put to it to disqualify all unsuitable candidates. Allocation of pensions by mere seniority would grant assistance to men who needed it least. The printing of all Acts, orders and regulations would prove a very expensive business, especially if it included local and temporary rules which were constantly made, altered and rescinded to meet changing needs and conditions.

Having heard argument on both sides the Common Council by an Act of 24 January 1822 embarked on the Fellowship's reform. As an interim solution it confirmed life tenure to the existing Rulers, now eleven, ordering the nomination and election by the whole membership within a month of one additional Ruler to be chosen from candidates of twenty-one years' standing to serve for three years. Once all life Rulers had been replaced, one-third of a court of twelve elected Rulers would retire every three years in order of seniority, but be re-eligible. All Porters of twenty-one years' standing could become candidates for rulership on condition of paying £2 towards election expenses. Out of Fellowship revenues £100 per year was allowed to defray the costs of court meetings. Annual accounts as well as the number and names of new admissions had to be furnished to the Common Council, the former also to be exhibited in Fellowship Hall. Like other Rulers, William Griffin, the Pennyman, was confirmed in office for life, but his successors were to be nominated and elected annually from among the Court of Rulers by the whole membership. In addition to his salary of £36 as a Ruler he had an allowance of £60 a year for giving full-time daily attendance at Fellowship Hall, but only one further Ruler had to attend every day at the Corn Meters' office, though he could call on other Rulers to give assistance, if required, without reward for this emergency help. The eight senior Quartermen should be appointed Corn Porters at once; henceforth the number to be so promoted annually would amount to one-eightieth of the total membership.

No leases of shifts should be granted in future, but Shifters would become Fellowship employees appointed by the Common Council, obliged to take up membership of the Fellowship and to employ Fellowship Porters as their clerks. They were entitled to inspect, though not to publish, the books and accounts of all Meters for the purpose of collecting porterage dues and would look to the Fellowship for the capital necessary to operate the shift. Net Fellowship revenue was to be added to capital stock invested in 5% Navy Bank Annuities until it amounted to £8,000; during the period of such accumulation, annual expenditure on current account should not exceed £1,300. Any distribution required the Common Council's prior authority. Once the £8,000 target had been reached, all net revenue would become available for increasing relief by raising either the scale of payments or the number of recipients, at the Court of Rulers' discretion. Acts, rules, orders and regulations of the Common Council and the Court of Rulers' standing orders were to be printed at Fellowship expense and copies given to all existing members free of charge, whereas new members acquired them on admission at a price of 2s. 6d. Special orders of the Court of Rulers merely had to be entered in a book kept at Fellowship Hall for the inspection of members. Rulers henceforth met this awkward regulation by passing two types of resolutions, the majority entered in the public, but a few in a private, minute book which has not survived, though there are allusions to its contents.

As the Clerk to the Fellowship pointed out subsequently, the Act of 1822 rendered the position of the Rulers analogous to that of directors of a joint-stock company, liable to removal by discontented share-holders to whom they are responsible. Unlike directors of a joint-stock company, however, Rulers of the Fellowship exercised disciplinary power over members and had to order reluctant Porters to perform unremunerative jobs. For discharging these functions properly, they incurred the enmity of dissatisfied Porters, who combined to prevent their re-election. Nor were elections to the court always well con-ducted; approximately 1,400 members participated, contests were fierce, and much money was dispensed in order to buy votes. No Court of Rulers could function effectively in such conditions, and unless its members became independent of election, they could not exercise their responsibility to the public.

Agitation died down after the passage of the Act. Irregularities occurred in the Fellowship accounts for eighteen months from March 1825 to September 1826, in which an excess of receipts over expendi-ture, amounting to over £20, remained unaccounted for. The Rulers exonerated from blame the Pennyman (still William Griffin, confirmed for life in 1822) who recorded monthly receipts and expenditure, but not the disposal of the monthly balance in accordance with directions received from the Court of Rulers, also because the Hollamby experiment (from being a member of the ginger group,* Hollamby had become a Ruler) had confused the general accounts with those of the fruit shift.† In 1828 three Billingsgate Porters presented themselves to the Court of Rulers as a deputation from a general meeting of the Fellowship. Thomas Higham was the only one among them who had figured prominently among the pressure group of former days. The Court of Rulers refused to receive them, on the plea that it did not recognize general meetings of Fellowship Porters, unless called by itself, nor would it receive any communication from Billingsgate Porters not couched in the form of a petition and presented by its signatories. On the other hand the Court of Rulers forestalled

* See p. 272 above.   † See pp. 240–241 above.

criticism by making several bonus distributions to pensioners: in 1828 £1 each to the hundred senior pensioners on Midsummer Day and a shirt, a pair of socks and stockings to all pensioners at Christmas; £3 to the fifty senior men, £2 to the next fifty and 30s. to the fifty junior men in 1831.*

In the following year the Rulers initiated the practice by which four of them, acting in rotation, met on the eve of court day to audit the accounts and received the 7s. allowance for such duty. They rode roughshod over Charles Abbott, a Deputy Corn Meter who, like all Deputy Corn Meters, was a Billingsgate Porter. He considered the Fellowship funds mismanaged and pressed for investigation and remedy, rendering himself obnoxious to the Rulers, who thereupon accused him of misdemeanour. Two investigations of his conduct took place, one by the Board of Corn Meters in Trust which exonerated him, one by a Fellowship Court of Rulers which dismissed him from the Fellowship, thus depriving him of his livelihood. The Board of Corn Meters in Trust insisted on a rehearing of Abbott's case by the Court of Rulers, but, though the Deputy Governor consented, he refused to call seven witnesses who attended to give evidence in Abbott's favour. Abbott asked the Common Council for redress, but that body returned the case to the Corn Meters in Trust. This was the period of peak employment for Billingsgate Porters. In every winter season between 1835 and 1839 and again in 1842–43 and 1843–44, the potato trade required the daily attendance of a Ruler on the south shore,† certain Rulers discharging this duty on a weekly roster, and throughout 1838 two Rulers had to be at Tower Street every day to deal with corn work.[78]

In the 1840s when members of the old ginger group had either died or reached the stage of applying for superannuation, a new pressure group arose. It used more raucous and intemperate language than its predecessor, adopting a more truculent and impertinent tone. In one respect its character differed from that of the earlier ginger group: the men who composed it were not newcomers to the Fellowship, but discontented members of some twenty years' standing who looked upon themselves as spokesmen for some 400 Porters working regularly

* See p. 268 above. † See pp. 242–243 above.

at corn labour. In this capacity they printed a number of documents, usually characterized by verbose abuse of the Rulers. Typical is the passage in a handbill circulated and signed by Joseph Hawthorn:

> Brothers, after many of you have read and carefully perused this wholesome advice written with the printer's ink it is more than probable that some of the tribe of interested clap-traps of the used-up Court will begin to exclaim, with their accustomed war-whoop, if I were the Rulers I would cancel their bonds. do those execrable ignoramuses, who are a disgrace to any civilized community, know that the author of this, as well as of others of the same tendency, in behalf of a much injured and neglected body, is a British Subject.

With John McDowell and John Stephenson, Hawthorn headed the opposition to the Court of Rulers in the 1840s and 1850s, but eventually secured election to that Court, whereupon deliberations degenerated into a tug-of-war between two parties which did not see eye to eye on any point.

Complaining in 1845, the pressure group described an annual salary of £36 for Rulers, representing payment at the rate of £3 for each court day, as an exorbitant sum for labouring men for whom £1 a court day would constitute adequate remuneration. The same applied to the Beadle, who should have his wage reduced to £12 p.a., while £96 was an excessive annual salary for a Pennyman, another working man who ought to be satisfied with £72. The allowance for dinner and wine for twelve meetings of the Court of Rulers amounted to £100, but was not in fact so spent; a surplus remained which the Rulers divided among themselves, and a reduction to £50 would be justified. Other expenses of the Court of Rulers had equally risen out of all proportion, rendering an extravagant and superfluous court a drain on Fellowship funds. The Clerk drew £150 a year for which he attended for a few hours each on twelve court and two election days, receiving separate fees for all law charges: £100 would remunerate him adequately for his exertions. From extravagance the ginger group passed to unauthorized expenditure. The Beadle was entitled to reside at Fellowship Hall. Since 1829 he had not chosen to do so, receiving instead an annual allowance of £10 for house rent; why should he have an option and be compensated for exercizing it? In 1825 £4 4s., in all subsequent years £10 10s. had been paid out of Fellowship funds to a servant for the Pennyman, who had also received free coal, candles and house rent. Which regulations provided the Pennyman with a servant or these other allowances? Quoting figures from Fellowship balance-sheets for the period 1833 to 1837, the pressure group alleged a deficiency of £1,830 unaccounted for, all the more serious since two Pennymen had died, owing to Fellowship funds considerable amounts which had never been allowed to appear in the annual accounts. The ginger group therefore demanded competent and qualified Pennymen as well as annual audit of accounts. Suspicions of jobbery informed the insistence that nobody should receive a pension from Fellowship funds while working as a Porter. The office of Beadle should not be a Rulers' prerogative, but thrown open to the whole Fellowship body. After the Hollamby experiment the Court of Rulers had been weak enough to let the fruit shift to Hurles at an annual rent of £130;* this expanding field of work might now have swelled Fellowship revenues by £400 or £500 a year. Lastly they objected to the frequency of 'running on the job' by junior Porters, for which the Court fined offenders a mere £1 1s., amounting to little more than a licence fee.

The Court of Rulers did not deny the substance of many of these accusations, though it placed upon them a different interpretation. To gain office as a Ruler had become a very expensive process: a candidate had to pay canvassers, print and distribute cards, bills, handbills and addresses for months prior to the election, and 'amongst a body of working men, dry canvassing is not always practised'. By depending on re-election, Rulers faced with insubordination were in an extremely vulnerable position. Only once or twice in the twenty years since the passing of the 1822 Act had an outgoing Ruler secured re-election without stout opposition; whenever an unpopular move by the Court was attributed to an individual Ruler, he was certain to be dropped when next his term of office expired. The Beadle had been removed from Fellowship Hall because of the inconvenience experienced in accommodating there two families, the Beadle's as well as the Pennyman's.

* See pp. 239–241 above.

The disclosures contained partly in the ginger group's allegations, partly in the Court of Rulers' reply, were sufficiently serious for the Governor and Deputy Governor hurriedly to devise a scheme to do away with the worst abuses. They proposed that, once elected, Rulers should hold office during capacity and good behaviour, thus being spared the necessity of seeking re-election. Capacity and good behaviour could be called in question at meetings held by the Governor and Deputy Governor at least once a year or whenever requisitioned by twelve members, when Governor and Deputy Governor would hear complaints and wield powers of suspending or discharging Rulers. Equally an appeal against any decision of the Court of Rulers would lie to the Governor and Deputy Governor, with authority to fine individual Porters up to £5 or suspend them from labour wholly or partially for periods within their discretion.

Except where it concentrated final power in the Governor's and Deputy Governor's hands, this plan formed the basis of a scheme of reform elaborated by the Common Council's General Purposes Committee. Against the verdict discharging a Ruler from office, appeal could be made to the Court of Aldermen. A special court for hearing complaints about Rulers would require requisition from a hundred, not from twelve Billingsgate Porters, unless Governor and Deputy Governor thought it necessary. No salary or gratuity should in future be paid to either Governor or Deputy Governor. The number of Rulers should be reduced from twelve to six now that they were to become full-time irremoveable Rulers at a salary of £100 a year and disqualified from working as Fellowship Porters, though continuing to receive 7s. for any day spent on full-time duties other than attendance at court. Two new categories of officers were suggested: Assistant Rulers would be working Porters acting as Rulers only upon requisition signed by two Rulers; elected and continued in office in the same manner as Rulers, they would be allowed 20s. for each court attendance and 7s. for every day spent on rulership duties. Two working Porters would be elected to audit accounts and furnish written reports on the audit. Candidates for these new offices should be Porters of twenty-one years' standing, pay £2 towards the expenses of their election and could be vetoed by the Governor or Deputy for unsuitability. The quorum of the new Court of Rulers composed of six Rulers and six Assistant Rulers would be seven, provided at least four of them were Rulers. The court's annual expenses should be reduced from £100 to £50. Retaining his special £60 allowance, the Pennyman would be annually elected from among the Rulers and enjoy a total remuneration of £160 per year. To disqualify from voting outliers, defined for this purpose as members who had done no Fellowship labour for twelve months, was considered, but dismissed as impracticable.

On a number of issues Rulers voiced dissatisfaction with these proposals. Only Rulers working as Porters, they maintained, could keep intimately acquainted with the labour and conditions of the Fellowship. The number of six Rulers was too high for slack periods, too low for busy ones when at least one Ruler had to attend at the Tower Street Corn Office, one at the Legal Quays on the north bank, one at the sufferance wharves on the south shore, one in the potato market at Tooley Street, one at Horselydown to superintend granary work, one in charge of Porters labouring in the Commercial and East Country Docks and the Grand Surrey Canal, one at Billingsgate to supervise the landing of oysters and other fish, and one at each brewhouse whenever large quantities of malt were unloaded—an enumeration of duties which made it difficult to visualize how even twelve Rulers had hitherto managed to do justice to them all. Nor did the Rulers consider their disciplinary powers adequate: any court meeting should be authorized to suspend Porters from labour in certain places or branches for periods exceeding a fortnight upon proof of misconduct. No large section of Porters desired the division of the court into Rulers and Assistant Rulers, which would merely engender jealousy and partisanship. For the meals following court meetings £50 represented an inadequate allowance; Rulers had made fair and economical use of their £100 by occasionally inviting to dinner in the interests of the Fellowship employers of porterage labour who could thus meet the Governor, Deputy Governor and members of the Court. To abandon the remuneration to the Deputy Governor was a gratuitous meanness which would constitute a disgrace to the Fellowship, considering the frequent calls, not only on the Deputy's time, but also on his purse. Independent outside auditors were acceptable, but auditors elected from the Fellowship body would subordinate Rulers to yet another group of men over whom they were supposed to rule, nor were working Porters by education or ability fitted to conduct effective audits. The Rulers insisted on a permanent Pennyman, as a change in this office caused much inconvenience. Qualifications for the receipt of a pension remained as obscure as ever—whether seniority alone, infirmity or destitution or a combination of the two latter.

Some of the committee's proposals had gone some way towards meeting the ginger group's criticism, but not nearly far enough for the liking of its members. They wanted to make certain that Rulers would hold no other offices or employments, but devote their time exclusively to the discharge of rulership duties. They bitterly opposed permanent tenure of rulership; indeed, they preferred annual to the present triennial election. The least they demanded was a total dissolution of the present Court of Rulers, starting the new régime with a freshly constituted body. Special courts to hear complaints against Rulers should be held at quarterly intervals—their one suggestion which the Common Council adopted. Fourteen years' standing would be an adequate qualification for rulership, but candidates should be men of less than fifty years of age, and Deputy Corn Meters expressly excluded. The 'useless and expensive' innovation of Assistant Rulers came in for wholesale condemnation, justified by the astonishing assertion that no need existed for the supervision of working Porters. They objected to the retention of the present Pennyman, partly on the ground that he had been illegally and improperly elected, partly that he was too old and infirm to discharge his office personally. Future Pennymen should be one of, not additional to, the six Rulers. Outliers should be disqualified from voting, as they were retained in the Fellowship only for the purpose of outvoting working Porters. Annual promotion of forty Quartermen to the rank of Corn Porters, irrespective of the total number of members (which by this time had begun to fall, owing to the restriction on new admissions*), would rejuvenate the corn labour force and speed up the discharge of corn cargoes. All salaries and

* See p. 258 above.

expenses allowances were criticized as too lavish, that for a Clerk being described as totally unnecessary since a lawyer could be retained when required. The capital advanced to Ruston, the Corn Shifter below Bridge, could safely be halved.

Two members of the ginger group, John Stephenson and George Wildash, stood for election as Rulers in 1847 and 1848, but were beaten on both occasions. George Wildash in the latter year was a candidate not only for rulership, but also for relief, stating that he suffered from paralysis attributed by the surgeon to 'changes from a hot to a cold temperament in his labour'. A fellow member of his group, John McDowell, at the same time asked for relief in respect of an accident, but the Court of Rulers turned down both petitions, the first because it disclosed a condition not coming within the Fellowship's accident rules, the second because it was unaccompanied by a surgeon's certificate.

Though the ginger group urged its reform suggestions upon the Common Council in a variety of documents containing a wealth of detail, it was extremely critical of the two-years' delay which full consideration entailed. An echo of Chartist rumblings pervades the group's warning in 1848 that the Common Council might well halt elections to vacant rulerships 'to prevent confusion and disturbance in the vicinity of Fellowship Hall, Billingsgate Ward, excitement and agitation among the Members and unnecessary expense and loss of time to the Candidates at the ensuing Election time (Midsummer day)', and promptly appropriate the salaries thus saved to pensions for another six aged and infirm Porters.[79]

(d) The Missed Opportunity of Root-and-Branch Reform

In spite of the hint, reform hung fire for another four years. When endeavours were at last resumed in 1852, the most radical scheme of reorganization ever mooted formed the basis—a scheme under which Rulers, Shifters and independent Meters alike would be replaced by officers salaried by the City Corporation; a multiplicity of corn trade charges would be simplified and standardized at 1d. a quarter for metage and another 1d. for porterage for heavy grains ex ship, with corresponding reductions for light grains or work ex granary, all payable by the

U

seller. The author of this plan, Henry Muggeridge, an Alderman as
well as a corn factor, could rally support from his fellow merchants as
easily as catch the ear of the City parliament. Muggeridge alleged that
the City levied charges on the corn trade under twenty-five distinct
heads, a complication as unnecessary as burdensome at a time when
railway transport had established easy communications and a nation-
wide market so that London, on account of its system of charges, lost
trade to other ports. On principle, discharge of cargoes from vessels
arriving in port fell to the responsibility of their masters and crews.
This applied in all ports generally and in the Port of London to commodities other than corn, thus subjecting the London corn business to
burdens unparalleled either in outports or in kindred branches of
London trade. Muggeridge attacked metage as much as porterage:
London metage charges reduced to 2,000 quarters of corn the weekly
quantity now measured in granaries by sworn Meters, whereas they
had dealt in 20,000 to 30,000 quarters a few years ago. Among 147
parties interested in the corn trade who backed Muggeridge by ap-
pending their names to his petition, appear such well-known firms as
Baring Brothers and Rothschilds. For working purposes the corn
factors appointed a committee of ten members to watch proceedings
and act on their behalf. In response to their representations the
Common Council set on foot the fullest examination yet conducted
into the privileges, practices and charges of the Fellowship Porters.
The General Purposes Committee, strengthened by the addition of
three members (among them Henry Muggeridge, who during the
investigation, except for a short appearance as a witness, consistently
acted the part of Counsel for the prosecution), held more than thirty
hearings over a period lasting two years. To the evidence elicited at
these hearings we owe much detailed knowledge of Fellowship work.

At the end of March 1854 the committee formulated its recommendations. While not proposing to abolish Fellowship labour on
corn ships, it suggested the limitation of the team accompanying the
Meter with the bushel to three Porters, the ship's company providing
any additional labour required. Metage, fillage, lastage and porterage
would be amalgamated into a single charge on corn, amounting to
2d. per quarter if the quantity exceeded, 3d. per quarter if it did not

exceed fifty quarters; if the vessel lay more than ten miles from London Bridge, another 1d. per quarter increased the fee which would fall entirely on the seller or importer. Metage would be compulsory only for corn which was imported if foreign, or sold if home-produced; a granary keeper could have his grain measured at an inclusive charge of 1d. a quarter if he employed a Meter only, or 2d. a quarter if in addition to the Meter he called for a team of three Fellowship Porters. Powers should be sought from Parliament permitting the Corporation to weigh as well as measure corn where desired by customers, at an additional charge to be agreed. This was rather a small mouse to be born from such mountainous investigations, nor nearly as radical a reorganization as Henry Muggeridge and his fellow corn factors had hoped. Perhaps for that reason the recommendations fell flat. The Common Council listened, adjourned consideration and ordered them to be printed and circulated. They were never heard of again.

(e) Reduction in Rulers' Numbers

Had a reform acceptable to the corn trade been devised, Billingsgate Porters might have retained or even increased their hold on corn handling in the Port of London. In the absence of satisfactory arrangements, the corn trade had alternatives: it withdrew more and more from open wharves and quays to the security of the docks to which the Porters could not penetrate, or transported its grain by rail to termini where the Fellowship's writ did not run. As corn porterage diminished, fruit remained the sole substantial strand of labour to which Billingsgate Porters clung, but only a small number could make their living by working in or for the Orange Gang. Like Charles II the Fellowship of Porters was an unconscionable time a-dying, but from the 1850s onwards, when its revenues dipped seriously and permanently, death sentence could only be suspended, not averted. The Court of Rulers stopped monthly dinners in order to economize, and the Common Council once again pruned Fellowship administration to save expenses by reducing the number of Rulers to seven, inclusive of the Pennyman, the quorum of the court to four instead of seven, and extending the Rulers' period of office to four years. Rulers remained working Porters subject to re-election at the end of their term of office.

While a step in the right direction, such reforms achieved little. By 1860 some hundred Porters of whom the oldest had been Fellowship members for fifty years petitioned the Common Council not to replace a Ruler who had just died. Fellowship labour now provided a scanty living for no more than eighty to a hundred men, while the possibility of a new election was 'bringing forward a number of speculative adventurers competing for the sinecure whereby they may become legitimate claimants for compensation for loss of place and emoluments in the event of the abolition of the body by legislative enactment'. The thought of Rulers claiming compensation for loss of office filled the Common Council with apprehension. Given firmness in resisting pressure for the authorization of new admissions, abolition of the Fellowship had become merely a question of time; compensation claims would introduce an element of complication. The General Purposes Committee at this stage did not propose to yield to the request for a smaller Court of Rulers, but recommended that new Rulers in future be made upon appointment to sign a declaration renouncing all claims to compensation in respect of loss of rulership. Some members of the Common Council favoured more drastic action. The report was referred back for reconsideration; when it re-emerged, renunciation of compensation was accompanied by a reduction to six of the number of Rulers, the two points forming the substance of a short Common Council Act.

A survivor of the ginger group of the late 1840s, John McDowell, found further opportunities for attacking the Court of Rulers in 1862. Had he really been forty-four years of age and a member since 1820, as he alleged, he would have engaged in porterage labour from the age of two onwards; as it was, his standing made him the most senior of the ninety Porters who denounced 'our expensive Government so as to preserve and economize our remaining Funds, which are being absorbed by a staff of overpaid Officials unsuitable to the Revenue'. For reasons best known to itself, the City Corporation had ceased to support Billingsgate Porters' privileges, and revenues did not suffice to replenish 'their remaining capital being absorbed by a paralyzed Government who have no legal power of action to enforce their Rights'. For the first time, a pressure group acknowledged that in the light of prevailing free trade principles Fellowship Porters were generally considered to have outlived their utility, whatever the value of their services in the past. While therefore calling upon the Corporation to succour them by protecting their privileges, the petitioners placed more emphasis on the alternative of honourable termination of the Fellowship's existence, accompanied by generous compensation so that support of aged pensioners could continue. Before the Common Council could take any action, it received a counter-petition from 300 Fellowship Porters denying the right of the first petitioners to speak for the Fellowship at large, owing to the smallness of their number, describing them as unrepresentative of working members and bent only on injuring the Fellowship, in contrast with those associated with their own petition, men who had for many years earned a living in this hard but honourable employment and whom a termination of all Fellowship privileges would deprive of their sole livelihood. Opposing views demanded yet another lengthy investigation from which nothing new emerged; no changes were in prospect. Too many past ginger groups had been becalmed in similar circumstances. The dissatisfied Porters took their grievance to Parliament. A motion in the House of Commons called for a Select Committee to enquire into the treatment of Fellowship Porters by the Corporation of London. Discussion took place in July 1863, too late in the parliamentary session for any effective progress to be made. Two members speaking to the motion attacked the City of London, described by one as having 'only one merit, that of ancient descent—an apostolic succession for anything he knew', for oppressing the Porters and mulcting them of one-twelfth of their daily earnings without rendering any effective services in return. Of two opposing members one put the majority view among the Billingsgate Porters, whereas the other favoured taking the controversy to law rather than to Parliament. As an agency for immediate remedial measures the House of Commons proved no more effective than the Common Council.

The administration of the Fellowship required periodical adaptation to its shrinking size. The Common Council Act of 1868 turned Rulers into full-time officials by cancelling all their allowances and attendance monies and replacing these by an annual salary of £100. If an adequate number of Rulers gave attendance at Fellowship Hall, the Corn Meters' office and the Fruit Office during working hours, this did not leave any to continue doing Fellowship labour. Extension of their terms of office to six years limited ordinary elections to one Ruler a year. Maintenance of a capital stock of £8,000 remained the Fellowship's aim. The returns hitherto furnished to the Common Council by the Rulers were now to be made to the Board of Corn Meters in Trust, a body replaced four years later by the Corporation's Metage on Grain Committee under an Act of Parliament* which provided for the appointment of two persons connected with London's corn trade as Rulers, designating as suitable the directors respectively of the Corn Exchange Company and of the London Corn Exchange Company. Two of these trade Rulers joined the court, subject neither to the limitation on Rulers' numbers nor to duty at any of the stations where a small number of Porters still reported for work.[80]

(f) *Dishonesty of Rulers*

Administration of an organization without hope of rescuing it from financial ruin is a demoralizing experience. If the effort is denounced and misrepresented by those administered, no incentive remains towards conscientious, let alone beneficial, discharge of duties. For the last twenty years of the Fellowship's existence, the Court of Rulers set an example of fecklessness and mismanagement, of malversation of funds and travesty of administration. Its moral fibre, never very strong, had been completely rotted by the atmosphere of decay pervading the Fellowship. Differences within the court brought the abuses to light. I. I. Wilkinson, a Ruler acting as temporary Pennyman, aroused suspicions when denounced by a fellow Ruler for showing a resolution of the court to ordinary Fellowship members. He defended himself by reference to the regulation that all resolutions of the court should be entered in a book kept at Fellowship Hall for the inspection of Porters,† but was assured that this applied only to orders concerning Porters' methods of work, not to ordinary resolutions. By the end of 1873 Wilkinson resigned as Pennyman because of differences with one of the other Rulers concerning finance. Two Rulers not implicated

* See p. 222 above.   † See p. 281 above.

in the controversy presented a special report in 1876 when the Court voted on some of the points raised or alternatives suggested by them: did the Court accept as satisfactory the explanations of the diminution of the Fellowship capital put forward by the Rulers Pink and Piner, Wilkinson's opponents? The Court did. It decided against reducing admission fees to the Fellowship from £5 5s. to £2 2s., but unanimously approved suggestions to restrict admission to men sufficiently literate to make out fairly accurate bills, to appoint a clerk for the Fellowship's office work and to abolish the post of hall-keeper.

Remnants of the old pressure group pursued time-honoured tactics. Three of them—Hawthorn, Wyld and Hayes—suspecting the Court of Rulers of concealing irregularities, asked for an enquiry into the Fellowship's affairs, followed by reconstruction on more economical principles. Wyld and Hawthorn, applying for pensions in their individual capacity, were awarded a mere £20 a year each, whereupon they 'expressed dissatisfaction & used language amongst the Body derogatory to the Court', leading to disciplinary proceedings and threats of pension withdrawal. Meanwhile the Rulers called a general meeting of Porters to vote on two suggestions also embodied in a petition to the Common Council: the number of Rulers to be reduced from six to five and the salary of the sixth Ruler to be distributed among the other five. The Porters' meeting and the Common Council unanimously voted for the reduction, but allocated the £100 saved to general Fellowship funds.

Was it dishonesty or mere incompetence which had led the Court of Rulers to place on record its satisfaction with the explanations furnished for the dwindling of the Fellowship's capital? Holford, the Ruler who had first quarrelled with Wilkinson, managed to borrow over £23 from the Fellowship. His private pursuits apparently required not only money but also time: his absences from work aggregated three weeks in February, two each in May, June, November and December of 1878 as well as several whole days at other times; when he attended at all during the second half of the year he was late for work almost every morning and frequently drunk. However, he was a mere petty thief, compared to Richard Piner, Ruler and

Pennyman, who decamped in the following year to Ireland with the princely sum of £1,840 embezzled from Fellowship funds. Though eventually apprehended, brought back and sentenced to six months' imprisonment, he did not restore any of the Fellowship's lost capital. These disclosures destroyed confidence in the Rulers; even those whose own honesty had not been impugned had completely failed to discover and prevent the frauds of their fellow Rulers.

Would-be reformers pressed for further reduction in the number of Rulers to either four or three. As a result of limiting candidates to Porters of twenty-one years' standing, Rulers were drawn from too narrow a circle; fifteen years' standing should be sufficient. Accounts were audited, but not in public, nor did they show receipts and expenditures of individual Rulers, but obscured the picture by recording net balances only; members were denied facilities for seeking additional information or explanations of items in the accounts. Expenditure on court meetings appeared to run in excess of the sum authorized. Relief paid was inadequate and precarious where a proper administration would provide handsome insurance for old age, accident, disease and death. £300 had become too large a contribution to the expenses of a diminished corn shift.* Inexpediency, if not injustice, arose from the system of Rulers sitting in judgment upon complaints preferred by themselves without ready appeal from their decisions to a tribunal of known impartiality. As customary, the Court of Rulers was invited to answer these charges. On the number of Rulers, while assigning responsibility to the Common Council, it contented itself with asserting that a reduction at the present moment would be disadvantageous. Undaunted by the disasters of the last two years, it affirmed that twenty-one years' standing formed a guarantee of mature judgment and blameless character of candidates for ruler-ship, nor had it ever heard objections to the procedure of adjudication upon complaints, believing the constitution of the Court of Rulers itself to preclude serious partiality. On financial matters members had deluded themselves by calculations based on a gross shift revenue of £4,000 a year in comparison with a real figure over the last nine years of £1,300—insufficient even for the entire interest on invested capital

* See p. 233 above.

to be appropriated to pensions, as some of it was needed to defray current expenditure.

So once again the General Purposes Committee delved into the Fellowship's affairs. It attributed the fall in Fellowship income to causes not entirely outside the Porters' control; without authority from anybody, Billingsgate Porters had introduced what they called overtime charges for work after 5 p.m. No such overtime was charged inside the docks, where after 5 p.m. therefore porterage could be performed more cheaply than at the wharves; while Fellowship Porters forever complained of losing work to the docks, their own practice drove the trade to the cheaper service offered by the docks. The Rulers produced accounts in support of their figures, but soon afterwards a Ruler faced criminal charges for defalcation which these accounts had not disclosed. So far as the committee could see, one economy measure had been introduced: though a salary of £150 had been stipulated for the Fellowship Clerk, the present holder of the office drew only £100. It was more than offset by allowances of £36 each to the two Rulers representing the corn trade, though the Act of Parliament appointing them had not provided for any remuneration. However, they had taken office by virtue of national legislation and could not be tampered with.

The City Solicitor suggested economies by

	£ p.a.
discontinuing the Court's table expenses . .	50
reducing working Rulers from five to four .	100
reducing the Clerk's salary officially . . .	50
reducing the contribution to shift expenses . .	150
	£350 p.a.

the last measure being justified by the fact that the office collected a far greater amount of grain dues than porterage, hence should have the larger part of its expenses defrayed from grain dues. In order to improve membership discipline, the City Solicitor also proposed rendering Rulers less dependent on frequent re-election by extending their terms of office from five to seven years. In accepting all these proposals, the General Purposes Committee added one of its own:

professional auditors selected by the Common Council's Metage on Grain Committee should audit the accounts annually, every member being entitled to a copy of the audited balance-sheet and accounts on payment of 3d.

Though enacted by the Common Council in 1884, this did not stop the rot. Relying on check clerks to attend to their clerical duties, Rulers ceased altogether to present themselves for daily work. They came to court meetings, where proceedings remained as unsatisfactory as before: by the time Porters were admitted, complaints against them had already been discussed and virtually prejudged, nor were defendants allowed to call any witnesses except Fellowship members, a limitation not imposed upon Rulers' witnesses. The Pennyman was improperly elected in opposition to the main body of Porters. John Pink, late Pennyman, who had received a sum of £200 credited as porterage in excess of the proper amount, could not be made to account for it before he relinquished office. Books ordered to be available for general inspection remained closed to all members until the middle of 1885 when, after repeated applications and considerable pressure, the cause and minute books but none of the account books became available; copies could be obtained of balance-sheets for 1879 and 1880, but not for the three following years. In a letter accompanying the accounts for the last nine months of 1884, William Cash, F.C.A., the outside Auditor appointed by the Metage on Grain Committee, focussed attention on a number of irregularities revealed by his audit. Instead of attending personally to receive monies due to the Fellowship from the Shifters, the Rulers had left this duty to be performed by the check clerk. Of funds thus received on the Fellowship's behalf, the check clerk had made away with £167 19s. 9d.; only the fortuitous repayment to the Fellowship of a private debt owed to the check clerk had diminished this deficiency to £142 1s. 9d. A sum of £36 4s. 10d. represented unauthorized expenditure paid by the Rulers to themselves, partly for doing the check clerk's work, partly for expenses and overtime, none of which they had any right to claim.

The Common Council's imagination was exhausted. No magic wand could transform the Fellowship of Porters or its Court of Rulers into a solvent or honest organization. In 1887 it reduced the working Rulers to three, shortened their terms of office to three years and requested trade Rulers to exercise greater supervision over the keeping and rendering of accounts; the clerkship was to remain vacant, the duties to be performed at no extra charge by the working Rulers. The Court was empowered to sell or let the Fellowship Hall at St. Mary-at-Hill; by-laws and standing orders could be neither made nor changed nor rescinded without confirmation by the Common Council. At best, this could obviate gross abuses, but not secure a livelihood for the Fellowship.[81]

With dishonesty irrepressible, work dwindling and capital diminishing, the years of the Fellowship were numbered. But for the embarrassment of having to provide for members still clinging to the remnants of work, it would long have been put into liquidation. Such scruples worried members of the City Corporation, but not outsiders who believed a test action the best way of giving the Fellowship the *coup de grâce* by having it declared void and of no effect. Precisely this had been the judgment pronounced by Mr. Commissioner Kerr, a judge in the City of London Court, overruled in the Court of Appeal. If it were possible to bring a test action before the same judge without allowing the case to go to appeal, the Fellowship would be defeated. The plan was ingenious. Its promoters remained in the shadows. They bribed Charles Henry Harrod, a Billingsgate Porter, to deface a notice issued by the Court of Rulers—an offence calculated to lead to his dismissal from the Fellowship. No sooner had this penalty been visited upon Harrod than he began an action in the City of London Court against the Fellowship's Governor, claiming 5s. for work done and damages for wrongful dismissal. Albert Grey, a barrister accustomed to act for Porters involved in litigation with the Rulers, took charge of Harrod's case, whereas the City Solicitor conducted the defence. Mr. Commissioner Kerr, however, disappointed expectations. He declared himself bound by the decision of the higher court which had overruled his own, hence entered a non-suit at common law against the plaintiff. The attempt to strangle the Fellowship quickly had failed. Within a year Harrod, the conspiracy's tool, was petitioning for re-instatement in the Fellowship.

These events had happened in 1886 and 1887, the years during which the Court of Rulers ceased to keep a record of its meetings. In 1887 for the last time, it listed in its minute book fifty-two standing orders then in force, but did not pass any further minutes modifying or adding to these orders. For all practical purposes the Rulers had ceased to rule. Indeed, they paid no attention to the Governor. Two of them, Piner and Hilditch, treated their situations as freehold property to be used for their own advantage; they followed precedent by falsifying accounts and misappropriating funds. In 1888 they applied to the Common Council to appoint an associate of theirs, Thomas Stagg, the Fellow-ship's check clerk. The Common Council refused, whereupon in open defiance of that verdict they engaged Stagg as Beadle in the following year at a salary of £26, subsequently bestowing on him the clerkship at a salary of £80, all without authority. Only when enquiries had proceeded sufficiently far to make the formulation of precise criminal charges imminent, did Piner and Hilditch take the hints dropped to them and resign their offices. The third Ruler, Prestage, was not convicted of any dishonesty, though he admitted knowledge of wrong entries in the balance-sheet; he claimed that he disagreed with his colleagues' malpractices, though he had done nothing at all to prevent them. His saving grace consisted of a considerable dose of ill-health which had justified long absences from work during the first half of 1890 when the irregularities were coming to light. Reporting on the accounts for 1889, the Auditor drew attention to the following amounts paid by Rulers to themselves which were not authorized and accordingly illegal: salaries of £10 to the Pennyman and £2 2s. to Thomas Stagg, the latter for doing six days' duty on behalf of Prestage who was away ill; £3 to themselves in connection with drawing dividends or selling out Fellowship stock; £8 to Hilditch of which £6 referred to shovels and bushels bought, £2 to office expenses carried over from 1888. The last two items might be genuine, but no vouchers had been produced to substantiate them, no more than for an item of £82 described as strike expenses.

The Rulers printed the accounts of the Fellowship for 1889, as was their duty, but omitted, not without good reason, the greater portion of the Auditor's certificate. When at last Hilditch relinquished office as Pennyman, an amount of £92 10s. could not be recovered. It is not surprising that the circumstances prompted the Governor and Deputy Governor to urge an enquiry into the whole position of the Fellowship. The Common Council still would not grasp the nettle. It suggested disqualifying working Rulers from re-election for at least a year after completing a term of office and appointing two ordinary Fellowship members annually to inspect accounts and vouchers. It fell to the City Solicitor to voice what must long have been in the minds of all concerned.

> Altho' the present Rulers [he wrote in 1891] are considered to be as good men as could be chosen from the Fellowship, yet it is doubtful whether the system would ever work satisfactorily . . . the class of men concerned are so uneducated that they will never trust one another & that the present system had, therefore, better be discontinued, if possible.

(g) Dissolution of the Fellowship

A general meeting attended by 160 Billingsgate Porters took place in 1892 to discuss the possibility of disbanding the Fellowship. The Governor presided; Alderman Knill, Lord Mayor-elect and one of the chief employers in the fruit trade, was present; so were the working Rulers. A majority opposed liquidation of the Fellowship, but equally objected to elections of further working Rulers, substituting a committee of Porters to have binding powers of action on the Fellowship's behalf and to keep in touch with the City Solicitor. It is alleged that thereupon the Governor himself took steps to bring matters to a head by warning Porters of the risks they ran in persisting with an organization which incurred an annually increasing deficit. He persuaded, almost ordered, them to ask for liquidation, promising that the Corporation would in that contingency supplement the Fellowship's small assets by a generous donation, coupled with his personal contribution of £5,000 to enable men to start afresh. The evidence for such behind-the-scenes assurances rests on the unsupported recollection of an aged Porter thirty-eight years after the event; but the Common Council received through the Governor a petition, signed by over 180 Billingsgate Porters, setting forth the impossibility of making any longer a living at Fellowship labour, in spite of all attempts to adapt the Fellowship constitution to modern conditions. As the Fellowship could no longer enforce its rights and privileges, it should be wound up, subject to reasonable compensation. Even at that late date this did not represent the views of the whole membership, as proved by a prompt counter-petition from seventy signatories who described Fellowship labour as their only means of livelihood, of which they did no wish to be deprived. They believed the promoter of the petition for disbandment to be a man with an independent livelihood secured to him, who had obtained signatures by misleading supporters into thinking that on the Fellowship's abolition aged Porters would receive a pension, junior Porters a large bonus from the City Corporation.

Even at this stage the Common Council persisted in attempts to put the Fellowship on a functioning basis. In mid-1892 it reduced the number of working Rulers to two, turning the Pennyman into an appointed clerk at a salary of £52 a year, subject to a week's notice of dismissal. But this did not satisfy those working for the abolition of the Fellowship. When they renewed their petition in September they had collected over 340 signatures. According to their pleas, many members were facing starvation: some had entered workhouses, others had been compelled to accept parish out-relief. They demanded a scheme for equitable division of the funds.

The decision to put an end to the Fellowship was at last taken in 1893. The path had been cleared of a number of obstacles: of Porters old enough not to have signed, in one form or another, a declaration renouncing all claims to compensation for loss of Fellowship rights, only seven or eight survived; nothing in national legislation impeded the Common Council's powers to effect the dissolution; of the four firms employing the Orange Gang, three proclaimed themselves indifferent to the Fellowship's existence, only one preferring its continuance in being. The corn trade as represented by the trade Rulers manifested lack of interest, whereas working Rulers along with a majority of members favoured liquidation.

Once the principle had been accepted, the Governor called another general meeting to which he put a proposition of distributing to each member of the Fellowship £8 in full satisfaction of claims. The meeting was in a rebellious mood. After indignantly refusing such compensation as entirely inadequate, Billingsgate Porters took the opportunity to prefer 'a series of charges of gross, brutal and wantonly cruel acts of abuse of his authority' against William Nicholas, outgoing Ruler, and to express loud disapproval of the last two holders of the office of Ruler whom they assured of their inability to secure re-election; they also protested against the appointment of the last Pennyman. This wholesale condemnation of the ruling body was in the best Fellowship tradition. To ease the transition, the Common Council reduced the number of elected Rulers to one as from Midsummer Day 1893 and had the Fellowship's assets valued. These amounted to £8,600; the Fellowship called upon the City Corporation to augment them by a £48,000 grant, in view of the large sums of money derived by the Corporation from commodities handled by Fellowship labour. The audacity of the demand convinced the City authorities that no scheme they could devise for the distribution of assets had any chance of proving acceptable to the Billingsgate Porters; in the circumstances, the disposal of funds was left to the operation of the law. The bill dissolving the Fellowship became an Act on 15 March 1894, the disbandment dating from Midsummer Day of that year. The amount paid to each member consisted of a refund in full of all quarterage he had paid to the Fellowship, plus his share, amounting to £10 17s. 6d., of the collective assets—only a little more than the sum suggested by the Governor which the general meeting of Billingsgate Porters had rejected out of hand. For the first time in three centuries, the Port of London after mid-1894 harboured no privileged Porters.[82]

The end of the Fellowship of Porters was not the last to be heard of Billingsgate Porters. For another thirty-five years, former members strained their ingenuity to devise grounds for demanding money from the City Corporation. In 1908 they suggested a refund to them of sums laid out for taking up their freedom, an expense incurred merely in order to qualify for admission to the Fellowship. At the same time, they requested preferential consideration for porterage employment in markets under the Corporation's control. The City's two Market Committees discussed this demand, but no preference was granted, nor was redemption money refunded.

There remained appeals to charity. From the widowed daughter of a Porter trying her luck in 1901 to joint petitions by surviving Billingsgate Porters in 1914 and 1922, they proved in vain; but in 1924 the most energetic of the former Fellowship Porters, William C. Murphy, took a hand. He discovered an amount of £61 15s. 1d. still remaining in an account at the Midland Bank to the credit of the Fellowship of Porters. There being no body of this name in existence, the Bank refused to part with the money, except against an indemnity from the City Corporation. By energetic lobbying, Murphy obtained this indemnity; forty-nine survivors received 25s. each, the balance compensating Murphy for his expenses. In the following year Murphy organized another petition, but without the success which had attended his previous action. Undaunted, he tried again in 1926, and though a number of Common Councilmen endeavoured to have the matter dismissed, a compassionate grant of £3 each was made to thirty-nine survivors on condition that they signed undertakings to bother the Corporation no further. A sympathizer, Sir Harry Bird, persuaded his fellow Councilmen not to insist on this pledge; grants were made to former Billingsgate Porters of £1 each in 1928 and 1929, £2 each in 1930, 1931, and 1932. In the latter year, the survivors numbered sixteen, among them the indefatigable Murphy, who by an appeal to the City public in the correspondence columns of the *City Press* at Christmas in 1930 raised sufficient funds to provide all old Fellowship Porters with substantial Christmas dinners, coal and money for another three weeks' maintenance. A true last outpost of a ginger group, Murphy was not satisfied. The petition to the Common Council which he had drawn up to acquaint its members with the Billingsgate Porters' case had not been read out in full court, but hushed up by being confined to an inner circle of members. Murphy demanded no less than that the whole court, sitting as a committee, should give consideration to the petition. The Fellowship of Billingsgate Porters might have disappeared, but as long as any member survived, nobody could say that it had struck its flag of defiance.[83]

NOTES

Abbreviations used

B.M.	British Museum
C.J.	Journals of the House of Commons
Co. Co.	Court of Common Council, City of London
Co. Co. Jls.	Journals of the Court of Common Council, City of London
Co. Co. Print. Mins.	Printed Minutes of the Court of Common Council, City of London
Comm.	Committee
Ec. Hist. Rev.	Economic History Review
Engl. Law Rep.	English Law Reports
Fin.	Finance
Gen. Purp. Comm.	General Purposes Committee
G.L.M.R.	Guildhall Library Muniment Room, City of London
G.L.R.O.	Guildhall Library Record Office, City of London
P.R.O.	Public Record Office
R.C. Mun. Corp.	Royal Commission on Municipal Corporations in England and Wales, 2nd Report, British Parliamentary Papers 1837, xxv.
Reps.	Repertories of the Court of Aldermen of the City of London
S. C. Accomm.	Select Committee on Accommodation for Trade and Shipping in the Port of London, Report 1796, British Parliamentary Papers 1793–1806, xiv.
S. P. Dom.	State Papers Domestic

REFERENCES

1. E.g. W. Elkan, *An African Labour Force* (East African Studies No. 7, 1956), p. 40.

2. E. M. Leonard, *The Early History of English Poor Relief* (1900), pp. 98, 100. Reps. xix, fo. 204b. Co. Co. Jls. xxx, fo. 227 (Lord Mayor's Proclamation concerning Porters).

3. 7 Ric. II, cap. 37 (1383), quoted from the City Solicitor's copy of 1824 of Chancery Court records kept in the Tower of London.

4. T. F. T. Plucknett, *A Concise History of the Common Law* (5th ed. 1956), pp. 449, 480. E. G. M. Fletcher, *The Carrier's Liability* (1932), p. 153. I am very grateful to Professor Plucknett for his assistance in dealing with the legal complication of the Porters' position.

5. Co. Co. Jls. xx (2), fo. 481b, 506 (corrected and amended by Letter Book Y, fo. 341–341b). Privy Council Proceedings and Ordinances (n.s.) xi, pp. 88, 220–221. Letter Books A, fo. 130; C, fo. 54; D, fo. 158; F, fo. 164; S, fo. 20b. Calendar of Letter Books of the City of London (ed. R. R. Sharpe), Book F, pp. 193–194. *Liber Albus*: The White Book of the City of London (transl. H. T. Riley, 1861), pp. 211–214, supplemented from *Liber Custumarum*. Reps. iv, fo. 30b–31; v, fo. 163; x, fo. 215b, 266b; xii (2), fo. 261; xiii (1), fo. 255, 277–277b; xiv. fo. 179b, 374b; xv, fo. 195; xvi, fo. 48b, 50–56; xxi, fo. 114b–115. H. B. Dale, *The Fellowship of Woodmongers* (n.d. [1922–23], p. 5.

6. Dale, *loc. cit.* Charters in W. de Gray Birch, *The Historical Charters and Constitutional Documents of the City of London* (rev. ed. 1887). G.L.R.O. MS.101.3; Porters' Case Book 1716–1724, pp. 81–91 (Duncan Dee). 2 Will. & Mary, sess. I, cap. 8, sect. 2–4, 14. Engl. Law Reps. *Cuddon* v. *Eastwick*, 1704 (1 Salkeld 143 and 6 Modern 123); *Robinson* v. *Webb* (1 Barnadiston K.B.76). S.C. Accomm. pp. 247–443 (the table is extracted from Apps. D, G and H). Anon., *A General Description of all Trades digested in Alphabetical Order* (London 1747), p. 171. Reps. xxix, fo. 17b; xxxi(1), fo. 143b; xxxi(2), fo. 299, 306b; xxxii, fo. 104; xxxiv, fo. 439b; xxxviii, fo. 187; xlii, fo. 22–22b; xlvii, fo. 361–361b; lxxxiii, fo. 321. Co. Co. Jls. xxiv, fo. 285b–286, 288b (corrected and amended by Letter Book AA, fo. 176–178); xxvii, fo. 144b–146; xxx, fo. 227. P.R.O. S.P.Dom. Chas. I, ccclxxxvi, Nos. 10–12; 44–235 (Will. & Mary Entry

Book No. 1), p. 179. R. Davis: 'Seamen's Sixpences: An Index of Commercial Activity, 1697–1828', *Economica* (n.s.) xxiii (1956), pp. 328–343.

7. The story of the woad trade is admirably explained in Professor E. M. Carus-Wilson's article: '*La guède française en Angleterre: un grand commerce du Moyen Age*', *Revue du Nord*, xxxv (1953), pp. 89–105. Porters' references are to Calendar of Letter Books of the City of London, Books A, p. 219; C. p. 135; F. p. 192. The Little Red Book of Bristol (ed. F. B. Bickley), i, p. 55; ii, pp. 16–22. P.R.O. Calendar of Close Rolls, A.D. 1279–1288, p. 121 (9 Edw. I). W. Maitland and others, *The History of London*, i (1756), p. 83, make the not uncommon mistake of reading 'wood' for 'woad'.

8. This description follows E. Lipson, *The Economic History of England: I. The Middle Ages*, 8th ed. 1945, pp. 516–526, 609. M. M. Postan: 'The Economic and Political Relations of England and the Hanse (1400 to 1475)', in *Studies in English Trade in the Fifteenth Century* (ed. E. Power and M. M. Postan, 1933), pp. 113, 115, 140. E. Daenell, *Die Blütezeit der Deutschen Hanse* (Berlin, 1905), i, pp. 48–68; ii, pp. 1–47, 126–132. The following sources have been consulted: Calendar of Letter Books of the City of London, Books G, p. 30; K, p. 46. *Liber Albus* (ed. H. T. Riley, 1862), i, pp. 418–424. 6th Charter of Edw. III to London (4 Dec. 1376) in Birch, *op. cit.*, pp. 67–69. 9 Hen. III, cap. 30. P.R.O. Privy Council Proceedings and Ordinances (n.s.), iii, pp. 110–112. *Hanserezesse* (Leipzig 1872–93), 1st ser. ii, Nos. 37, sect. 13, 44 sects. 18, 20, 106, 107 sects. 12–13, 15, 142 sects. 3, 7, 12, 15. *Hansisches Urkundenbuch* (ed. K. Höhlbaum and K. Kunze, Halle and Leipzig 1879–1905), ii, No. 31 sect. 7 and n.; iv, Nos. 516, 569–572, 603, 645, 647, 671, 673, 697; v, Nos. 348, 387, 828, 843, 1114; vi, Nos. 144, 332, 334, 337, 482, 515–516, 529, 613, 658; ix, Nos. 71, 80, 211–212, 433–434.

9. W. Maitland and others, *op. cit.*, p. 106. G.L.R.O. Charter 18 Edw. IV, MS.108.6; *Mayor of London* v. *London Dock Company and West India Dock Company* (London Sessions of the Peace 1822), Shelf 481. Co. Co. Jls. xiv, fo. A–C; xx (2), fo. 183 (corrected and amended by Letter Book Y, fo. 341–341b); xxiv, fo. 285b–286, 288b (corrected and amended by Letter Book AA, fo. 176–178); xli*, fo. 156b–157. 1 Hen. VII, cap. 2 (1485); 22 Hen. VIII, cap. 8 (1530). Charters 16 Chas. I (1640) and 15 Chas. II (1664) in Birch, *op. cit.*

10. B.M. Harl. MS.1878, fo. 37–39. Reps. iv, fo. 183b; cxxvii, fo. 27–30, 37–39. P.R.O. S.P.Dom. Chas. I, cccxlii, Nos. 33–35; ccclxxvii, No. 89;

Chas. II, Entry Books lxxi, fo. 81; cccxxxv, fo. 369. Co. Co. Jls. xli*, fo. 76, 151b–152; lix, fo. 36–38, 346–346b; lxiv, fo. 321–323, 346b–348b; lxv, fo. 301b–302b, 327b–331b; lxxiv, fo. 21b–22, 155b–156b. G.L.R.O. Alchin's Coll. 3.81; indentures of leases of the office of Aliens' Packer and Porter in Deed Box 90.1 and Box 5, Shelf 149 and on Shelf 481.

11. Reps. x, fo. 342; xxxiv, fo. 98, 134; lxi, fo. 1, 37b–38, 89–89b, 142, 147. Co. Co. Jls. xxiv, fo. 285b–286, 288b (corrected and amended by Letter Book AA, fo. 176–178); xxvii, fo. 144b–146; lxxvii, fo. 442b–454. G.L.R.O. Porters' Case Book 1716–1724, pp. 74–75 (Duncan Dee); *Petition by the Registers and Rulers of the Society of Tackle House and Ticket Porters to the Court of Aldermen*, n.d. [1 Feb. 1694], Box 5, Shelf 149; *Mayor of London* v. *London Dock Company and West India Dock Company* (London Sessions of the Peace 1822), Shelf 481. P.R.O. S.P.Dom. Chas. I, xxi, No. 40; cccxiv, No. 51; cccxlii, No. 33; ccccxxi, No. 157. 12 Chas. II, cap. 4, esp. rule or article 20.

12. Reps. xiv, fo. 525b; xxiv, fo. 388b–389; lviii (1), fo. 47b; xcviii, fo. 126–127, 142–143, 240, 278–279. Co. Co. Jls. xx(2), fo. 483, 506 (corrected and amended by Letter Book Y, fo. 341–341b); xxiv, fo. 285b–286, 288b (corrected and amended by Letter Book AA, fo. 176–178); xxvii, fo. 52b–54, 144b–146; xxxi, fo. 123b–124; xli*, fo. 156b–157. 13 & 14 Chas. II, cap. 11. G.L.R.O. *The Case of the Tackle Porters of the Waterside commonly called the Packers Porters addressed to the Court of Aldermen*, n.d. [1694], Box 3, Shelf 149; *Petition by the Registers and Rulers of the Society of Tackle House and Ticket Porters to the Court of Aldermen*, n.d. [1 Feb. 1694], *Complaint of the Registers and Rulers of the Society of Tackle House and Ticket Porters to the Court of Aldermen*, printed, n.d. [17 April 1694], Box 5, Shelf 149.

13. 12 Chas. II, cap. 18, sect. 9; 13 & 14 Chas. II, cap. 11, sect. 10; 24 Geo. III, Sess. II, cap. 16, sect. 3. G.L.R.O. *Petition by Col. Pearce on behalf of his Porters to the Court of Aldermen*, 9 Jul. 1706, Box 3, Shelf 149; Porters' Case Book 1716–1724, pp. 76–79 (Tho. Pengelly); Alchin's Coll. 5.8. City Lands Comm. Jls. 1, fo. 74b–75, 79b–80; li, fo. 93b–94. Co. Co. Jls. lvii, fo. 43–43b; lviii, fo. 379–381; lix, fo. 36–38, 346–346b; lxi, fo. 262b–263; lxiv, fo. 321–323, 346–348b; lxv, fo. 295–295b, 301b–302b, 327b–331. Reps. xxxi(1), fo. 139b; lxv, fo. 91b; cx, fo. 165, 167b; cxxi, fo. 468, 582–583.

14. G.L.R.O. *The Case of the Tackle House Porters belonging to the Primary Companies, especially the Mercers', Drapers' and Goldsmiths' Companies, against the Ticket Porters, presented to the Common Council*, printed, n.d. [1711], Box 1, Shelf 149. *A Brief Story of the Worshipful Company of*

Vintners, pamphlet (Vintners' Hall, London, n.d.). R.C. Mun. Corp. pp. 210–212. P. J. Bowden: 'Wool Supply and the Woollen Industry', *Ec. Hist. Rev.* 2nd ser. ix, 1 (Aug. 1956), p. 57. Reps. xix, fo. 95, 157b, 284b, 310b–311b; xxi, fo. 104, 108, 114b–115; lxvi, fo. 78–79. Co. Co. Jls. xx(2), fo. 483, 506 (corrected and amended by Letter Book Y, fo. 341–341b); xxiv, fo. 285b–286, 288b (corrected and amended by Letter Book AA, fo. 176–178); lxxvii, fo. 442b–454b.

15. Co. Co. Jls. xxvii, fo. 329b; xl, fo. 126b–128; lviii, fo. 379–381; lxxiv, fo. 37b–42, 59b–60b. Reps. liv(1), fo. 224–224b, 243; liv(2), fo. 163b–164; xciii, fo. 194b; cx, fo. 150–150b, 152b–153, 157b–158; clxxiii, fo. 159–161. G.L.M.R. Abstract of Tacklehouse Porters made and Companies nominating them, 1738–1831, MS.916. G.L.R.O. Letter [from a lawyer to the Clerk of the Skinners' Company], 3 Aug. 1688, *The case of the Tackle-house Porters of the Twelve Primary Companies*, printed, n.d. [1707], *The Case of the Tacklehouse Porters belonging to the Primary Companies, especially the Mercers', Drapers' and Goldsmiths' Companies, against the Ticket Porters, presented to the Common Council*, printed, n.d. [1711], Box 1, Shelf 149; *Petition by the Ticket Porters to the General Purposes Committee of the Common Council*, read 23 Jan. 1794, Box 3, Shelf 149. P.R.O. T.76 (Proceedings of the Port of London Compensation Commissioners)/5, fo. 786–788, 881–883, 890–892; T.76/6, fo. 1075–1076, 1116; T.76/7, fo. 1485–1489; T.76/8, fo. 288–289; T.76/9, fo. 16–19, 509–510; T.76/10, fo. 177/182, 282–284. C.J. li, p. 487.

16. Reps. xxi, fo. 114b–115; xxiii, fo. 369b–371; xxvi(2), fo. 521b–524; xxxii, fo. 320b–321; xlvii, fo. 402–402b; xlviii, fo. 246b; il, fo. 122–122b; lvii(2), fo. 168b; lviii(2), fo. 143b; lix, fo. 25–25b, 184b–185; lxv, fo. 60. Co. Co. Jls. xxiv, fo. 285b–286, 288b (corrected and amended by Letter Book AA, fo. 176–178) xxvii, fo. 142b–146; xl, fo. 126b–128, 194–196; lv, fo. 353–355; lxx, fo. 116b–117; lxxiv, fo. 37b–42, 57–59b; lxxvii, fo. 442b–454b. G.L.M.R. MSS.913, 2836/5, 3455, 3456 (Minutes of the Court of Rulers of the Society of Tacklehouse and Ticket Porters). H. Llewellyn Smith: 'Chapters in the History of London Waterside Labour. I. Waterside Porters', *Economic Journal*, ii (1892), p. 603. P. Colquhoun, *A Treatise on the Commerce and Police of the River Thames* (London 1800), p. 75. G.L.R.O. Porters' Case Book 1716–1724, pp. 79–81 (Rich. Richardson), 81–91 (Duncan Dee). P.R.O. T.76/4, fo. 93–94; T. 76/5, fo. 881–883; T. 76/6, fo. 1075–1076; T.76/10, fo. 275–276, 297–298, 301–303, 391–392; T.76/11, fo. 185–186. *A General Description . . .* p. 171.

17. Reps. xxvii, fo. 176, 183b, 191, 199b–200; xxix, fo. 41–42b, 102b; xxx, fo. 391; xxxi(1), fo. 108; xxxi(2), fo. 246b; xxxviii, fo. 174; lxxii, fo. 79b; lxxx, fo. 237. G.L.M.R. MSS. 913, 2836 (Registers' Account Books of the Society of Tacklehouse and Ticket Porters)/8, 2836/10, 3455, 3456. Co. Co. Jls. xl, fo. 126b–128; lv, fo. 353–355; lxxiv, fo. 37–42, 61–62b, 66b–67; lxxvii, fo. 442b–454b. G.L.R.O. *Petition by the Tackle Porters to the Court of Aldermen*, n.d. [1681–82], Box 5, Shelf 149; *Petition by the Ticket Porters to the General Purposes Committee of the Common Council*, read 21 March 1793, Box 3, Shelf 149. *A General Description* . . . p. 172.

18. Reps. lxxii, fo. 69–69b; cxcv, fo. 257–263. G.L.M.R. MSS. 913, 3455. G.L.R.O. Lord Mayor's Waiting Book iii, no pag., 6 Feb. 1667; *Petition by the Tackle Porters to the Court of Aldermen*, n.d. [1681–82], *The Case of the Ticket Porters against the Tackle House Porters presented to the Court of Aldermen*, n.d. [1707], Box 5, Shelf 149; *Reasons and Allegations offered to the Common Council by the Ticket Porters against the Tackle House Porters*, n.d. [officially dated c. 1682], P.D. 9.3; *The Case of the Tackle House Porters belonging to the Primary Companies, especially the Mercers', Drapers' and Goldsmiths' Companies, against the Ticket Porters, presented to the Common Council*, printed, n.d. [1711], Box 1, Shelf 149; petitions by the Ticket Porters to the Co. Co., 23 Feb. 1712, and to Gen. Purp. Comm., Co. Co., 21 March 1793 and another read 23 Jan. 1794, Box 3, Shelf 149. Colquhoun, *op. cit.*, pp. xxxi–xxxii. Co. Co. Jls. xl, fo. 126b–128; lix, fo. 81–82; lxx, fo. 116b–117.

19. G.L.M.R. MSS. 913, 2076, 2836/1–2836/11, 2933/1, 3455. Co. Co. Jls. xl, fo. 104b, 126b–128; xli*, fo. 47, 55, 57; lv, fo. 353–355; lxvi, fo. 182–183b; lxx, fo. 116b–117; lxxiv, fo. 57–59b; lxxvi, fo. 132–132b, 249–250, 292b; lxxvii, fo. 222–222b, 240, 357b, 442b–454b; lxxviii, fo. 241b–242. Reps. xxxvi, fo. 4b–5, 31b–32b; liv, fo. 334b–336; lv, fo. 16–16b, 165b, 416b, 438–438b; lvii(1), fo. 151b; cciii, fo. 259–275. G.L.R.O. *Petition by the Tackle Porters to the Court of Aldermen*, n.d. [1681–82], Box 5, Shelf 149; petitions by the Ticket Porters to the Co. Co., 23 Feb. 1712, and to Gen. Purp. Comm., Co. Co., read 23 Jan. 1794, Box 3, Shelf 149; Porters' Case Book 1716–1724, pp. 81–91 (Duncan Dee).

20. Co. Co. Jls. xl, fo. 126b–128, 194–196; lv, fo. 353–355. Reps. xxxvi, fo. 31b–32b; lxiv, fo. 218; lxv, fo. 1–1a; lxvi, fo. 78–79; cxi, fo. 124–125, 131, 137–138, 167, 179. G.L.R.O. *Reasons and Allegations offered to the Common Council by the Ticket Porters against the Tackle House Porters*,

n.d. [officially dated *c.* 1682], P.D. 9.3 ; *Petition by the Tackle Porters to the Court of Aldermen,* n.d. [1681–82], *The Case of the Ticket Porters against the Tackle House Porters, regarding goods from Scotland,* n.d. [May–June 1707], Box 5, Shelf 149; *The Case of the Tackle House Porters belonging to the Primary Companies, especially the Mercers', Drapers' and Goldsmiths' Companies, against the Ticket Porters, presented to the Common Council,* printed, n.d. [1711], Box 1, Shelf 149; minutes of Co. Co. comm. preparing bill on the Tacklehouse and Ticket Porters, 15 and 20 May 1712, Box 3, Shelf 149; draft Act for the better government of the Tacklehouse and Ticket Porters, n.d. [*c.* 1797], Box 2, Shelf 149. G.L.M.R. MSS. 913, 3455.

21. G.L.R.O. Petition by the Ticket Porters to Gen. Purp. Comm., Co. Co., read 23 Jan. 1794, Box 3, Shelf 149. Co. Co. Jls. lxxvii, fo. 442b–454b; lxxviii, fo. 241b–242. Reps. xxvi(2), fo. 521b–524; xcvii, fo. 309; clxv, fo. 312–314; cciii, fo. 259–275. G.L.M.R. MS. 2838 (Quarterage Account Books of the Society of Tacklehouse and Ticket Porters). P.R.O. T.76/6, fo. 1106–1107; T.76/11, fo. 182–183.

22. Reps. xxxvi, fo. 31b–32b; lxxxi, fo. 56–56b, 88–89, 145; c, fo. 16b–17; civ, fo. 264, 297, 309; cxxvii, fo. 413–415; cciii, fo. 222–223, 259–275. Co. Co. Jls. xl, fo. 126b–128; lv, fo. 353–355. G.L.M.R. MSS. 913, 3455. G.L.R.O. London Sessions Book 1674–75, no pag., 17 Feb. 1675; *The Case of the Tacklehouse Porters belonging to the Primary Companies, especially the Mercers', Drapers' and Goldsmiths' Companies, against the Ticket Porters, presented to the Common Council,* printed, n.d. [1711], Box 1, Shelf 149; minutes of Co. Co. comm. preparing bill on the Tacklehouse and Ticket Porters, 15 and 20 May 1712, Box 3, Shelf 149. P.R.O. T.76/3, no pag., evidence 17 Feb. and 17 March 1806; T.76/4, fo. 32–34, 67–70, 105–116; T.76/6, fo. 1106–1107, 1167–1176; T.76/9, fo. 153–154, 213–214, 265–267; *Report of the Compensation Commissioners for the West India, London and East India Docks to the Treasury,* printed, 17 June 1824, apps. II, V. Colquhoun, *op. cit.,* pp. xxxi–xxxii, 77, 80, 104n., 105–106. S.C. Accomm., p. 310.

23. Co. Co. Jls. xxiv, fo. 285b–286, 288b (corrected and amended by Letter Book AA, fo. 176–178); xxvii, fo. 144b–146; xxxi, fo. 123b–124; lv, fo. 353–355; lix, fo. 81–82, 346–346b; lxvi, fo. 182–183b; lxxviii, fo. 241b–242. Reps. xxi, fo. 114b–115, 369b–371; li, fo. 49; lxxiv, fo. 183b; lxxviii, fo. 15b, 278–278b, 305; xciii, fo. 158b–159, 160; xcv, fo. 175b; cxxi, fo. 7–12. G.L.R.O. *Petition by the Tackle Porters to the Court of Aldermen,* n.d. [1681–82], Box 5, Shelf 149; Porters' Case Book 1716–1724, pp. 74–75, 81–91 (Duncan Dee and Rich. Richardson): *Petition of*

the Registers and Rulers of the Society of Tackle House & Ticket Porters to the Court of Aldermen, n.d. [1692], petition by the Ticket Porters to Gen. Purp. Comm., Co. Co., read 23 Jan. 1794, Box 3, Shelf 149. G.L.M.R. MS. 913. 39 Geo. III, cap. lviii, sect. 12.

24. Reps. xvi, fo. 50–56; lxv, fo. 1–1a, 112–113; lxvi, fo. 78–79; lxxxiii, fo. 19b–20; xcviii, fo. 497; ic(1), fo. 24, 308–310. Co. Co. Jls. xxxi, fo. 225b–228b; lv, fo. 353–355; lxxvii, fo. 442b–454b; lxxix, fo. 302b–304b; lxxx, fo. 25–27b. G.L.R.O. Alchin's Coll. 6.56; *Reasons and Allegations offered to the Common Council by the Ticket Porters against the Tackle House Porters,* n.d. [officially dated *c.* 1682], P.D. 9.3; *Petition by the Tackle Porters to the Court of Aldermen,* n.d. [1681–82], *The Case of the Ticket Porters against the Tackle House Porters, presented to the Court of Aldermen,* n.d. [1707], Box 5, Shelf 149; petition by a large number of Ticket Porters to the same, 11 Apr. 1676, petition by the Tacklehouse Porters belonging to the 12 Primary Companies to the same, 26 June 1707, rough draft of an agreement between the Tacklehouse and Ticket Porters, amended by a Co. Co. comm., 14 Oct. 1712, petition by the Ticket Porters to Gen. Purp. Comm., Co. Co., read 21 March 1793, Box 3, Shelf 149; *The Case of the Tackle-house Porters of the Twelve Primary Companies,* printed, n.d. [1707], Box 1, Shelf 149; Porters' Case Book 1716–1724, pp. 91–93 (John Lingard). G.L.M.R. MSS. 913, 1703, 3455.

25. Reps. xxviii, fo. 271; lxvi, fo. 78–79; lxxxii, fo. 164b; c, fo. 180b, 182–182b; cxx, fo. 349–350; cxxi, fo. 7–12; cxxii, fo. 166–167; cxliv, fo. 60–61. G.L.M.R. MSS. 913, 3455. G.L.R.O. *Reasons and Allegations offered to the Common Council by the Ticket Porters against the Tackle House Porters,* n.d. [officially dated *c.* 1682], P.D. 9.3; *The Case of the Tackle House Porters belonging to the Primary Companies, especially the Mercers', Drapers' and Goldsmiths' Companies, against the Ticket Porters, presented to the Common Council,* printed, n.d. [1711], Box 1, Shelf 149; petition of the Tacklehouse Porters belonging to the 12 Primary Companies to the Court of Aldermen, 26 June 1707, petition by the Ticket Porters to the Co. Co., 23 Feb. 1712, minute of Co. Co. comm. preparing bill on the Tacklehouse and Ticket Porters, 14 Oct. 1712, rough draft of an agreement between the Tacklehouse and Ticket Porters, amended by a Co. Co. comm. 14 Oct. 1712, petition to the Co. Co. comm. preparing the Porters' Act by several merchants trading in Spanish iron, read 11 Nov. 1712, *The Case of the Ticket Porters,* printed, n.d. [1716], petition by the Ticket Porters to Gen. Purp. Comm., Co. Co., read 21 March 1793, proposition of a division of labour between Tacklehouse and Ticket Porters settled

at a meeting of their Rulers, read in Select Comm., Co. Co., 29 Oct. 1793, objections offered by the Tacklehouse Porters to the claims of the Ticket Porters, submitted to Select Comm., Co. Co., 4 July 1794, Box 3, Shelf 149; *The Case of the Tackle House Porters in answer to a Petition by the Ticket Porters*, printed, n.d. [Jan. 1740], Box 5, Shelf 149; draft Act for the better government of the Tacklehouse and Ticket Porters, n.d. [*c.* 1797], Box 2, Shelf 149. Co. Co. Jls. lv, fo. 353–355; lxxvii, fo. 442b–445b.

26. Reps. lxxxii, fo. 162, 202b; cii, fo. 157, 164–165; cx, fo. 150–150b; cxi, fo. 181. G.L.R.O. *Reasons and Allegations offered to the Common Council by the Ticket Porters against the Tacklehouse Porters*, n.d. [officially dated *c.* 1682], P.D. 9.3; *Petition by the Tackle Porters to the Court of Aldermen*, n.d. [1681–82], *The Case of the Ticket Porters against the Tackle House Porters, regarding goods from Scotland*, n.d. [May–June 1707], Box 5, Shelf 149; petition of the Tacklehouse Porters belonging to the 12 Primary Companies to the Court of Aldermen, 26 June 1707, certificate from London traders with Scotland to the same, read 15 July 1707, petition by the Ticket Porters to Co. Co., 23 Feb. 1712, rough draft of agreement between Tacklehouse and Ticket Porters, amended by a Co. Co. comm., 14 Oct. 1712, objections offered by the Tacklehouse Porters to the claims of the Ticket Porters, submitted to Select Comm., Co. Co., 4 July 1794, letter from W. Ramsay (Secretary, East India Company) to the City Solicitor, 26 Oct. 1796, Box 3, Shelf 149. Co. Co. Jls. lv, fo. 353–355; lxxiv, fo. 57b–59b; lxxvii, fo. 442b–454b; lxxix, fo. 302b–304b; lxxx, fo. 5–6. Colquhoun, *op. cit.*, pp. 29–30. P.R.O. T.76/7, fo. 1508–1511; T. 76/8, fo. 87–89.

27. Reps. xxiii, fo. 369b–371; xxvi, fo. 521b–524; xxxvi, fo. 31b–32; liv, fo. 224–224b, 334b–336; lxxx, fo. 193–193b; lxxxv, fo. 125b; cciii, fo. 259–275. Co. Co. Jls. xl, fo. 126b–128; lxxvi, fo. 249–250, 292b; lxxvii, fo. 222–222b, 442–454b. G.L.R.O. *Reasons and Allegations offered to the Common Council by the Ticket Porters against the Tackle House Porters*, n.d. [officially dated *c.* 1682], P.D. 9.3; *The Case of the Tackle-house Porters of the Twelve Primary Companies*, printed, n.d. [1707], Box 1, Shelf 149; minute of Co. Co. comm. preparing bill on the Tacklehouse and Ticket Porters, 20 May 1712, petition by the Ticket Porters to Gen. Purp. Comm., Co. Co., read 21 March 1793, extract of minutes of meeting of West India merchants, London, 20 Dec. 1793, letters from Beeston Long (Chairman, Committee of West India Merchants in London) and Edward Ogle (Chairman, Proprietors and Lessees of Legal Quays and Warehouses

in the City) to the City Solicitor, 1796, Box 3, Shelf 149. G.L.M.R. MS. 913.

28. G.L.R.O. *Stanford* v. *Stagg et al.* Sm.S. 13.11. B.M. Lansd. MS. 84, No. 15; Add MS. 12503, fo. 266–267. Charter of Henry III in Birch, *op. cit.* A. Pulling, *A Practical Treatise on the Laws, Customs, Usages and Regulations of the City and Port of London* (2nd ed. 1844), p. 354. Letter Books A, fo. 130; C, fo. 54; D, fo. 158; F, fo. 164; S, fo. 20b. Calendar of Letter Books of the City of London, Book F, pp. 193–194. *Liber Albus*, pp. 211–214, supplemented from *Liber Custumarum*. Reps. iv, fo. 30b–31; v. fo. 163; xii(2) fo. 261; xiii(1), fo. 277–277b; xiv, fo. 179b. Dale, *op. cit.*, pp. 1, 9, 14. Co. Co. Jls. cxxxix, fo. 73–74b.

29. Reps. xvi, fo. 50–56; lxxxiii, fo. 259b–260; clxi, fo. 180–183; clxxxiii, fo. 222; cxciv, fo. 421–422; cxcv, fo. 37. Co. Co. Jls. xxxi, fo. 225b–228b (corrected and amended by Letter Book GG, fo. 274–279b). G.L.R.O. Lord Mayor's Waiting Book iii, no pag., 26 and 27 Apr. 1668; MS. 101.3; Petition by the Corn Porters to a Co. Co. Comm. arranging for a bounty on foreign wheat, 5 May 1773, Box 1, Shelf 149; book of Fellowship Acts etc., printed 1822, Box 2, Shelf 149; Alchin's Coll. 6.56. Co. Co. Print. Mins. 1819, pp. 39–49. G.L.M.R. MS. 1702 (Minutes, Rules and Orders of the Fellowship Porters)/1. Charles Welch: 'Fellowship Porters', *Middlesex and Hertfordshire Notes and Queries*, i (1895), pp. 46–52. P.R.O. S.P.Dom. Chas. II, cccvii, No. 49.

30. Co. Co. Jls. xxxi, fo. 225b–228b (corrected and amended by Letter Book GG, fo. 274–279b); xli*, fo. 70b, 83b–85. Reps. xvi, fo. 50–56; xxii, fo. 57–61; lvi, fo. 46–50b; lxi, fo. 8–8b; lxii, fo. 129b–135. G.L.M.R. MSS. 444, 1591, 1702/1. G.L.R.O. MS. 9.30; bill for the better Regulation of the Fellowship of Porters of Billingsgate, 27 Oct. 1708, Alchin's Coll. 6.56; book of Fellowship Acts etc., printed 1822, Box 2, Shelf 149. Co. Co. Print. Mins. 1819, pp. 39–49.

31. Co. Co. Jls. xxxi, fo. 225b–228b (corrected and amended by Letter Book GG, fo. 274–279b); xli*, fo. 83b–85; lvi, fo. 109, 150b, 192b. Co. Co. Print. Mins. 1819, pp. 39–49. G.L.M.R. MSS. 1699 (Accounts of the Fellowship of Billingsgate Porters)/1, 1700, 1702/1. G.L.R.O. MS. 101.3; *Petition of the Salt Porters called Quartermen of Billingsgate to Sir Francis Child and the Court of Aldermen*, n.d. [1698], correspondence in bundle 3, Box 1, Shelf 149; Alchin's Coll. 3.61, 6.56. Reps. xvi, fo. 50–56, 524; xxii, fo. 57–61b; xxxiii, fo. 65–65b; xxxiv, fo. 19b; xxxix, fo. 28b, 83–83b; xl, fo. 404–404b; lii, fo. 185, 235, 237–237b; lviii(1), fo. 88b; lxxxvii, fo. 51, 60b, 108b, 127b; cxviii, fo. 312–313.

32. Reps. xvi, fo. 50–56; xxii, fo. 57–61b. G.L.R.O. Lord Mayor's Waiting Book, iii, no pag., 26 and 27 Apr. 1668; articles of agreement, 18 Dec. 1708, Deed Box 30, No. 11; bill for the better Regulation of the Fellowship of Porters of Billingsgate, versions of 27 Oct. 1708 and 16–20 Dec. 1709, Alchin's Coll. 6.56; *Clissold et al.* v. *Beeston et al.*, 1718–19, L.S. Box 1.14. Co. Co. Jls. xxxi, fo. 225b–228b (corrected and amended by Letter Book GG, fo. 274–279b). G.L.M.R. MSS. 444, 1699/1, 1700, 1702/1, 1703, 4790.

33. Co. Co. Jls. xxxi, fo. 225b–228b (corrected and amended by Letter Book GG, fo. 274–279b); liv, fo. 611–612, 614, 692, 702, 707; lv, fo. 69b, 156b–157. Reps. xv, fo. 362b; xviii, fo. 11b, 29; xxxi(1), fo. 44b, 61b, 67b, 91, 95b, 97b; xxxii, fo. 89b; xxxv, fo. 198b; xxxviii, fo. 59b, 113, 180b–181; xl, fo. 178; xliii, fo. 162, 167; xlv, fo. 212, 455–455b; xlviii, fo. 454b–455; lvii(2), fo. 59b–60; lxiii, fo. 39, 326–326b, 383b–384; lxv, fo. 59b–60; lxvi, fo. 24; lxvii, fo. 130; lxviii, fo. 58b; lxxix, fo. 270, 324–324b; lxxxi, fo. 261, 287; lxxxiv, fo. 45b; lxxxv, fo. 63–63b, 68b; lxxxvi, fo. 186; lxxxvii, fo. 114–114b; xcvi, fo. 138, 429; xcvii, fo. 44; xcviii, fo. 402–403, 412–413; c, fo. 193; cii, fo. 377; ciii, fo. 3, 25–30, 31, 214; cv, fo. 101–102, 375–376; cvii, fo. 509, 540; cviii, fo. 263–265; cix, fo. 457, 495–496; cx, fo. 6–7, 8–9, 83–83b, 116b, 122, 125–127b, 182; cxi, fo. 13–14, 24, 33–34, 59, 116; cxiv, fo. 87–88; cxv, fo. 15; cxvi, fo. 74; cxix, fo. 169–170, 176, 243, 281; cxxi, fo. 41–42, 52, 76; cxxii, fo. 195–196; cxxv, fo. 493–494; cxlvi, fo. 418–419; cl, fo. 393–394. G.L.R.O. Lord Mayor's Waiting Book, iii, no pag., 26 and 27 Apr. 1668; Report by John Peake and Nath. Hawes, Alderman and Deputy of Billingsgate Ward, to the Court of Aldermen, 1 Dec. 1691, statement by Thomas Tyler and William Aris to the same, n.d. [1706], attaching statement of charges, *Petition of the Society of Corn and Salt Porters to the Court of Aldermen*, read 23 Jan. 1710, *Petition by the Upper Ruler, Rulers and Assistants of the Fellowship of Billingsgate Porters to the Court of Aldermen*, n.d. [1718], *Fazackerly* v. *Wiltshire*, handwritten copy, 1721, Box 1, Shelf 149; petition by the Corn Meters to the Lord Mayor, read 17 July 1733, Box 3, Shelf 149; Proceedings of City Corporation Comms. ccccxxvii, fo. 12, 20–22, 27; bill for the better Regulation of the Fellowship of Porters of Billingsgate, 27 Oct. 1708, Alchin's Coll. 6.56.

34. G.L.M.R. MSS. 1700, 1702/1. S.C. Accomm. pp. 302–303. G.L.R.O. Lord Mayor's Waiting Book, iii, no pag., 26 and 27 Apr. 1668; statement by Thomas Tyler and William Aris to the Court of Aldermen, n.d. [1706], Box 3, Shelf 149; petition by the Corn Porters to a Co. Co. comm.

arranging for a bounty on foreign wheat, 5 May 1773, Box 1, Shelf 149; book of Fellowship Acts etc., printed 1822, pp. 52–53, Box 2, Shelf 149; statements by William Ruston, Corn Shifter below Bridge, to the Coal and Corn Comm., Co. Co., read 10 Apr. 1818, Box 4, Shelf 149. Co. Co. Jls. xxxi, fo. 225b–228b (corrected and amended by Letter Book GG, fo. 274–279b); xlviii, fo. 416–416b; lxxxiii, fo. 258b–261b. Co. Co. Print. Mins. 1818, pp. 133–139. 1 Anne cap. 26, esp. sect. 4. Reps. xvi, fo. 48b, 50–56; xxx, fo. 325b, 338b–339, 356b–357; xxxix, fo. 132; lxxix, fo. 99b; lxxxiii, fo. 228, 267b–268; xci, fo. 17–18; xcii, fo. 57, 105–107; ccxxi, fo. 632–642. Colquhoun, *op. cit.*, pp. 131, 138–139. Pulling, *op. cit.*, pp. 469–470.

35. Reps. xvi, fo. 48b, 50–56; xxxix, fo. 115b–116; xlv, fo. 455–455b; lv, fo. 42–42b; lvi, fo. 46–50b. Co. Co. Jls. xxxi, fo. 225b–228b (corrected and amended by Letter Book GG, fo. 274–279b); xl, fo. 5, 151; xli*, fo. 84–85, 94–95. G.L.M.R. MSS. 444, 1591, 1700, 1702/1.

36. Co. Co. Jls. xxxi, fo. 225b–228b (corrected and amended by Letter Book GG, fo. 274–279b); xlvi, fo. 22–24b; lii, fo. 26b–29b; lvii, fo. 290–291, 315, 317b, 319, 321, 331b. Reps. xvi, fo. 48b, 50–56; xxxiv, fo. 219b, 244b–245b; lxxviii, fo. 205; c, fo. 4b, 12b, 90b, 101b–102, 111, 120–120b, 125, 129b–130, 132, 135b–144, 170b–171, 174–174a; ciii, fo. 157, 184–185; cxvii, fo. 290. P.R.O. S.P.Dom. Chas. II, Entry Book lv, pp. 135, 299; Will. & Mary vi, Nos. 67–68, Entry Books i, p. 62, ii, p. 107, lxxiii, p. 8; Anne Entry Book ccxxxix, pp. 125–126. H. B. Dale: 'The Worshipful Company of Woodmongers and the Coal Trade of London', *Journal of the Royal Society of Arts*, lxx (1922), pp. 816–823. Dale, *op. cit.*, pp. 35, 39, 41, 63–65, 79–80, 82–85, 90–93. G.L.R.O. Petition by a number of Fellowship Porters to the Court of Aldermen, read 9 Sept. 1740, Box 3, Shelf 149. C.J. xxviii, p. 259; xxix, pp. 766–767; xxxii, pp. 300, 422–423, 736, 788, 833, 867, 877, 894, 972, 975, 980. 19 Geo. II, cap. 35; 31 Geo. II, cap. 76; 7 Geo. III, cap. 23; 10 Geo. III, cap. 53; 26 Geo. III, cap. 14; 43 Geo. III, cap. cxxxiv, esp. sect. 37; 47 Geo. III, sess. II, cap. lxviii, esp. sect. 139. G.L.M.R. MSS. 444, 1591, 1700, 1702/1. Colquhoun, *op. cit.*, pp. xxxi–xxxii, 142–144, 181. For a fuller description of the London coal trade see T. S. Ashton and J. Sykes, *The Coal Trade in the Eighteenth Century*, pp. 203–210.

37. T. S. Ashton and J. Sykes, *op. cit.*, pp. 207–208. M. D. George: 'The London Coal-Heavers: Attempts to regulate Waterside Labour in the Eighteenth and Nineteenth Centuries', *Economic Journal: Economic History Supplement No. 2* (May 1927), pp. 229–248. Dale, *op. cit.*, pp. 15–18.

Dale, article *cit.*, pp. 816–823.   P.R.O. S.P.Dom. Jas. I, 14–141; Chas. II, Entry Book x, pp. 50–54; Jas. II, Entry Book lv, p. 392.   Reps. cxvi, fo. 238–243; cxvii, fo. 16–18; cxviii, fo. 153–213, 299, 313–314, 372–373; cxix, fo. 174.   Co. Co. Jls. xli*, fo. 76, 84–85.   G.L.M.R. MSS. 1700, 1702/1.   Colquhoun, *op. cit.*, pp. 142–144.   S.C. Accomm., p. 331.

38. Reps. xvi, fo. 48b, 50–56; xxii, fo. 57–61b; xlii, 280–280b; cviii, fo. 263–265; cx, fo. 6–7.   G.L.R.O. Minute of the Mayor, 23 Sept. 1662, book of Fellowship Acts etc., printed, 1822, p. 39, Box 2, Shelf 149; bill for the better Regulation of the Fellowship of Porters of Billingsgate, versions of 27 Oct. 1708 and 16–20 Dec. 1709, Alchin's Coll. 6.56.   Co. Co. Jls. xxxi, fo. 225b–228b (corrected and amended by Letter Book GG, fo. 274–279b).   G.L.M.R. MSS. 444, 1591, 1699/1, 1700, 1702/1, 1703, 4790.

39. On the general question of City privileges and commercial development in the Port of London around 1800, see W. M. Stern: 'The First London Dock Boom and the Growth of the West India Docks', *Economica*, n.s. xix (1952), pp. 59–77.

40. G.L.R.O. Petition by the Registers and Rulers of the Society of Tacklehouse and Ticket Porters to the Co. Co., read 16 May 1792, Box 3, Shelf 149; *Mayor of London* v. *London Dock Company and West India Dock Company* (London Sessions of the Peace 1822), Shelf 481; minutes of evidence taken before Gen. Purp. Comm., Co. Co., 8 June 1833, Porters' Box 1.4.   Co. Co. Jls. lxx, fo. 116b–117; lxxv, fo. 262b–263.   G.L.M.R. MSS. 914 (Minutes of the Court of Rulers of the Society of Tacklehouse and Ticket Porters), 1702/2, 1702/3.   Reps. ccii, fo. 260–263, 358–361; cciii, fo. 114–119.   Dale, *op. cit.*, pp. 93–96, 100.   1 & 2 Will. IV, cap. lxxvi, esp. sects. 38, 39, 43, 60; 1 & 2 Vict., cap. ci; 6 & 7 Vict., cap. ci, esp. sect. 10.

41. Reps. cxcv, fo. 195–196, 226, 257–263, 401–402; cxcvi, fo. 388–391.   G.L.R.O. Petition by a number of owners of oyster vessels coming to Billingsgate Market to the Court of Aldermen against Thomas Bolt, read 27 Sept. 1791, Box 3, Shelf 149; *Stennett* v. *Bolt* (1800), L.S. 6.13; *The Complaints of the Tackle House and Ticket Porters against Mr. Bolt*, 15 Dec. 1803, Box 4, Shelf 149; memorial by Garrard & Son, Grocers' Porters, to Gen. Purp. Comm., Co. Co., n.d. [1803–1804], Box 5, Shelf 149; *Mayor of London* v. *London Dock Company and West India Dock Company* (London Sessions of the Peace 1822), Shelf 481.   Co. Co. Jls. lxxiv, fo. 21b–22, 155b–156; lxxviii, fo. 88b–89; lxxxi, fo. 272b–274; lxxxii, fo. 130–131; lxxxvii, fo. 266–267; xc, fo. 29–30.   *Bolt* v. *Stennett*,

Engl. Law Rep. 8 T.R. 606–608 (20 June 1800). 39 & 40 Geo. III, cap. xlvii, sects. 110, 111; 43 Geo. III, cap. cxxiv, sect. 8; 46 Geo. III, cap. cxviii, sect. 1. G.L.M.R. MS. 914.

42. *Report of the Compensation Commissioners for the Construction of the West India, London and East India Docks to the Treasury*, printed, 17 June 1824, apps. I, II, claims Nos. 221, 611–613. P.R.O. T.76/3, no pag., 17 Feb. 1806 (George Jacobs), 17 March 1806 (John Lightly), 5 July 1811 (Alderman Atkins); T.76/4, fo. 318 (William Richards); T.76/6, fo. 1106–1107 (Andrew Chalmers); T.76/9, fo. 153–154 (Wiggins' Quay Gang). Reps. cxcvi, fo. 388–391; ccxxvi, fo. 870–878; ccxxvii, fo. 153–156, 232–235, 405–408, 585–587. Co. Co. Jls. lxxviii, fo. 88b–89. G.L.M.R. MS. 914. G.L.R.O. Complaint by Fellowship Rulers about Christopher Hill, printed, n.d. [1823], with handwritten addition [1824–25], memorial from the Rulers of the Fellowship Porters to the Coal and Corn Comm., Co. Co., n.d. [1824], letter by George Marten, Clerk of the Fellowship of Porters, to Gilpin Gorst, Chairman, Coal and Corn Comm., Co. Co., 7 Apr. 1825, Box 1, Shelf 149; note by Christopher Hill to Court of Aldermen, n.d. [1823], Box 5, Shelf 149; case stated by the Clerk of the Fellowship of Porters to Coal and Corn Comm., Co. Co., 1 March 1831, Box 4, Shelf 149. Co. Co. Print. Mins. 1825, pp. 68–71.

43. G.L.M.R. MS. 914. Co. Co. Jls. cii, fo. 284–286b; ciii, fo. 165–166. Co. Co. Print. Mins. 1828, pp. 28–29; 1829, pp. 3, 117–118. G.L.R.O. Minutes of evidence taken before Gen. Purp. Comm., Co. Co., 8 June 1833, Porters' Box 1.4.

44. Co. Co. Jls. cvi, fo. 6–7; cxvi, fo. 132b–133b; cxxi, fo. 325–325b; cxxxix, fo. 73–74b; clii, no pag., 18 June 1874; cliii, fo. 315–318; clvi, no pag., 16 May 1878. Co. Co. Print. Mins. 1828, pp. 44, 75–76, 102; 1831, p. 168; 1838, p. 344; 1843, p. 229; 1848, p. 18. G.L.M.R. MSS. 914, 1702/2, 1702/3. G.L.R.O. Minutes of evidence taken before Gen. Purp. Comm., Co. Co., 25 May 1833, Porters' Box 1.4; City Solicitor's report to Gen. Purp. Comm., Co. Co., 13 Dec. 1892, I.R.52.

45. W. M. Stern: 'The First London Dock Boom and the Growth of the West India Docks', *Economica*, n.s. xix (1952), pp. 59–77. Co. Co. Jls. lxxviii, fo. 279–280, 293b–296; lxxxi, fo. 3b–6, 64b–65; lxxxii, fo. 31b–33; lxxxiii, fo. 258b–261, 291–293; cxxv, fo. 199–199b. 39 Geo. III, cap. lxix, sects. 121, 128; 39 & 40 Geo. III, cap. xlvii, sect. 109; 43 Geo. III, cap. cxxvi, sect. 109; 44 Geo. III, cap. 100, sect. 11; 46 Geo. III, cap. cxiii, sects. 32, 40. G.L.R.O. *Stennett* v. *Long* (1806), L.S. 6.13; *Mayor of London* v. *Baynes* (1807), L.S. 6.14; *Mayor of London* v. *London Dock Company and*

West India Dock Company (London Sessions of the Peace 1822), Shelf 481; case stated by the Clerk of the Fellowship of Porters to Coal and Corn Comm., Co. Co., 1 March 1831, Box 4, Shelf 149; letter by Chas. R. Brown, Fellowship Porter, to the Lord Mayor, n.d. [1845], I.R.72. G.L.M.R. MS. 1702/2. W. M. Stern: 'The Isle of Dogs Canal. A Study in Early Public Investment', *Ec. Hist. Rev.* 2nd ser. iv, 3 (1952), pp. 359–371.

46. 39 Geo. III, cap. lxix, sects. 121, 122, 128, 130, 131; 39 & 40 Geo. III, cap. xlvii, sects. 109–111, 114, 141; 46 Geo. III, cap. cxxxii, sects. 8–11, 13. P.R.O. T.76/3, no pag., 2 Aug. 1805, 3 Feb., 10 March, 12 Nov. 1806, 7 Jan., 26 Aug., 16 Sept., 7 Oct., 23 Dec. 1807, 6 Jan. 1808, 18 Jan., 27 Sept., 29 Nov. 1809, 21 Sept. 1810, 1 May, 5 July 1811, 27 May, 4 Nov. 1812, 4 Feb. 1813, 17 June 1824; T.76/4, fo. 52–53; T.76/5, fo. 975–976; T.76/7, fo. 1497–1501; T.76/9, fo. 16–19; T.76/11, fo. 182–183, 509–510. *Report of the Compensation Commissioners for the Construction of the West India, London and East India Docks to the Treasury*, printed, 17 June 1824, esp. pp. v, 1, apps. I, II, V. Reps. ccxiv, fo. 170.

47. P.R.O. T.76/3, no pag., 19 Aug. 1807, 12 Jan., 1 Feb., 25 March, 1 June; 1 Aug., 8 Oct., 15 Nov. 1814, 3 Jan. 1815, 20 June 1820, 25 March, 30 Apr., 7 May 1822, 3 and 31 Jan., 6 May 1823; T.76/8, fo. 193/194, 212–214, T.76/11, fo. 524, 575–579. G.L.R.O. Annual accounts of the Porter of Aliens' Goods, 1802–1833, Shelf 481; copy covenant of Aliens' Porter's lease granted to William Stennett, 25 Dec. 1803, indenture between City Corporation and the same, 20 Dec. 1811, L.S. 6.13; indenture of deputation of the office of Aliens' Packer and Porter, 15 Dec. 1821, Deed Box 90, No. 26; *Mayor of London* v. *London Dock Company and West India Dock Company* (London Sessions of the Peace 1822), Shelf 481. Co. Co. Jls. lxxxvi, fo. 231b–232; lxxxvii, fo. 64–64b, 413b–414; lxxxviii, fo. 191b–192; lxxxix, fo. 167b–168; xc, fo. 66b–67, 385b–386; xci, fo. 341–341b; xcii, fo. 324–325; xciii, fo. 331b–332; xciv, fo. 305–306; xcvi, fo. 27b–28. 3 & 4 Will. IV, cap. lxvi. R.C. Mun. Corp. p. 232. H. Mayhew, *London Labour and the London Poor*, iii (1861), pp. 364–367.

48. G.L.M.R. MSS. 914, 1700, 1702/2, 1702/3. 50 Geo. III, cap. ccvii, sect. 83; 51 Geo. III, cap. clxxi, sect. 53; 6 Geo. IV, cap. cxviii; 13 & 14 Vict., cap. li, sects. 25, 47. G.L.R.O. *Representations by the Rulers of the Fellowship Porters to the Committee on the South London Docks Bill*, printed, n.d. [1825], Box 1, Shelf 149; case stated by the Clerk of the Fellowship of Porters to Coal and Corn Comm., Co. Co., 1 March 1831, Box 4, Shelf 149; Gen. Purp. Comm., Co. Co., hearings relative to Fellowship Porters, *passim* and

pts. viii (10 July) and xxi (23 Nov. 1852), Porters' Boxes 7 and 8; City Solicitor's report to Gen. Purp. Comm., Co. Co., 7 Nov. 1882, I.R.52. Co. Co. Jls. cxxv, fo. 199–199b, 358b–362b; cxxxviii, no pag., 13 Sept. 1860. Co. Co. Print. Mins. 1861, pp. 102–103.

49. Reps. ccx, fo. 3, 324–326, 444–445. Co. Co. Jls. lxxxvi, fo. 173b–174b; xciii, fo. 109–110. Co. Co. Print. Mins. 1821, p. 36; 1825, p. 122. G.L.M.R. MS. 914. G.L.R.O. *Minutes of Evidence, Documents, etc. on the Petition of the Innholders*, Gen Purp. Comm., ordered to be printed 13 Oct. 1819, pp. 3–4, 50–52, 55–56.

50. Co. Co. Print. Mins. 1831, p. 185; 1832, pp. 70–71; 1833, pp. 120, 168–169. G.L.R.O. Letters from George Marten, Clerk of the Fellowship of Porters, to the Town Clerk, 10 Apr., and from James Smith to —— Evans, 25 June 1832, Gen. Purp. Comm., Co. Co., report on Tacklehouse, Ticket and Fellowship Porters, printed, 12 Dec. 1833, Box 1, Shelf 149; case stated by the Clerk of the Fellowship of Porters to Coal and Corn Comm., Co. Co., 1 March 1831, Box 4, Shelf 149; minutes of evidence taken before the Gen. Purp. Comm., Co. Co., 2, 8, 16 May 1832, 11 June 1833, Porters' Box 1.4. G.L.M.R. MS. 916: letter from Miles & Bracker, meat traders, to the Governor and Rulers of the Tacklehouse and Ticket Porters, 8 Dec. 1828, complaint by nine Ticket Porters at Leadenhall Market, n.d. [1840].

51. Co. Co. Print. Mins. 1834, pp. 4–5, 43, 134–136; 1851, p. 209. G.L.R.O. Memorandum on steam packet burdens, 1808, statements by Ticket and Fellowship Porters to a Court of Aldermen comm. on burthen labour, n.d. [1823], certificate by salesmen of Leadenhall and Newgate Markets to Gen. Purp. Comm., Co. Co., 2 Apr. 1834, Box 4, Shelf 149; minutes of evidence taken before Gen. Purp. Comm., Co. Co., 5 June 1832, 8 June 1833, Porters' Box 1.4; report of Gen. Purp. Comm., Co. Co., on Tacklehouse, Ticket and Fellowship Porters, printed, 12 Dec. 1833, Box 1, Shelf 149. G.L.M.R. MSS. 914, 916 (draft petition by Ticket Porters at Leadenhall Market to Court of Aldermen, 26 July 1836), 3846 (letter from the Housekeeper, Custom House, to the Alderman of the Ward of Tower, 15 July 1851). Reps. ccxxvii, fo. 579–585; ccxl, fo. 467–468, 539; ccxli, fo. 33; ccxlii, fo. 151–152.

52. G.L.R.O. Minutes of evidence taken before Gen. Purp. Comm., Co. Co., 11 Jan., 25 May 1833, Porters' Box 1.4; report of Gen. Purp. Comm., Co. Co., on Tacklehouse, Ticket and Fellowship Porters, printed, 12 Dec. 1833, Box 1, Shelf 149; brief for the defendants, *Stanford* v. *Stagg et al.* (1885), Sm.S. 13.11. Co. Co. Print. Mins. 1834, p. 16. R.C. Mun.

Corp. pp. 19–20, 207–210. *Bims* v. *Studley*, reported in *The Star*, 6 Jan. 1891, p. 3.

53. G.L.M.R. MSS. 914, 3456, 3846. Reps. ccxxxi, fo. 768–770. Colquhoun, *op. cit.*, p. 75. G.L.R.O. Minutes of evidence taken before Gen. Purp. Comm., Co. Co., 5 June 1832, Porters' Box 1.4; Gen. Purp. Comm., Co. Co., hearings relative to Fellowship Porters, pt. xxix (3 May 1853), Porters' Boxes 7 and 8. Co. Co. Jls. xcv, fo. 8b–10. Co. Co. Print. Mins. 1820, p. 134.

54. Mayhew, *op. cit.*, pp. 364–367. G.L.M.R. MSS. 914, 916, 3846 (petition of 52 Ticket Porters to the Court of Registers and Rulers of their Society, n.d. [1823]). Reps. ccxxiii, fo. 14–16; ccxxxii, fo. 631–633; ccxxxviii, fo. 402–405; cclxv, fo. 137–140, 153–156. Co. Co. Jls. xcvii, fo. 238–244. Co. Co. Print. Mins. 1815, p. 43. Roundabout Doctors' Commons—Walter Dexter: 'About Its Whereabouts'; Percy T. Carden: 'About the Doctors and the Courts', *The Dickensian*, xxvii (1931), pp. 7–17. Charles Dickens, *The Posthumous Papers of the Pickwick Club* (Chapman & Hall, Works, i), pp. 145–146. 20 & 21 Vict., cap. lxxvii, sects. 4, 105–106, 116–117. M. D. Slatter: The Study of the Records of the Court of Arches', *Journal of the Society of Archivists*, i, 2 (1955), pp. 29–30.

55. R.C. Mun. Corp. pp. 210–212. G.L.M.R. MSS. 914, 3846. Co. Co. Print. Mins. 1834, pp. 136, 152, 166; 1835, pp. 119, 140, 143 and app.; 1837, p. 255; 1838, pp. 36, 159–160, 175–176; 1841, pp. 49–50, 133; 1843, p. 51; 1849, p. 114; 1853, p. 85. Co. Co. Jls. xcvii, fo. 238–244; cix, fo. 365b–367; cxxvi, fo. 384b–385; cxxvii, fo. 137b–138; cxxix, fo. 93b–94, 130–130b, 330. G.L.R.O. Minutes of evidence taken before Gen. Purp. Comm., Co. Co., 8 June 1833, Porters' Box 1.4; *Bill for conferring upon Billingsgate Porters the privilege of unshipping, carrying, loading and warehousing of dried and pickled fish imported into the Port of London*, printed, n.d. [1837], Box 1, Shelf 149; Gen. Purp. Comm., Co. Co., hearings relative to Fellowship Porters, pt. xxix (3 May 1853), Porters' Boxes 7 and 8.

56. G.L.M.R. MSS. 914, 915 (Registers' Receipt Books), 916, 2836/11 (Registers' rough Account Books), 2933 (Registers' Account Books)/1, 2933/2, 2934, 3456, 3846. Reps. ccxiv, fo. 170; ccxix, fo. 499–500; ccxxii, fo. 608–609, 621–622; ccxlvii, fo. 372, 389–393. Co. Co. Jls. lxxxvi, fo. 243–244b; xcvi, fo. 168b–169b; xcvii, fo. 238–244; cxii, fo. 237b–238. Co. Co. Print. Mins. 1837, p. 56; 1838, pp. 266, 330. R.C. Mun. Corp. pp. 210–212. G.L.R.O. Minutes of evidence taken before

Y

Gen. Purp. Comm., Co. Co., 5 June 1832, 25 May 1833, Porters' Box 1.4; Gen. Purp. Comm., Co. Co., hearings relative to Fellowship Porters, pt. xxix (3 May 1853), Porters' Boxes 7 and 8.   *Fellowship Porters: Petitions and Statements submitted to the General Purposes Committee of the Common Council*, printed, 1878–79, pp. 3–4.   W. W. Glenny: 'The Fruit and Vegetable Markets of the Metropolis', *Journal of the Royal Agricultural Society*, 3rd ser. vii (1896), p. 51.

57. I am greatly indebted to the Worshipful Company of Vintners and its Clerk, Mr. W. H. Lloyd Mead, B.Sc.(Econ.), A.C.A., for access to its Wine Porters' Minute Books I to III and its files connected with the wine porterage business from which this account has been compiled. In addition, P.R.O. T.76/5, fo. 890–892; T.76/7, fo. 1485–1489, have been used.

58. G.L.M.R. MSS. 1697 (Causes heard by the Court of Rulers of the Fellowship Porters), 1702/1, 1702/2, 1702/3, 1702/4.   G.L.R.O. Memorial of the Fellowship Porters in answer to the Rulers' written statement, n.d. [second half 1817], Box 4, Shelf 149; Thomas Kidder, *Remarks on the Fellowship Porters*, to Coal and Corn Comm., Co. Co., 18 Jan. 1821, Box 1, Shelf 149; Gen. Purp. Comm., Co. Co., hearings relative to Fellowship Porters, pts. xx (16 Nov. 1852), xxxi (10 May 1853), Porters' Boxes 7 and 8.

59. G.L.M.R. MSS. 1702/1, 1702/2, 1702/3, 1702/4.   Reps. ccxxi, fo. 632–642.   G.L.R.O. Statement by William Ruston, Corn Shifter below Bridge, to Coal and Corn Comm., Co. Co., read 10 Apr. 1818, Box 4, Shelf 149; observations of the Court of Rulers of the Fellowship Porters to the same, Feb. 1820, Thomas Kidder, *Remarks on the Fellowship Porters*, to the same, 18 Jan. 1821, statement by John Henry Liquorish, James Hollamby and John Christey, Fellowship Rulers, to the same, read 12 June 1824, Box 1, Shelf 149; Gen. Purp. Comm., Co. Co., hearings relative to Fellowship Porters, pts. v (6 July), xiv (14 Sept. 1852), xxxi (10 May 1853), Porters' Boxes 7 and 8; P.A.R. Book viii, No. 63.   Co. Co. Print. Mins. 1824, pp. 35–39.   Co. Co. Jls. xcii, fo. 4–6b.

60. G.L.M.R. MSS. 1702/1, 1702/2, 1702/3, 1702/4.   R.C. Mun. Corp. pp. 207–210.

61. Co. Co. Print. Mins. 1818, pp. 133–139. G.L.M.R. MSS. 1697, 1702/1, 1702/2. Reps. ccxxi, fo. 632–642. G.L.R.O. Statement by William Ruston, Corn Shifter below Bridge, to Coal and Corn Comm., Co. Co., read 10 Apr. 1818, Box 4, Shelf 149; specimens of bills shifted with the Corn Shifter, I.R.72; Gen. Purp. Comm., Co. Co., hearings relative to Fellowship Porters, pt. xxiii (4 Dec. 1852), Porters' Boxes 7 and 8;

Fellowship Porters: Petitions and Statements submitted to the General Purposes Committee of the Common Council, printed, 1878–79, pp. 2–3, 5, Box 2, Shelf 149. Sir James Sexton, *Sir James Sexton, Agitator: The Life of the Dockers' M.P.* (London, 1936), pp. 110–111. Co. Co. Jls. xcvi, fo. 31–44. 46 & 47 Vict., cap. 31, sects. 2, 3.

62. Co. Co. Print. Mins. 1824, pp. 35–39, 57–58, 173–182, 208; 1826, p. 100; 1827, pp. 89–90, 120–121; 1848, p. 125. G.L.R.O. Minutes of evidence taken before Gen. Purp. Comm., Co. Co., 25 May 1833, Porters' Box 1.4.

63. G.L.R.O. Complaint of charges payable for grain porterage in London, printed, n.d. [1822], statement by the Rulers of the Fellowship Porters to the Coal and Corn Comm., Co. Co., 1823, statement by John Henry Liquorish, James Hollamby and John Christey, Rulers of the Fellowship Porters, to the same, 4 Feb. 1823, letter from Barclay, Perkins & Co. to the Town Clerk, 29 Jan. 1824, letter from William Ruston, Corn Shifter below Bridge, to C. A. Savage, 29 Nov. 1824, Box 1, Shelf 149; memorial by the Rulers of the Fellowship of Billingsgate Porters to the Coal and Corn Comm., Co. Co., 13 Sept. 1827 (duplicate in Box 2), broadsheet headed *To Fellowship Porters*, Aug. 1830, cases stated on behalf of the Court of Rulers of the Fellowship Porters for the opinion of Thos. Denman, Common Serjeant, and Russell Gurney, Common Pleader, 28 Sept. 1830, and by the Clerk to the Fellowship of Porters to Coal and Corn Comm., Co. Co., read 1 March, 1831, Box 4, Shelf 149. Co. Co. Jls. xcvi, fo. 316–318; civ, fo. 393–397b; cix, fo. 375–378. G.L.M.R. MSS. 1702/1, 1702/2, 1702/3, 1702/4. Reps. ccxxi, fo. 632–642. Co. Co. Print. Mins. 1824, pp. 35–39, 173–182.

64. G.L.M.R. MSS. 1698 (Fellowship porterage accounts), 1702/1, 1702/2, 1702/3, 1702/4. G.L.R.O. Memorial of the Fellowship Porters in answer to the Rulers' written statement, n.d. [second half 1817], cases stated on behalf of the Court of Rulers of the Fellowship Porters for the opinion of Thos. Denman, Common Serjeant, and Russell Gurney, Common Pleader, 28 Sept. 1830, and by the Clerk of the Fellowship Porters to Coal and Corn Comm., Co. Co., read 1 March 1831, broadsheet headed *To Fellowship Porters*, Aug. 1830, Box 4, Shelf 149; Gen. Purp. Comm., Co. Co., hearings relative to Fellowship Porters, pts. i (29 June), iv (6 July), x (15 July), xxi (23 Nov.), xxiv (14 Dec. 1852), xxxi (10 May 1853), Porters' Boxes 7 and 8; printed reports of comm., appointed at a general meeting of corn factors of the City of London on 21 Oct. 1852 and of Gen. Purp. Comm., Co. Co., on metage of corn, 24 March 1854,

Box 2, Shelf 149; Coal, Corn and Finance Comm., Co. Co., papers, Nov. 1930. Sir James Sexton, *loc. cit.* 1 & 2 Geo. IV, cap. 87, sects. 40, 45; 7 & 8 Geo. IV, cap. 58, sect. 39; 9 Geo. IV, cap. 60, sect. 47; 35 & 36 Vict., cap. c. R.C. Mun. Corp. pp. 83, 102, 137. Co. Co. Jls. lxxix, fo. 285b–286b; lxxxiii, fo. 258b–261b; cix, fo. 375–378; cxxv, fo. 199–199b. Co. Co. Print. Mins. 1868, app. 37.

65. W. H. Beveridge, *Unemployment: a Problem of Industry* (London, 1909). G.L.R.O. Memorial of the Fellowship Porters to Coal and Corn Comm., Co. Co., written and printed copies, n.d. [Dec. 1817], Box 4, Shelf 149; observations of the Court of Rulers of the Fellowship Porters to the same, read 17 May 1820, complaint of charges payable for grain porterage in London, printed, n.d. [1822], statement by the Rulers of the Fellowship Porters to Coal and Corn Comm., Co. Co., 1823, petition by John Henry Liquorish, James Hollamby and John Christey, Rulers of the Fellowship Porters, to the same, n.d. [1823], letter from William Ruston, Corn Shifter below Bridge, to C. A. Savage, 29 Nov. 1824, Box 1, Shelf 149; memorial by the Rulers of the Fellowship of Billingsgate Porters to the Coal and Corn Comm., Co. Co., 13 Sept. 1827, Box 2 (duplicate in Box 4), Shelf 149; scale of grain porterage charges after 3 May 1852, I.R.72; report of comm. appointed at a general meeting of corn factors of the City of London on 21 Oct. 1852, printed, Box 2, Shelf 149; Gen. Purp. Comm., Co. Co., hearings relative to Fellowship Porters, pts. viii (10 July), xxi (23 Nov.), xxii (30 Nov.), xxiv (14 Dec. 1852), xxix (3 May 1853), Porters' Boxes 7 and 8. Co. Co. Print. Mins. 1824, pp. 35–39, 173–182. Co. Co. Jls. lxxix, fo. 144b–145b, 285b–286b; lxxx, fo. 32b–34; lxxxv, fo. 380b–382, 410b–411b; lxxxvi, fo. 66b–67b.

66. G.L.R.O. Gen. Purp. Comm., Co. Co., hearings relative to Fellowship Porters, pt. xxiii (4 Dec. 1852), Porters' Boxes 7 and 8; answers of a deputation of Fellowship Porters to the replies of their Rulers, June 1885, Box 5.1, Shelf 149; City Solicitor's report to Gen. Purp. Comm., Co. Co., 13 Dec. 1892, I.R.52. G.L.M.R. MSS. 1697, 1700, 1702/2, 1702/3, 1702/4.

67. Co. Co. Print. Mins. 1818, pp. 133–139; 1827, pp. 142–145; 1829, pp. 100–101; 1860, pp. 141–142; 1861, pp. 102–103; 1866, pp. 161–162; 1868, pp. 112, 210, 224–225, 230–233, apps. 14, 37. G.L.M.R. MSS. 1697, 1700, 1702/1, 1702/2, 1702/3, 1702/4. G.L.R.O. Memorial of Fellowship Porters to Coal and Corn Comm., Co. Co., n.d. [late 1817], statement by William Ruston, Corn Shifter below Bridge, to the same, read 10 Apr. 1818, Corn Shifter's accounts, 1820–1830, Box 4, Shelf 149; resolution of the Court of Rulers of the Fellowship Porters relating to the salary and

duties of a Paymaster, n.d. [1827], memorial from the same to Coal and Corn Comm., Co. Co., read 29 Nov. 1827, Box 1, Shelf 149; specimens of bills shifted with the Corn Shifter by Fellowship Porters, details of corn shift 1820–1826 supplied by William Ruston, Corn Shifter below Bridge, to Coal and Corn Comm., Co. Co., read 24 Nov. 1827, I.R.72; Gen. Purp. Comm., Co. Co., hearings relative to Fellowship Porters, pts. xxi (23 Nov.), xxii (30 Nov.), xxiv (14 Dec. 1852), Porters' Boxes 7 and 8; *Fellowship Porters: Petitions and Statements submitted to the General Purposes Committee of the Common Council*, printed, 1878–79, p. 5, Box 2, Shelf 149. R.C. Mun. Corp. pp. 83, 137. Co. Co. Jls. lxxix, fo. 285b–286b.

68. G.L.R.O. Letter from Zachariah Rye and Jno. Cs. Barrell, Fellowship Porters, to John Bumstead, Chairman, Coal and Corn Comm., Co. Co., 9 Apr. 1818, statement by William Ruston, Corn Shifter below Bridge, to Coal and Corn Comm., Co. Co., read 10 Apr. 1818, Box 4, Shelf 149; *City Corporation* v. *William Clay*, 1830–31, Alchin's Coll. 6.56; minutes of evidence taken before Gen. Purp. Comm., Co. Co., 8 June 1833, Porters' Box 1.4; report of the same on Porters, printed, 12 Dec. 1833, Box 1, Shelf 149; Gen. Purp. Comm., Co. Co., hearings relative to Fellowship Porters, pts. xi (22 July), xix (6 Nov. 1852), Porters' Boxes 7 and 8; P.A.R. Book viii, No. 63. Co. Co. Jls. lxxxv, fo. 380–382b, 410b–411b; lxxxvi, fo. 66b–67b; civ, fo. 399b–401; cv, fo. 307b–309; cix, fo. 375b–378. Co. Co. Print. Mins. 1818, pp. 133–139; 1824, pp. 173–182; 1830, pp. 157–158; 1856, p. 38. G.L.M.R. MSS. 1700, 1702/1, 1702/2, 1702/3. Reps. ccxvi, fo. 551–559; ccxvii, fo. 657; ccxxi, fo. 576–579, 632–642; ccxxvi, fo. 257–260; ccxxvii, fo. 400–403. R.C. Mun. Corp. pp. 83–84, 138. H. B. Dale: 'The Worshipful Company of Woodmongers and the Coal Trade of London', *Journal of the Royal Society of Arts*, lxx (1922), pp. 816–823.

69. G.L.R.O. Statement by William Ruston, Corn Shifter below Bridge, to Coal and Corn Comm., Co. Co., read 10 Apr. 1818, memorial by the Rulers of the Fellowship of Billingsgate Porters to the same, 13 Sept. 1827 (duplicate in Box 2), Box 4, Shelf 149; Gen. Purp. Comm., Co. Co., hearings relative to Fellowship Porters, pts. xviii (26 Oct.), xix (6 Nov.), xxi (23 Nov. 1852), xxxi (10 May 1853), Porters' Boxes 7 and 8; P.A.R. Book viii, No. 63; *Fellowship Porters: Petitions and Statements submitted to the General Purposes Committee of the Common Council*, printed, 1878–79, p. 5, Box 2, Shelf 149. Co. Co. Print. Mins. 1818, pp. 133–139; 1827, pp. 142–145; 1834, pp. 16–17; 1861, pp. 16, 102–103; 1875, p. 197. G.L.M.R. MSS. 1700, 1702/1, 1702/2, 1702/3, 1702/4. Co. Co. Jls.

lxxxv, fo. 380–382b, 410b–411b; lxxxvi, fo. 66b–67b; cv, fo. 307b–309; cxxiv, fo. 38–41. R.C. Mun. Corp. pp. 83, 137–138.

70. G.L.R.O. Memorandum by the Orange Porters to Coal and Corn Comm., Co. Co., read 22 Feb. 1831, letter from John Finch, Solicitor to the Orange Porters, to the Town Clerk, 13 Oct. 1831, letter from William Payne, Clerk to the Society of Tacklehouse and Ticket Porters, to Coal and Corn Comm., Co. Co., 17 Oct. 1831, Box 4, Shelf 149; *Fellowship Porters: Petitions and Statements submitted to the General Purposes Committee of the Common Council*, printed, 1878–79, Box 2, Shelf 149; Gen. Purp. Comm., Co. Co., hearings relative to Fellowship Porters, pts. iii (29 June), xi (22 July), xviii (26 Oct.), xxi (23 Nov), xxiv (14 Dec. 1852), xxxi (10 May 1853), Porters' Boxes 7 and 8; memorandum by C. P. Lucas, representing Fellowship Porters' Protection Union, 22 Jan. 1891, minutes of sub-comm., Gen. Purp. Comm., Co. Co., pencilled, 18 March and 18 Nov. 1891, fruit traders' petition to Gen. Purp. Comm., Co. Co., 20 Oct. 1891, letter from City Solicitor to the same, 11 Nov. 1891, reports by the same to the same, 16 Dec. 1891, 26 Jan. and 13 Dec. 1892, letter from W. C. Murphy, Fellowship Porter, to H. J. McAuliffe, member of Coal, Corn and Finance Comm., Co. Co., 17 Dec. 1923, I.R.52; letter from the same to C. S. Giddins, Co. Co., 11 Nov. 1930, Coal Corn and Finance Comm. papers, Nov. 1930. G.L.M.R. MSS. 1697, 1700, 1702/1, 1702/2, 1702/3, 1702/4, 3833, 3834. Reps. ccxxxiv, fo. 311–313. Co. Co. Jls. civ, fo. 397b–399b; clvii, no pag., 12 Dec. 1878; clxx(1), fo. 23–26. Co. Co. Print. Mins. 1832, p. 31; 1883, app. 45. *The Star*, 10 Sept. 1880, p. 3, 13 Sept. 1889, p. 3, 18 Sept. 1889, p. 1, 29 Aug. 1891, p. 3, 7 Sept. 1891, p. 3. *The City Press*, 11 Sept. 1889, p. 5, 14 Sept. 1889, p. 3, 2 Sept. 1891, p. 2; 5 Sept. 1891, p. 5. 46 & 47 Vict., cap. 31, sects. 2, 3. H. Llewellyn Smith: 'Chapters in the History of London Waterside Labour. I. Waterside Porters', *Economic Journal*, ii (1892), pp. 593–607.

71. G.L.M.R. MSS. 1700, 1702/2, 1702/3. Co. Co. Print. Mins. 1818, pp. 133–139; 1823, p. 127. G.L.R.O. Reports by the Markets Comm. to the Co. Co., one printed, read 27 Feb. 1840, another 8 July 1850, I.R.72; Gen. Purp. Comm., Co. Co., hearings relative to Fellowship Porters, pts. xii (27 July 1852), xxv (8 March), xxvii (24 March 1853), Porters' Boxes 7 and 8. R.C. Mun. Corp. pp. 84, 138, 206–207. *Laybourn and Others* v. *Crisp and Others*, Engl. Law Reps. 4 M. & W. 320–330 (15–16 June 1838). S. Gwynn: 'Billingsgate', *Country Life*, 1928, pp. 303–306. T. J. Dove: 'Two Famous London Markets: II. Billingsgate', *The Listener*, 13 Apr. 1939, p. 771.

72. Co. Co. Print. Mins. 1818, pp. 133–139; 1819, pp. 39–49; 1824, pp. 35–39, 173–182; 1835, p. 143 and app.; 1836, pp. 5, 81–82, 189–190; 1837, pp. 16, 86–87; 1838, pp. 61–62, 159, 265, 330; 1839, pp. 12, 28; 1840, p. 308; 1841, p. 243; 1849, pp. 61–62. G.L.R.O. Thomas Kidder, *Remarks on the Fellowship Porters*, to Coal and Corn Comm., Co. Co., 18 Jan. 1821, letter from William Ruston, Corn Shifter below Bridge, to C. A. Savage, 29 Nov. 1824, nominal roll of Fellowship Porters admitted Apr. 1830–June 1837, Box 1, Shelf 149; answer by the Court of Rulers of the Fellowship Porters to Gen. Purp. Comm., Co. Co., read 16 Apr. 1846, memorandum from John McDowell, John Stephenson, Jos^h. Hawthorn and Chas. Brown, Fellowship Porters, to the same, read 18 Apr. 1848, letter from the Clerk of the Fellowship of Porters to the Town Clerk, 18 July 1850, letters from Wm. Lyal and other potato merchants to the same, 18–29 July 1850, I.R.72; Gen. Purp. Comm., Co. Co., hearings relative to Fellowship Porters, pts. xx (16 Nov. 1852), xxx (7 May, 1853), Porters' Boxes 7 and 8. R.C. Mun. Corp. pp. 207–210. G.L.M.R. MSS. 1702/3, 3831 (Quarterage books of the Fellowship of Porters)/1, 3831/2, 3831/3. Co. Co. Jls. cix, fo. 375–378; cxxv, fo. 199–199b; cxxxix, fo. 73–74b.

73. G.L.R.O. Memorial by James Hollamby, Zachariah Rye, John Henry Schleicher and John Christey, Fellowship Porters, to Coal and Corn Comm., Co. Co., 18 Jan. 1821, Thomas Kidder, *Remarks on the Fellowship Porters*, to the same, 18 Jan. 1821, letter from William Ruston, Corn Shifter below Bridge, to C. A. Savage, 29 Nov. 1824, Box 1, Shelf 149; memorial of the Fellowship Porters in answer to the Rulers' written statement, n.d. [second half 1817], case stated by the Clerk to the Fellowship of Porters to Coal and Corn Comm., Co. Co., read 1 March, 1831, Box 4, Shelf 149; Gen. Purp. Comm., Co. Co., hearings relative to Fellowship Porters, pts. xx (16 Nov.), xxii (30 Nov. 1852), Porters' Boxes 7 and 8; *Fellowship Porters: Petitions and Statements submitted to the General Purposes Committee of the Common Council*, printed, 1878–79, p. 6, Box 2, Shelf 149; *Stanford v. Stagg et al.*, 21 Dec. 1885, Sm.S. 13.11. Co. Co. Print. Mins. 1818, pp. 133–139; 1868, app. 37. G.L.M.R. MS. 1697. Co. Co. Jls. xcii, fo. 4–6b; xcvi, fo. 31–44. Reps. ccxx, fo. 978–981; ccxxi, fo. 65–66, 643–649.

74. Co. Co. Print. Mins. 1818, pp. 133–139; 1868, pp. 112, 210, 224–225, 230–233, app. 37. G.L.M.R. MSS. 1697, 1700, 1702/1, 1702/2, 1702/3, 1702/4. Reps. ccxxi, fo. 632–642. G.L.R.O. Observations of the Court of Rulers of the Fellowship Porters to Coal and Corn Comm., Co. Co.,

Feb. 1820, Thomas Kidder, *Remarks on the Fellowship Porters*, to the same, 18 Jan. 1821, Box 1, Shelf 149; Gen. Purp. Comm., Co. Co., hearings relative to Fellowship Porters, pts. xx (16 Nov.), xxi (23 Nov. 1852), Porters' Boxes 7 and 8. R.C. Mun. Corp. pp. 207–210. Co. Co. Jls. xcvi, fo. 31–44; cxxiv, fo. 38–41.

75. Co. Co. Print. Mins. 1818, pp. 133–139; 1819, pp. 39–49; 1835, p. 152; 1836, pp. 63, 295; 1837, p. 156; 1841, p. 242; 1842, pp. 30, 223; 1843, p. 40; 1845, p. 167; 1853, pp. 20–21; 1855, pp. 58, 73; 1861, p. 15; 1868, app. 37. G.L.M.R. MSS. 1696, 1700, 1702/1, 1702/2, 1702/3, 1702/4, 3833 (ledger of the Fellowship of Porters, 1880–1890). Reps. ccxxi, fo. 632–642. G.L.R.O. Observations of the Court of Rulers of the Fellowship Porters to Coal and Corn Comm., Co. Co., Feb. 1820, Thomas Kidder, *Remarks on the Fellowship Porters*, to the same, 18 Jan. 1821, memorial by James Hollamby, Zachariah Rye, John Henry Schleicher and John Christey, Fellowship Porters, to the same, 18 Jan. 1821, Box 1, Shelf 149; returns of capital stock of the Fellowship of Porters, 1832–1835, certified by the Clerk, Box 4, Shelf 149; annual statements of Fellowship capital stock and annual accounts, Boxes 4 and 5, Shelf 149, I.R.52 and 72; memorandum by Thos. Jones, Chas. Willett, John Wilkinson and William Willett, Fellowship Porters, to Gen. Purp. Comm., Co. Co., read 30 Apr. 1846, I.R.72; Gen. Purp. Comm., Co. Co., hearings relative to Fellowship Porters, pts. xx (16 Nov.), xxi (23 Nov. 1852), xxix (3 May 1853), Porters' Boxes 7 and 8; *Scheme of Distribution of Fellowship Porters' Assets*, prepared by W. Sutton, printed, 11 Oct. 1893, I.R.52. Co. Co. Jls. xcii, fo. 4–6b; xcvi, fo. 31–44; cxxiii, fo. 336b–337b; cxxiv, fo. 38–41; cxxxix, fo. 73–74b; cli, no pag., 29 May 1873.

76. Reps. ccxxi, fo. 476–487. Co. Co. Jls. xcii, fo. 4–6b. Co. Co. Print. Mins. 1818, pp. 133–139. G.L.R.O. Memorial by Fellowship Porters (read in Aldermen's comm., 28 Oct. 1817), 8 Oct. 1817, Box 1, Shelf 149; memorials of the Fellowship Porters in answer to the Rulers' written statement and to Coal and Corn Comm., Co. Co., n.d. [late in 1817], petition by James Hollamby, Zachariah Rye, Thomas Higham and John Christey, Fellowship Porters, to the same, 1 Apr. 1818, memorial from James Hollamby, Zachariah Rye and John Christey to the same, 17 Aug. 1819, memoranda by James Hollamby, Zachariah Rye, John Christey and John Henry Schleicher to the same, 13 and 17 Nov. 1820, Box 4, Shelf 149.

77. G.L.R.O. Certificate of potato merchants to Coal and Corn Comm., Co. Co., n.d. [1817], copy of notice put up in Corn Office by authority of the Rulers, n.d. [1817], petitions by Fellowship Porters to Coal and Corn

Comm., Co. Co., 3 Feb. and 27 May 1818, statements by William Ruston, Corn Shifter below Bridge, to the same, read 10 Apr. 1818, *Answer of the Upper Ruler and Rulers of the Fellowship of Corn and Salt Porters to the Petition presented to the Common Council on the 22nd January, 1818*, read 10 Apr. 1818, Box 4, Shelf 149; observations of the Court of Rulers of the Fellowship Porters to Coal and Corn Comm., Co. Co., Feb. 1820, Thomas Kidder, *Remarks on the Fellowship Porters*, to the same, 18 Jan. 1821, Box 1, Shelf 149. Reps. ccxxi, fo. 632–642. Co. Co. Print. Mins. 1818, pp. 133–139.

78. Co. Co. Print. Mins. 1818, pp. 133–139, 180; 1819, pp. 39–49, 78. G.L.R.O. Letter from James Hollamby, Zachariah Rye and John Christey, Fellowship Porters, to Coal and Corn Comm., Co. Co., printed, 17 May 1819, and amendments proposed by the same to the same in respect of the bill prepared, received 17 May 1820, observations of the Court of Rulers of the Fellowship Porters to the same, Feb. 1820, memorial by James Hollamby, Zachariah Rye, John Henry Schleicher and John Christey to the same, 18 Jan. 1821, Box 1, Shelf 149; case stated by the Clerk to the Fellowship of Porters to the same, read 1 March 1831, Box 4, Shelf 149. Co. Co. Jls. xcvi, fo. 31–44; cvii, fo. 3–4b. R.C. Mun. Corp. pp. 207–210. G.L.M.R. MSS. 1700, 1702/2, 1702/3.

79. G.L.R.O. Bill prepared by Gen. Purp. Comm., Co. Co. to revise regulations for Fellowship Porters, 7 Dec. 1848, Box 1, Shelf 149; memorial by J. McDowell, G. Wildash, J. Stephenson, J. Hawthorn, R. Richards, Fellowship Porters, to Gen. Purp. Comm., Co. Co., printed, n.d. [18 Dec. 1845], answer by the Court of Rulers of the Fellowship Porters to the same, read 16 Apr. 1846, loose papers of Gen. Purp. Comm., Co. Co., for Oct. 1846, objections to the draft bill by J. McDowell, J. Hawthorn, J. Stephenson and C. Brown, printed, n.d. [1849], and by the Court of Rulers, read 13 July 1850, letter addressed to Co. Co. purporting to embody resolutions adopted at a general meeting of Fellowship Porters held at the *King's Head* tavern, Great Tower Street, 7 June 1852, letter by J. Hawthorn, J. Stephenson, C. Brown, to the members of the City Corporation, printed, n.d. [1852–53], I.R.72; Gen. Purp. Comm., Co. Co., hearings relative to Fellowship Porters, pts. xxi (23 Nov.), xxiv (14 Dec. 1852), xxix (3 May), xxx (7 May), xxxi (10 May 1853), Porters' Boxes 7 and 8. Co. Co. Jls. cxxiv, fo. 38–41; ccxxv, fo. 21b–22b, 464–465; ccxxvi, fo. 238–239. G.L.M.R. MSS. 1702/2, 1702/3.

80. G.L.R.O. Memorandum by Alderman Henry Muggeridge to Gen. Purp. Comm., Co. Co., 27 May 1852, *Report by the Committee of Corn Factors on*

the Metage Question, printed, 11 Jan. 1853, Box 5, Shelf 149; Gen. Purp. Comm., Co. Co., hearings relative to Fellowship Porters, pt. xx (16 Nov. 1852), Porters' Boxes 7 and 8; report by Gen. Purp. Comm., Co. Co., on metage of corn, printed, 24 March 1854, Box 2, Shelf 149. Co. Co. Jls. cxxx, fo. 351b–352b; cxxxviii, no pag., 13 Sept. 1860, 18 Oct. 1860; cxxxix, fo. 73–74b; cxl, fo. 116–117b, 166–167b, 201–202b. Co. Co. Print. Mins. 1852, p. 129; 1855, app. 5; 1861, p. 15; 1863, pp. 100, 166; 1868, app. 37; 1883, app. 45. *Hansard* (3rd ser.) clxxii, cols. 815–817 (14 July 1863). 35 & 36 Vict. cap. c, esp. sect. 19. G.L.M.R. MS. 1702/4.

81. G.L.M.R. MSS. 1702/4, 3833 (ledger of the Fellowship of Porters, 1880–1887). Co. Co. Print. Mins. 1876, pp. 127, 207–208, 231, 237, 252; 1878, p. 114; 1882, p. 193; 1883, app. 45; 1884, app. 29; 1886, pp. 221–222, 237–238; 1887, pp. 138, 149–150 and app. 22. Co. Co. Jls. clxii(2), fo. 1866–1867. G.L.R.O. Petition of members of the Fellowship of Porters to Co. Co., 24 Apr., and reply by the Court of Rulers, 21 May 1879, Box 2, Shelf 149; City Solicitor's report to Gen. Purp. Comm., Co. Co., 7 Nov. 1882, memorandum by a deputation of Fellowship Porters to Co. Co., 16 Nov. 1884, letter from William Cash, F.C.A., to the Metage on Grain Comm., Co. Co., 11 May 1885, I.R.52; answers of a deputation of Fellowship Porters to the replies of their Rulers, June 1885, and of their Court of Rulers to the petition presented to Co. Co. by Sir Charles Read and others, n.d. [between 1879 and 1883], Box 5.1, Shelf 149; letter from Wm. C. Murphy, Fellowship Porter, to C. S. Giddins, Co. Co., 11 Nov. 1930, Coal, Corn and Finance Comm. papers for Nov. 1930.

82. Co. Co. Jls. clxiv(1), fo. 366–368, clxiv(2), fo. 797–798 clxvi(1), fo. 25–26, 272–273; clxx(2), fo. 871–874, 1334–1335; clxxxvi(2), fo. 1548–1550. Co. Co. Print. Mins. 1888, pp. 271, 317; 1890, pp. 15, 168; 1891, pp. 63, 156; 1892, pp. 155, 161 and app. 26; 1893, p. 67, apps. 5 and 29; 1894, pp. 33–34, 42, 52, 69–70 and app. 13. G.L.M.R. MS. 1700. G.L.R.O. Notes of sub-comm. of Gen. Purp. Comm., Co. Co., on enquiry into Fellowship Porters, pencilled, 20, 23 and 28 May 1890, memorandum by C. P. Lucas representing Fellowship Porters' Protection Union, 22 Jan. 1891, accompanied by covering letter from City Solicitor to Gen. Purp. Comm., Co. Co., 27 Jan. 1891, City Solicitor's report to the same, 26 Jan. 1892, copy of minutes of special general meeting of Fellowship Porters held 19 May 1893, letter from T. Thurlow, Fellowship Porter, to Chairman, Gen. Purp. Comm., Co. Co., 22 May 1893, I.R.52; letter from Wm. C. Murphy, Fellowship Porter, to C. S. Giddins, Co. Co., 11 Nov. 1930, Coal,

Corn and Finance Comm., Co. Co., papers for Nov. 1930; summary of Fellowship Porters' history, typed, April 1934, MS. 135.1.

83. Co. Co. Print. Mins. 1901, p. 427; 1908, pp. 120, 351; 1909, p. 23; 1914, p. 238; 1922, p. 260; 1924, p. 108; 1925, pp. 21, 87; 1926, pp. 168, 231, 281, 349. Co. Co. Jls. clxxxvi(2), fo. 1548–1550, 1712–1713. G.L.R.O. City Solicitor's report to Coal, Corn and Finance Comm., Co. Co., 7 July 1924, I.R.52; summary of Fellowship Porters' history, typed, April 1934, MS. 135.1; letter from Wm. C. Murphy, Fellowship Porter, to C. S. Giddins, Co. Co., 11 Nov. 1930, Coal, Corn and Finance Comm., Co. Co., papers for Nov. 1930.

INDEX

1. GENERAL

Accidents, 7, 199, 247, 250, 268–72, 289, 296

Aliens, 18, 22–7, 33–5, 37, 67, 83, 123, 126, 138, 139, 156, 224

Aliens' Porters, 13–16, 22, 27, 30–7, 40, 42, 67, 127

Apples, 134, 209, 212

Arnotto, 75

Ashes, 66

Backing work, 95, 100, 202, 205, 227

Badge. *See* Tally

Bailiffs, 9

Bakers, 98

Balliage, 26, 32

Barge(master)s, 99, 124, 133 215, 216, 221, 224, 227, 228, 236

Bargemen, 93, 102

Barley, 100, 101, 135

Basket men, 109, 112, 237, 238

Beans, 101

Beef, 76

Beer, 109, 226, 228, 251

Beer corn, 101

Boat. *See* Vessel

Brandy, 78, 81, 89

Brewers, Breweries, Brewhouses, 98, 192, 207, 218, 226–8, 287; Barclay & Perkins, 227; Calvert's, 228; City of London, 227; Combe, Delafield & Co., 134, 135, 192; Courage & Donaldson, 228; Hoare's, 228; Reid & Co., 228; Whitbread's, 227.

Bushel, 83, 101, 107, 115, 221, 222, 246, 255–7, 290, 300

Butter, 124, 154

Cables, 66

Carmen, Carts, 3, 4, 13, 14, 27, 78, 136, 153, 154, 159, 160, 165, 236, 238, 244, 245, 256

Carrots, 114, 209

Catching burdens, 69, 70, 114, 164

Charters, Royal, 15, 22, 24, 82, 84; *of 1338*, 82; *of 1478*, 26; *of 1605*, 15; *of 1638*, 15; *of 1640*, 31, 36

Cheese, 124

City of London

Aldermen, 7, 9, 14, 19, 20, 42, 43, 47, 54, 62, 63, 68, 70, 73, 78, 79, 84, 85, 88, 92, 101, 107, 114, 121, 122, 129, 142, 156, 164, 191, 219, 251, 272, 291, 301

Aliens' Porter. *See* Packer and Porter of Aliens' Goods

area (geographical), 3, 5, 16, 26, 32, 36, 37, 42, 59, 65, 70, 78, 82, 83, 102, 107, 111, 123, 124, 126, 139, 144, 149, 153, 161, 163, 165, 173, 174, 177, 179, 181, 194, 197, 216, 218, 219, 225, 236, 237, 294

arms, 50, 178

authorities, 7, 11, 13, 28, 31, 36, 37, 50, 53, 65–7, 79, 86, 95, 107, 108, 127, 131, 133, 134, 179, 187, 272, 303

boundaries, 7

chamber, 28–30, 107, 108, 235, 254, 269

Chamberlain, 16, 20, 68, 84, 85, 91, 99, 132, 133

Common Council, 9, 10, 16, 29, 33, 34, 39, 50, 53, 54, 72, 74, 80, 81, 86, 89, 91, 99, 106, 108, 110, 114, 128, 130–33, 135–7, 147, 152, 158, 161, 162, 166, 178, 182, 186–9, 191, 192, 195, 207, 212–16, 218, 219, 222–6, 229, 230, 232, 233, 235, 237, 238, 240–42, 245, 247, 248, 258–60, 269, 270, 272–3, 277–81, 283, 288–96, 298–304

Acts (By-laws), 9, 11, 38, 74, 80, 99, 130, 158, 166, 212, 217, 261, 273, 276–81; *of 1597*, 30, 33, 39, 42, 65, 66; *of 1606*, 33; *of 1608*,

333

z

2. NAMES OF PERSONS AND COMPANIES

3. PLACES